D1588496

AMERICAN TRANSCENDENTALISM

American Transcendentalism

AN ANTHOLOGY OF CRITICISM

Edited by
BRIAN M. BARBOUR

UNIVERSITY OF NOTRE DAME PRESS
NOTRE DAME
LONDON

Library of Congress Cataloging in Publication Data

Barbour, Brian M   1943-   comp.
    American transcendentalism.

    CONTENTS: Barbour, B. M. Introduction.—Bowers, D. Democratic
vistas.—Carpenter, F. I. Transcendentalism.—Hochfield, G. An introduction
to transcendentalism. [etc.]—Bibliography (p.   )
    1. American literature—19th century—History and criticism. 2. Tran-
scendentalism (New England)
I. Title.
PS217.T7B3   141'.3   72-12640
ISBN 0-268-00492-7
ISBN 0-268-00494-3 (pbk.)

Manufactured in the United States of America by
NAPCO Graphic Arts, Inc., New Berlin, Wisconsin

Nature seems to exist for the excellent.
The world is upheld by the veracity of
good men: They make the earth wholesome.
They who lived with them found life
glad and nutritious.

Emerson
Representative Men

Preface

MY PURPOSE HAS BEEN TO BRING TOGETHER THE BEST WORK DONE
on a subject of importance, work not always available, especially in smaller
libraries. I hope that four classes of readers will benefit from the book,
members of the intelligent public, undergraduates, graduate students, and
professional scholars. Of course, not all will use it in the same way. The first
two will profit most from Part One and from such essays as Miller's,
Goddard's, Hutchison's, Smith's, and James's. For graduate students it should
prove useful for a variety of purposes from survery courses to the Compre-
hensives and beyond. They will also find material helpful to them as they
begin their lives as teachers. Professional scholars should find the gathering
convenient (and, I hope, provocative) and the Bibliography invaluable. Seeing
what has been done, perhaps they will find a stimulus to fresh effort. There is
still no history of the American Transcendental movement since Frothingham's, now nearly a century old. And there is not enough first-rate work on
Transcendentalism's relationship to the society out of which it grew, and
none on the odd Transcendental attitude toward creative literature.

   I owe a good deal to others. Miss Emily Schossberger and Mr. John
Ehmann of Notre Dame Press encouraged me from the beginning. Miss Ann
Rice took the manuscript in hand and showed me what an editor should be.
Professor Richard W. Alsfeld read and criticized my Introduction, mending

where and what he could. The tares that remain are of course my responsibility. I am grateful to the Reverend Ernest A. Hogan, O.P., Mr. Joseph H. Doherty, and Miss Maureen Whelan of the Phillips Memorial Library, Providence College, for providing me with materials through Inter-Library Loan. Professor Robert E. Spiller and Professor Richard M. Ludwig graciously assisted me on a matter of information. Mrs. Etta DiMauro helped me with the physical preparation of the manuscript. Mr. Eugene R. Gousie, Mr. Dean M. Lobello, and Mr. Kresten Jespersen assisted me with the proofs and Index. Finally, my greatest debt is to my wife June, who, through it all, never stopped being herself.

Providence, Rhode Island   B.M.B.
January 19, 1973

Contents

Contributors

BRIAN M. BARBOUR is Assistant Professor of English, Providence College. His criticism has appeared in *The Southern Review.*

ROBERT C. ALBRECHT is Associate Professor of English and Associate Dean of the College of Liberal Arts, the University of Oregon. He has written a critical study, *Theodore Parker,* and his articles on American Literature have appeared in a number of journals.

DAVID BOWERS was, at the time of his death, Associate Professor of Philosophy at Princeton, where he helped found the American Civilization program and edited its first publication, *Foreign Influences in American Life.*

A. ROBERT CAPONIGRI is Professor of Philosophy at Notre Dame, where he is also Chairman of the Committee on the Humanities. His publications include *Time and Idea: The Theory of History in Giambattista Vico; History and Liberty: The Historical Writings of Benedetto Croce;* and articles in a wide variety of journals.

FREDERICK I. CARPENTER is retired as Research Associate in English, University of California (Berkeley). His books include *Emerson and Asia,*

American Literature and the Dream, Robinson Jeffers, Eugene O'Neill, and *Laurens van der Post.*

CHARLES R. CROWE is Professor of History, the University of Georgia. Besides many articles, he has written or edited *George Ripley: Transcendentalist and Utopian Socialist; A Documentary History of American Thought and Society;* and *The Age of Civil War and Reconstruction: A Book of Interpretative Essays.*

The late H. C. GODDARD taught at Swarthmore College where he was for many years Chairman of the Department of English. Besides *Studies in New England Transcendentalism,* he wrote *The Meaning of Shakespeare* and a well-known article on *The Turn of the Screw.*

GEORGE HOCHFIELD is Professor of English, the State University of New York at Buffalo, and he has held Fulbright Lectureships to both Italy and Yugoslavia. Besides editing *Selected Writings of the American Transcendentalists,* he has written *Henry Adams: An Introduction and Interpretation* and has edited a volume of Adams' essays.

WILLIAM R. HUTCHISON, educated at Oxford and Yale, is Charles Warren Professor of the History of Religion in America, Harvard Divinity School. His books include *The Transcendentalist Ministers* (which won the Brewer Prize from the American Society of Church History), *American Protestant Thought: The Liberal Era,* and *How New is the New Religious Radicalism?*

HENRY JAMES knew Emerson from his own childhood on. In the winter of 1872-73 they toured the Louvre and the Vatican Museum together on Emerson's last visit to Europe. James's books dealing directly with New England include two novels, *The Europeans* and *The Bostonians,* and a critical study, *Hawthorne.*

GEORGES JOYAUX is Professor of French and Comparative Literature, Michigan State University. He has held a Guggenheim Fellowship, and his work has appeared in *The French Review, Yale French Studies, Modern Language Journal, Revue d'Histoire de l'Amerique Francaise,* and *African Studies Review.*

The late PERRY MILLER was Powell M. Cabot Professor of American Literature at Harvard. Among his many publications were *Orthodoxy in Massachusetts, 1603-1650; The New England Mind* (two volumes); *Jonathan Edwards; The Raven and the Whale; Errand into the Wilderness; Nature's*

Nation; The Transcendentalists; and *The Life of the Mind in America: From the Revolution to the Civil War,* which received a Pulitzer Prize.

ARTHUR M. SCHLESINGER, JR., Special Assistant to Presidents Kennedy and Johnson, is Albert Schweitzer Professor of the Humanities, CUNY. He has twice won a Pulitzer Prize, once in History (for *The Age of Jackson*) and once in Biography (for *A Thousand Days: John F. Kennedy in the White House*). He has also written *Orestes A. Brownson: A Pilgrim's Progress; The Age of Roosevelt* (three volumes of which have been published); *The Bitter Heritage;* and *Paths of American Thought* (edited with Morton White).

HENRY NASH SMITH is Professor of English, University of California (Berkeley). He is a past President of the Modern Language Association and a Fellow of the American Academy of Arts and Sciences. His books include *Virgin Land: The American West in Symbol and Myth* (which received both the Bancroft Award and The John H. Dunning Prize from the American Historical Association); *Mark Twain: The Development of a Writer;* and *Popular Culture and Industrialism, 1865-1890.* He co-edited *The Mark Twain-Howells Letters.*

TONY TANNER is a Fellow of King's College, Cambridge. His books include *The Reign of Wonder; Saul Bellow;* and *City of Words: American Fiction, 1950-1970.* He contributes regularly to journals on both sides of the Atlantic.

CAMERON THOMPSON teaches English and Philosophy at Pine Manor Junior College. He has edited *Philosophy and Literature* and has written a number of pieces for *The New England Quarterly.*

RENÉ WELLEK, Sterling Professor of Comparative Literature at Yale, has received honorary degrees from nine universities, including Harvard, Oxford, Louvain, and Rome. He has written *Kant in England, The Rise of English Literary History, Theory of Literature* (with Austin Warren), *Concepts of Criticism, Confrontations, Discriminations,* and *A History of Modern Criticism* (of which four volumes have appeared to date).

The late YVOR WINTERS taught at Stanford from 1928 until 1966. He was both critic and poet, and his *Collected Poems* won the Bollingen Prize in 1960. His personal and disturbing criticism can be found in *Primitivism and Decadence; Maule's Curse; The Anatomy of Nonsense; Edwin Arlington Robinson; In Defense of Reason; The Function of Criticism;* and *Forms of Discovery.*

Introduction

BRIAN M. BARBOUR

TRANSCENDENTALISM WAS THE MOST IMPORTANT FORCE IN American intellectual life during the great middle-third of the nineteenth century, but it is separated from us by the strangeness of its idiom, the confidence of its odd metaphysics, and a set of religious and social conditions which are gone forever. Such a barrier not only insures that Transcendentalism can be comfortably ignored by the complacent and abused by the ignorant; it also means that we have lost continuity with a vital positive force in our tradition. If the three main themes of Transcendentalism were, as Perry Miller said, a search for faith, a reaction against Unitarianism, and a revulsion against commercialism, we have not yet superseded our need for the first; and while "revulsion" is not helpful in the face of the commercial and technological drives rampant in our civilization, the sincerity and integrity of the accents in which the Transcendentalists and especially Emerson preached a turn to Idealism and a spiritual criterion for living, should not be lost on us. If we cannot take over the message, we have great need for the strength of character that provided the accent.

The first aim of criticism, Matthew Arnold noted, should be "to see the object as in itself it is." With Transcendentalism this is especially difficult both for the reasons cited and because it is hard to say precisely what Transcendentalism was. Transcendental thinkers deliberately set out to blur

1

the inherited (and, to them, wholly artificial) distinctions between philosophy and theology. In an oft-repeated image, they hoped to "marry" the two. Their basic insight was epistemological, and they hoped to use it to provide a new basis and a different kind of certitude for both. They believed that they could know all of spiritual reality.

This collection of essays divides along the traditional lines between intellectual disciplines. Its bias is historical and critical. The five sections view the phenomenon in the network of its historical relationships. The essays are concerned with where it came from and how it arrived, and what its effects were. They are all attempts at definition.

Those in the first section are prefatory and nonspecialized. They introduce us to the Transcendental world and the peculiar Transcendental vocabulary, while surveying the phenomenon in a broad way and locating its major significances. All agree that the emancipation from the past and the exploitation of the new democratic impulse—the discovery and elevation of the common man—were the keys to the energy it released. Bowers and Tanner are concerned with its philosophical side. Bowers argues that it effected a philosophical reorientation which, by awakening interest in the fundamental questions of human nature and destiny, provided the basic humanistic framework within which all the great literature of the age was created. For him, *Moby-Dick* is as characteristic a product of the new forces as *Walden*. Tanner, writing as an Englishman, sees the Transcendentalists following Wordsworth in developing "a new attitude towards nature, a new point of view." By emphasizing the direct apprehension of reality, they freed themselves from traditional learning—which was knowledge gained at second hand—and pushed the democratic principle so far that not merely the common man but the uneducated child symbolized their faith that spiritual truth was immediately available to all. Carpenter is in general agreement with Bowers, but he tries to trace more closely the philosophical and religious sources on which the Transcendentalists drew, and he places the movement within the wider context of Romanticism.

Hochfield sees it as a response to "the immediate cultural and intellectual predicament" of the time: religion had become impoverished and defensive and the Enlightenment had mechanized human consciousness. He lays major stress on the gradual liberalizing and rationalizing of theology that took place throughout the eighteenth century and which left men, by the 1820s, with little they could believe in and nothing they could feel. The Transcendental doctrine of Reason exploded the received tradition. It "divinized man and endowed him with a dynamic and expansive energy"—this last by way of the notion of continuous organic growth. But any religious tradition became with Transcendentalism discontinuous. For as he points out, it was not a criticism of religion but a rejection of all churches, of any form of mediation between the individual soul and the Divine. It pushed the Protestant principle to the extreme of its logic and, full of optimism, left man there. Yet one of the many paradoxes that resulted was a new emphasis on social reform.

The second group of essays has for its matrix what we usually call the history of ideas. The first of these is a classic piece by the greatest historian of the American mind, Perry Miller. How did New England produce the Transcendentalism of Emerson less than a century after it had known the Calvinism of Jonathan Edwards? Since there is no organic evolution of ideas from Edwards (Transcendentalism's roots are in the Arminianism he abhorred) what continuities persisted in the culture to so completely reshape the radical tradition? As Miller said on another occasion, "What is persistent . . . is the Puritan's effort to confront, face to face, the image of a blinding divinity in the physical universe, and to look upon that universe without the intermediacy of ritual, of ceremony, of the Mass and the confessional."

Everyone knows that John Locke was America's philosopher (the phrase is Merle Curti's), and everyone knows too that the Transcendentalists revolted against the sense-impression basis of his epistemology. What we all know in a general way, Thompson knows intimately. Locke, and through him the Scottish "Common Sense" philosophers, dominated the schools and seminaries of the early National period. If the Transcendentalists were to be able to justify their cardinal point—that through Reason all men had immediate access to the Divine—the older philosophy had to be dethroned. The hero of innate ideas they found to enter the battle behind was Coleridge, and their weapon Marsh's edition (1829) of *Aids to Reflection* (now, happily, reprinted). Locke restricted the extent and nature of human knowledge because he limited its basis. "The soul," *The Dial* said, "is against him."

The two essays which follow uncover the European analogues of the new philosophy. To say "sources" would be misleading, since by and large what the Transcendentalists sought from Europe was not so much information as corroboration. Their central drive was native; only their idiom was borrowed. Wellek starts with the advantage of firsthand knowledge of the relevant German philosophers, and he is able to determine who among the New Englanders knew what, and he discusses how important each influence was. His concern is with Alcott, Ripley, Parker, Brownson, and Margaret Fuller. Of these only Brownson seems to have been able to really study the Germans with critical power, and Wellek concludes that for the rest firsthand contact was not great. The real influence came through Coleridge. Kant they used more for sloganeering than for understanding. The French influence is rightly seen as minor in comparison with the German. But there was a French Eclectic influence, which Joyaux fully documents, though he cautiously points out that it was more a stimulus to speculation than a transference of doctrine.

The essays in the first group all emphasize the positive nature of the democratic impulse in Transcendentalism. Schlesinger, however, is not so confident. Writing as a historian and a champion of Jackson, he is unhappy with the practical side of Transcendental life—or rather the impractical side, for the Transcendentalists could never descend to the ordinary level of day-to-day party politics. Their complete individualism made them democrats but not Democrats. They were poor Party men and Schlesinger deprecates them thus: "The headlong escape into perfection left responsibility far behind for a magic domain where mystic sentiment and gnomic utterance exorcised the rude intrusions of the world." Perry Miller's essay "Emersonian Genius and the American Democracy" (see Bibliography) should be consulted.

Literary histories often link Transcendentalism with such social experiments as Brook Farm, while in fact they represent different impulses. Crowe's essay is a necessary reminder that the union between nonconformists and collectivists could not but be unstable. Anarchists are unsuited to socialist discipline. George Ripley tried heroically to make the two impulses compatible and for a time succeeded, but any success was bound to be temporary. What both Schlesinger and Crowe point to is how little insight Transcendentalism offered into the nature and structure of society, how "unworldly" (in the bad sense) it was. This, more than its famous inability to announce a metaphysics of evil, seems to me its radical weakness.

The third section provides a theological perspective. The essays by Goddard and Hutchison are long and fully developed. Goddard reviews the historical development of Unitarianism from the King's Chapel break-off of 1785, through the work of Channing, to the 1830s and the Transcendental revolt. Hutchison focuses on Emerson's "Divinity School Address" and makes clear why it provoked so bitter an attack from Andrews Norton. He delineates the issues and personalities that were prominent in Massachusetts theological circles in the 1830s, and shows just what is at stake in Emerson's assurance that Christian faith need not depend on the historical truth of Christ's miracles for evidence. By that time there was little other objective evidence left, and Emerson's offer to remove the grounds of faith into the soul's certainty meant, as Norton saw, the end of historical Christianity. The "miracles question" was the central issue and on it everything else divided.

Albrecht has the melancholy duty of recording the Transcendental response to the Civil War. The horrors of that war could not be denied; neither could they be fitted to a philosophy which taught that man and the Universe were perfect and evil merely privative. Transcendentalism did not survive the war. In the gilded age it ceased to matter.

Part IV is concerned with Emerson as the foremost Transcendentalist. Smith traces the problem that attended his resignation from the ministry in 1832—or rather problems, for there were two. The first had been his struggle with the established order and its threat to his self-realization. He had only to settle that problem to be threatened with one more subtle and more severe: how was he to justify his apparent idleness in a strenuous age? How was he to keep from becoming just another Massachusetts crank or social reformer? The Party of the Future could be as sinister as the Party of the Past. His answer was to work out a distinction between Actors and Students and create himself as the American Scholar.

Caponigri, writing as a professional philosopher, sets Emerson off against Orestes Brownson and shows how their careers developed out of their divergent positions on nature and history. Emerson's "peculiar philosophic preoccupation," he says, was "the discrediting of history." His weapon was nature. The Soul, living completely in the present, receiving the Divine Influx through Reason, finds history—the past and all traditions—expendable. It becomes a duty to ignore them since they interfere with the business of living with new intuitions. History is expendable because nature is all-sufficient. Brownson's development is from a Transcendental ahistorical position toward an acceptance of the reality of the past, the contingency of Being, and the radical distinction between man and God.

A basic criticism that must be made is that the Transcendentalists took no interest in fiction. They were interested in moral *statement* and failed utterly to appreciate the novel's capacity for *dramatizing* the ambiguities and con-flicts of the moral life. Emerson's triumph is a triumph of character, the product of keeping his attention forever fixed on virtue and never taking a sidelong glance at anything else. Henry James, a great critic and one of the greatest novelists in the language, was in a unique position to respond with all his gifts to Emerson. He knew Emerson personally through his father, and he had the great novelist's interest in the moral makeup of the New England milieu. His discriminations are the essential ones: no one has surpassed Emerson's "particular faculty," he said, "for speaking to the soul in a voice of direction and authority," but "there were certain complications in life which he never suspected."

Part V contains a sharper criticism made from a somewhat different perspective. Winters boldly lays the blame for Hart Crane's suicide on his adherence to ideas that came to him from Emerson by way of Whitman. He sees the ahistorical belief leading to historical tragedy and the assertion of self-realization as an absolute as destructive of all standards of morality. What kept Emerson from the logic of Crane's position was the Calvinist constraint he continued to feel long after he had separated himself from any creed. By Crane's time no check was present. The argument seems excessively rational-istic and much sport has been made with it in some quarters. But Winters is offering something important. He was a great critic and his views should be attended.

PART I
The Overview

Democratic Vistas

DAVID BOWERS

1

IN QUALITY OF STYLE, AND PARTICULARLY IN DEPTH OF PHILO-
sophic insight, American literature has not yet surpassed the collective
achievement of Emerson, Thoreau, Hawthorne, Melville, and Whitman. Having freed itself in these writers from its earlier tendencies either blindly to
imitate or blindly to reject European models, American literature here for the
first time sloughed off provincialism, and, by being itself—by saying only
what it wanted to say and as it wanted to say it—attained, paradoxically, the
rank and quality of world literature, a literature authentic not only in
America but everywhere the English tongue is understood.

The release was both material and social. There was, to begin with, the
increasing social fluidity of the mid-nineteenth century in the East, with its
accompanying sense of unlimited cultural possibilities. While the West was
expanding and experimenting, those parts of the country which had by now
been settled for more than two hundred years began to lose their sharp social
and regional contrasts and to settle into a cultural homogeneity more like that

of the older civilizations of Europe, though built firmly on a democratic base.

The social stratification of the seaboard colonies, with their mercantile and landed aristocracies, their small farmers, their squatters, and their slaves, had begun to disintegrate during the Revolution, but was not yet reshaped into the industrial class structure of the future. Regionally, colonial distinctions had also broken down with the mounting pressure of populations to the eastward—from Europe to the Atlantic seaboard and from the seaboard to the frontier. The slow process of eroding these regional differences, so important in colonial assemblies, had already achieved, by the intermingling of ideas and of local customs, the national feeling which was to culminate later in a simpler, more inclusive, division of the country into the North, the South, and the West.

Moreover, this flux of institutions and people was marked not by a sense of loss or confusion but by a sense of potentiality and expectancy. The era of good feeling following the War of 1812—a war which at first seemed lost but was miraculously retrieved—had affected all levels of the national life and, blinding men to the risk of the American experiment, revealed only its adventure. And this spirit of self-confidence had been fed by other fires: by the material promise of timber, land, and waterway, convertible at a touch into ready wealth; and by the technological promise—already apparent—of American mechanical and social invention.

Yet neither the general confidence nor the manifold promises of the period can alone explain the peak reached by American literature at this time. For this we must turn to a third and more decisive factor: the reorientation of literature under the influence of New England transcendentalism. For, by reawakening—even among its critics—an interest in the great problems of human nature and destiny, transcendentalism conferred upon American literature a perspective far wider and deeper than that proposed by its own formulated doctrines, the perspective of humanity itself. This perspective it is which gives common purpose and meaning to the otherwise divergent achievements of Emerson, Thoreau, Hawthorne, Melville, and Whitman, and accounts in great part for their manifest superiority to predecessors like Irving and Bryant whose interests were less profound and more superficially literary.

2

Transcendentalism emerged as a full-fledged movement of New England thought between 1815 and 1836. The first date marks the maturing of the liberalizing ministry of William Ellery Channing; the second, the publication of Emerson's *Nature,* the original—and probably the best—systematic expression of the transcendentalist philosophy. Thereafter the movement continued to expand, first as a revolt against the sterile Unitarian orthodoxy, then as a protest against the continuing cultural dependence of America on Europe, and finally as a profound exploration of the spiritual foundations and moral implications of the new democracy. From the beginning it attracted eccentrics no less than men of genius, and after the Civil War it gave way to weaker forms of idealism. But at its zenith in the writings of Emerson, Thoreau, and Alcott—and by its challenge to fresh speculation in Hawthorne, Melville, and Whitman—its vitalizing effect upon American art and literature and, indeed, upon the development of American democracy as a whole, remains unrivaled.

The source of this vitality lies in the intellectual background of transcendentalism: in its appropriation of certain insights of Puritan, Quaker, and other colonial theologies as they had been refracted through the secular and equalitarian ideology of the Revolution; and in its reexpression of these insights in the vocabulary of contemporary European philosophy. For in spite of its oft proclaimed rejection of authority and its frankly nationalistic bias transcendentalism was rooted both in the American past and in the Europe of that day.

To Puritanism in the broadest sense, for example, it owed among other things its pervasive moralism. Like all those early pioneers who sought freedom of conscience in a new land, the transcendentalists were ever disposed to interpret life ethically, to subordinate the aesthetic, intellectual, and even political and economic aspects of human nature to man's significance as a moral agent. Once again, after two centuries and more this conception was used as a means of dignifying all phases of human activity, even the most humble. Thus, just as the Mathers, Edwards, Penn, Woolman, and even Franklin had alike maintained that each man is "called" to perform as faithfully as he can the duties of his particular station in life, so Emerson argued that every act of the individual springs from his inner nature as a unique embodiment of humanity, and hence no occupation is inherently ignoble.

A similar affinity may be discovered between transcendental "intuition" and the doctrine of the "inner light." For each of these theories interpreted material nature mystically as a "veil" or symbol of the divine; and each maintained that every individual can penetrate the veil to discover divine truth for himself without the aid of traditional authority or even of logic.

But none of these doctrines had been transmitted in its original form. The Puritan orthodoxy of New England had from the earliest times been subject to the filtering process of dissent, and had finally succumbed as a rigid and dominant system to the less precise and more rationalized theology of the Unitarians. The tendencies thus manifest on the level of religious thinking were even stronger on that of secular radicalism during the Revolutionary epoch. The worldliness and "common sense" of a Franklin or a Jefferson had apparently made a clean break with earlier orthodoxies while retaining their zeal for moral enlightenment; and the same tendency had but recently moved even further from theological sanction in the equalitarian theory of Jacksonian democracy. These latter-day and transplanted expressions of the

Reformation and the Enlightenment, which had coalesced in the preachings of William Ellery Channing and other predecessors of the transcendental movement in New England, had in some instances added to, but in all instances had transformed, the orthodox teachings of the early religious and secular leaders.

This is illustrated in the new meanings given to the old doctrine of the sovereignty of ethics. For one thing, the equalitarian implications of the doctrine were secularized and broadened to a degree hitherto unknown in this country. Whereas in the orthodox Puritan interpretation the doctrine of the equality of man with man was largely theoretical—being restricted to a mere hypothetical equality before God and the law—and, even in the political philosophy of the Revolution, had accepted social stratification, Jacksonian individualism demanded that it be applied as a practical principle of social reform calling for local autonomy, free public education, and universal suffrage on a scale undreamed of even by Jefferson. Coincidentally, the scope of the principle had been broadened. In place of the old invidious distinction between the elect and the damned which had suggested that only a chosen few were to be admitted to spiritual equality, the Unitarian and Universalist emphasis on the brotherhood of man proclaimed the perfectibility of all.

Still more subtly, this leveling process reoriented the very concept of ethics itself. For although it was still insisted that moral obligation is transcendent in origin—is determined by more than personal whim or habit—that obligation could no longer be construed in abstract universal terms or continue to be rooted in the will of an arbitrary God. Under the influence of Unitarianism, Deity was reduced to a kind of immanent principle implicit in man everywhere, and man himself thereby was made the true source of the moral law. Also, instead of continuing to conceive moral obligation legalistically—as a kind of ritualistic observance of a general code—it was now argued that no single code fits all situations adequately and that each individual must be left perfectly free to judge for himself what his actual duty on any given occasion is. Thus theology made its final effort to provide religious sanction for equalitarian tendencies inherent in the republic from the start.

Equally radical was the transformation of the doctrine of the inner light brought about by the acknowledgment of the autonomous power of secular reason, in part aided by the accelerating conquests of natural science. For this acknowledgment—validated anew by the role of reason in formulating the principles of the Revolution, and manifested concretely both in the rationalism of Unitarian theology and in the pragmatism of frontier thought—had undermined belief in the inner light at two points.

In the first place, it challenged the theoretical competence of the inner light. Although often authoritarian in spirit itself, the new emphasis on reason was wholly antiauthoritarian in implication. Holding with Locke that all knowledge is perceptual in origin, it demanded that every truth be held subject to the test of experiment and observation. And this was a test which, with its implicit mysticism, the doctrine of the inner light as the word of God could not hope to sustain.

In the second place, the new emphasis on reason challenged the doctrine of the inner light on the score of its immediate utility. For while the older doctrine could promise only the quietistic value of bringing man face to face with God, the reason, practically applied, promised a control of nature itself and thereby the immediate satisfaction of human needs.

Yet neither the period generally, nor Unitarianism and democracy in particular, was so pragmatically inclined as to deny the possibility of religious insight entirely. The hold of the Christian tradition upon belief and imagination was still too strong. Nevertheless, certain changes in the conception of the inner light were effected. One of these was to restrict the scope of the inner light to the moral and speculative sphere and to concede to observation priority in the understanding of nature. Another and more important change was the transformation of the inner light into a wholly natural organ. Instead of being dependent, as in the early orthodoxies, upon divine Grace—upon a kind of flooding of the mind by light from without—the power of the inner light was now grounded in the nature of the mind itself, becoming merely one mental faculty among others and subject, therefore, to the same degree of individual control. It was converted, in other words, from a "revelation," an act and agency of God, into an "intuition," an act and agency of man.

It is doubtful whether these transformations of the Puritan ethic and theory of knowledge ever could have become more than vague intellectual tendencies of the time or could have achieved the degree of articulate formulation they subsequently did without the stimulus of contemporary European philosophy. There had emerged in Germany an intellectually sophisticated movement elaborately embodied in the systems of Fichte, Schelling, Schleiermacher, and Hegel, and—at a further remove—in the thought of Coleridge, Carlyle, and Victor Cousin. This movement, idealistic in nature, had its specialized formulas and idioms, its accepted premises and methods. In literature it took the form of romanticism.

It was also a movement whose influence began to be felt in New England about 1820. New England interest in German thought generally goes back much further to William Bentley who acted as cultural ambassador between the merchants of Hamburg and of Salem in the late years of the eighteenth and the early years of the nineteenth century; and, beyond Bentley, to the correspondence of Cotton Mather with the Pietistic theologians of Halle. The interest was not widespread until after the War of 1812, when it became intellectually fashionable for younger New England to make the grand tour or to enroll in German universities, and when particular notice began to be taken of German philosophy as reflected in the writings of its English and French disciples. Later, many of the transcendentalists were to make some pretense of studying German philosophy directly; but their initial—and probably most enduring—impression of the movement was derived from such secondary sources as Marsh's edition (1829) of Coleridge's *Aids to Reflection,* Linberg's translation (1832) of Cousin's *Introduction to the History of Philosophy,* and Carlyle's *Sartor Resartus* (1836).

What was important in this influence was the fact that it made available to the New England writers and through them to American writers generally an elaborate symbolic construction capable not only of expressing the general metaphysical hesitancy of the period—its inability either to retreat into frank supernaturalism or to advance to a bold materialism—but also of providing principles and distinctions whereby this midway position could be explored and defended.

Thus, the doctrine of human individuality as both self-transcending and self-asserting—as both acknowledging its oneness with and obligation to something higher than itself, and yet ever cherishing its uniqueness and independence as a distinct being—and the further conception that individual happiness depends upon the successful synthesis of these twin tendencies, provided an almost perfect theoretical framework for a new effort to discover supernatural sanction for the swift-moving and constantly changing panorama of American life.

Similarly, the distinction found in Coleridge and Emerson alike, between the reason and the understanding—which, by a curious distortion of terminology, identified the reason with intuition and imagination, and the understanding with logic and induction—could express and justify the transcendentalist's desire to retain both the mysticism of the past and the empiricism of the present, and to assign each a sphere in experience proper to its character.

Finally, the idealistic view of the universe as an embodiment of a single, cosmic psyche, now manifesting itself as man, now as nature, and achieving through the interaction of the two in history its own secret intent, permitted the self-asserting impulse of the individual—his determination to be himself at all costs—to be explained as the consciousness of his identity with the world-psyche, while his self-transcending or outgoing impulses could be attributed to the consciousness of his own finitude, to the fact of his awareness that he is only one fragmentary expression of the world-psyche among others. The theory could also account for and validate the distinction between the intuitive and the inductive, interpreting the first of these faculties as the necessary condition for conscious union with the world-psyche, and the second as the necessary condition for survival as a separate expression of that psyche.

The initial function of this movement was thus to act as a kind of model and repository of ideas from which American, and in particular New England, writers could borrow in their self-imposed task of creating a new metaphysic for democracy out of the theological and intellectual materials of the American past. Without slavishly imitating this model, but still inspired by it in various degrees, Emerson, Thoreau, Whitman, and even, by contraries, Hawthorne and Melville were able to achieve a curious blending of the alien and the native, a blending in which specific traditional conceptions were adjusted to specific American use. This fusion is apparent, for example, in Emerson's appeal to the Over-Soul as a sanction for Yankee self-reliance, in Thoreau's discovery that Walden recapitulated the universe in small, and—by its failure— in Melville's ambiguities. It is also apparent in Whitman's *Democratic Vistas,* which preached a new brotherhood of man in terms of the mystic unity of creation, "the divine central idea of All."

But European idealism was to act as more than a mere model for New England transcendentalism. For, working in and through transcendentalism— and reinforced a little later by the influx of roughly similar teachings from the Orient—its influence leavened American literature as a whole, including even the writings of men like Hawthorne and Melville who were actively opposed to transcendentalism proper. The general leavening consisted not so much in the transmission and implanting of specific borrowings—although this also occurred—as it did in the setting of problems and perspectives like the nature of the universe, the origin of evil, and the meaning of experience, which were destined to give American literature a universal import and eventually swing it into the orbit of world literature.

3

At first sight, Emerson, Thoreau, Hawthorne, Melville, and Whitman seem to differ from one another more than they agree. For one thing, they are divergent in temperament. Thoreau, Whitman, and—above all—Emerson are prevailingly optimistic. Hawthorne, on the other hand, is at least fatalistic in point of view; while Melville seems to have run the entire emotional gamut from optimism through pessimism to final resignation. Again, all of them differ widely in their choice of subject matter and literary form. Primarily novelists, Hawthorne and Melville are concerned with the psychological and allegorical analysis of certain types of human personality and moral situations; primarily poets and essayists, Emerson, Thoreau, and Whitman focus, each in his own way, upon the underlying relation of man to nature. Most widely of all, they differ in their interest and capacity for sustained philosophical thought. None of them could be described as interested in philosophical theory for its own sake—not even Emerson, who is less intolerant of abstract reasoning than the rest. But even within these limits their divergency is still great. For although we can find at least traces of a comprehensive philosophical system in Emerson, the traces become progressively more rudimentary in Thoreau, Melville, and Whitman, until at last in Hawthorne they almost disappear.

Yet this incommensurability is not absolute. Common to them as to all great writers, is a profound sense of the human predicament, of the questions that beset man as man, and of the relation of these problems to man's defects and potentialities. Their common concern surmounts all differences, as may be seen in Emerson's and Hawthorne's treatment of the problem of evil. When Emerson proclaims the non-existence of evil in an ultimate form and Hawthorne rejects this conception as tragically blind, neither writer is proceeding on the assumption that the problem of evil itself is unreal or trivial. For Hawthorne, as we know, it is the most pressing of all problems, while for Emerson—as the haunting overtones of "Experience" intimate—it is a problem which can be optimistically resolved only after the most desperate of inward struggles and only after attaining a serenity almost stripped of emotion. In other words, the difference between the two lies not in their conception of the importance of the problem but only in their conception of its proper solution.

Common also to all these writers is the framework of ideas within which they seek to understand the problem of man. Even when it provides quite divergent solutions the framework or perspective is in all instances radically humanistic.

Its basic premise is that man is the spiritual center of the universe and that in man alone can we find the clue to nature, history, and ultimately the cosmos itself. Without denying outright the existence either of God or of brute matter, it nevertheless rejects them as exclusive principles of interpretation and prefers to explain man and his world so far as possible in terms of man himself. This is expressed most clearly in the transcendentalist principle that the structure of the universe literally duplicates the structure of the individual self, and that all knowledge therefore begins with self-knowledge. But it is no less evident in the moral earnestness of Hawthorne and Melville, which leads them to dwell ceaselessly upon the allegory of the human soul and to personalize impersonal nature itself as an allegory of human experience. It is because of this, for example, that few incidents in their plots ever turn out to be wholly fortuitous or to be without symbolic significance for the characters involved in them.

This common perspective is also, in all cases, radically universalized. Its emphasis is almost never upon man as particular—as European, say, or as American—but almost always upon man as universal, upon man as freed from the accidents of time and space as well as from those of birth and talent and reduced to his common humanity. It is apparent not only in Emerson and Thoreau but also in Hawthorne, Melville, and Whitman; none of them even in the most concrete and practical moments can ever quite forget that the drama of man is clothed with the aspect of eternity. Thus, for Emerson, the "American Scholar" turns out to be simply "Man Thinking"; while, for Whitman, the song of himself merges imperceptibly into a song of all the "children of Adam," where "every atom belonging to me as good belongs to you." Thus also, in spite of a frequently high degree of individualization, the characters and situations of Hawthorne and Melville are fundamentally impersonal, emerging at their best as a fusion of particular and type but at their worst as types only.

This turning away from the current scientific view of the world and regression under the impetus of European idealism to the Neo-Platonic conception of nature as a living mystery full of signs and portents, revives a conception with which some of the five were already familiar from their reading in the literature of the seventeenth century and of religious mysticism. At the same time, a principle of correspondence is evolved which promises the reconciliation rather than the rejection of science.

Nor can we overestimate the practical importance of this conception from either the literary or the social point of view. In terms of literature, for instance, its construing of nature as inherently symbolic invests the natural faculty of imagination with a new prestige, dissolving the older literary emphasis upon wit, sentiment, and rationality, and preparing the way for the symbolist literature to come. Even more far-reaching are the social implications of the conception. For by postulating, as it does, an identity between the categories of impersonal nature and the categories of human psychology— and thereby also the unity of creation—the conception provides a metaphysical basis for the belief in democratic equality to which the social philosophy of Emerson, Thoreau, and Whitman can and does appeal.

The second assumption common to all five writers is the belief that individual virtue and happiness depend upon self-realization, and that self-realization, in turn, depends upon the harmonious reconciliation of two universal psychological tendencies: first, the expansive or self-transcending impulse of the self, its desire to embrace the whole world in the experience of a single moment and to know and become one with that world; and second, the contracting or self-asserting impulse of the individual, his desire to withdraw, to remain unique and separate, and to be responsible only to himself.

The current theory of self as expounded by Coleridge and other Europeans was adaptable here, and its importance was more than theoretical because it stated in universal terms the central goal and problem of democracy itself. On the one hand, democracy as a moral and political doctrine implied an ethic of extreme individualism, one which preserved to the individual a maximum degree of freedom and self-expression. On the other hand, the democratic self was divided. There was, first, the conflict between its traditional sense of duty to God and its new-found sense of duty to man. There was, second, the conflict between the duty to self as implied by the concept of liberty and the duty to society as implied by the other two concepts of the revolutionary triad, equality and fraternity. Hence, a doctrine which recognizes the divisions in the self and insists that their reconciliation is necessary for true self-realization defines not only the democratic ethic in general but also the specific hope of democracy that the self can be realized without sacrificing any side of its nature, altruistic as well as egoistic.

There can be no doubt that all five of the writers define the ethical ideal in these terms, although, characteristically, they disagree both on *how* the ideal is to be actualized and on the degree to which it is actualizable. Thus Emerson, Thoreau, and Whitman, who accept its actualization as a real possibility because they have assumed to begin with that the self and the cosmos express one and the same spiritual force, disagree on what specific course of action will convert their inner harmony into an outward fact. For while Emerson and Thoreau believed the harmony can be fully realized by the simple, though paradoxical, expedient of forgetting the world and being true only to oneself, Whitman seems to hold that there is needed an unlimited love of creation as such, a love that will include the self and the world as one.

In contrast to these three stand Hawthorne and Melville, who doubt whether a genuine harmony between the individual and his cosmos is possible at all. For although both assume that the destiny of man is ever to seek such a harmony, they are also deeply convinced that the self and the cosmos are victim to tragic flaws which prevent their ever realizing it. Hawthorne discovers the flaws both in the spiritual pride and spiritual weakness of the individual and in the intractability of his social environment. And Melville identifies them with a defect in the universe at large, symbolized in the inscrutability of the white whale.

But both writers hold that the flaws, in all cases, effectively block a final rapport between the individual and the world. For although the conflict between these two protagonists is sometimes susceptible of an emotional resolution—either by a daemonic assertion of the will, as in Captain Ahab, or by the will's abnegation, as in Hester Prynne and Billy Budd—the resolution is only partial since it is at the cost of eliminating either the world or the self from final moral consideration. In other words, where Emerson, Thoreau, and Whitman discover in the romantic theory of self-realization grounds for ultimate hope, Hawthorne and Melville draw from it only tragic irresolution.

The third assumption common to the five writers is that intuition and imagination offer a surer road to truth than abstract logic or scientific method. It is a corollary to their belief that nature is organic, and corresponds to the technical distinction between the reason as intuition and the understanding as logical analysis. In the specific form of this distinction, the assumption appears frequently in Emerson. But as a general principle underlying both theory and practice it is present in all.

It is illustrated by their emphasis upon introspection—their belief that the clue to outer nature is always to be found in the inner world of individual psychology—and by their constant interpretation of experience as in essence symbolic. For both these stresses presume an organic relationship between the self and the cosmos of which only intuition and imagination can properly take account.

Finally, in terms of the third assumption, all five writers were able to deduce a consequence of immense practical importance not only for their own work but for the subsequent course of American literature as a whole. Not only could the belief in the primacy of imagination be used to justify their own tendency toward the concrete, the metaphorical, and the didactic; it also had the wider implication of attaching greater significance to the craft of literature generally. Once the faculty of imagination is placed on a par with the faculty of reason, the writer as the primary exponent of the imagination acquires an importance in society at least equal to that of the scientist, the philosopher, and the theologian. All equally can then claim to be engaged in the same pursuit: the search for truth.

It is undoubtedly their faith in the imagination and in themselves as practitioners of imagination that enabled Emerson, Thoreau, Hawthorne, Melville, and Whitman to achieve supreme confidence in their own moral and metaphysical insights. It is this also that led them to conceive of the writer as a seer, and thus to exemplify in their attitude toward literature the emphasis upon its responsibility to life which is characteristic of our own day.

4

The close affinity between the idealism of contemporary European philosophy and the romanticism of Emerson, Thoreau, Melville, Hawthorne, and Whitman must not be pressed to the point of identity or to the exclusion of other influences. The sharing between European and American thinkers of common concepts and a common idiom for their expression is merely one more evidence that the young nation was beginning to lose its provincialism and to take its place in the main flow of Western culture. American philosophical thinking had remained true to its own origins, which were of course European in the first instance, through the periods of settlement, early development, and now a first maturity. Once more it could look to Europe for a confirmation by parallel of its own conclusions.

There were, however, significant differences as well as similarities. Where the Europeans of the eighteenth and nineteenth centuries were predominantly intellectual and aesthetic in their interests, the Americans were predominantly moral; and where the Europeans often tended to underscore the role of hierarchy and institutional stability in human affairs, the Americans stressed the ideas of equality and freedom from state interference.

Nor was European philosophy the only such force to act as a catalyst on the nineteenth century American mind. Its importance was taken for granted even though it was not fully understood by the earlier critics of New England transcendentalism. Recently there has been a tendency to underestimate it in favor of the obvious influences of Neo-Platonic and Oriental kinds of idealism in giving new forms and a new vocabulary to American thinkers. Historians have demonstrated the catalytic effect of Plato and Plotinus on Emerson and of the Bhagavad-Gita and other Oriental tales and poems on Emerson and Thoreau. But more often than not such influences out of the past were shared by American writers with their European contemporaries, and the precise channels or directions of their flow can be distinguished only with the greatest difficulty. The minds of Emerson, Whitman, and Melville were characteristically American in their willingness to appropriate usable ideas wherever they might be found, without too much concern for logical consistency, and it is safer to assume that these men obtained many of their principal assumptions—or at least the language in which such ideas found expression—through their alert interest in the dominant intellectual movements of the time rather than from any single source in the past.

Whatever the sources or channels of their common feeling, the fact remains that there existed between these five Americans and their European contemporaries a community of interest based upon the use of a common philosophical idiom and upon the discovery, as a result of the common vocabulary, of a common set of problems approached in a common spirit. This community helps explain the promptness with which Emerson, Thoreau, and others of the group were "discovered" and acclaimed abroad. It also helps explain the almost proprietary sense these writers themselves had in European literary and philosophical movements.

Of even greater moment was the fact that contact with European philosophy and literature established a spiritual continuity not only with their contemporaries but with the great literary and philosophical traditions of the past. For in rediscovering such fundamental conceptions of Western culture as the correspondence between man and nature and the doctrine of the poet as seer, these writers acquired something more than a set of inert principles. Rather, by means of these ideas—by accident of the fact that the ideas had been perennial to Western thought—they acquired that spirit of universality which has characterized Western literature at its greatest moments, even making it capable of absorbing the best of the Orient. Thus the preoccupation with local customs, local legends, and local scenes characteristic of the earlier writers in the seaboard states, and again of those of the frontier, was generalized, at least for a moment of literary fulfillment, into a profound concern with human nature, while democracy itself instead of continuing to be construed as a mere experiment in government was now subjected to a more thorough examination of its fundamental moral and metaphysical meanings.

In other words, European philosophical theory, acting as a primary catalyst for forces already deeply indigenous to the American mind, had effected and accelerated a reorientation of literature which was tantamount to raising it to a new plane. Having revealed the American character and experience as identical in form and substance with the character and experience of man everywhere, it had created the conditions whereby American literature without ceasing to be national could become a part of world literature. And it is one measure of the genius of Emerson, Thoreau, Hawthorne, Melville, and Whitman that they were able to transmute this possibility into an opportunity.

2

Transcendentalism

FREDERICK IVES CARPENTER

"TRANSCENDENTALISM MEANS, SAYS OUR ACCOMPLISHED MRS. B., with a wave of her hand, *a little beyond.*" So Emerson half-humorously described the idea in his *Journals* for October 6, 1836. And five years later, on October 8, 1841, he added a second half-humorous description: "The view taken of Transcendentalism in State Street is that it threatens to invalidate contracts." Somewhere between these two extremes the idea developed in New England. Like the word, "Yankee," "Transcendental" was first applied with mild contempt but soon was accepted with cheerful defiance. If Transcendentalism seemed sometimes vague and immaterial, it also seemed sometimes revolutionary and practical.

Writing of *Transcendentalism in New England,* its first historian thus described the idea:

> With some truth it may be said that there never was such a thing as Transcendentalism out of New England. In Germany and France there was a transcendental philosophy . . . but it never affected society in its organized institutions or practical interests. In old England, this philosophy influenced poetry and art, but left the daily existence of men and women

From *Emerson Handbook* by Frederick Ives Carpenter (New York: Hendricks House, 1953). Reprinted by permission of Hendricks House, Inc.

untouched. But in New England, the ideas entertained by the foreign thinkers took root in the native soil and blossomed out in every form of social life.[1]

That is, Transcendentalism in New England took many different forms. First, it paid lip-service to the formal philosophy of Immanuel Kant, but greatly modified it. Second, it developed the Puritan religion of its own New England past in new ways. Third, it applied this philosophic idealism and this religious enthusiasm to the practical reform of American social institutions. And, finally, it stimulated a "renaissance" in American literature—a renaissance whose first exponent was Ralph Waldo Emerson. We shall consider its manifestations in philosophy, in religion, in society, and in literature.

a. In Philosophy. In the first paragraph of his famous essay on "The Transcendentalist," Emerson defined the idea as accurately as possible: "What is popularly called Transcendentalism among us is Idealism; Idealism as it appears in 1842."[2] Broadly, he compared it with "the very oldest of thoughts . . . Buddhism is an expression of it." Only later did he specify that:

> The Idealism of the present day acquired the name Transcendental from the use of that term by Immanuel Kant, of Königsberg, who replied to the skeptical philosophy of Locke, which insisted that there was nothing in the intellect which was not previously in the experience of the senses, by showing that there was a very important class of ideas or imperative forms, which did not come by experience, but through which experience was acquired; that these were intuitions of the mind itself; and he denominated them Transcendental forms.[3]

Because the *name* "Transcendentalism" had always been associated with Kant, historians (especially historians of philosophy) have often sought to identify New England Transcendentalism with Kantianism. But Emerson did not make this identification, either in theory or in practice. Only the name was Kantian.

Emerson's Transcendentalism derived from oriental mysticism, from Neoplatonic idealism, and from a diluted form of Kant's philosophy as interpreted by Coleridge, Carlyle, and other amateur philosophers. It included some religious and philosophical elements of mysticism, which were largely lacking in Kant. It included a monistic idealism, which the Neoplatonists had grafted upon Platonism. And it blurred the sharp distinction between "Pure Reason" and "Practical Reason" which Kant had made.

The chief idea which Emerson derived from Kant was the distinction between the transcendental "Reason" and the empirical "understanding." "Reason" described "the intuitions of the mind itself," as opposed not only to sensational empiricism but to mechanical logic and rationalism as well. This intuitive "Reason" resembled that perfect "reason" which Swift imputed to the Houyhnhnms, beloved by Gulliver, rather than the logical reason that we now associate with the word. Finding this idea in Coleridge,[4] Emerson elaborated it, first in his Journals and Letters[5] and then in his first book, *Nature*. This intuitive "Reason"—and the religions, poetic, or symbolic "truth" to which it promised access—formed the very foundation of his transcendental philosophy.

But Kant had warned that this "pure" Reason could not be applied practically to the world of the senses. Coleridge repeated this warning[6] and then partially disregarded it, sometimes using the idea for his own purposes. Emerson noted these warnings, and at first heeded them. But soon Emerson began equating transcendental "intuition" with "instinct." And at the end of *Nature* he wrote that "if [Man] have elemental power . . . it is not conscious power . . . it is instinct." Thereafter, Emerson often used the words "intuition" and "instinct" almost interchangeably. And practically this confusion converted Emerson's Transcendentalism into a naturalistic philosophy. Disregarding or ignoring the subtle distinctions of Kantian logic, Emerson kept the language and the sanctions of transcendental idealism, but changed their meanings and used them in new ways.

When he equated transcendental "Reason" or intuition with "instinct," Emerson opened a Pandora's box of primitivistic and romantic delusions. For this he has justly been attacked and condemned.[7] But although Emerson's confusion of intuition with instinct was logically dangerous, it also suggested the pragmatic path which modern philosophy has taken in reconciling mystical idealism with empirical naturalism.

If the transcendental "intuitions" are considered as "hypotheses"—to be tested and corrected by later observation and experiment, rather than to be accepted uncritically as absolute truth—they offer the only possible path to discovery of scientific laws. So Charles Sanders Peirce[8] later emphasized and prepared the way for Pragmatism and the modern philosophy of science. So Bertrand Russell suggested when he related the intuitions of the mystics to the hypotheses of the scientists. So George Santayana implied when he first criticized Emerson's idealism as subjective and "genteel," but then added that Transcendentalism "is a plan of those avenues of inference by which our ideas of things must be reached . . . In other words, transcendentalism is the critical logic of science . . . Transcendental logic, the method of discovery for the mind, was to become also the method of evolution in nature and history. Transcendental method, abused, produced transcendental myth."[9]

Emerson's Transcendentalism, therefore, was not philosophically pure but was compounded of "Reason" and of "myth." He lived between two worlds—the supernatural and the natural—striving constantly to reconcile them. If he had not cared so much for the actual "conduct of life," he might have become a pure logical philosopher. If he had not cared so much for the eternal truths, he might have remained merely a successful pastor, like his father and grandfather before him. As it was, he constantly explored the unknown ways of thought that promised to lead from supernaturalism to naturalism, and often lost his way. But as Joseph Warren Beach has written: "Transcendentalism was an absolutely necessary step in the transition from supernaturalism to naturalism . . . But the transcendentalists themselves did not develop the possibilities of naturalism. They approached it from the wrong side."[10]

Nevertheless, from this "wrong side" Emerson constantly caught vistas of the truths which modern thinkers have explored, and threw out suggestions which they have followed. Perhaps because Emerson's Transcendentalism was not philosophically pure, it has proved more fruitful than the more logical thought of less imaginative men.

b. In Religion. One of the causes of the impurity of Emerson's philosophy was the fact that "Transcendentalism in New England" was a religion before it was a philosophy. Whereas in Germany Kant's logic was the determining element, in America Emerson and his associates were men of religion, both by training and by temperament. Their Transcendentalism developed the religious idealism of their own Puritan past primarily and only borrowed the forms and phrases of German thought secondarily. As O. B. Frothingham justly observed: "It requires an effort to forget that the speculative basis of their faith was not the natural basis of the philosopher but the supernatural one of the believer." Suggesting that Jonathan Edwards himself was "transcendental" in part, Frothingham concluded:

> Indeed, whenever orthodoxy spread its wings and rose into the region of faith, it lost itself in the sphere where the human soul and the divine were in full concurrence. Transcendentalism simply claimed for all men what Protestant Christianity claimed for its own elect.[11]

And H. C. Goddard, the second major interpreter of the movement, emphasized that: "They were Puritans to the core. This . . . was the signally American contribution to transcendentalism."[12]

In other words, American Transcendentalism was primarily religious rather than philosophical. Its inspirational force was what Emerson called "the religious sentiment," rather than the Kantian "Reason" on the one hand, or the merely practical desire to reform society on the other. It developed the "piety" of the early Puritans rather than their logical theology or their social "moralism." When Andrews Norton attacked Emerson's "Divinity School Address," he justly compared its sentiment to the earlier mysticism and emotionalism of Edwards. American Transcendentalism was primarily a reassertion of the mystical basis of all religion.

But historically, of course, New England Transcendentalism was a specific reassertion of this religious sentiment, in reaction first against the rationalism of the Unitarians, and second against the pessimism of the Calvinists.

By origin, New England Transcendentalism was merely a branch of Unitarianism. Indeed, the latest *Encyclopaedia Britannica*[13] article on "Unitarianism" still describes Emerson as one of the leaders of the "second period" of Unitarianism and goes on to describe "the third period" beginning "about 1885" as one of "recognition of universal religion." Whether Transcendentalism be defined as a separate sect or as a part of Unitarianism, the facts remain that the leading Transcendentalists were Unitarian ministers by training, and that many continued in this profession throughout their lives. It is probable that today Emerson is quoted more often from Unitarian pulpits and from the pulpits of "the Community Church" movement than from academic lecture platforms.

Specifically, Transcendentalism shared three fundamental ideas which Unitarianism had emphasized in its attack on Calvinism. Emerson might even have subscribed to the exact words with which William Ellery Channing, the greatest Unitarian, announced these tenets.

First, Unitarianism, as its name implies, rejected the idea of the Trinity and declared its belief that "there is One God, even the Father; and that Jesus Christ is not this One God, but his son and messenger."[14] By denying the divinity of Jesus and by emphasizing his humanity, Unitarianism and Transcendentalism both implied that human individuals might ultimately hope to realize the Christian ideal in this actual world.

Second, Unitarianism and Transcendentalism both opposed the exclusive and sectarian nature of Calvinism and of Catholicism alike:

> Our aim is not sectarian . . . Far from us be this spirit of exclusion, the very spirit of antichrist, the worst of all the delusions of Popery and of Protestantism. We hold nothing to be essential but the simple and supreme dedication of the mind, heart, and life to God and to his will.[15]

Emphasizing that *all* men may hope to realize this Christian ideal through perfect self-dedication, Emerson and Channing both looked forward to an inclusive Universal Religion.

Third, Unitarianism and Transcendentalism both opposed most emphatically the Calvinist emphasis on sin, and on its violent punishment in hell-fire. So Channing attacked the "abject and slavish fear" of one "whose spirit has been broken to this creed"; and in its place emphasized that "the ultimate reliance of a human being is and must be on his own mind . . . Conscience is the highest faculty given us by God."[16] Emerson's "Self-Reliance" stemmed directly from this Unitarian liberalism but placed less emphasis on the "mind," and more on "the religious sentiment."

Indeed, New England Transcendentalism diverged from Unitarianism for the same reason that it diverged from Kantian Transcendentalism: it exalted man's "heart" and soul above his mere "mind" (Hawthorne to the contrary notwithstanding). It reasserted the "piety" of the old Puritan religion and

even justified that religious "enthusiasm" which Edwards had shared with
Whitefield and the eighteenth century revivalists. In the words of Professor
Perry Miller, it declared man's "refusal to live by decorum and sobriety
alone."[17]

Specifically, Transcendentalism left behind all the forms and traditions of
the Unitarian Church, placing its reliance on the conscience, intuition, or
"inner light." In his farewell sermon on "The Lord's Supper," Emerson had
borrowed many of his arguments against formal religion from the Quakers.[18]
In his "Divinity School Address," he went on to reject "Historical Christianity" itself in favor of "the religious sentiment" in the soul of man. Going
beyond Unitarianism and all institutionalized churches, he sought to make
religion effective by ending the separation between Sabbath religion and
secular life.

Inevitably, since Transcendentalism undermined institutional Unitarianism, even while enlarging many of its religious ideas, many practical Unitarians opposed it. But orthodox Unitarians opposed it for other reasons as well:
when Andrews Norton attacked Emerson's "Divinity School Address" as
"The Latest Form of Infidelity," he denounced its "pantheistic" ideas. For
Emerson not only rejected the authority of the Church as an institution. He
also rejected the authority of the Bible as Revelation; and, finally, he even
rejected the traditional, anthropomorphic concept of God as a "person,"
exalting rather the impersonal laws of science and the impersonal beauty of
nature. Small wonder that Calvinists gloated:

> Step by step the Unitarian theology has come down from the true position
> as to the inspiration of the scriptures, and thus having abandoned the only
> sure footing, those who are foremost in the descent have found themselves
> among the ooze and quicksands of atheistic philosophy.[19]

But if the orthodox were right in pointing to the non-theistic nature of
Emerson's Transcendentalism, they were wrong in declaring that "there is
nothing of the scriptures in it."[20] Transcendentalism merely sought to reassert
the mysterious nature of God ("I am that I am") and to rediscover His
manifestations in nature and in the soul of man. In so doing, it sometimes
rejected and sometimes continued the religious ideas of Puritan and of
Unitarian Christianity. But it always went "a little beyond."

c. In Society. Emerson's editorial introduction to the first issue of *The
Dial* described the social constituency of Transcendentalism perfectly. The
passage is worth quoting at length:

> No one can converse much with different classes of society in New
> England without marking the progress of a revolution. Those who share in
> it have no external organization, no badge, no creed, no name. They do
> not vote, or print, or even meet together. They do not know each other's

faces or names. They are united only in a common love of truth, and love of its work. They are of all conditions and constitutions. Of these acolytes, if some are happily born and well bred, many are no doubt ill-dressed, ill-placed, ill-made, with as many scars of hereditary vice as other men. Without pomp, without trumpet, in lonely and obscure places, in solitude, in servitude, in compunctions and privations, trudging beside the team in the dusty road or drudging a hireling in other men's cornfields, school-masters, who teach a few children the rudiments for a pittance, ministers of small parishes of the obscurer sects, lone women in dependent condition, matrons and young maidens, rich and poor, beautiful and hard-favored, without concert or proclamation of any kind, they have silently given in their several adherence to a new hope, and in all companies do signify a greater trust in the nature and resources of man, than the laws or the popular opinions will well allow.

This spirit of the time is felt by every individual with some differences— to each one casting its light upon the objects nearest to his temper and habits of thought; to one, coming in the shape of special reforms in the state; to another, in modifications of the various callings of men and the customs of business; to a third, opening a new scope for literature and art; to a fourth, in philosophical insight; to a fifth, in the vast solitudes of prayer. It is in every form a protest against usage, and a search for principles. In all its movements, it is peaceable. . . .[21]

Naturally a spontaneous movement as individualistic and anti-institutional as Transcendentalism lacked official, social forms and organizations of its own. Nevertheless, an informal discussion group known afterwards as the "Transcendental Club" had been organized in 1836 to bring together the leaders of the group. And the famous magazine, *The Dial*, gave it a voice from 1840 to 1844. If to these we add Alcott's Temple School, the ideal "communities" indirectly associated with the movement, and various reform "conventions" attended by many of its members, the list is complete.

The "Transcendental Club"[22] originated informally as a group of liberal intellectuals meeting in turn at the various homes of its members. It was first known as "Hedge's Club" after Frederic Henry Hedge, Unitarian minister and later Professor of Ecclesiastical History and German Literature at Harvard. It met first at the home of George Ripley, later the head of Brook Farm, and next at the Boston home of Bronson Alcott. Theodore Parker, Henry Thoreau, Margaret Fuller, and other leading Transcendentalists later attended its irregular meetings irregularly. The "Club," however, did furnish a meeting ground for the discussion of the new ideas, and from it emerged *The Dial* after many uncertainties. Here "the communities" were discussed and partly planned, though with many dissenting voices. Then, after producing these concrete results, it ceased to be.

Probably *The Dial* was the most typical and tangible product of New

England Transcendentalism, and certainly Emerson was its leading spirit. Although Margaret Fuller was editor for the first two years, and George Ripley was its first business manager, Emerson contributed more voluminously and more consistently than any other author and also helped continuously with its business affairs. For its last two years he was both editor and business manager, and, finally, even financial "angel."

The Dial illustrates both the bad and the good qualities of pure Transcendentalism. It was, as Carlyle (and many others) complained, "too ethereal." It never came to grips with the problems of "the times," in spite of a few topical articles by Emerson and Parker on reform and labor movements, and by Margaret Fuller on women's rights; but it concentrated on "the eternities." It printed many translations, many dull critical essays, and much poor poetry—both in prose and verse. It suffered (partly of necessity) from inbreeding (for instance, printing various excerpts from the writings of Emerson's ill-fated younger brothers and some poems of his first wife, Ellen).

But *The Dial* probably published more famous articles and poems by more famous men of letters than any other American magazine of its small scope and brief span. Besides Emerson, many of whose poems and essays first saw print in its pages, it introduced Thoreau to the reading public, as well as several minor poets like Jones Very and Ellery Channing. It gave Margaret Fuller and Alcott a new voice. And, beyond personalities, it helped to introduce two new realms of literature to the American public: most obviously, the writings of the German romantic poets and Transcendental philosophers; but perhaps more important, the "ethnic scriptures" or religious literatures of the East. Going beyond "the times" to "the eternities," it helped stimulate the American Renaissance.

Meanwhile Brook Farm and Alcott's "Fruitlands" had attempted to institutionalize the social idealism of the Transcendental movement. But Emerson remained skeptical of these and all other utopias. In practice he would go only a "little beyond," although in theory he sympathized with the perfectionists. Perhaps his half-humorous essay reporting the "Chardon Street Convention of Friends of Universal Reform" best suggests his attitude toward social Transcendentalism:

> If the assembly was disorderly, it was picturesque. Madmen, madwomen, men with beards, Dunkers, Muggletonians, Come-outers, Groaners, Agrarians, Seventh-day Baptists, Quakers, Abolitionists, Calvinists, Unitarians, and Philosophers—all came successively to the top, and seized their moment, if not their hour, wherein to chide, or pray or preach, or protest. The faces were a study.[23]

Although Transcendentalism stimulated social reform, Emerson remained an individualist.

Nevertheless, Emerson remained the leader of the Transcendentalists cause he best gave expression to their ideals—both religious and social—even he did not try to realize them at once. His books became the bible of the social reformers of his day and of many practical-minded men and women who were not interested in philosophy or religion. The testimony of Charles Dickens, novelist and reformer, is perhaps typical of all these:

> There has sprung up in Boston [wrote Dickens in his *American Notes*] a sect of philosophers known as Transcendentalists. On inquiring what this appellation might be supposed to signify, I was given to understand that whatever was unintelligible would be certainly Transcendental. Not deriving much comfort from this elucidation, I pursued the inquiry still further, and found that the Transcendentalists are followers of my friend Mr. Carlyle, or I should rather say, of a follower of his, Mr. Ralph Waldo Emerson. This gentlemen has written a volume of Essays, in which among much that is dreamy and fanciful, if he will pardon me for saying so, there is much more that is true and manly, honest and bold. Transcendentalism has its occasional vagaries (what School has not?), but it has good healthful qualities in spite of them . . . If I were a Bostonian, I think I would be a Transcendentalist.[24]

d. In Literature. Although Transcendentalism in America purported to be a logical philosophy and to develop the ideas of Immanuel Kant, and although it did develop the religious ideas and attitudes of Puritanism and Unitarianism, and although it actually contributed to the social reforms and experiments of the times, its greatness lay primarily in its contribution to American literature. (Emerson and his associates used the abstract ideas of philosophy, the emotional faith of religion, and the forms of democratic society to create a literature that was new and challenging.)

The literary significance of Transcendentalism has only begun to be appreciated, partly because of its confusion with Kantian philosophy and partly because of its confusion with literary Romanticism (which we shall consider in the next section). This significance was suggested by Professor F. O. Matthiessen, who pointed out that Transcendentalism stimulated "The American Renaissance" by calling into question and reexamining all the old assumptions and ideas which Western European civilization had come to consider either axiomatic or proven. And it was first clearly defined by Professor David Bowers,[25] who pointed out that Transcendentalism in America developed a series of "Democratic Vistas," whose framework gave form and meaning not only to the writings of Emerson, Thoreau, and Whitman, who optimistically believed in the actual realization of the democratic dream, but also to the writings of Hawthorne and Melville, who symbolically described its tragic defeat.

Superficially, American Transcendentalism reproduced the literary charac-

icism, praising intuition rather than logic, poetry rather
re rather than the society of man. Moreover it shared the
the past and the romantic idealization of the common

ranscendentalism converted the romantic revolt from the
assertion of the independence of American literature and culture
the European past. And it converted the romantic idealization of the
common man into an assertion of the infinite potentialities of all men and of
their equality before God. The first assertion received classic expression in
Emerson's address on "The American Scholar." The second gave form and
significance to all the literature of "The American Renaissance."

Fundamentally, American Transcendentalism was, as Professor Bowers has
described it, "a profound exploration of the spiritual foundations and moral
implications of the new democracy."[26] It attempted to explore the "metaphysics of democracy" by developing the equalitarian implications of the
doctrine of "the inner light," or the intuitive reason. In Emerson's words, it
gave its "adherence to a new hope . . . a greater trust in the nature and
resources of man, than the laws or the popular opinions will well allow."[27]
Declaring that "all things are possible," it called into question the orthodox
dogmas and the classical formulations of religion and philosophy. Believing in
the ability of man to govern himself and eventually to determine his own
destiny, it suggested a whole new philosophy of life and scale of values, and it
explored the implications of this in imaginative literature.

The Transcendental belief in the infinite potentialities of the common man
gave greatness to the writings of Emerson—and after him, Thoreau and
Whitman. American Transcendentalism first fully explored the psychological
implications of this belief, which has also been called "The American
Dream." But this complex idea can only be described in a later section.

NOTES

1. O.B. Frothingham, *Transcendentalism in New England* (New York, 1876), p. 105.

2. *The Complete Works of Ralph Waldo Emerson,* Centenary Edition, 12 vols. (Boston, 1903-04), I, 329.

3. *Ibid.,* pp. 339-40.

4. See Coleridge, *Aids to Reflection,* "On the Difference in Kind of Reason and the Understanding."

5. *The Journals of Ralph Waldo Emerson,* ed. Edward Waldo Emerson and Waldo Emerson Forbes, 10 vols. (Boston, 1909-14), III, 235-39; *The Letters of Ralph Waldo Emerson,* ed. Ralph L. Rusk, 6 vols. (New York, 1939), I, 412-13.

6. See Coleridge, *loc. cit.;* and *The Cambridge History of English Literature,* article on Coleridge, XI, 137.

7. See Yvor Winters, *In Defense of Reason,* chapter on "Jones Very and Emerson" (Denver, 1947), pp. 262-82.

8. See F. I. Carpenter, "C. S. Peirce: Pragmatic Transcendentalist," *New England Quarterly,* XIV (March 1941), 34-48.

9. George Santayana, *Winds of Doctrine* (New York, 1912), pp. 194-95, essay on "The Genteel Tradition in American Philosophy."

10. J. W. Beach, "Emerson and Evolution," *University of Toronto Quarterly,* III (1934), 474-97.

11. Frothingham, *Transcendentalism in New England,* p. 108.

12. H. C. Goddard, *Studies in New England Transcendentalism* (New York, 1908), p. 188.

13. John H. Lathrop, "Unitarianism: United States," *Encyclopaedia Britannica,* 14th ed.

14. W. E. Channing, address delivered at the dedication of the Second Congregational Unitarian Church, New York, 1826.

15. *Ibid.*

16. W. E. Channing, *The Moral Argument Against Calvinism,* 1820.

17. Perry Miller, ed., *The Transcendentalists* (Cambridge, Mass., 1950).

18. M. C. Turpie, "A Quaker Source for Emerson's Sermon on the Lord's Supper," *New England Quarterly,* XVII (March 1944), 95-101.

19. From an anonymous review of Emerson's *Essays: First Series* in *Biblical Repertory and Princeton Review,* XIII, 544. The controversy which centered on Emerson's "Divinity School Address" is outlined by Clarence Faust, "The Background of the Unitarian Opposition to Transcendentalism," *Modern Philology,* XXXV (February 1938), 297-324. Some of these controversial documents are reprinted in Miller, *The Transcendentalists.*

20. Faust, *loc. cit.*

21. *Uncollected Writings: Essays, Addresses, Poems, Reviews and Letters by Ralph Waldo Emerson* (New York, 1912), pp. 32-33.

22. The best, though brief, account of this club occurs in Ralph L. Rusk's *The Life of Ralph Waldo Emerson* (New York, 1949), pp. 243 ff.

23. Emerson, *Works,* X, 374. (First published in *The Dial,* July 1842).

24. O. W. Holmes, *Ralph Waldo Emerson* (Boston, 1884), p. 119.

25. Bowers, "Democratic Vistas," in Spiller, Thorp, Johnson and Canby, *The Literary History of the United States,* 3rd. ed., rev. (New York, 1963), I, 345-57.

26. *Ibid.,* p. 346.

27. See note 23 above.

An Introduction
to Transcendentalism

GEORGE HOCHFIELD

1

LIKE THOSE OF ALL MOVEMENTS IN INTELLECTUAL HISTORY, THE
outlines of American Transcendentalism are indistinct. Its beginnings merge
with the liberal tendencies of Boston Unitarianism; its endings are a confused
record of unforeseeable careers, ephemeral publications, and a historical
influence that still affects the intellectual life of contemporary America.
Despite this vagueness at the edges, however, Transcendentalism was a real
and significant event, a somewhat provincial and peculiar manifestation of the
more general phenomenon of Romanticism. During its heyday—roughly the
decade 1836-1846—it exerted a fascination over most of the active literary
minds of the country, whether in sympathy or repulsion. It flowered brilliant-
ly in the masterpieces of Emerson, Thoreau, and Whitman; the problems it
raised concerning knowledge, freedom, nature, art, democracy obsessed the
minds of Poe, Hawthorne, and Melville. And possibly of equal importance
with its strictly literary manifestations, Transcendentalism made a lasting
impression on the American character. It gave shape and meaning to a certain

From *Selected Writings of the American Transcendentalists* by George
Hochfield. Copyright © 1966 by George Hochfield. Reprinted by arrange-
ment with The New American Library, Inc., New York, New York.

inchoate American idealism. The portrait of the self-reliant man, the follower of his conscience, the divinely inspired democratic individual, which is passionately delineated in the writings of the whole Transcendentalist group, helped to create and identify an American type that seems to have become a permanent element of the national life. It is hard to imagine the forms American rebellion might have taken during the past one hundred and twenty years if Brook Farm had not existed, *The Dial* had not been published, and works like "Civil Disobedience" had not been written.

Transcendentalism was, of course, as much a product of its time and place as an influence upon them. I have called it a manifestation of Romanticism, and its debt to certain key ideas that swept Europe in the early nineteenth century is unmistakable. The divinity of nature, the glory of human aspiration and freedom, the power of intuition as opposed to reason, the creative energy of the poetic imagination—these are some of the themes imported into America by writers like Hedge, Brownson, Ripley, and Fuller, as well as Emerson. Indeed, Transcendentalism, as a radical and innovating movement, invented the typical American avant-garde strategy of allying itself with European masters as both an offensive and a defensive measure against conservative resistance at home. Some of the most important acts of self-assertion by members of the group took the form of an exposition of foreign ideas or a tribute to a foreign hero. By such means the names and the thought of a whole range of writers, from Kant and Goethe to Cousin, Wordsworth, Coleridge, and Carlyle, entered into the discussion of American issues and broadened the scope of American literary culture.

But foreign influences did not create Transcendentalism; they would have been quite meaningless if they had not responded to a prior need stemming from an immediate cultural and intellectual predicament. This predicament, which may be defined as the impoverishment of religion and the mechanization of consciousness as a result of eighteenth-century rationalism and empiricism, was one, of course, which Europe shared. But in America, against the background of a successful democratic revolution and the subsequent release of enormous physical energy, it was a predicament which came to be felt with special acuteness as involving anomalies and limitations of thought intolerable in the light of social realities. What the young men who came of age in the 1820's and 1830's—the first intellectual generation born after the completion of the revolutionary struggle and the founding of the nation—what these young men felt most deeply was that a radically new world was taking shape around them, requiring for its comprehension and its fulfillment a new vision of man. It was the need for such a vision, and the literary means of defining it, that caused them to turn to the great European Romantics for inspiration; it was this need, more fundamentally, which called Transcendentalism into being and gave it its distinctive American character.

For in its essence Transcendentalism was an attempt to complete in the world of thought what the American revolution had begun in the world of action. If one may attribute, for the sake of definition, a single overriding motive to the Transcendentalist group, it was no less than the creation of a new literature, the literature, in a word, of democracy. Democracy had already taken political shape in America, and the democratic ideals of equality and liberty were already deeply implanted in the American spirit, but the inmost meaning of democracy—its new conception of the nature of man, his place in the world, and his relation to the divine—had hardly been thought about as yet and never adequately expressed. For the Transcendentalists, whether they understood themselves in these terms or not, the immediate duty and the prospective glory of literature was to bring into consciousness this inmost meaning which the life of society was already shadowing forth. This is not to suggest that they had a common program, nor that their concern with the meaning of democracy was only a variety of literary nationalism. Although they sometimes wrote of America as though its destiny was to be a messiah among the nations, the main tendency of their thought was universal, toward a new humanism that embraced all mankind and obliterated the petty distinctions of nationality. America, having found the path of democracy, might lead the way to millennium, but millennium was the age-old dream of the emancipation and unity of man.

2

The first distinguishable signs of what came to be called Transcendentalism appeared as expressions of dissatisfaction with the philosophic underpinnings of the reigning New England churches, both "orthodox" (i.e., Calvinist) and Unitarian. The theme of this dissatisfaction was the churches' reliance upon Lockian empiricism (what the Transcendentalist critics called "sensualism") as a way of explaining the origin and formation of ideas in the mind, including ideas about religion. But the real meaning of the attack on Locke, at first only hinted at but soon frankly asserted, was an impatience with the sterility and complacence of the churches, their failure to make religion a vital part of the lives of their communicants. The complaint, at bottom, was that New England piety was dying, and that a false philosophy was killing it. The churches had lost their power to inspire an active faith; they were absorbed in arid theological wrangling and hair-splitting, or they were simply, as Emerson said of Boston Unitarianism, "corpse-cold."

Locke was vulnerable to attack because his immensely influential theory of knowledge—which had become part of New England Calvinism through the agency of Jonathan Edwards, and which was the cornerstone of Unitarian apologetics—had become increasingly identified during the course of the eighteenth century with purely natural and rationalistic ways of thinking. Locke conceived of the mind as a blank page on which ideas of the external world were inscribed through the senses, or as a kind of mechanical organizer of sensations which were fed to it by "experience." This view appeared very well suited to explain the processes of scientific classification and experiment or the formation of common-sense judgments on practical matters, but it tended to create the assumptions that only the physical, the tangible, the measurable were real, and that consciousness was a prisoner of the senses. Locke had no intention of casting doubt on religion; he thought that religion could be defended by the means of common sense; but his epistemology proved to be a potent weapon of religious skepticism. The history of eighteenth-century religious thought shows the impossibility of making Christianity meet the standards of common sense. It is a history of steady drift, through all the forms of rational or "natural" religion, away from the ancient sanctions of revelation and dogma toward the open seas of mechanism or pantheism, idealism, materialism, antinomianism, or outright atheism.

The Romantic movement was, in one of its major aspects, a violent reaction against the assumptions created by Lockian epistemology. Stimulated by Kant and his followers in Germany, and by the revival of various forms of Platonism and intuitionism, the Romantics sought to free consciousness from the tyranny of sensation and to restore it as an active, generative force in the achievement of knowledge. By this means they hoped to reestablish communication with a realm of truth from which science and common sense had seemed fatally to divide man: the realm of inward illumination and spiritual insight, of value and meaning not given directly to the senses. Romanticism was not necessarily linked to a revival of orthodox Christianity—the Enlightenment had done its work too well for that—but it brought a fresh awareness of the spiritual possibilities in man that reawakened religious instincts all over Europe. It encouraged the emergence of a new kind of religious individualism, and it set in motion currents of renovation that troubled the peace of those churches especially which had most fully come to terms with the Age of Reason.

Such a church was the Unitarianism of Boston and eastern Massachusetts in the first third of the nineteenth century. Unitarianism was probably at the farthest limit to which Christianity, in an organized form, could go in the direction of liberal, rationalized religion. Even before his conversion to Catholicism, Orestes Brownson referred to it as "the jumping-off place from the church to absolute infidelity." During its evolution in the eighteenth century from Calvinist origins, Unitarianism had gradually stripped itself of traditional dogma and ritual: the sovereign and potent God of the Puritans was transformed into a benevolent Father whose creation followed strict rules of cause and effect; the iron law of predestination was repealed in favor of a thoroughgoing Arminianism; Christ became a type of human perfection, a teacher and exemplar of the ideal life, no longer a person of the Trinity. The motive behind these changes was the same that shaped deism and all the other forms of rational religion in that period. Human reason grounded in natural experience had become the arbiter of truth; human dignity was no longer compatible with submission to a dogmatic, irrational faith. Yet the Unitarians insisted that they were faithful Christians. All they had done was remove the last vestiges of obscurantism and superstition clinging to the simple teachings of Christ. But they never meant to question the divine authority of these teachings—which they understood to refer primarily to conduct—or the right of Christ to speak on God's behalf. Not only was his character perfect and his message intrinsically beautiful, but his ministry was plainly vouched for by the miracles he had performed which were recorded in sacred Scripture.

The miracles of Christ had been a matter of considerable debate throughout the eighteenth century. Skeptics like Hume had dismissed them as incredible deviations from the observable order of experience, while a long line of Anglican apologists tried to defend them as consistent with the fundamental rationality of Christian belief. To the latter, this argument acquired a painful importance because miracles increasingly seemed to mark the dividing line between a faith that was specifically Christian and a merely natural religion, or no religion at all. At stake, so it appeared, was the validity of the Scriptural claim to divine revelation, the claim of Christianity to be something more than natural religion. The miracles of Christ stood as the one unmistakable body of evidence that the Author of nature was also the Author of the Christian religion.

The Unitarians of New England were deeply committed to this compromise position, as it may be considered. To free the religion of Christ from the toils of Calvinist theology, to refine and purify it so that the word of God became transparent in the light of human reason—that was one thing. But to give up the last remaining assurance that reason could ultimately rely on divine authority was quite another. Even the most liberal of Christians had their limits! As the eighteenth-century debates had shown, however, this compromise was far from secure. Once reason and experience were acknowledged to be the standards of Scriptural interpretation, it was well-nigh impossible to set a limit to their application. Why should miracles be sacrosanct? The Unitarians gave much thought to working out a line of defense on this question that would not betray them into either dogmatism or skepticism. Their chief mentor was William Paley, whose "inestimable work" (as William Ellery Channing called it), *Evidences of the Christian Religion,* was used as a textbook at Harvard. Channing's own Dudleian Lecture on the miracles is an able exposition of the viewpoint derived from Paley; its mild, thoughtful, firm tone is partly Channing's own, but in part it also reflects the confidence of Unitarian leaders that they had hit upon an ideal form of Christianity. Scripture and common sense were sweetly reconciled; the drift away from barbarous superstition was halted at just the right point: they felt themselves very nearly impregnable.

3

What they did not expect, and were wholly unprepared for, was rebellion within the ranks. The young men who eventually came to be called, and to call themselves, Transcendentalists, almost all grew up within the Unitarian communion. Many of them went to Harvard College and the Harvard Divinity School, which were solidly Unitarian institutions, and many of them served as Unitarian ministers for part or all of their careers. And when they began to complain that Unitarianism was cold and lifeless, that it did not satisfy their idea of Christianity at all, then the Unitarian church faced a threat it did not know how to resist, and its careful compromise started to break down.

For it was precisely the compromise itself that the young rebels denounced and not merely the arguments that upheld it. In seeking to define their position, they were drawn to the question of miracles because it illustrated for them the fatal incompatibility of the elements which Unitarianism had tried to bind together. To rest the authority of Christ on miracles, while appealing to the natural reason as the only arbiter of the credibility of miracles, was not to solve the problem of religion but to render it insoluble. Reason educated by the senses could never admit the certainty of miracles. The Unitarians thought they had circumscribed reason, but instead they had been trapped by it. No wonder their faith had lost its warmth and piety its zeal. To the budding Transcendentalists the issue was clear: choose Locke and the sensual reason or choose the religion of Christ—you cannot have both!

The restoration of religion, then, was the immediate purpose of the "new school" among the Unitarian clergy. To accomplish this purpose, they began to exploit a new idea—or an old one in new form—that seemed to them so effective and so much what the occasion demanded, that they fell in love with it. The idea was that consciousness itself is a reliable source of spiritual insight, that in man's mind, by virtue of its native, inherent capacities, the fundamental truths of religion can be found. Man possesses a faculty or a power—following Coleridge, they usually called it Reason—which can give him immediate access to super-sensual knowledge. Thus the testimony of miracles can be dispensed with as misleading and irrelevant; men have a touchstone within themselves by which to judge the truth of Christ's ministry. "The divine message of the Gospel," said George Ripley, "corresponds to the divine instincts of the soul." Thus, too, Locke's analysis of the human understanding could be relegated to its own proper sphere, that in which mental experience was indeed conditioned by the senses (the sphere of the Understanding). The strategy of the Transcendentalists did not require the complete overthrow of Locke; they merely wished to redraw his map of the mind with greatly extended boundaries, so as to include much, in effect, of what he had excluded when he denied the existence of innate ideas.

The conception of a super-sensual Reason as the Transcendentalists understood it was derived in simplified form from Coleridge—in Brownson's case, from Cousin—who had derived it, with suitable modifications, from Kant and his successors in German philosophy. Inevitably there were gross changes and distortions along this line of descent, but what is most interesting from our perspective is not the history of the idea but the use to which it was put in the American context. Kant had been primarily concerned with the epistemological problems raised by British empiricism; Coleridge was looking for a means of reviving confidence in the certainty of spiritual truth within a framework of Anglican orthodoxy. But the Transcendentalists, having become interested in the epistemological question for immediate reasons very similar to Coleridge's, quickly went on to an affirmation that was uniquely their own, namely that Reason was the very essence of the democratic idea. It was Reason that created the peculiar value of human nature, and the value of human nature was the justification of democracy.

In thus discovering the link between Reason and democracy the Transcendentalists discovered their mission, which was to elaborate the meaning of democracy as a new unfolding of the human spirit. In this context, it should be observed, the word "democracy" takes on a far broader and vaguer significance than it usually has. The Transcendentalists were not especially interested in concrete political systems. More than anything else, democracy meant for them an ideal of human perfection which was implicit in the nature of man and in American society and institutions. The democracy so far achieved in America, however, was no more than a tentative groping toward the ideal, a very partial realization of what men were capable of. For this reason their writings are obsessed by the theme of freedom. Freedom was the key to progress toward the ideal; it was the means and the end of Reason's vision; it was the quintessence of paradise to be regained! In the history of American thought Transcendentalism is the nearest thing we have to an absolutism of freedom. Once they had seized upon this theme the Transcendentalists were carried a long way beyond their initial goal of revitalizing the New England churches.

Reason was not the only motive of the Transcendentalist quest for freedom. One other idea, intimately related to the theme of freedom, was at work in Transcendentalist thought almost without the awareness of the thinkers. This was what has been called the "organic metaphor," the tendency to conceive of reality in terms suitable to living things, to interpret the world by means of analogies with plant and animal life. Among the salient characteristics of such life are growth and change, potentiality and ripeness, creativity, and the interconnection of parts within a complex unity. Thus in Emerson's eyes—he was the most deliberate and subtle of American writers in exploiting this metaphor—nature was not a vast machine but a marvelously integrated diversity, a growing, dynamic, harmonious union of all beings in a single living Body. The Transcendentalists absorbed the organic metaphor from their German and English sources and used it with varying degrees of perspicuity, but its most important meaning for them was in the view it gave of human development. Human beings, to be sure, are living creatures, but, as we have seen, it had not been customary to think of human intelligence as an organic growth. Locke discussed the operations of the mind in essentially mechanical terms; it was with a shock of delight, therefore, that the Transcendentalists realized that the mind *grew*. As Sampson Reed put it, "The mind of the infant contains within itself the first rudiments of all that will be hereafter and needs nothing but expansion, as the leaves and branches and fruit of a tree are said to exist in the seed from which it springs." Later writers, with greater sophistication, substituted the word "Reason" for "the first rudiments of all that will be hereafter," and thus arrived at the formula which linked together the two basic elements of the Transcendentalist theory of consciousness, Reason and organic growth. The combination was to prove explosive.

4

It was explosive because it both divinized man and endowed him with a dynamic and expansive energy. The attribution of Reason was not a mere change in epistemological theory; it was a new definition of human nature, the implications of which grew irresistibly. Once they had decided that men were capable of ascertaining divine truth by an examination of their own minds, the Transcendentalists saw that this capacity must be of the same nature as divinity itself. Men knew God because in some fashion God was within them—how else could the phenomenon of Reason be explained? Furthermore, this innate divinity, the "divine instincts" in Ripley's phrase, was an organic power, something that grew as men found ways of revealing it to themselves, something that pressed against all artificial constraints and demanded acknowledgment in the world. If men were divine, why should they everywhere be in chains?

Taken all in all, and despite some failings on the side of acerbity (Brownson) or self-righteousness (Parker), the Transcendentalists were a mild-mannered and kindly tempered set of revolutionaries. But revolutionaries they were, though it seems to have been a more or less inadvertent development from their premises. What happened was that the fusion of Reason with the organic metaphor generated a certain spontaneous millenarianism that gradually became the atmosphere of their thinking. The most striking evidence for this state of mind can be found in the conclusion of Brownson's *New Views,* which is an excited vision of redeemed society glimpsed by the eye of Reason. As they fastened their attention more and more on the latent possibilities of man's nature, and their conviction grew that "God look[s] out from human eyes," they became dazzled by the enormous opportunity that awaited mankind to remake its world from God's viewpoint. And not unnaturally, they were progressively disillusioned with the world as they found it. From a somewhat academic band of ecclesiastical rebels, the Transcendentalists were thus metamorphosed into the most thoroughgoing critics of society that had yet appeared on the American scene.

It is worth examining this process more closely. In criticizing the miracles of Unitarian theology, the Transcendentalists had begun by appealing to man's innate certainty of religious truth. Christianity was verified for them not by displays of magical power (which might very well have actually taken place), but by its "correspondence," as Ripley said, "with the divine spirit in man." It was true because men instinctively believed it; its evidence was in its own perfection, not in visible signs. The spirit of man, therefore, which they called Reason when they wanted to think of it as an instrument of knowledge, was or could be an infallible guide to eternal wisdom. At this point the question could not help but pose itself as to what eternal wisdom consisted of. What did men actually find in their consciousness with respect to Christianity or religious truth generally?

The Transcendentalists, for the most part, were in agreement that Christianity must be a divine revelation, but since Reason was the ground of their belief, they had necessarily to deny the right of any church or sect, however liberal, to impose a doctrinal formulation on the Christian message. Christ had spoken directly to what was godlike in every man and his words were very simple—he was the master, as Alcott said, of the art of conversation. Hence religious truth was contained in the plain sense of Christ's own words, which did not require the elucidations of Andrews Norton, or Calvin, or St. Thomas Aquinas, or even St. Paul. Men recognized by the blaze of their hearts in response that the Sermon on the Mount was an oracle. Churches and doctrines had only created obscurity and dissension in twisting the simple message to their own ends. Hence the Transcendentalists found themselves at war with what they persisted in calling "historical Christianity"—an expression that irritated their more orthodox opponents no end.

By "historical Christianity" they meant all the forms with which the pure, essential truth of Christ had been clothed ever since its original pronouncement. By these forms, without exception, the pristine Word had been adulterated, confused, betrayed. The history of Christianity was a history of the struggle to liberate the Word from the forms which imprisoned it. And Reason was obviously the force designed to accomplish this liberation once and for all. The Transcendentalists thus placed themselves at the vanguard of a new and final purification of religion; it was the first step on the path of iconoclasm to which they had set their feet.

This thesis concerning history, and the end of history, was the subject of many of the most important and notorious Transcendentalist declarations. Best known, of course, is Emerson's "Divinity School Address," which brought down upon him the unexpected violence of Boston's disapproval. But even earlier Ripley had preached his sermon "Jesus Christ, the Same Yesterday, Today, and Forever"; Brownson had published his outrageous *New Views*, which perhaps were too new to stimulate much of a response; and as late as 1841 Theodore Parker raised a storm with his "Discourse of the Transient and Permanent in Christianity." All of these pieces illustrate two significant points about Transcendentalism which are often overlooked and are worth dwelling upon for a moment. First of all, it was a movement distinctly Protestant in character, with roots that went deep into the Puritan soil of New England. Indeed, one might well regard Transcendentalism, as Brownson did after his conversion, as the ultimate form of Protestant dissent. It had the passion for simplification, for going back to the primitive origins of religion, that repeatedly has marked Protestant history. It longed for a naked confrontation with the divine; it demanded that religion consume the soul, alter the affections, change men's lives from top to bottom. It conceived of faith as a thoroughgoing, heartfelt *piety,* in the manner of the Augustinian fathers of New England, and its millenarian spirit was an echo of the Puritan dream of a church of visible saints.

At the same time, it is true, however paradoxical it may appear, that the Transcendentalists were heirs of the eighteenth-century Enlightenment. The content they gave to religion did not differ in any marked respect from the natural religion of the previous century. Since they relied on universal Reason as their guide to truth, they were not encouraged to deduce complex systems of belief. On the contrary, so far as articles of faith were concerned, Reason led to pretty much the same conclusions as the despised reason of the Unitarians. That there was a perfect God; that He created the universe out of love and governed it benevolently; that He endowed men with immortal souls; and that morality was the essential substance of religion: these were the certainties the Transcendentalists found ingrained in human consciousness. Of course, the intuitional basis of certainty produced an element of mysticism, and, unlike the Unitarians, the Transcendentalists welcomed enthusiasm as a sign of the genuineness of faith. But these and other differences do not obscure the fact that they continued a tradition with which they were in large measure at odds. Since it was a tradition incompatible with the kind of piety they wished to promote, it may well have been a contributing factor in the rather rapid decline of the movement.

In the beginning, however, the Protestant impulse combined with natural religion and backed by Reason all pointed together to the churches, to "historical Christianity," as the great obstacle standing in the way of Christ's reign on earth. The widening of the issue from miracles to historical Christianity marked a decisive change in the character of the Transcendentalist movement. Not only did it directly affect the lives of a number of people— Emerson and Ripley resigned from the Unitarian ministry; Brownson moved away (temporarily) to his own post-Unitarian church, "The Society for Christian Union"; and Parker came as near being excommunicated as was possible among Unitarians—but it impelled them to examine the relations between church and society and gradually to extend the scope of their criticism beyond what any of them had originally foreseen.

5

At bottom, the Transcendentalist position which pitted the "divine spirit in man" against "historical Christianity" was not merely a criticism of the churches but a total rejection of them. It is a testimony rather to the millenarian temper of the movement than to its intellectual discipline. But the inner dynamic of this position was very hard to resist. Once they had defined Reason as the source of religious truth, and equated it with the truth of Christ, there was nothing for the Transcendentalists to do but assert the absolute incompatibility of Christ and Reason on one side and Christianity on the other.

They did so, as we might expect, in the name of democracy in religion. The churches, they came to see, by denying man's power to derive religious truth from his own consciousness, were really anti-democratic institutions. When Andrews Norton defended the miraculous evidence of Christianity on the basis of Lockian psychology, he was only falling back on the age-old view of man's fallibility, his depravity, his need of priestly guidance into the mysteries. The real meaning of the struggle between old and new in the Boston churches, then, was the question of whether man was to be trusted or not, whether he was to be *free.* Consistency with the principle of democracy required that the churches submit to the same process that was already under way in American political life. Out of unfettered human nature, not out of the priest's manipulation of evidence, would come the sanctification of human life on earth. From the Unitarian point of view, this was democracy with a vengeance!

But the Transcendentalists were by no means ready to stop at this point.

Many of them, in fact, realized fairly soon that the democratization of the churches was after all only a peripheral issue for them. It was the democratization of society as a whole, a true reign of sanctity, that they were compelled to seek. Having committed themselves to a redemptive mission, there was no drawing a line between church and society. To confine themselves within the churches would, perhaps, have meant the salvation of a few souls at best, but, as Ripley saw it, "The purpose of Christianity . . . is to redeem society as well as the individual from all sin." It is no coincidence that this remark concerning the purpose of Christianity comes from a letter addressed by Ripley to his parishioners explaining the reasons for his resignation from the ministry.

To redeem society from all sin: this can well be taken as the ultimate expression of Transcendentalist motives. Not that they supposed it could be accomplished overnight, but their fondness for the expression, "It is the mission of the age . . ." gives a measure of the confidence they felt that their hopes were practicable and within reach. And why not? It was an age of confidence, of hope and progress. The powerful tide of democracy seemed to be releasing fresh energies every day, and it was already a habit in America to anticipate the emergence of a new man in whom the splendor of human nature would at last be vindicated. The Transcendentalists were perhaps the first to enshrine this democratic Adam in their temple, but it was not necessary to be a Transcendentalist in 1838 to share the sentiments expressed by Orestes Brownson:

> . . . here is virgin soil, an open field, a new people, full of the future, with unbounded faith in ideas, and the most ample freedom. Here, if anywhere on earth, may the philosopher experiment on human nature and demonstrate what man has it in him to be when and where he has the freedom and the means to be himself.

Language like this shows how close Transcendentalism was to a native American vision. Indeed, it was the fullest, most radical, rashest expression of that vision we have had: the "American dream" at its moment of greatest intensity and innocence.

What were the experiments which these philosophers proposed to try on human nature? How did they expect to redeem society and free man to be himself? We may briefly examine, for the sake of illustration, two of their answers to these questions under separate heads.

Education. It is quite possible that the most lasting influence of Transcendentalism has been exercised upon the theory and practice of American education. This subject rose to the surface of Transcendentalist social criticism very quickly, forced up, we may suppose, by the pressure of conflicting assumptions about human nature. We can see the outlines of a new theory emerging in that fascinating proto-Transcendentalist work, Sampson Reed's "Observations on the Growth of the Mind," but the major prophet in this field was undeniably Bronson Alcott. Whatever reservations his colleagues may have had about Alcott, and however flatulent his soaring prose may strike the modern reader, he was a man profoundly in tune with his age, and his educational writings as well as his practical experiments reveal the inner meaning of Transcendentalism as surely as anything else written or done during the period.

Alcott's basic idea was very simple, and he discovered it for himself long before he knew Emerson or became a member of the Transcendental Club. It was that education is a calling forth and cultivation of the divinity within man, not an imposition of external forms upon a passive intellect. "The province of the instructor," he wrote in his journal in 1828, "should be . . . awakening, invigorating, directing, rather than the forcing of the child's faculties upon prescribed and exclusive courses of thought. He should look to the child to see what is to be done, rather than to his book or his system. The Child is the Book. The operations of his mind are the true system." From this kernel grew Alcott's more fully developed theory in "Human Culture" and his experiments like the one at Temple School, as revolutionary and undertaking in its way as Brook Farm.

Alcott's method of teaching forms a striking complement to the quite independent body of ideas being hammered out by Brownson and Ripley during the very years of the Temple School's operation. Brownson's excitement over Cousin came from the fact that Cousin made psychology ("an exact classification of the mental phenomena") the "first part, the foundation" of philosophy. From such a beginning Cousin could go on to define the nature of Universal Reason and show how it "reveals to us God and the world on precisely the same authority as our own existence." Alcott would not have felt much sympathy with Brownson's enthusiasm—his own genius spoke to him in less complex language—but he too was basing his work on psychology, a direct approach to mental phenomena. Instead of teaching, he probed the contents of his pupils' minds (for the most part, very sensitively), confident that by this means he could strengthen and purify the light of Reason innate in them. His lessons may now seem to us loaded with preconceptions and more forcibly controlled than he was aware, but the evidence suggests that by treating young minds as though they were capable of growth and not simply accumulation, he found a way of making learning an active pleasure. It was an accomplishment valuable enough to entitle him to his place as the patron saint of American progressive education.

Labor. But the redemption of American society posed a far more difficult problem than the reform of the schools. At the heart of the matter, the Transcendentalists came slowly but inevitably to realize, was the question of property and the relations between those who had little of it and those who had much. None of them was equipped to deal with this subject professionally, of course; they were ministers whose training and interests were primarily literary. But they were drawn to it by what has come to seem a characteristic necessity of modern intellectual life: the necessity to make some relation between the sphere of value derived from religion and literature and the sphere of economic organization. Their sensitivity to the widening gap between these two spheres is one of the measures of their relevance to the history of American thought. They belonged to an age of burgeoning industrialism, and they were among the first Americans to see that this new social fact cast a problematic and threatening light on the hope for democratic fulfillment.

Although the Transcendentalists frequently brought to their discussion of economics a rhetoric of Christian idealism that cannot help but seem vague and sentimental in that context, their thinking was informed by certain hard insights. Most crucially, they saw that the private ownership of property, especially the means of capitalist production, was incompatible with the democratic ideal of individual freedom. Private property tended to destroy the social equality on which freedom was based; it seemed to be creating a new class system and new forms of dependency in which masses of men were the helpless victims of economic power controlled by a few. The factory system, which was hardly a widespread phenomenon in the America of the 1830's, was thus early recognized, particularly by Brownson, who was the most prescient in these matters of the Transcendentalist group, as the most ominous fact of American life. Brownson did not think it absurd to compare the conditions of factory labor in the North with slave labor in the South and to give the advantage to slavery. His grim pages on this subject, and on the gulf between factory owner and factory worker, in "The Laboring Classes" are among the earliest signs of awareness in the United States that a dangerous contradiction was evolving out of the unexamined assumptions of American democracy.

Two other aspects of nascent capitalism disturbed the Transcendentalists: the competitive spirit which it encouraged, and its use of machinery. Although competition had not yet become an article of faith in a full-fledged business ideology, the Transcendentalists felt its presence as a cause of anxiety and insecurity; it threatened, in their eyes, to revive a state of primitive warfare in the midst of civilized society. Toward machinery they were generally hostile, but not without ambivalence, as Theodore Parker's "Thoughts on Labor" illustrates. On the one hand, they felt that machine labor disrupted the "natural" character of work, while its only social purposes seemed to be the increase of profits for a small minority of owners and the stimulation of trivial forms of consumption among the working class. But on the other hand, machines promised an eventual release from drudgery for the mass of mankind, and unprecedented leisure for "study, social improvement, the pursuit of a favorite art." These tentative attitudes have since, of course, become the stuff of cliches, but in the 1830's and 1840's they were, especially insofar as they expressed reservations about the tendency of American development, the heterodoxies of an intellectual vanguard.

In their responses to the problem of labor, the Transcendentalists again foreshadowed the solutions which would be proposed by later generations of American radicals. Two conflicting views emerged in their work: one essentially political, aimed at reforming the structure of society; the other Utopian, aimed at changing the quality of life. The first of these views was held in somewhat desperate isolation by Brownson, whose talent for pushing things to their logical conclusion often led him to brilliant diagnoses and utterly impractical remedies. Brownson saw more clearly than any of his contemporaries that money had become the only real source of power in the world, and that the only social distinction of importance was between those who possessed money and those who did not. He deduced that class warfare was in the offing, the object of which would be a redistribution of wealth, and so he made his perfectly rational proposal that hereditary property be abolished. It was rational because it followed "from the admitted premises of the American people."

> Hereditary property is either a privilege or it is not. If it is not, if it confer no social advantage on him who inherits it over him who does not, then there can be no harm in seeking to abolish it, for what we propose to abolish is declared to be valueless. . . . But hereditary property, unless the amount inherited by each individual could be rendered equal, is unquestionably a privilege. It gives, and always must give, to one portion of the community an advantage over the rest to which they are entitled by no natural superiority of intellect or of virtue. Will the public conscience, then, of the American people tolerate it?

This suggestion seems to have been offered, at least on second thought, as an alternative to bloodshed, but Brownson knew that any serious attempt to carry it out would involve violence, and he came dangerously close to justifying the necessity of violence in the cause of a more perfect democracy. Despite this passing ideological fury, however, Brownson's zeal never became detached from its original source. It is an idea of Man that sustains his passion, not a system of power; it is the longing "to prove what man may be, when and where he has free and full scope to act out the almightiness that slumbers within him." In "The Laboring Classes," then, Transcendentalism showed itself capable of producing some quite tough-minded social analysis and contemplating, if need be, extreme operations on the existing body politic.

Although Brook Farm has the look of an even more radical approach to social experiment, it was in fact animated by a different, less political spirit than Brownson's. Only at the end, when it converted itself into a Fourierist phalanstery, did it adopt an aggressive tone with respect to the society around it. Up till then, if we may judge by George Ripley's public and private statements, Brook Farm turned its attention inward upon the perfection of a style of life that would solve in miniature the problems of the world at large and thus provide a model for the rest of mankind. Ripley's main concern was to find a natural balance and harmony between intellectual and physical labor. He had in mind an ideal of wholeness like that propounded in Emerson's "American Scholar," in which action and thought did not exclude one another but formed a unity presided over by Nature. This, or something like it, was what lay behind the striking remark concerning Brook Farm in one of his letters: "We are striving to establish a mode of life which shall combine the enchantments of poetry with the facts of daily experience." Nothing could sound less subversive, but all the radical hopes of Transcendentalism are summed up in these mild words, and they conceal just as strong an impulse for change as Brownson's demand for the emancipation of the "proletaries."

Ripley's description of Brook Farm, which of course is deeply colored by his anticipation of the results it would achieve, is probably as close as we may come to a concrete vision of the sort of world dreamed of by Transcendentalist idealism. The interesting thing to note about this world is its fluidity and formlessness. There are no roles into which men must fit; they are to equally at home in the field and in the study; and social distinctions of every sort vanish before the human dignity elicited by a way of life in which soul and body are equally satisfied. It is a perfect democracy, where washerwomen may walk with philosophers indeed, where washerwomen may *be* philosophers, and philosophers do the laundry. This is what Ripley meant by combining "the enchantments of poetry with the facts of daily experience." It is so complete an integration of the physical with the spiritual that all actions are holy and all men divine. It is no wonder that Ripley could not resist thinking of Brook Farm, albeit in quotation marks, as a "city of God."

6

The genuine Transcendentalist note is one of intense, almost limitless optimism, a feeling that arises out of the sense of living on the threshold of profound and glorious change. For the generation of Emerson, Ripley, Parker, and Brownson the American and French revolutions were still sending shock waves through the frame of society, and the inspiration of European Romanticism was fresh and tonic. When the optimism faded, Transcendentalism began to die; it was alive only so long as it could believe in its vision of a new man and a redeemed society.

Transcendentalism was, in its way, an attempt to solve the most acute and troubling problems of its century. Like other greater, though equally perishable, systems of nineteenth-century thought, it aimed at a synthesis of the rapidly fragmenting mind of its age. In the idea of Reason the Transcendentalists believed they had found the key to such a synthesis. It reconciled for them science and religion and made the resuscitation of Christianity in a new and viable form seem possible; it healed the split between mind and matter and restored the intellectual to a place in the world of action; it provided the basis for a new social order in which human dignity and freedom might triumph over the power of money and machines. The faith of the Transcendentalists in their premises and their prospects was certainly naive, almost incredibly so; and their vision of a future America, in which "the almightiness that slumbers within" man was to awake in a new age of liberty and brotherhood, can only be contemplated with the most generously ironic indulgence. But despite all their limitations, they wrote an irreplaceable chapter of American history. They were among the first of a breed which has played a decisive role in our culture: the unattached, committed intellectual who confronts the problems of society as a literary free agent. For this reason as well as the others that have been mentioned, they remain one of the important sources of our intellectual tradition. Both their example and their dreams continue to haunt us.

4

Saints Behold: The Transcendentalist Point of View

TONY TANNER

A HOSTILE AMERICAN REVIEWER OF WORDSWORTH NOTED THAT 'he tries to look on nature as if she had never been looked on before' and he bemoaned that fact that the poet seemed to be attracting an 'ever increasing school of devoted disciples'[1] in America. Now, what he blames Wordsworth for accurately sums up the ambition of many of the Transcendentalists. There is no need here to disentangle the indigenous emotional drive from the imported European ideas in Transcendentalist thought.[2] But it is important to stress how eager the Transcendentalists were to develop a new attitude towards nature, a new point of view. Picking up the Wordsworthian hint they developed it for their own purposes. Thus Theodore Parker echoes Wordsworth in describing the correct way to respond to the world. He is discussing terrestial beauty.

> Now to many men, who have but once felt this; when heaven lay about them, in their infancy, before the world was too much with them, and they laid waste their powers, getting and spending, when they look back upon it across the dreary gulf, where Honor, Virtue, Religion have made

From *The Reign of Wonder: Naivety and Reality in American Literature* by Tony Tanner, published by Cambridge University Press, 1965. Reprinted by permission of the publisher.

53

shipwreck and perished with their youth, it seems visionary, a shadow, dream-like, unreal. They count it a phantom of their experience; the vision of a child's fancy, raw and unused to the world. Now they are wiser. They cease to believe in inspiration. They can only credit the saying of the priests, that long ago there were inspired men; but none now; that you and I must bow our faces to the dust, groping like the Blind-worm and the Beetle; nor turn our eyes to the broad, free heaven; that we cannot walk by the great central and celestial light that God made to guide all that come into the world, but only by the farthing-candle of tradition. . . . Alas for us if this be all.[3]

An awareness of the divine beauty of the world should not be made dependent on 'tradition', nor on any inherited and institutionalized modes of thought or belief. It would be apprehended directly by any one who could maintain the requisite reverence of attitude and recapture a personal conviction that the world was 'instinct with the Divine Spirit'.[4] 'When this day comes, man will look on Nature with the same eye, as when in the Eden of primitive innocence and joy.'[5] It was the privilege of unmediated admiration and response which the Transcendentalists were determined to secure for their age. It was for this reason they took issue with the Unitarians with their Lockean materialism and passionless contention that only through the biblical miracles was God revealed to man. Such an attitude seemed to impoverish the present world.

> It is negative, cold, lifeless, and all advanced minds among Unitarians are dissatisfied with it, and are craving something higher, better, more living and lifegiving. . . . Society as it is, is a lie, a sham, a charnelhouse, a valley of dry bones. O that the Spirit of God would once more pass by, and say unto these dry bones, 'Live!' So I felt, and so felt others.[6]

Thus Orestes Brownson described the original thrust behind the movement. The Transcendentalists refused to see the world as 'a mute and dead mass of material forms': rather, it was 'a living image, speaking forth the glory of God'.[7] At least, it was that if it was looked at properly. The eye which was 'purified of the notes of tradition'[8] would see God in all things. Here. Now. That thralldom to old and cramping ways of thought, which inhibited and policed the individual response, would be broken. It was such a release from tradition that the Transcendentalists sought to achieve so that they might indulge a proper admiration for a present America neither subservient nor inferior to Europe. And the most forceful concept with which to challenge the traditional eye was clearly the innocent eye.

> Innocent, the soul is quick with instincts of unerring aim; then she knows by intuition what lapsed reason defines by laborious inference; her appetites and affections are direct and trustworthy. . . . By reasoning the soul

strives to recover her lost intuitions; groping amidst the obscure darkness of sense, by means of the fingers of logic, for treasures present always and available to the eye of conscience. Sinners must needs reason: saints behold.[9]

So Bronson Alcott summed up the extremity of his position. For him 'thought disintegrates and breaks'[10] the unity of soul a child enjoys with the world. The prescribed cure was obvious: unlearn reason and behold the world with child-like passive admiration. The word recurred in much Transcendentalist writing. 'Wisdom does not inspect but behold'[11] wrote Thoreau; while Emerson recommended for the 'habitual posture of the mind—beholding'. [12] Saints behold, and so do children. The way back into a divine nature was through the innocent eye. Alcott himself was an educational experimenter of some audacity and he took his beliefs to their logical conclusion. He held conversations with children on the gospels and made their response a test of the validity of Christianity. 'If these *testimonies of children,* confirm the views of adults—that *Christianity is grounded in the essential Nature of Man*—than shall I add to its claim upon our faith.'[13] It is hard to imagine Wordsworth making so literal an application of his poetic assertion that the child was a prophet and philosopher. There was much more interest in the child's point of view in America than in Europe at the time. It was revered to an unusual degree. Thus Miss Peabody, who worked in Alcott's experimental school, could observe:

It was very striking to see how much nearer the kingdom of heaven . . . were the little children, than those who had begun to pride themselves on knowing something. We could not but often remark to each other, how unworthy the name of knowledge was that superficial acquirement, which has nothing to do with self-knowledge; and how much more susceptible to the impressions of genius, as well as how much more apprehensive of general truths, were those who had not been hackneyed by a false education.[14]

There is knowing and knowing. The knowledge which is a mere accumulation of data will tend to support the *tabula rasa* theories of the psychological sensationalists and make man the sport of matter. But the knowledge which seems to deliver itself as unharassed intuition, which seems to be the result of a generous impressionability and an out-reaching sense of spiritual qualities shared by perceiver and perceived, this knowledge will justify the Transcendentalists in their assertions. 'The mind must grow, not from external accretion, but from an internal principle',[15] in the words of Sampson Reed. Given this emphasis on the 'internal principle', the process of true knowing, and the diminished concentration on the thing known, then clearly the child's mind can be expected to attract novel focus. The interest, that is to say, is in a cognitive stance, a stance of reverent response and assimilation. There is far less interest in the end results of analysis and prolonged inquiry, such as finished doctrine, intricate theology, or logical demonstration. For the Transcendentalists the central question was: how should a man look at the world to recover and retain a sense of its 'actual glory'? And for many of them the answer was—behold it with wonder, like a child.

Just as the child was used as a positive image to set up against the claims of tradition, so the claims and rights of the uneducated vernacular type were pushed against the aristocratic hegemony of Europe over American thought. 'We are now the literary vassals of England, and continue to do homage to the mother country. Our literature is tame and servile, wanting in freshness, freedom, and originality. We write as Englishmen, not as Americans. . . . Moreover, excellent as is the English literature, it is not exactly the literature for young republicans. England is the most aristocratic country in the world.'[16] Orestes Brownson continuously stressed the democratic implications of transcendentalist thought. He insisted that 'the light which shines out from God's throne, shines into the heart of every man'.[17] The relevance of this for the writer was brought out by George Ripley: 'The most sublime contemplations of the philosopher can be translated into the language of the market.'[18] So he instructs the American writer: 'He is never to stand aloof from the concerns of the people; he is never to view them in the pride of superior culture or station as belonging to a distinct order from himself.' [19] Clearly a totally new perspective, disregardful of the past and the accumulated precedents of culture, was being sought and required. The call was for the point of view of the uninstructed: the eye of the child, the language of the market. The optimism involved in this idealization of the untutored need not be underlined. But there is one further implication of Transcendentalist thought which should be brought out. Many of the Transcendentalists were Unitarians who became dissatisfied with the mere observance of orthodox and seemly forms. They were more interested in sentiment than institutions and there was current enmity between them. So Brownson wrote: 'The sentiment now breaks away from that form, which, if one may so speak, has become petrified.'[20] Perhaps this attitude was most significantly dramatized by Emerson's resignation from the Unitarian ministry in 1832. 'I am not engaged to Christianity by decent forms' he explained later, 'what I revere and obey in it is its reality, its boundless charity, its deep interior life. . . . Its institutions should be as flexible as the wants of man. That form from which the life and suitableness have departed should be as worthless in its eyes as the dead leaves that are falling around us.'[21] I think one may take this as a more general apostasy from all formalism—in art as well as in religion. Because if all nature is good and the unmediated inner impulse of man reliable, then there is no need for life to be transmuted and reworked into art: art must rather emulate nature; flow with it, grow like it. Such an art—it is characteristic of much American writing—can display an almost unique breadth of hospitality, a spontaneous generosity of inclusion, a free-ranging wonder and compassionate attention which more than justify its daring neglect of accredited forms. For indeed there are forms which the instinct of health will cry out to scatter and demolish; forms which condone mental sloth, which perpetuate habitual responses, which flatter old complacencies, which smother all emerging novelty. But if we may adapt Emerson's words a little and say that the Transcendentalist felt that form could afford to be, indeed ought to be, as flexible as sentiment, then we could fairly point out that this might involve them in problems of organization. The vivifying enthusiasm and stimulus of the Transcendentalists provided the essential impetus for the development of a genuine American literature. But their own well-warranted animus against forms has often, for subsequent writers, changed into the real and often arresting problem of how to assemble and contain their material. An excess of flexibility may well let everything in, but at the cost of not being able to hold very much together.

The Transcendentalists themselves could hold everything together by mystical generalizations. They disliked Unitarianism because 'it cannot pass from the Particular to the General'.[22] Transcendentalism could do exactly this, with effortless confidence. But it should here be pointed out that the Transcendentalist, by relying so much for his poise and faith on fervent but vague feelings and generalizations, does expose himself to the risk of a shockingly abrupt disillusion, a very sudden sense of blighting deprivation, an impotent gloom which is the residue of an evaporated enthusiasm. And indeed the Transcendentalists at times revealed the precariousness of their position. Consider these two quotations from George Ripley.

> The creation in itself, without reference to the Almighty Spirit from which it sprung, is formless and without order—a mass of chaotic objects, of whose uses we are ignorant, and whose destiny we cannot imagine. It is only when its visible glory leads our minds to its unseen Author, and we regard it as a manifestation of Divine Wisdom, that we can truly comprehend its character and designs. To the eye of sense, what does the external creation present? Much less than we are generally apt to suppose. . . .
> Merely the different arrangements of matter, the various degrees and directions in which the light falls on the object admired, and the change of position with regard to space. This is all that is seen. The rest is felt. The forms are addressed to the eye, but the perception of beauty is in the soul. And the highest degree of this is perceived, when the outward creation suggests the wisdom of the Creator. Without that, it is comparatively blank and cold and lifeless.[23]

Without that—everything depends on religious conviction. There are no compromise assurances, no working rules, no limited certainties, no veracities attainable by the senses alone. It is all or nothing. Again:

> Without religion, we are buried in this world as in a living tomb. Mystery—Darkness—Death—Despair—these are the inscriptions which are born on the portals of our gloomy prison-house. Doomed and unhappy orphans, we know not whence we came, why we are here, nor whither we go. . . . All is blank, and desolate, and lifeless, for to our darkened eye no God is present there. And God, my friends, is necessary to man.[24]

Some of these images have a prophetic air. The lost child becomes a frequent figure in American literature, and images of confinement and imprisonment obtrude themselves in the works of writers as remote as Poe and Sherwood Anderson. The journey of which the path and destination are no longer sure becomes a common theme (it is in Melville and Mark Twain), and the material world as chaos instead of God's order is the insistent tenor of the work of Henry Adams. One could say that Pragmatism was a necessary solution to the dangerous extremism of response countenanced by Transcendentalist thought.

Perhaps the simplest definition of what Transcendentalism meant to those who embraced it is given by Ripley: 'It thirsts after the primitive, absolute, all pervading Truth. It is not contented with the knowledge of barren insulated facts.'[25] They believed you could take a single discrete fact and infer from it some absolute truth: hence the continual shift from particularization to generalization in their writing. But take away that all-maintaining confidence in God, and man is left surrounded by 'barren insulated facts' with only the 'eye of sense' to help him. The Transcendentalists asserted that a man who could not see God everywhere was blind. The blind men of a later age duly had to return to a braille-like reading of the world.

NOTES

1. Perry Miller, ed., *The Transcendentalists: An Anthology* (Cambridge, Mass., 1950), p. 98.

2. Perry Miller's illuminating inquiries into this subject are too well known to need enumerating here; but see in particular his *Errand Into The Wilderness* (Cambridge, Mass., 1956), p. 184 *et seq.*

3. Miller, ed., *Transcendentalists,* pp. 322-23.

4. Ibid., p. 165.

5. Ibid., p. 165.

6. Ibid., p. 46.

7. Ibid., pp. 136-37.

8. Ibid., p. 309.

9. Ibid., p. 306.

10. Ibid., p. 312.

11. Ibid., p. 330.

12. Quoted by Charles Fiedelson, Jr., in *Symbolism and American Literature* (University of Chicago Press, 1953), p. 128.

13. Miller, ed., *Transcendentalists,* p. 152.

14. Ibid., p. 146.

15. Ibid., p. 54.

16. Ibid., pp. 189-90.

17. Ibid., p. 208.

18. Ibid., p. 295.

19. Ibid., p. 296.

20. Ibid., p. 85.

21. Emerson, *Complete Works,* Centenary Edition, 12 vols. (Boston, 1903-04), XI, 21.

22. Miller, ed., *Transcendentalists,* p. 317.

23. Ibid., p. 135.

24. Ibid., pp. 292-93.

25. Ibid., p. 292.

PART II
The History of Ideas

From Edwards to Emerson

PERRY MILLER

RALPH WALDO EMERSON BELIEVED THAT EVERY MAN HAS AN inward and immediate access to that Being for whom he found the word "God" inadequate and whom he preferred to designate as the "Over-Soul." He believed that this Over-Soul, this dread universal essence, which is beauty, love, wisdom, and power all in one, is present in Nature and throughout Nature. Consequently Emerson, and the young transcendentalists of New England with him, could look with complacence upon certain prospects which our less transcendental generation beholds with misgiving:

> If the red slayer thinks he slays,
>   Or if the slain think he is slain,
> They know not well the subtle ways
>   I keep, and pass, and turn again.

Life was exciting in Massachusetts of the 1830's and '40's; abolitionists were mobbed, and for a time Mr. Emerson was a dangerous radical; Dr. Webster committed an ingenious murder; but by and large, young men were not called upon to confront possible slaughter unless they elected to travel the Oregon

From *The New England Quarterly*, 13 (1940), 589-617. Reprinted by permission.

Trail, and the only scholar who did that was definitely not a transcendentalist. Thus it seems today that Emerson ran no great risk in asserting that
should he ever be bayoneted he would fall by his own hand disguised in
another uniform, that because all men participate in the Over-Soul those who
shoot and those who are shot prove to be identical, that in the realm of the
transcendental there is nothing to choose between eating and being eaten.

It is hardly surprising that the present generation, those who are called
upon to serve not merely as doubters and the doubt but also as slayers and
slain, greet the serene pronouncements of Brahma with cries of dissent.
Professors somewhat nervously explain to unsympathetic undergraduates that
of course these theories are not the real Emerson, much less the real Thoreau.
They were importations, not native American growths. They came from
Germany, through Coleridge; they were extracted from imperfect translations
of the Hindu scriptures, misunderstood and extravagantly embraced by Yankees who ought to have known better—and who fortunately in some moments did know better, for whenever Emerson and Parker and Thoreau
looked upon the mill towns or the conflict of classes they could perceive a
few realities through the haze of their transcendentalism. They were but
transcendental north-north-west; when the wind was southerly they knew the
difference between Beacon Hill and South Boston. I suppose that many who
now read Emerson, and surely all who endeavor to read Bronson Alcott, are
put off by the "philosophy." The doctrines of the Over-Soul, correspondence, and compensation seem nowadays to add up to shallow optimism and
insufferable smugness. Contemporary criticism reflects this distaste, and
would lead us to prize these men, if at all, for their incidental remarks, their
shrewd observations upon society, art, manners, or the weather, while we put
aside their premises and their conclusions, the ideas to which they devoted
their principal energies, as notions too utterly fantastic to be any longer taken
seriously.

Fortunately, no one is compelled to take them seriously. We are not
required to persuade ourselves the next time we venture into the woods that
we may become, as Emerson said we might, transparent eyeballs, and that
thereupon all disagreeable appearances—"swine, spiders, snakes, pests, mad-
houses, prisons, enemies"—shall vanish and be no more seen. These afflictions
have not proved temporary or illusory to many, or the compensations always
obvious. But whether such ideas are or are not intelligible to us, there remains
the question of whence they came. Where did Emerson, Alcott, Thoreau, and
Margaret Fuller find this pantheism which they preached in varying degrees,
which the Harvard faculty and most Boston businessmen found both discon-
certing and contemptible? Was New England's transcendentalism wholly
Germanic or Hindu in origin? Is there any sense, even though a loose one, in
which we can say that this particular blossom in the flowering of New

England had its roots in the soil? Was it foolishly transplanted from some desert where it had better been left to blush unseen? Emerson becomes most vivid to us when he is inscribing his pungent remarks upon the depression of 1837, and Thoreau in his grim comments upon the American blitzkrieg against Mexico. But our age has a tendency, when dealing with figures of the past, to amputate whatever we find irrelevant from what the past itself considered the body of its teaching. Certain fragments may be kept alive in the critical test tubes of the Great Tradition, while the rest is shoveled off to potter's field. The question of how much in the transcendental philosophy emerged out of the American background, of how much of it was not appropriated from foreign sources, is a question that concerns the entire American tradition, with which and in which we still must work. Although the metaphysic of the Over-Soul, of self-reliance, and of compensation is not one to which we can easily subscribe, yet if the particular formulations achieved by Emerson and Thoreau, Parker and Ripley, were restatements of a native disposition rather than amateur versions of *The Critique of Pure Reason,* then we who must also reformulate our traditions may find their philosophy meaningful, if not for what it held, at least for whence they got it.

Among the tenets of transcendentalism is one which today excites the minimum of our sympathy, which declared truth to be forever and everywhere one and the same, and all ideas to be one idea, all religions the same religion, all poets singers of the same music of the same spheres, chanting eternally the recurrent theme. We have become certain, on the contrary, that ideas are born in time and place, that they spring from specific environments, that they express the force of societies and classes, that they are generated by power relations. We are impatient with an undiscriminating eclecticism which merges the Bhagavad-Gita, Robert Herrick, Saadi, Swedenborg, Plotinus, and Confucius into one monotonous iteration. Emerson found a positive pleasure—which he called "the most modern joy"—in extracting all *time* from the verses of Chaucer, Marvell, and Dryden, and so concluded that one nature wrote all the good books and one nature could read them. The bad books, one infers, were written by fragmentary individuals temporarily out of touch with the Over-Soul, and are bad because they do partake of their age and nation. "There is such equality and identity both of judgment and point of view in the narrative that it is plainly the work of one all-seeing, all-hearing gentleman." We have labored to restore the historical time to Chaucer and Dryden; we do not find it at all plain that they were mouthpieces of one all-seeing agency, and we are sure that if there is any such universal agent he certainly is not a gentleman. We are exasperated with Emerson's tedious habit of seeing everything *sub specie aeternitatis.* When we find him writing in 1872, just before his mind and memory began that retreat into the Over-Soul which makes his last years so pathetic, that while in our day we have

witnessed great revolutions in religion we do not therefore lose faith "in the
eternal pillars which we so differently name, but cannot choose but see their
identity in all healthy souls," we are ready to agree heartily with Walt
Whitman, who growled that Emerson showed no signs of adapting himself to
new times, but had "about the same attitude as twenty-five or thirty years
ago," and that he himself was "utterly tired of these scholarly things." We
may become even more tired of scholarly things when we find that from the
very beginning Emerson conceived the movement which we call transcendentalism as one more expression of the benign gentleman who previously had
spoken in the persons of Socrates and Zoroaster, Mohammed and Buddha,
Shakespeare and St. Paul. He does not assist our quest for native origins,
indeed for any origins which we are prepared to credit, when he says in 1842,
in the Boston Masonic Temple, that transcendentalism is a "Saturnalia of
Faith," an age-old way of thinking which, falling upon Roman times, made
Stoic philosophers; falling on despotic times, made Catos and Brutuses; on
Popish times, made Protestants; "on prelatical times, made Puritans and
Quakers; and falling on Unitarian and commercial times, makes the peculiar
shades of Idealism which we know." Were we to take him at his word, and
agree that he himself was a Stoic revisiting the glimpses of the moon, and that
Henry Thoreau was Cato redivivus, we might then decide that both of them
could fetch the shades of their idealism from ancient Rome or, if they
wished, from Timbuktu, and that they would bear at best only an incidental
relation to the American scene. We might conclude with the luckless San
Francisco journalist, assigned the task of reporting an Emerson lecture, who
wrote, "All left the church feeling that an elegant tribute had been paid to
the Creative genius of the First Cause," but we should not perceive that any
compliments had been paid to the intellectual history of New England.

Still, to take Emerson literally is often hazardous. We many allow him his
Stoics, his Catos and Brutuses, for rhetorical embellishment. He is coming
closer home, however, when he comes to Puritans and Quakers, to Unitarian
and commercial times. Whether he intended it or not, this particular sequence
constitutes in little an intellectual and social history of New England: first
Puritans and Quakers, then Unitarians and commercial times, and now transcendentalists! Emerson contended that when poets spoke out of the transcendental Reason, which knows the eternal correspondence of things, rather
than out of the shortsighted Understanding—which dwells slavishly in the
present, the expedient, and the customary, and thinks in terms of history,
economics, and institutions—they builded better than they knew. When they
were ravished by the imagination, which makes every dull fact an emblem of
the spirit, and were not held earthbound by the fancy, which knows only the
surfaces of things, they brought their creations from no vain or shallow
thought. Yet he did not intend ever to dispense with the understanding and

the fancy, to forget the customary and the institutional—as witness his constant concern with "manners." He would not raise the siege of his hencoop to march away to a pretended siege of Babylon; though he was not conspicuously successful with a shovel in his garden, he was never, like Elizabeth Peabody, so entirely subjective as to walk straight into a tree because "I saw it, but I did not realize it." Could it be, therefore, that while his reason was dreaming among the Upanishads, and his imagination reveling with Swedenborg, his understanding perceived that on the plain of material causation the transcendentalism of New England had some connection with New England experience, and that his fancy, which remained at home with the customary and with history, guided this choice of words? Did these lower faculties contrive, by that cunning which distinguishes them from reason and imagination in the very moment when transcendentalism was being proclaimed a saturnalia of faith, that there should appear a cryptic suggestion that it betokened less an Oriental ecstasy and more a natural reaction of some descendants of Puritans and Quakers to Unitarian and commercial times?

I have called Emerson mystical and pantheistical. These are difficult adjectives; we might conveniently begin with Webster's dictionary, which declares mysticism to be the doctrine that the ultimate nature of reality or of the divine essence may be known by an immediate insight. The connotations of pantheism are infinite, but in general a pantheist holds that the universe itself is God, or that God is the combined forces and laws manifested in the existing universe, that God is, in short, both the slayer and the slain. Emerson and the others might qualify their doctrine, but when Professor Andrews Norton read that in the woods "I become a transparent eyeball; I am nothing, I see all; the currents of the Universal Being circulate through me; I am part or particle of God," in his forthright fashion he could not help perceiving that this was both mysticism and pantheism, and so attacking it as "the latest form of infidelity."

Could we go back to the Puritans whom Emerson adduced as his predecessors, and ask the Emersons and Ripleys, not to mention the Winthrops, Cottons, and Mathers, of the seventeenth century whether the eyeball passage was infidelity, there would be no doubt about the answer. They too might call it the "latest" form of infidelity, for in the first years of New England Winthrop and Cotton had very bitter experience with a similar doctrine. Our wonder is that they did not have more. To our minds, no longer at home in the fine distinctions of theology, it might seem that from the Calvinist doctrine of regeneration, from the theory that a regenerate soul receives an influx of divine spirit, and is joined to God by a direct infusion of His grace, we might deduce the possibility of receiving all instruction immediately from the indwelling spirit, through an inward communication which is essentially mystical. Such was exactly the deduction of Mistress Anne Hutchinson, for

which she was expelled into Rhode Island. It was exactly the conclusion of
the Quakers, who added that every man was naturally susceptible to this
inward communication, that he did not need a special and supernatural
dispensation. Quakers also were cast into Rhode Island or, if they refused to
stay there, hanged on Boston Common. Emerson, descendant of Puritans,
found the descendants of Quakers "a sublime class of speculators," and wrote
in 1835 that they had been the most explicit teachers "of the highest article
to which human faith soars [,] the strict union of the willing soul to God &
so the soul's access at all times to a verdict upon every question which the
opinion of all mankind cannot shake & which the opinion of all mankind
cannot confirm." But his ancestors had held that while the soul does indeed
have an access to God, it receives from the spirit no verdict upon any
question; only a dutiful disposition to accept the verdict confirmed by
Scripture, by authority, and by logic. As Roger Clap remarked, both Anne
Hutchinson and the Quakers "would talk of the Spirit, and of revelations by
the Spirit without the Word, . . . of the Light within them, rejecting the holy
Scripture"; and the Puritan minister declared that the errors of the Anti-
nomians, "like strong wine, make men's judgments reel and stagger, who are
drunken therwith." The more one studies the history of Puritan New England, the more astonished he becomes at the amount of reeling and staggering there was in it.

These seventeenth-century "infidels" were more interested in enlarging the
soul's access to God from within than in exploring the possibilities of an
access from without, from nature. But if we, in our interrogation of the
shades of Puritans, were to ask them whether there exists a spirit that rolls
through all things and propels all things, whose dwelling is the light of setting
suns, and the round ocean, and the mind of man, a spirit from whom we
should learn to be disturbed by the joy of elevated thoughts, the Puritans
would feel at once that we needed looking after. They would concede that
the visible universe is the handiwork of God, that He governs it and is present
in the flight of every sparrow, the fall of every stone, the rising and setting of
suns, in the tempests of the round ocean. "Who set those candles, those
torches of heaven, on the table? Who hung out those lanterns in heaven to
enlighten a dark world?" asked the preacher, informing his flock that although we do not see God in nature, yet in it His finger is constantly evident.
The textbook of theology used at Harvard told New England students that
every creature would return into nothing if God did not uphold it—"the very
˄essation of Divine conservation, would without any other operation present-
y reduce every Creature into nothing." In regard of His essence, said Thomas
Hooker, God is in all places alike, He is in all creatures and beyond them,
"hee is excluded *out* of no place, included *in* no place." But it did not follow
that the universe, though created by God and sustained by His continuous

presence, was God Himself. We were not to go to nature and, by surrendering to the stream of natural forces, derive from it our elevated thoughts. We were not to become nothing and let the currents of Universal Being circulate through us. Whatever difficulties were involved in explaining that the universe is the work of God but that we do not meet God face to face in the universe, Puritan theologians knew that the distinction must be maintained, lest excitable Yankees reel and stagger with another error which they would pretend was an elevated thought. The difficulties of explanation were so great that the preachers often avoided the issue, declaring, "this is but a curious question: therefore I will leave it," or remarking that the Lord fills both heaven and earth, yet He is not in the world as the soul is in the body, "but in an incomprehensible manner, which we cannot expresse to you." Thomas Shepard in Cambridge tried to be more explicit: the Godhead, he said, is common to everything and every man, even to the most wicked man, "nay, to the vilest creature in the world." The same power that made a blade of grass made also the angels, but grass and angels are not the same substance, and so the spirit of God which is in the setting sun and the round ocean is not the same manifestation which He puts forth as a special and "supernatural" grace in the regenerate soul. "There comes another spirit upon us, which common men have not." This other spirit teaches us, not elevated thoughts, but how to submit our corrupt thoughts to the rule of Scripture, to the law and the gospel as expounded at Harvard College and by Harvard graduates.

The reason for Puritan opposition to these ideas is not far to seek. The Renaissance mind—which was still a medieval mind—remembered that for fifteen hundred years Christian thinkers had striven to conceive of the relation of God to the world in such a fashion that the transcendence of God should not be called in question, that while God was presented as the creator and governor of the world, He would always be something other than the world itself. Both mysticism and pantheism, in whatever form, identified Him with nature, made Him over in the image of man, interpreted Him in the terms either of human intuitions or of human perceptions, made Him one with the forces of psychology or of matter. The Renaissance produced a number of eccentrics who broached these dangerous ideas—Giordano Bruno, for instance, who was burned at the stake by a sentence which Catholics and Calvinists alike found just. The Puritans carried to New England the historic convictions of Christian orthodoxy, and in America found an added incentive for maintaining them intact. Puritanism was not merely a religious creed and a theology, it was also a program for society. We go to New England, said John Winthrop, to establish a due form of government, both civil and ecclesiastical, under the rule of law and Scripture. It was to be a medieval society of status, with every man in his place and a place for every man; it was to be no utopia of rugged individualists and transcendental freethinkers.

But if Anne Hutchinson was correct, and if men could hear the voice of God within themselves, or if they could go into the woods and feel the currents of Universal Being circulate through them—in either event they would pay little heed to governors and ministers. The New England tradition commenced with a clear understanding that both mysticism and pantheism were heretical, and also with a frank admission that such ideas were dangerous to society, that men who imbibed noxious errors from an inner voice or from the presence of God in the natural landscape would reel and stagger through the streets of Boston and disturb the civil peace.

Yet from the works of the most orthodox of Calvinists we can perceive that the Puritans had good cause to be apprehensive lest mystical or pantheistical conclusions arise out of their premises. Anne Hutchinson and the Quakers commenced as Calvinists; from the idea of regeneration they drew, with what seemed to them impeccable logic, the idea that God imparted His teaching directly to the individual spirit. With equal ease others could deduce from the doctrines of divine creation and providence the idea that God was immanent in nature. The point might be put thus: there was in Puritanism a piety, a religious passion, the sense of an inward communication and of the divine symbolism of nature. One side of the Puritan nature hungered for these excitements; certain of its appetites desired these satisfactions and therefore found delight and ecstasy in the doctrines of regeneration and providence. But in Puritanism there was also another side, an ideal of social conformity, of law and order, of regulation and control. At the core of the theology there was an indestructible element which was mystical, and a feeling for the universe which was almost pantheistic; but there was also a social code demanding obedience to external law, a code to which good people voluntarily conformed and to which bad people should be made to conform. It aimed at propriety and decency, the virtues of middle-class respectability, self-control, thrift, and dignity, at a discipline of the emotions. It demanded, as Winthrop informed the citizens of Massachusetts Bay in 1645, that men forbear to exercise the liberty they had by nature, the freedom to do anything they chose, and having entered into society thereafter, devote themselves to doing only that which the authorities defined as intrinsically "good, just and honest." The New England tradition contained a dual heritage, the heritage of the troubled spirit and the heritage of worldly caution and social conservatism. It gave with one hand what it took away with the other: it taught men that God is present to their intuitions and in the beauty and terror of nature, but it disciplined them into subjecting their intuitions to the wisdom of society and their impressions of nature to the standards of decorum.

In the eighteenth century, certain sections of New England, or certain persons, grew wealthy. It can hardly be a coincidence that among those who were acquiring the rewards of industry and commerce there should be progressively developed the second part of the heritage, the tradition of reason and criticism, and that among them the tradition of emotion and ecstasy should dwindle. Even though a few of the clergy, like Jonathan Mayhew and Lemuel Briant, were moving faster than their congregations, yet in Boston and Salem, the centers of shipping and banking, ministers preached rationality rather than dogma, the Newtonian universe and the sensational psychology rather than providence and innate depravity. The back country, the Connecticut Valley, burst into flame with the Great Awakening of the 1740's; but the massive Charles Chauncy, minister at the First Church, the successor of John Cotton, declared that "the passionate discovery" of divine love is not a good evidence of election. "The surest and most substantial Proof is, *Obedience to the Commandments of God,* and the *stronger* the Love, the more uniform, steady and pleasant will be this *Obedience.*" Religion is of the understanding as well as of the affections, and when the emotions are stressed at the expense of reason, "it can't be but People should run into Disorders." In his ponderous way, Chauncy was here indulging in Yankee understatement. During the Awakening the people of the back country ran into more than disorders; they gave the most extravagant exhibition of staggering and reeling that New England had yet beheld. Chauncy was aroused, not merely because he disapproved of displays of emotion, but because the whole society seemed in danger when persons who made a high pretense to religion displayed it in their conduct "as something wild and fanciful." On the contrary, he stoutly insisted, true religion is sober and well-behaved; as it is taught in the Bible, "it approves itself to the Understanding and Conscience, . . . and is in the best Manner calculated to promote the Good of Mankind." The transformation of this segment of Puritanism from a piety to an ethic, from a religious faith to a social code, was here completed, although an explicit break with the formal theology was yet to come.

Charles Chauncy had already split the Puritan heritage. Emerson tells that Chauncy, going into his pulpit for the Thursday lecture (people at that time came all the way from Salem to hear him), was informed that a little boy had fallen into Frog Pond and drowned. Requested to improve the occasion,

> the doctor was much distressed, and in his prayer he hesitated, he tried to make soft approaches, he prayed for Harvard College, he prayed for the schools, he implored the Divine Being "to—to—to bless to them all the boy that was this morning drowned in Frog Pond."

But Jonathan Edwards felt an ardency of soul which he knew not how to express, a desire "to lie in the dust, and to be full of Christ alone; to love him with a holy and pure love; to trust in him; to live upon him; to serve and follow him; and to be perfectly sanctified and made pure, with a divine and heavenly purity." To one who conceived the highest function of religion to be the promotion of the good of mankind, Jonathan Edwards stood guilty of fomenting disorders. Chauncy blamed Edwards for inciting the populace, and was pleased when the congregation at Northampton, refusing to measure up to the standards of sanctification demanded by Edwards, banished him into the wilderness of Stockbridge. Edwards, though he was distressed over the disorders of the Awakening, would never grant that a concern for the good of mankind should take precedence over the desire to be perfectly sanctified and made pure. In his exile at Stockbridge he wrote the great tracts which have secured his fame for all time, the magnificent studies of the freedom of the will, of the nature of true virtue, of the purpose of God in creating the universe, in which Chauncy and Harvard College were refuted; in which, though still in the language of logic and systematic theology, the other half of the Puritan heritage—the sense of God's overwhelming presence in the soul and in nature—once more found perfect expression.

Though the treatises on the will and on virtue are the more impressive performances, for our purposes the eloquent *Dissertation Concerning the End for which God Created the World* is the more relevant, if only because when he came to this question Edwards was forced to reply specifically to the scientific rationalism toward which Chauncy and Harvard College were tending. He had, therefore, to make even more explicit than did the earlier divines the doctrines which verged upon both mysticism and pantheism, the doctrines of inward communication and of the divine in nature. It was not enough for Edwards to say, as John Cotton had done, that God created the world out of nothing to show His glory; rationalists in Boston could reply that God's glory was manifested in the orderly machine of Newtonian physics, and that a man glorified God in such a world by going about his rational business: real estate, the triangular trade, or the manufacture of rum out of smuggled molasses. God did not create the world, said Edwards, merely to exhibit His glory; He did not create it out of nothing simply to show that He could: He who is Himself the source of all being, the substance of all life, created the world out of Himself by a diffusion of Himself into time and space. He made the world, not by sitting outside and above it, by modeling it as a child models sand, but by an extension of Himself, by taking upon Himself the forms of stones and trees and of man. He created without any ulterior object in view, neither for His glory nor for His power, but for the pure joy of self-expression, as an artist creates beauty for the love of beauty. God does not need a world or the worship of man; He is perfect in Himself. If He bothers to create, it is out of the fullness of His own nature, the overflowing virtue that is in Him. Edwards did not use my simile of the artist; his way of saying it was, "The disposition to communicate himself, or diffuse his own fulness, which we must conceive of as being originally in God as a perfection of his nature, was what moved him to create the world," but we may still employ the simile because Edwards invested his God with the sublime egotism of a very great artist. God created by the laws of His own nature, with no thought of doing good for anybody or for mankind, with no didactic purpose, for no other reason but the joy of creativeness. "It is a regard to himself that disposes him to diffuse and communicate himself. It is such a delight in his own internal fulness and glory, that disposes him to an abundant effusion and emanation of that glory."

Edwards was much too skilled in the historic problems of theology to lose sight of the distinction between God and the world or to fuse them into one substance, to blur the all-important doctrine of the divine transcendence. He forced into his system every safeguard against identifying the inward experience of the saint with the Deity Himself, or of God with nature. Nevertheless, assuming, as we have some right to assume, that what subsequent generations find to be a hidden or potential implication in a thought is a part of that thought, we may venture to feel that Edwards was particularly careful to hold in check the mystical and pantheistical tendencies of his teaching because he himself was so apt to become a mystic and a pantheist. The imagery in which a great thinker expresses his sense of things is often more revealing than his explicit contentions, and Edwards betrays the nature of his insight when he uses as the symbol of God's relation to the world the metaphor that has perennially been invoked by mystics, the metaphor of light and of the sun:

> And [it] is fitly compared to an effulgence or emanation of light from a luminary, by which this glory of God is abundantly represented in Scripture. Light is the external expression, exhibition and manifestation of the excellency of the luminary, of the sun for instance: it is the abundant, extensive emanation and communication of the fulness of the sun to innumerable beings that partake of it. It is by this that the sun itself is seen, and his glory beheld, and all other things are discovered; it is by a participation of this communication from the sun, that surrounding objects receive all their lustre, beauty and brightness. It is by this that all nature is quickened and receives life, comfort, and joy.

Here is the respect that makes Edwards great among theologians, and here in fact he strained theology to the breaking point. Holding himself by brute will power within the forms of ancient Calvinism, he filled those forms with a new and throbbing spirit. Beneath the dogmas of the old theology he discovered a different cosmos from that of the seventeenth century, a dynamic world, filled with the presence of God, quickened with divine life, pervaded with joy and ecstasy. With this insight he turned to combat the rationalism of Boston, to argue that man cannot live by Newtonian schemes and mathematical calculations, but only by surrender to the will of God, by reflecting back the beauty of God as a jewel gives back the light of the sun. But another result of Edwards's doctrine, one which he would denounce to the nethermost circle of Hell but which is implicit in the texture, if not in the logic, of his thought, could very easily be what we have called mysticism or pantheism, or both. If God is diffused through nature, and the substance of man is the substance of God, then it may follow that man is divine, that nature is the garment of the Over-Soul, that man must be self-reliant, and that when he goes into the woods the currents of Being will indeed circulate through him. All that prevented this deduction was the orthodox theology, supposedly derived from the Word of God, which taught that God and nature are not one, that man is corrupt and his self-reliance is reliance on evil. But take away the theology, remove this overlying stone of dogma from the wellsprings of Puritan conviction, and both nature and man become divine.

We know that Edwards failed to revitalize Calvinism. He tried to fill the old bottles with new wine, yet none but himself could savor the vintage. Meanwhile, in the circles where Chauncy had begun to reëducate the New England taste, there developed, by a very gradual process, a rejection of the Westminster Confession, indeed of all theology, and at last emerged the Unitarian churches. Unitarianism was entirely different wine from any that had ever been pressed from the grapes of Calvinism, and in entirely new bottles, which the merchants of Boston found much to their liking. It was a pure, white, dry claret that went well with dinners served by the Harvard Corporation, but it was mild and was guaranteed not to send them home reeling and staggering. As William Ellery Channing declared, to contemplate the horrors of New England's ancestral creed is "a consideration singularly fitted to teach us tolerant views of error, and to enjoin caution and sobriety."

In Unitarianism one half of the New England tradition—that which inculcated caution and sobriety—definitely cast off all allegiance to the other. The ideal of decorum, of law and self-control, was institutionalized. Though Unitarianism was "liberal" in theology, it was generally conservative in its social thinking and in its metaphysics. Even Channing, who strove always to avoid controversy and to appear "mild and amiable," was still more of an enthusiast than those he supplied with ideas, as was proved when almost alone among Unitarian divines he spoke out against slavery. He frequently found himself thwarted by the suavity of Unitarian breeding. In his effort to establish a literary society in Boston, he repaired, as Emerson tells the story, to the home of Dr. John Collins Warren, where

> he found a well-chosen assembly of gentlemen variously distinguished; there was mutual greeting and introduction, and they were chatting agreeably on indifferent matters and drawing gently towards their great expectation, when a side-door opened, the whole company streamed in to an oyster supper, crowned by excellent wines; and so ended the first attempt to establish aesthetic society in Boston.

But if the strain in the New England tradition which flowered so agreeably in the home of Dr. Warren, the quality that made for reason and breeding and good suppers, found itself happily divorced from enthusiasm and perfectly enshrined in the liberal profession of Unitarianism, what of the other strain? What of the mysticism, the hunger of the soul, the sense of divine emanation in man and in nature, which had been so important an element in the Puritan character? Had it died out of New England? Was it to live, if at all, forever caged and confined in the prison house of Calvinism? Could it be asserted only by another Edwards in another treatise on the will and a new dissertation on the end for which God created the universe? Andover Seminary was, of course, turning out treatises and dissertations, and there were many New Englanders outside of Boston who were still untouched by Unitarianism. But for those who had been "liberated" by Channing and Norton, who could no longer express their desires in the language of a creed that had been shown to be outworn, Calvinism was dead. Unitarianism rolled away the heavy stone of dogma that had sealed up the mystical springs in the New England character; as far as most Unitarians were concerned, the stone could now be lifted with safety, because to them the code of caution and sobriety, nourished on oyster suppers, would serve quite as well as the old doctrines of original sin and divine transcendence to prevent mankind from reeling and staggering in freedom. But for those in whom the old springs were still living, the removal of the theological stopper might mean a welling up and an overflowing of long suppressed desires. And if these desires could no longer be satisfied in theology, toward what objects would they now be turned? If they could no longer be expressed in the language of supernatural regeneration and divine sovereignty, in what language were they to be described?

The answer was not long forthcoming. If the inherent mysticism, the ingrained pantheism, of certain Yankees could not be stated in the old terms, it could be couched in the new terms of transcendental idealism, of Platonism, of Swedenborg, of "Tintern Abbey" and the Bhagavad-Gita, in the eclectic and polyglot speech of the Over-Soul, in "Brahma," in "Self-Reliance," in *Nature*. The children of Puritans could no longer say that the visible fabric of nature was quickened and made joyful by a diffusion of the fullness of God, but they could recapture the Edwardsean vision by saying, "Nature can only be conceived as existing to a universal and not to a particular end; to a universe of ends, and not to one,—a work of *ecstasy*, to be represented by a circular movement, as intention might be signified by a straight line of definite length." But in this case the circular conception enjoyed one great advantage—so it seemed at the time—that it had not possessed for Edwards: the new generation of ecstatics had learned from Channing and Norton, from the prophets of intention and the straight line of definite length, that men did not need to grovel in the dust. They did not have to throw themselves on the ground, as did Edwards, with a sense of their own unworthiness; they could say without trepidation that no concept of the understanding, no utilitarian consideration for the good of mankind, could account for any man's existence, that there was no further reason than "*so it was to be.*" Overtones of the seventeenth century become distinctly audible when Emerson declares, "The *royal* reason, the Grace of God, seems the only description of our multiform but ever identical fact," and the force of his heredity is manifest when he must go on to say, having mentioned the grace of God, "There is the incoming or the receding of God," and as Edwards also would have said, "we can show neither how nor why." In the face of this awful and arbitrary power, the Puritan had been forced to conclude that man was empty and insignificant, and account for its recedings on the hypothesis of innate depravity. Emerson does not deny that such reflections are in order; when we view the fact of the inexplicable recedings "from the platform of action," when we see men left high and dry without the grace of God, we see "Self-accusation, remorse, and the didactic morals of self-denial and strife with sin"; but our enlightenment, our liberation from the sterile dogmas of Calvinism, enables us also to view the fact from "the platform of intellection," and in this view "there is nothing for us but praise and wonder." The ecstasy and the vision which Calvinists knew only in the moment of vocation, the passing of which left them agonizingly aware of depravity and sin, could become the permanent joy of those who had put aside the conception of depravity, and the moments between could be filled no longer with self-accusation but with praise and wonder. Unitarianism had stripped off the dogmas, and Emerson was free to celebrate purely and simply the presence of God in the soul and in nature, the pure metaphysical essence of the New England tradition. If he could no longer publish it as orthodoxy, he could speak it fearlessly as the very latest form of infidelity.

At this point there might legitimately be raised a question whether my argument is anything more than obscurantism. Do words like "New England tradition" and "Puritan heritage" mean anything concrete and tangible? Do they "explain" anything? Do habits of thought persist in a society as acquired characteristics, and by what mysterious alchemy are they transmitted in the blood stream? I am as guilty as Emerson himself if I treat ideas as a self-contained rhetoric, forgetting that they are, as we are now discovering, weapons, the weapons of classes and interests, a masquerade of power relations.

Yet Emerson, transcendental though he was, could see in his own ideas a certain relation to society. In his imagination transcendentalism was a saturnalia of faith, but in his fancy it was a reaction against Unitarianism and in his understanding a revulsion against commercialism. We can improve his hint by remarking the obvious connection between the growth of rationalism in New England and the history of eighteenth-century capitalism. Once the Unitarian apologists had renounced the Westminster Confession, they attacked Calvinism not merely as irrational but as a species of pantheism, and in their eyes this charge was sufficient condemnation in itself. Calvinism, said Channing, robs the mind of self-determining force and makes men passive recipients of the universal force:

> It is a striking fact that the philosophy which teaches that matter is an inert substance, and that God is the force which pervades it, has led men to question whether any such thing as matter exists. . . . Without a free power in man, he is nothing. The divine agent within him is every thing, Man acts only in show. He is a phenomenal existence, under which the One Infinite Power is manifested; and is this much better than Pantheism?

One does not have to be too prone to economic interpretation in order to perceive that there was a connection between the Unitarian insistence that matter is substance and not shadow, that men are self-determining agents and not passive recipients of Infinite Power, and the practical interests of the society in which Unitarianism flourished. Pantheism was not a marketable commodity on State Street, and merchants could most successfully conduct their business if they were not required to lie in the dust and desire to be full of the divine agent within.

Hence the words "New England tradition" and "Puritan heritage" can be shown to have some concrete meaning when applied to the gradual evolution of Unitarianism out of the seventeenth-century background; there is a continuity both social and intellectual. But what of the young men and young women, many of them born and reared in circles in which, Channing said, "Society is going forward in intelligence and charity," who in their very adolescence instinctively turned their intelligence and even their charity against this liberalism, and sought instead the strange and uncharitable gods of transcendentalism? Why should Emerson and Margaret Fuller, almost from their first reflective moments, have cried out for a philosophy which would reassure them that matter is the shadow and spirit the substance, that man acts by an influx of power—why should they deliberately return to the bondage from which Channing had delivered them? Even before he entered the divinity school Emerson was looking askance at Unitarianism, writing in his twentieth year to his southern friend, John Boynton Hill, that for all the flood of genius and knowledge being poured out from Boston pulpits, the light of Christianity was lost: "An exemplary Christian of today, and even a Minister, is content to be just such a man as was a good Roman in the days of Cicero." Andrews Norton would not have been distressed over this observation, but young Emerson was. "Presbyterianism & Calvinism at the South," he wrote, "at least make Christianity a more real & tangible system and give it some novelties which were worth unfolding to the ignorance of men." Thus much, but no more, he could say for "orthodoxy": "When I have been to Cambridge & studied Divinity, I will tell you whether I can make out for myself any better system than Luther or Calvin, or the *liberal besoms* of modern days." The "Divinity School Address" was forecast in these youthful lines, and Emerson the man declared what the boy had divined when he ridiculed the "pale negations" of Unitarianism, called it an "icehouse," and spoke of "the corpse-cold Unitarianism of Harvard College and Brattle Street." Margaret Fuller thrilled to the epistle of John read from a Unitarian pulpit: "Every one that loveth is born of God, and knoweth God," but she shuddered as the preacher straightway rose up "to deny mysteries, to deny second birth, to deny influx, and to renounce the sovereign gift of insight, for the sake of what he deemed a *'rational'* exercise of will." This Unitarianism, she argued in her journal, has had its place, but the time has now come for reinterpreting old dogmas: "For one I would now preach the Holy Ghost as zealously as they have been preaching Man, and faith instead of the understanding, and mysticism instead &c—." And there, characteristically enough, she remarks, "But why go on?"

A complete answer to the question of motives is probably not possible as yet. Why Waldo and Margaret in the 1820's and '30's should instinctively have revolted against a creed that had at last been perfected as the ideology of their own group, of respectable, prosperous, middle-class Boston and Cambridge—why these youngsters, who by all the laws of economic determinism ought to have been the white-headed children of Unitarianism, elected to become transcendental black sheep, cannot be decided until we know more about the period than has been told in *The Flowering of New England* and more about the nature of social change in general. The personal matter is obviously of crucial importance. The characters of the transcendentalists account for their having become transcendental; still two facts of a more historical nature seem to me worth considering in the effort to answer our question.

The emergence of Unitarianism out of Calvinism was a very gradual, almost an imperceptible, process. One can hardly say at what point rationalists in eastern Massachusetts ceased to be Calvinists, for they were forced to organize into a separate church only after the development of their thought was completed. Consequently, although young men and women in Boston might be, like Waldo and Margaret, the children of rationalists, all about them the society still bore the impress of Calvinism: the theological break had come, but not the cultural. In a thousand ways the forms of society were still those determined by the ancient orthodoxy, piously observed by persons who no longer believed in the creed. We do not need to posit some magical transmission of Puritanism from the seventeenth to the nineteenth century in order to account for the fact that these children of Unitarians felt emotionally starved and spiritually undernourished. In 1859 James Cabot sent Emerson *The Life of Trust,* a crude narrative by one George Muller of his personal conversations with the Lord, which Cabot expected Emerson to enjoy as another instance of man's communion with the Over-Soul, which probably seemed to Cabot no more crackbrained than many of the books Emerson admired. Emerson returned the volume, accompanied by a vigorous rebuke to Cabot for occupying himself with such trash:

> I sometimes think that you & your coevals missed much that I & mine found: for Calvinism was still robust & effective on life & character in all the people who surrounded my childhood, & gave a deep religious tinge to manners & conversation. I doubt the race is now extinct, & certainly no sentiment has taken its place on the new generation,—none as pervasive & controlling. But they were a high tragic school, & found much of their own belief in the grander traits of the Greek mythology,—Nemesis, the Fates, & the Eumenides, and, I am sure, would have raised an eyebrow at this pistareen Providence of . . . George Muller.

At least two members of the high tragic school Emerson knew intimately and has sympathetically described for us—his stepgrandfather, the Reverend Ezra Ripley, and his aunt, Mary Moody Emerson. Miss Emerson put the essence of the Puritan aesthetic into one short sentence: "How insipid is fiction to a mind touched with immortal views!" Speaking as a Calvinist, she anticipated Max Weber's discovery that the Protestant ethic fathered the spirit of capitalism, in the pungent observation, "I respect in a rich man the order of Providence." Emerson said that her journal "marks the precise time when the power of the old creed yielded to the influence of modern science and humanity"; still in her the old creed never so far yielded its power to the influence of modern humanity but that she could declare, with a finality granted only to those who have grasped the doctrine of divine sovereignty, "I was never patient with the faults of the good." When Thomas Cholmondeley once suggested to Emerson that many of his ideas were similar to those of Calvinism, Emerson broke in with irritation, "I see you are speaking of something which had a meaning once, but is now grown obsolete. Those words formerly stood for something, and the world got good from them, but not now." The old creed would no longer serve, but there had been power in it, a power conspicuously absent from the pale negations of Unitarianism. At this distance in time, we forget that Emerson was in a position fully to appreciate what the obsolete words had formerly stood for, and we are betrayed by the novelty of his vocabulary, which seems to have no relation to the jargon of Calvinism, into overlooking a fact of which he was always aware—the great debt owed by his generation "to that old religion which, in the childhood of most of us, still dwelt like a sabbath morning in the country of New England, teaching privation, self-denial and sorrow!" The retarded tempo of the change in New England, extending through the eighteenth into the nineteenth century, makes comprehensible why young Unitarians had enough contact with the past to receive from it a religious standard by which to condemn the pallid and unexciting liberalism of Unitarianism.

Finally, we do well to remember that what we call the transcendental movement was not an isolated phenomenon in nineteenth-century New England. As Professor Whicher has remarked, "Liberal ideas came slowly to the Connecticut Valley." They came slowly also to Andover Theological Seminary. But slowly they came, and again undermined Calvinist orthodoxies as they had undermined orthodoxy in eighteenth-century Boston; and again they liberated a succession of New Englanders from the Westminster Confession, but they did not convert them into rationalists and Unitarians. Like Emerson, when other New Englanders were brought to ask themselves, "And what is to replace for us the piety of that race?" they preferred to bask "in the great morning which rises forever out of the eastern sea" rather than to rest content with mere liberation. "I stand here to say, Let us worship the mighty and transcendent Soul"—but not the good of mankind! Over and again the rational attack upon Calvinism served only to release energies which then sought for new forms of expression in directions entirely opposite to rationalism. Some, like Sylvester Judd, revolted against the Calvinism of the Connecticut Valley, went into Unitarianism, and then came under the spell of Emerson's transcendentalist tuition. Others, late in the century, sought out new heresies, not those of transcendentalism, but interesting parallels and analogues. Out of Andover came Harriet Beecher Stowe, lovingly but firmly underlining the emotional restrictions of Calvinism in *The Minister's Wooing* and *Oldtown Folks,* while she herself left the grim faith at last for the ritualism of the Church of England. Out of Andover also came Elizabeth Stuart Phelps in feverish revolt against the hard logic of her father and grandfather, preaching instead the emotionalism of *Gates Ajar.* In Connecticut, Horace Bushnell, reacting against the dry intellectualism of Nathaniel Taylor's Calvinism just as Margaret Fuller had reacted a decade earlier against the dry rationalism of Norton's Unitarianism, read Coleridge with an avidity equal to hers and Emerson's, and by 1849 found the answer to his religious quest, as he himself said, "after all his thought and study, not as something reasoned out, but as an inspiration—a revelation from the mind of God himself." He published the revelation in a book, the very title of which tells the whole story, *Nature and the Supernatural Together Constituting One System of God,* wherein was preached anew the immanence of God in nature: "God is the spiritual reality of which nature is the manifestation." With this publication the latest—and yet the oldest—form of New England infidelity stalked in the citadel of orthodoxy, and Calvinism itself was, as it were, transcendentalized. At Amherst, Emily Dickinson's mental climate, in the Gilded Age, was still Emerson's; the break-up of Calvinism came later there than in Boston, but when it had come the poems of Emily Dickinson were filled with "Emersonian echoes," echoes which Professor Whicher wisely declines to point out because, as he says, resemblances in Emerson, Thoreau, Parker, and Emily Dickinson are not evidences of borrowings one from another, but their common response to the spirit of the time, even though the spirit reached Emily Dickinson a little later in time than it did Emerson and Thoreau. "Their work," he says, "was in various ways a fulfillment of the finer energies of a Puritanism that was discarding the husks of dogma." From the time of Edwards to that of Emerson, the husks of Puritanism were being discarded, but the energies of many Puritans were not yet diverted—they could not be diverted—from a passionate search of the soul and of nature, from the quest to which Calvinism had devoted them. These New Englanders—a few here and there—turned aside from the doctrines of sin and predestination, and thereupon sought with renewed fervor for the accents of the Holy Ghost in their own hearts and in woods and mountains. But now that the restraining hand of theology was withdrawn, there was nothing to prevent them, as there had been everything to prevent Edwards, from identifying their intuitions with the voice of God, or from fusing God and nature into the one substance of the transcendental imagination. Mystics were no longer inhibited by dogma. They were free to carry on the ancient New England propensity for reeling and staggering with new opinions. They could give themselves over, unrestrainedly, to becoming transparent eyeballs and debauchees of dew.

6

John Locke and New England Transcendentalism

CAMERON THOMPSON

1

The Great Mr. Locke, America's Philosopher. (Merle Curti)

THE PIVOTAL ROLE OF JOHN LOCKE IN THE PHILOSOPHICAL DE-velopment of Transcendentalism has not been asserted with sufficient emphasis. Some years ago, Odell Shepard remarked that "We may yet come to realize that the entire Transcendental Movement was a revolt against Locke and a rediscovery of his predecessors."[1] Since then, much has been written to correct the second half of this indictment, but equal justice has not been paid to the essential first half—nor to the additional fact that the "men of Locke" responded with vigor and point to the "revolt."

The revolt was against the philosophy dominant in academic and clerical institutions. This philosophy was empiricism, and its father was Locke. It was commonly—and not necessarily with depreciatory intention—called Sensationalism,[2] and it included not only Locke, but also the Scottish "common sense" philosophers: notably (in New England), Reid, Stewart and Brown. So typically cavalier an identification of the Scottish school with Locke prompted some contemporary indignation, and modern scholarship has given support to the protest. An evaluation of this peripheral controversy, however,

From *The New England Quarterly,* 35 (1962), 435-57. Reprinted by Permission.

is not part of the present essay. It will be enough to show that the Transcendentalists themselves considered the Scottish philosophy to be a mere "modification" of Locke—especially of his epistemology—designed to make the founder more palatable to current tastes.

The Transcendentalists were accurate in their appraisal of the prevalence of Sensationalism in influential quarters during the early part of the century. With respect to its esteem in education circles, the Reverend James Murdock, writing in 1842, is explicit: "Until within about twenty years, the empirical philosophy as taught by Locke and the Scotch writers . . . had dominion in all our colleges and schools and was regarded everywhere as the only true philosophy."[3] This relatively early judgment was to be corroborated by later studies. Indeed, with respect to Locke these studies reveal a reign for the celebrated *Essay* which in duration, as well as in extent, is astonishing. Noah Porter was to remember that "Locke's Essay on the Human Understanding [*sic*] was for a long time the well-studied text-book in the instruction of the youth at the most important of the American colleges,"[4] and a few years later C. Emory Aldrich supplied impressive additional testimony. Aldrich addressed "letters of inquiry . . . to gentlemen connected with ten of our oldest and best known colleges," and although in certain instances the replies were of little help because of incomplete records, taken together they constitute effective evidence on the sustained popularity of "Locke's Essay." Thus, it was used as a textbook at Yale from 1717 to 1825, when Stewart was introduced; at Dartmouth it appears to have been studied from 1769 to 1838 and to have been assigned as a text from 1822 to 1838, when it was replaced by Stewart; at Brown it was a text from 1783 to 1825, when Stewart was substituted. Harvard and Williams (in addition to colleges outside of New England, such as Princeton, Columbia, William and Mary) also furnished Aldrich with reports which, if more sketchy, support the conclusion that Locke's appeal was widespread and long continued.[5] Moreover, in the instance of Harvard, where the philosophical traditions are especially pertinent to this study, we are fortunate in having excellent confirmation of Aldrich's informal investigations, for Benjamin Rand has shown that the *Essay* was introduced in 1742 and held its own even after the weight of the Scottish influence began to be felt, some seventy-five years later, and he is led to assert that "No other text-book of modern philosophy has been used in this University for such an extended period of time."[6]

Finally, it is significant that when Locke began to lose his individual pre-eminence in the classroom it was the Scottish philosophers who inherited the mantle of authority.[7] James Marsh, writing to Coleridge in 1829, notes the new emphasis: "The works of Locke were formerly much read and used as text-books in our colleges; but of late have very generally given place to the Scottish writers; and Stewart, Campbell and Brown are now almost universally read as the standard authors on the subjects of which they treat."[8] These men, if they sought to combat the skepticism implicit in Locke, if they attempted to find a place for the "intuitions of common sense," were avowed empiricists in their presuppositions and in their methodology. In short, they offered what Noah Porter was later to describe as "the newly modified philosophy of Locke," and they therefore found a ready welcome in academic environments which had been long nurtured on Locke but were happy to have the oracle[9] brought up to date by the "realistic" interpretation.[10]

Turning to the correlative prestige of Sensationalism within the church, a reminder is necessary. While it will be shown that the clergy of New England (and we have, of course, particular reference to the Unitarian clergy) embraced Locke or the Scots so far as it rested its religious convictions on any philosophy at all, it should not be thought that this acceptance is indicative of any developed philosophical interests. On the contrary, Alexis de Tocqueville's observation, "I think that in no country in the civilized world is less attention paid to philosophy than in the United States,"[11] applies with particular force to the customary attitude of the ministry both toward philosophy and toward any expressed philosophical basis for religion. The explanation of this intellectual lethargy is not hard to find. Formalized religion—even so loosely formalized a one as Unitarianism—has often considered philosophical buttresses to be of dubious value, since these buttresses, erected as "the rational security of faith," have been known to develop an alarming independence. Behind this dubiety has commonly lain the suspicion that philosophy and religion ("reason" and "faith") are innately hostile to one another, and that in a marriage of the two the latter is all too likely to be relegated to a progressively uxorious position. That some such apprehension existed among the New England clergy, thereby discouraging philosophical inquiries of a more searching nature, is the charge of Marsh in his Introductory Essay to Coleridge's *Aids to Reflection:*

> No one, who has had occasion to observe the general feelings and views of our religious community . . . can be ignorant that a strong prejudice exists against the introduction of philosophy . . . in the discussion of theological subjects. The terms philosophy and metaphysics, even reason and rational, seem in the minds of those most devoted to the support of religious truth, to have forfeited their original, and to have acquired a new import, especially in their relation to matters of faith. By a philosophical view of religious truth would generally be understood a view, not only varying from the religion of the Bible . . . but at war with it; and a rational religion is supposed to be, of course, something diverse from revealed religion.[12]

There was, then, an inherent suspicion of philosophy as an ally of religion (a suspicion which predictably would be confirmed by any "philosophy," such as Transcendentalism, which emphasized the free play of "reason").[13] If we remember, in addition, that America had produced no philosophical literature of importance (always with the exception of Edwards'), it is readily understandable that the pedestrian New England clergyman of the day accepted, uncritically, the philosophy which he had imbibed at the colleges and the innocuousness of which was attested by the fact that it was taught at all in institutions administered, in large part, for and by the ministry.[14]

His confidence would be heightened by the evident compatibility of Sensationalism with conventional Unitarianism. At first blush, it may seem paradoxical that a religious movement which had had its stimulus and earlier momentum in dissatisfaction with the diminishing role to which orthodox Congregationalism (heavily Calvinistic in temper) had consigned the capacity of the individual for direct religious insight should have grown to marriage with a philosophy identified with the limitation of human knowledge to sense experience—and the potential skepticism of which had been demonstrated in the "infidelity" of deism.[15] But the seeming incongruity, although it was to be seized upon and exploited by the Transcendentalists, was pronounced illusory by Unitarians, and the very circumscription of the mind's capacities became for them warrant for a church, since by 1830—or thereabouts—Unitarianism had lost much of its previous character as a reaffirmation of the unmediated relationship with religious truths and was becoming increasingly doctrinal. The invigorating protests of its adolescent years were already becoming watered down to what Emerson was disdainfully to call "the pale negations of Boston Unitarianism" as age brought to the movement the sclerotic symptoms of an established sect. In short, Unitarianism was becoming "respectable,"[16] and in its respectability it found Sensationalism a congenial philosophy, for by its insistence that empirical knowledge was dependent on experience derived through the senses, Sensationalism encouraged the inference that the only source of supraempirical knowledge must be revelation. The question here is not the correctness of this interpretation of Locke's writings; it is enough to have established how so accommodating a reading cut the ground beneath the apparent anomaly of a union between religion and Sensationalism—a union which (it must be repeated) could be satisfying only to a Unitarianism which had drifted toward a traditional caste view of the functions of the clergy.[17]

So it was that " . . . in the Unitarian body . . . the philosophy of Locke had been accepted in its extremest form. . . ."[18] George Ripley's measured exposition of Andrews Norton's views affords a succinct description of the "correct" stance resulting from this acceptance:

> Adopting the cardinal positions of Locke and Hume in regard to the origin of knowledge and the foundation of belief, he pursued them with strict logical sequence to their natural conclusions. In his view there could

be but two sources of ideas—experience and testimony,—which in the final analysis were resolved into one. We have the teachings of experience in regard to the facts of the material universe; and concerning the realm of spiritualities, we are dependent on the authority of divine revelations. The human mind has no inherent faculty of perception in the sphere of facts which transcends the cognizance of the senses. We cannot rely upon the intuitions of reason as the ground of faith in the suggestions of the soul. The veracity of the human spirit as the condition of truth formed no part of his scheme of philosophy. . . . Intuition can inform us of nothing but what exists in our own minds . . . ; it is therefore a mere absurdity to maintain that we have an intuitive knowledge of the truths of religion.[19]

The declarations of a Unitarian clergyman, quoted by Frothingham as a typical example of the "Unitarian of a conservative stamp," are contributive here, as indicating that the platform of the formidable Norton was not unrepresentative of that adopted by the less conspicuous members of his persuasion:

The Christian minister is to preach the declarations and principles of the Gospel. In his view, religion is identified with Christianity, and he values Christianity because it gives him assurance of certain Truths which he regards as of infinite importance. These truths constitute his religion. . . . All our knowledge of Christ and Christianity is derived, not from consciousness or intuition, but from outward revelation. It is not innate, spontaneous and original with us, but extrinsic, derived, super-induced. . . . Once admit that the New Testament does not contain all the principles of spiritual Truth . . . and you open the door to all sorts of loose and crude speculations . . . the heathen sages, it is true, stumbled on some fortunate conjectures, but they could assert nothing with assurance; they could not speak with certainty and authority.[20]

2

Locke's mind will not always be the standard
for metaphysics. (Sampson Reed)

For a questing younger generation which had become increasingly disenchanted with the blandness of the established culture, the confident lucidities of the Andrews Nortons and the echoings of anonymous clergymen were sufficient irritants to incite repudiation. To a degree, the ground had been prepared for the Transcendentalists. Themselves Unitarians, so far as they retained ties to any church, they were members of a sect which had had its American birth in distaste for the "obnoxious" tenets of Calvinistic theology and which had reaffirmed the essentially Protestant principle of the worth, dignity, and capacity of the individual.[21] Moreover, if in its intellectual rationale Unitarianism seemed to have reached a sorry pass, there remained its heritage of tolerance and the encouragement of free enquiry to fortify those who would urge a philosophy more consonant with its intrinsic religious idealism.

Yet the past was at best preparatory. If there had been much in earlier expressions of Unitarian faith, notably in the sermons of Channing,[22] which voiced aspirations that the Transcendentalists were to reassert and augment, the present stimulus was first to come from the outside, for it was a Congregationalist, Marsh, who provided the Transcendentalists with their Old Testament.[23] In his Introductory Essay, the earlier (1821) prophetic opinion of Sampson Reed[24] on the future of Locke's influence is expanded, and the uncritical acceptance of Sensational philosophy is indicted as the principal cause of the deficiency of spiritual content evident in contemporary religion. Marsh named the enemy, exposed his baneful effects, and presented (in Coleridge) a new leader with an invigorating platform. His challenge was unequivocal: " . . . I do not hesitate to express my conviction, that the natural tendency of some of the leading principles of our prevailing system of metaphysics, and those which must unavoidably have more or less influence on our theoretical views of religion, are of an injurious and dangerous tendency. . . . Let it be understood . . . without farther preface, that by the prevailing system of metaphysics, I mean the system of which in modern times Locke is the reputed author, and the leading principles of which, with various modifications, more or less important, but not altering its essential character, have been almost universally received in this country. . . . If the spirit of the Gospel still exerts its influence; if a truly spiritual religion be maintained, it is in opposition to our philosophy, and not at all by its aid." Finally, in the concluding words of the Essay, Marsh anticipates the crux of the whole of Transcendentalism's religious-philosophical protest: "It may at length be discovered, that a system of religion essentially spiritual, and a system of philosophy which excludes the very idea of all spiritual power and agency, in their only distinctive and proper character, cannot be consistently associated together."[25]

It was as if Marsh's Essay, well timed as it was in its articulation of existing undercurrents of discontent, had sounded a clarion call for the young Unitarian liberals, and henceforth their identification of Locke (and, of course, the "derived" Scots) with all that they considered objectionable in contemporary Unitarianism is ubiquitous.[26] Remembering the initial meeting of the Transcendental Club in September, 1836, Cabot quotes a letter from F. H. Hedge recalling that "Mr Emerson, George Ripley, with one another, chanced to confer together on the state of current opinion in theology and philosophy, which we agreed in thinking very unsatisfactory. Could anything be done in the way of protest and introduction of deeper and broader views?

What precisely we wanted would have been difficult for any of us to state. What was strongly felt was dissatisfaction with the reigning sensuous philosophy, dating from Locke, on which our Unitarian theology was based." [27] Nor were the individual members of the Club, and those associated with them, less preoccupied with the iniquities of Locke, especially his guilt in the "materialization" of religion. Emerson speaks slightingly of "philosophers like Locke, Paley, Mackintosh and Stewart . . . men of the world who are reckoned accomplished talkers," [28] of "the skeptical philosophy of Locke"; [29] Alcott is released from "the Philosophy of Sense," [30] from being "a disciple of Experience," from those philosophers, including Locke, who "narrowed the range of the human faculties, retarded the progress of discovery by insisting on the supremacy of the Senses, and shut the soul up in the cave of the Understanding"; [31] Brownson finds Locke's philosophy "altogether unfriendly to religion" and doubts if Harvard will ever contribute much to society "so long as Locke is her text-book in Philosophy"; [32] James Freeman Clarke is rescued from the "wooden philosophy" of Locke by the "higher" thought of Coleridge; [33] George Ripley scores "the sensuous philosophy of Locke" as the cause for the divorce between religion and philosophy, [34] and elsewhere singles out the men of religion "who were led by the philosophy of Locke to attach an extravagant value to external evidence"; [35] Theodore Parker ironically compliments the Unitarians on being "consistent Sensationalists," [36] while he strenuously advances the claims of a more spiritual theology. Finally, it is F. H. Hedge who has given us one of the best summary statements of Transcendentalism's objection to Locke, for in the following comments, although as editor of an American edition of English writings he is directing his attention to theological developments in England, he clearly reflects the judgment of his fellow Transcendentalists on the essential danger to religion implicit in Sensationalism:

> The problem which mainly occupied the theological mind of the time (c. 1800) was the attempt to prove the Gospel by demonstrating the *external* relation between it and God. Christianity, whose fundamental postulate is the inner light by which it manifests itself as the Truth of God, was advocated on the ground of certain facts, which, if true, would prove God to be its Author. . . . The student of the history of opinions might trace here a legitimate result of the then prevailing philosophy of Locke. A germ of mischief lurked in the immortal "Essay," whose fructification had so infected the intellectual atmosphere of the time, so vitiated its conceptions, so dimmed and confused the consciousness of God, that instead of the divine Inpresence and informing Word of the old theologians, a prodigy in nature was held to be the only possible mediator between God and man, the only possible voucher and vehicle of revelation. Christianity was to be received on account of its miracles, not the miracles on account of the more commending Truth of Christianity . . . the very being of God

was no longer a self-evident truth, but a question of logic, to be tried and settled by the understanding.[37]

Here, in words fully applicable to New England Unitarianism, we have the Transcendental development of those seeds of insurrection first firmly planted by the popularity of Marsh's edition of the *Aids.*

But the Transcendentalists were far too emotionally involved to remain content in mere renunciation of their immediate past. If Sensationalism was permanently to be dethroned, a philosophy—particularly an epistemology— more contributive to their religious conviction must be convincingly adduced. Marsh had given them assurance that no satisfaction could be salvaged from the empirical tradition of Locke. They must, ironically, be Separatists, not Puritans. To them, dependence upon Locke as a starting point sanctioned but two eventualities: the "crass materialism" which his French followers had evolved, or, at best, the deceptive compromise of Scottish Realism. No, the epistemological implications of Locke could not be acceptably mitigated; the only promise of success lay in a bold challenge of the premises from which they flowed. If, in the final analysis, the unpardonable deficiency of Locke and his fellow Sensationalists was the limitation which they put upon the extent of human knowledge, this limitation of *extent* issued, irrevocably, from a limitation of *origin.* In short, once grant Locke's presuppositions, all the rest—including, it seemed, Boston Unitarianism—followed. This conclusion was to be given explicit (if naïve) statement in the *Dial:*

> Every system of theology grows out of and is shaped by the philosophical system of those by whom it is first digested, and scientifically taught . . . all systems of philosophy may be divided into two classes— those which recognize innate ideas and those which do not. . . . For those who do not accept innate ideas there is but one system of theology logically possible, and that is Unitarianism . . . which is the result of an attempt to explain Christianity by the sensual philosophy instigated by a desire to get rid of mystery and make everything clear and simple. If this philosophy is not true to psychology, then its interpretations of Christianity are wrong, and the soul is against them, and will finally triumph.[38]

"The soul is against them." Here, surely, is the very pulse of the Transcendental protest, and by the time the words were spoken, the movement had already contrived to bolster its certitude by means of a sympathetic philosophy of mind. The substantive concepts of this philosophy are too familiar to require exposition. The happy distinction between Reason and Understanding, which Emerson was once unabashed enough to call "philosophy itself"[39] (and which constituted the epistemological tenet most commonly identified with Transcendentalism in its early stages), the concepts of Spontaneous Reason, of Intuition, of Instinct—all were affirmations of the inadequacy of the Sensationalistic psychology. If each Transcendentalist seemed, at times, to be wedded to his private phraseology, and if some (notably Emerson)[40] seemed capable of oscillating between one vocabulary and another with an exasperating disregard for helpful definition, it was perfectly clear to Transcendentalists (and also to their critics) that running through all the differences of designation was a unifying agreement in maintaining a capacity within the mind to *transcend* "experience" and thereby luxuriate in direct and irrefutable contact with Truths whose very nature precluded discovery by way of sensuous channels. Given this confidence, it followed that the poverty of the Understanding was not merely the limitation of its epistemological reach; a more pernicious deficiency was that its inescapable preoccupation with empirical experience acted as an inhibiting factor on the free play of Reason, encouraging men toward contentment with the half-truths of the sensory world while obfuscating the light of those verities which only Reason (unfettered from the "iron lids" of the Understanding) could companionably grasp. The import of these contentions for Transcendentalism's expressed religious goals was evident: broadly speaking, it rendered the "necessary mediator" justification of the church baseless and proclaimed instead, if only by implication, that each man found his Church within his own soul, his Revelation within the voice of Reason itself.[41]

3

. . . a philosopher of some repute in his day. (Francis Bowen)

It could not be expected that the "men of Locke"—entrenched spokesmen for established Unitarianism—would be found weaponless against the sound and fury of such intransigency. They were powerfully numerous; they represented the ingrained acceptance of New England's current thinking; they were intellectually equipped to defend themselves with pungent vitality. Philosophically speaking, much of their defense was one by implication. The Transcendental "controversy" was, after all, in the first instance a religious contention, and such tiltings as those between George Ripley and Andrews Norton are sufficient witness of the extent to which it was the specifically religious issues which engaged the concern and resources of the interested parties, the extent to which the fate of rival philosophies rested upon the outcome of theological tussles. Nevertheless, even here the awareness that antagonistic philosophies were also involved was never far from the surface. Ripley was careful to note that the "radical defect" of Norton's theology " . . . proceeds from the influence of the material philosophy on which it is founded. The error with which it starts, that there is no faculty in human nature for perceiving spiritual truth, must needs give rise to the other errors which I have formerly pointed out";[42] and Norton, as has been shown, felt constrained to reassert the Sensationalistic principles which he embraced.

However, while the many excommunications of the "latest form of infidelity," along with the consistently caustic reviews of Transcendental writings (and the writings of such foreign "inspirers" as Coleridge and Cousin)[43] constituted cogent, if tacit, expressions of continued loyalty to the tradition of Locke, more explicit defenses were also at hand. As early as 1829, Edward Everett had published two articles in the *North American Review* on the history of philosophy. In the course of surveying the modern schools, he deals in terms of surprising moderation with the Transcendental philosophy in Germany; yet he feels compelled to score the alleged obscurity of this Idealism and its "unintelligible nomenclature," and in the end he emerges a "man of Locke," denying that Locke encourages the materialistic position to which his French followers had progressed and giving his appreciation of the *Essay* in no uncertain terms: "This great work is, and will probably always remain, the text-book of the noblest branch of human learning. What higher honor could mortal ambition attain or aspire to, than that of achieving it?" [44] In such unstinted eulogy, as in his attack on Idealism's "unintelligible nomenclature," Everett foreshadows much of the character of the opposition which Transcendentalism was to face. It is a character suggested again, two years later, by an unidentified contributor to the same periodical when, in answer to an *Edinburgh Review* article in which Locke's epistemology is dismissed as merely "mechanical," he asserts, "Give us Locke's Mechanism and we will envy no man's Mysticism. Give us to know the 'origin of our ideas,' to comprehend the phenomena 'which we see in the mind' and we will leave the question of the mind's essence to Transcendental speculation."[45]

These judgments were harbingers of more pointed rebuttals soon forthcoming. An article by the Reverend Leonard Withington in the *Quarterly Christian Review,* entitled "The Present State of Metaphysics,"[46] deprecates the value of philosophy in general, but at the same time appears to have been the first favorably to contrast Locke's views with those of a native Transcendentalism still in its germinal stage. It is noteworthy that Withington concentrates on the "psychological issue" involved. Charitably allowing that "Coleridge and his followers" really meant something by their "celebrated distinction" between Reason and Understanding, Withington proceeds to ask, "But what do they mean and how would an Englishman express the same thing?" Consideration leads him to the decision that " . . . The whole mystery seems to be this: the mind sometimes turns its eye on the material world, surveys its operation, learns its laws, and makes its powers subservient to its purposes; and sometimes it looks inward on itself, learns its own powers, and surveys the agreement or discrepancy among its own ideas . . . ," but to consider these two operations evidence of a distinction in mental faculties has as little propriety " . . . as a one-eyed man would call his eye two faculties, because it was sometimes turned towards the heavens and sometimes toward the earth." Again, "Either this 'reason,' this Transcendental and supersensuous faculty, is something so sublime as to be above our reach . . . or it means what has been far better seen, and more clearly expressed, by every sober writer since the days of Locke." Suggested here is an apologia for Locke's epistemology that was to become standard among the critics of Transcendentalism: namely, the contention that a correct reading of Locke would show him to have recognized the two *operations* of the mind which the Transcendentalists professed to have discovered and distinguished by the terms "Reason" and "Understanding," and that if the Transcendentalists meant to accomplish more than merely the elevation of acknowledged operations by bestowing resounding titles—if, in short, they were bent on transforming the twofold capacity of the mind into a dichotomy of faculties—they were talking arrant nonsense. Withington himself is unable to find Coleridge's Reason a contributive concept since Locke had long ago pointed out "two sources of our ideas— sensation and reflexion," and he questions whether Reason "is anything more than a reflexive mind, conscious of its own operations." His conclusion is uncompromisingly severe: " . . . we do not remember in the whole history of human delusions a more pompous profession ending in a more contemptible nothingism."[47]

More consequential than Withington's article were two by Francis Bowen. Bowen's objections to Transcendentalism are to be read as complementary to the rejoinders of Andrews Norton in his dialogue with George Ripley, since taken together they comprise the gist of the Sensationalist-Unitarian answer to the challenge of Transcendentalism. For our purposes, the Bowen articles alone contain, at least in nucleus, all the pertinent arguments which were to be recurrently leveled against Transcendentalism—arguments which in reducing the foe constituted implied reaffirmation of allegiance to conventional Unitarianism and its associated philosophy. The occasion of Bowen's first article[48] was the publication of Emerson's *Nature*. In reviewing it, he finds it representative of a class of writings and is led to observe that "Within a short period, a new school of philosophy has arisen. . . . It rejects the aid of observation, and will not trust to experiment. . . . General truths are to be attained without the previous examination of particulars, and by the aid of a higher power than the understanding. . . . The sphere of intuition is enlarged and made to comprehend the most abstruse and elevated propositions respecting the being and destiny of man." He notes that the adoption of such a novel philosophy entails the forging of a special vocabulary, a practice which must encourage an unwarranted obscurity of language: "It would avail but little, perhaps, with some Transcendentalists to assert that the deepest minds have ever been the clearest, and to quote the example of Locke and Bacon, as men who could treat the most abstruse subjects in the most familiar and intelligible terms." To his mind, one is well within one's right to "infer vagueness and incompleteness of thought from obscurity in language," and in support of this judgment he quotes with approval "a few homely remarks from the writings of a philosopher who enjoyed some repute in his day." The ironic allusion is, of course, to Locke.

Bowen's second article, coming shortly afterwards,[49] is a more sweeping censure of Transcendentalism. For purposes of summary, its content can be broken down into seven charges:

1. "There is *prima facie* evidence against it . . . for . . . it is abstruse in its dogmas, fantastic in its dress, and foreign in its origin."

2. Its passion for phraseological innovations leads not only to the "depravation of English style," but to a highly suspicious obscurity of thought.

3. As a necessary result of 1 and 2, it has "deepened the gulf between speculative and practical men," since clarity of philosophical language is "the only bridge which spans the chasm."[50]

4. It appeals from the authority of argument to that of "passion and feeling."

5. Its advocates include men familiar with the "sublimated atheism" of Fichte and the "downright pantheism" of Schelling. (Bowen merely hints these charges of atheism and pantheism; others are destined to make them familiar.)[51]

6. It does not recognize that . . . "there are mysteries in nature which human nature cannot penetrate; there are problems which the philosopher cannot solve."

7. Its touted distinction between Reason and Understanding either solely directs attention to two *aspects* of the mind's capacity, in which case it says nothing new; or it proclaims two *kinds* of mental faculties, in which case it is false. (This criticism is, of course, essentially the same as Withington's.)

The articles in the *Princeton Review* were still to be published, the formidable Norton was still to be heard from, innumerable random passages of hostile reference were still to be penned, but the future indictments of Transcendentalism had been sharply prefigured by Bowen. Prescient, too (as well as timely), was the title Bowen chose for his second article, "Locke and the Transcendentalists," for although disputation over Transcendentalism was to rage for many years, integral to its philosophical history was to remain the name of John Locke, symbol of commitments too diverse and too profoundly rooted to permit facile compromise.

NOTES

1. *The Journals of Bronson Alcott* (Boston, 1938). An abbreviated account of Locke's relationship to Transcendentalism is contained in Merle Curti's "The Great Mr. Locke, America's Philosopher (1783-1861)," *Huntington Library Bulletin,* XI (1937).

2. The mere pejorative designation "Sensualism" is also common in contemporary literature. Thus, in an article ascribed to Charles Mayo Ellis: "The old Philosophy is sensual; that is, it affirms that all knowledge . . . may be shown to have come into the body through the senses . . . the new is spiritual." *An Essay on Transcendentalism* (1842), (Gainesville, Fla., 1954), pp. 22-23. Andrews Norton protested the application of "Sensualism" to Locke's philosophy and cited the "barbarism" as an example of the importation of Germanic usages, incompletely understood and inaccurately translated. *Remarks on a Pamphlet Entitled " 'The Latest Form of Infidelity' Examined"* (Cambridge, Mass., 1839), p. 58.

3. *Sketches of Modern Philosophy* (Hartford, 1842), p. 34.

4. Friedrich Ueberweg, *A History of Philosophy,* translated by G. S. Morris, with additions by Noah Porter (New York, 1872), p. 451.

5. The Aldrich material is in "Report to the Council," *Proceedings of the American Antiquarian Association* (April 1879), pp. 22-39.

6. "Philosophical Instruction in Harvard University (1636-1906)," *Harvard Graduates Magazine,* XXXVII (1928-29), 36.

7. But not without protest from the more devout. As early as 1822, the Rev. Frederick Beasley, in the Dedication to his *A Search of Truth in the Science of the Human Mind* (Philadelphia), had maintained that Locke had been grossly misinterpreted by the Scottish philosophers, to whose claims of impressive innovations the bulk of his work is an energetic rebuttal. Edward Everett expressed his trust that Brown would not long be permitted to "usurp" the place "once occupied by the great master of intellectual science" (*North American Review,* XXIX, 1829), and the *Christian Examiner* (September 1834, p. 97) expressed its satisfaction that Giles had reintroduced the *Essay* as a textbook at Harvard.

8. *Memoir and Remains of the Rev. James Marsh,* edited by J. Torrey (Burlington, Vt, 1852), p. 136. There is abundant evidence of the Scottish authority at the time of the Transcendental revolt. E. W. Todd provides especially valuable information in his "Philosophy at Harvard College," *New England Quarterly,* XVI (1943), 63-90.

9. " . . . that justly celebrated oracle. . . ." The accolade is Benjamin Rush's.

10. As Channing put it in answer to the surprise expressed by Miss Peabody that Brown had been adopted in the Andover curriculum: "I think I understand it. It denotes a change of tone at Andover, that will not reach the

depth of their error, but make it a less noxious error." Elizabeth Palmer
Peabody, *Reminiscences of Reverend Wm. Ellery Channing* (Boston, 1880),
p. 140. From a very different quarter comes more specific assertion of the
derived character of Scottish philosophy: "Locke is the proper father of Reid
and Stewart with their school who, we must say, have rendered him but
scanty justice." Francis Bowen, *North American Review*, LIII (1841), 40.
Bowen had maintained this position from the first: in 1837 he used the word
"additive" ("Here everything is additive") to describe the relationship between the Scots and Locke. "Locke and the Transcendentalists," *Christian
Examiner*, XXIII (1837), 188.

11. *Democracy in America*, revised and edited from the twelfth edition of
the original, 1850, by Francis Bowen (Cambridge, Mass., 1864). G. Stanley
Hall has also noted the common indifference toward philosophical subjects
and he reminds us of a half-forgotten simile once applied to nineteenth-
century American thought: "philosophers in America are as rare as snakes in
Norway." "Philosophy in the United States," *Mind*, IV (1894), 89-105.

12. First American edition, edited by James Marsh (Burlington, Vt.,
1829). That this distrust of philosophical speculation was not limited to the
ministry of New England is made clear by one of John McVicker's professed
reasons for issuing his own edition of Coleridge's *Aids*, in 1839, without
Marsh's Essay. McVicker, an Episcopalian theologian at Columbia states of
the Essay that " . . . it circulates what is deemed a false and dangerous
principle, *viz.*, that some system of metaphysical philosophy is essential to
soundness in Christian doctrine." (An account of the rivalry between Marsh
and McVicker will be found in "American Comments on Coleridge a Century
Ago," by Alice D. Snyder, in *Coleridge: Studies by Several Hands on the
Hundredth Anniversary of his Death* [London, 1934].) Presbyterian conviction that the encouragement of philosophy endangers orthodox dependence
on revelation is found in an article by Samuel Tyler in the *Princeton Review*,
XV (1843), 249-50.

It may be observed that the alleged divorce between religion and philosophy constituted a strong incentive for the attacks of the Transcendentalists,
so we are not surprised to find numerous references to the effect that "the
bans of wedlock have been forbidden to religion and philosophy." *Dial*, vol. I,
no. 1 (1840); see also vol. I, no. 2, and vol. II, no. 1 (1841). Nine years after
Marsh's remarks, George Ripley was to notice that "the wedded union of
philosophy and religion . . . has not yet been consummated in the sanctuary
of our holiest thoughts. This is the true cause of the ominous fact that an
open dread of philosophy, and a secret doubt of religion, are not unfrequent
in the midst of us." *Specimens of Standard Foreign Literature* (Boston,
1838), I, 15. Fourteen years later, at least one Transcendentalist suggests that
the movement, now past its first great challenge, has failed to effect the
marriage: "You know the actual condition of the American church, that it
has a theology which cannot stand the test of reason; and accordingly it very
wisely resolved to throw reason overboard before it began the voyage"
(Theodore Parker, "Some Account of My Ministry," November 1852); where-

as it was Parker's conviction that " . . . a true method in theology marries the religious instinct to philosophical reflection and they will increase and multiply, replenishing the earth and subduing it; toil and thought shall dwell in their household, and desire and duty go hand in hand therein." ("A Sermon on True and False Theology," February 1858).

13. Representative are the sentiments of the elder Frothingham, spoken in 1834, in the midst of the furor over Transcendentalism, and quoted by his son: "The present era seems to be that of the apotheosis of human nature . . . give me back the simple form of a child's credulity, rather than mislead me into any philosophical refinement, that instructs me to presume, and leaves me to perish." O. B. Frothingham, *Boston Unitarianism: 1820-1850* (New York, 1890), p. 44.

14. G. Stanley Hall (*Mind*, IV, 89-105) considers the extent and effect of the control exercised over philosophical instruction by the nineteenth-century clergyman-professor. A. C. Armstrong states flatly that at the time in question " . . . the trend of philosophical instruction was controlled by dogmatic conviction." "Philosophy in the United States," *Education Review*, X (1895), 11.

15. Curti comments on Locke and American deism. He also says of Locke's *Essay* that " . . . its plea for reliance on sensory experience and reflection rather than on innate ideas and the 'mysterious' tended to undermine the traditional sanctions of orthodoxy. Locke's position was, in many respects, anticipatory of that maintained a hundred years later by the early Unitarians." "The Great Mr. Locke . . . ," p. 115. It should be pointed out, however, that by the time with which we are dealing Unitarianism had itself become comparatively "orthodox"; yet by emphasizing the restrictive aspect of Locke's epistemology in order to further the claim for revelation, it was able to continue, with happy consistency, its acceptance of the *Essay*.

16. As the *Dial* was to put it, "Religion has become chiefly and with the well-clad class of men, a matter of convention, and they write Christian with their name as they write 'Mr.' because it is respectable." Vol. I, no. 2 (1840).

17. This "caste" view was to be singled out for assault in the theological objections of the Transcendentalists, to whom it was a cardinal betrayal of the Protestant liberal tradition. Thus, in his controversy with Andrews Norton, George Ripley inveighs against his opponent's adoption and defense of "the exclusive principle": that is, "the assumption of the right for an individual, or any body of individuals, to make their own private opinions the measure of what is fundamental in the Christian faith." *"The Latest Form of Infidelity" Examined* (Boston, 1839).

In concluding this sketch of Unitarian acceptance of Locke's philosophy, it is interesting to note the understandable prevalence of contemporary writings claiming Locke himself to be a Unitarian: e.g., the *Christian Examiner*, XI (1831), and an American Unitarian Association reprint (Series I, no. 77, 1833) of an English pamphlet, *Religious Opinions and Example of Milton, Locke and Newton*, by the Rev. Henry Acton of Exeter.

18. Noah Porter in Friedrich Ueberweg, *A History of Philosophy*, p. 454.

O. B. Frothingham agrees: "The Unitarians as a class belonged to the school of Locke. . . ." *Transcendentalism in New England* (Boston, 1903), p. 109.

19. Quoted in *The Memorial History of Boston,* edited by Justin Winsor (Boston, 1881), IV, 300. Ripley has here been scrupulously accurate (except, of course, in his lumping together "the cardinal positions of Locke and Hume") in reproducing Norton's view; e.g., one compares the last sentence of his summation with the following: "There can be no intuition, no direct perception of the truths of Christianity. . . ." *A Discourse on the Latest Form of Infidelity* (Cambridge, Mass., 1839), p. 32. Indeed, all of Ripley's sentences seem to have been suggested by passages in the pamphlets which Norton issued during his controversy with Ripley. For a chronology of the Norton-Ripley altercation, see Clarence Gohdes, *The Periodicals of New England Transcendentalism* (Durham, 1931), pp. 59-60.

20. *Boston Unitarianism,* p. 169.

21. The "radical" inheritance of Transcendentalism is the subject of Perry Miller's "From Edwards to Emerson," *New England Quarterly,* XIII (1940), 589-617.

22. Schneider calls Channing's sermon, "Likeness to God" (1828), "one of the first American formulations of transcendentalism." Herbert W. Schneider, *A History of American Philosophy* (New York, 1946), p. 65.

23. The designation is Odell Shepard's in *Pedlar's Progress* (Boston, 1937), p. 159; Emerson's *Nature* was, of course, their New Testament.

24. "Oration on Genius"; it is reprinted in Kenneth W. Cameron's *Emerson the Essayist: an Outline of his Philosophical Development through 1836,* 2 vols. (Raleigh, N.C., 1945), II, 9-12.

25. Marsh, Introductory Essay in his edition of Coleridge's *Aids to Reflection.*

26. Marjorie Nicolson has presented some of the considerable evidence of the popularity enjoyed by Marsh's edition of the *Aids* (*Philosophical Review,* XXXIV [1925], 28-50). It was probably this enthusiastic reception which prompted Marsh, in his Preface to Coleridge's *The Friend* (Burlington, Vt.), two years later, to express the premature confidence that "It is no longer hazardous to one's reputation to call in question the authority of those philosophers who have been most popular among us."

27. J. E. Cabot, *A Memoir of Ralph Waldo Emerson* (Boston, 1887), I, 244.

28. *Works* (Boston, 1903), II, 287.

29. *Ibid.,* I, 340.

30. *The Journals of Bronson Alcott,* p. 66.

31. *Ibid.,* p. 39.

32. *Boston Quarterly Review,* II (1839), 105-12. However, the unpredictable Brownson, always an unreliable ally of the Transcendentalists, was to contribute (only three years later) a recantation of his many barbed criticisms of Locke: " . . . we are not ashamed to own that our respect for Locke is every day increasing and we would not repeat the severe things which the indiscreet zeal of admirers has, on some former occasions, induced us to say

of him. . . . The philosophy which commends itself by detracting from the imperishable glory of such a man as John Locke can be in vogue only for a day and must soon take its place with the things which are as if they had not been." *Ibid.,* V (1842), 181.

33. *The Autobiography of James Freeman Clarke,* edited by Edward Everett Hale (Boston, 1891), pp. 39, 89-90.

34. *Specimens of Standard Foreign Literature,* Introductory Notice.

35. *"The Latest Form of Infidelity" Examined.*

36. *"A Sermon on the Moral Condition of Boston,"* February 1849.

37. *Essays and Reviews* (New York, 1874). The volume reproduces Hedge's prefatory remarks of 1860 to the first American edition. For more on Hedge's background and opinion, see Ronald V. Wells, *Three Christian Transcendentalists* (New York, 1943).

In quoting the evaluations of Locke by the rebellious younger men, one should not overlook the judgment of the less engaged Channing: "Locke's philosophy has quenched spirituality in modern thought, and so brings men to enthrone logical abstraction above the spirit . . . " (Peabody, p. 140).

38. I (1841).

39. *The Letters of Ralph Waldo Emerson,* edited by Ralph L. Rusk (New York, 1939), I, 412.

40. The most satisfactory single volume on Emerson's "formal" position remains A. D. Grey's *Emerson: a Statement of New England Transcendentalism as Expressed in the Philosophy of its Chief Exponent* (Palo Alto, 1917).

41. "Revelation is the disclosure of the Soul." Emerson, *Works,* II, 282. "Each of us is a new born bard of the Holy Ghost." *Ibid.,* I, 146. " . . . experience of the soul is a revelation of God." Alcott, *Dial,* vol. I, no. 3 (1841).

42. *A Third Letter to Mr Andrews Norton* (Boston, 1840).

43. Cousin's most specific contribution to the Transcendental controversy was his *Lectures on Locke,* presented to America under the title of *Elements of Psychology* (translated and introduced by C. S. Henry, 1834). Of the book, which by 1855 had achieved a fourth edition, so qualified a commentator as Noah Porter has said, "This work openly raised the standard of revolt against the fundamental principles and methods of Locke" (Ueberweg, p. 453). In the light of the evidence attesting to the impact of Marsh's edition of the *Aids,* which preceeded the *Elements* by five years, and the marked lack of evidence which would confirm any comparable influence asserted for Cousin's work (except on Brownson, who at the time was a combative disciple of Cousin and who, it should be recalled, disassociated his Cousinism from Transcendentalism), we can say that Porter was in error if his evaluation is meant to claim *American* priority of significance for the *Elements.* The truth is that Cousin's "professional" analysis of Locke's deficiencies could only corroborate the already established objections of the Transcendentalists; in contrast, the chief reason for the greater effect of Marsh's Introductory Essay, aside from its precedence in time, was that Marsh articulated their highly emotional repugnance towards Locke's role in the spiritual life of New England.

This suggested weight of Cousin on Transcendentalism is a reminder that non-American sources of basic influence on the movement have been commonly overemphasized. Many such sources have indisputable claim for recognition, but it is always necessary to remember that to a considerable extent the Transcendentalists borrowed those European (and Asian) concepts and emphases which most satisfactorily expressed the core of their rebellion. The core itself had a strong indigenous history (as, of course, had American Unitarianism, as well). With respect to German philosophy, this view is supported by Wellek: "What attracted the American thinkers was . . . the fact that the German philosophy shared with them a common enmity to the methods and results of eighteenth century British empiricism and to the tradition of skepticism and materialism in general. . . . The Transcendentalists were merely looking for corroboration of their faith. They found it in Germany, but ultimately they did not need the confirmation. Their faith was deeply rooted in their minds and their own spiritual ancestry." Rene Wellek, "Emerson and German Philosophy," *New England Quarterly*, XVI (1943), 61-62.

44. The Everett articles are in vols. XVIII (1824) and XIX (1829). The quotations are from the second volume.

45. "Defence of Mechanical Philosophy," XXXIII (1831), 122.

46. December 1834.

47. That the Transcendentalists' reading of Locke could find in his "reflexion" nothing that would justify Withington's reduction of Reason to an idiosyncratic "translation" of Locke's concept is evident from the following passage: "It seems obvious at first sight that, in denying the mind any primary principles, and reflection being, by definition, only the notice which the mind, this blank piece of paper, takes of its own operations, reflection can add nothing to the stock of ideas furnished by sensation. It is a mere spectator; its office merely to note impressions." (*Dial*, vol. II, no. 1 [1841].)

In addition to the reference to be made to Francis Bowen's stand, warm agreement with Withington on the speciousness of the Reason-Understanding distinction may be found in an article by James W. Alexander and Albert Dod entitled "Transcendentalism" (*Princeton Review*, January 1839). This piece and one by Charles Hodge, entitled "The School of Hegel" (*Ibid.*, January 1840), were subsequently to be published together by Andrews Norton under the title *Two articles from the "Princeton Review," Concerning the Transcendental Philosophy of the Germans and of Cousin and Its Influence on Opinion in this Country* (Cambridge, Mass., 1840). Brownson is also critical of the distinction (*Boston Quarterly Review*, April 1842). Withington's article comes in for high praise in a pamphlet attributed to William Mitchell and entitled *Coleridge and the Moral Tendency of his Writings*, a vitriolic attack on the alleged moral and religious implications of Coleridge's thought.

48. *Christian Examiner*, XXI (1836), 371. Wells gives us the following statement on Bowen's own position: "Basically . . . Bowen's interest lay in demonstrating the validity of the principles of natural religion, whereas Marsh, Hedge, and Henry sought to re-establish Christian principles by means

of a marriage of philosophy to religion. This union Bowen considered the source of all evil both to religion and to philosophy." (*Three Christian Transcendentalists,* p. 8.)

Wells' summary calls for two comments. The first is that Bowen's interest in establishing the validity of natural religion is harmonious with Locke's own concern: e.g., "Locke believed that he had established, philosophically, the existence of God and 'natural' religion." (*Encyclopaedia Britannica,* 14th edition, XIV, 272.) The second is that, read out of context, the judgment that " . . . Marsh . . . sought to re-establish Christian principles by means of a marriage of philosophy to religion" could suggest a closer affinity of Marsh to the Transcendentalists of the Boston-Cambridge-Concord stamp than in point of fact existed. In truth, although Marsh's goal (" . . . a marriage of philosophy to religion") was the same as that of the Young Turks his edition of the *Aids* had awakened, his Andover Congregational training, his convictions (and, no doubt, his personality) could not permit him to be sympathetic with their perspective of this goal—or with their intemperate rhetoric. Thus: "There are, I am persuaded, but two thoroughly consistent [and] complete systems [and] these are, *the evangelical system,* which places the ultimate views of truth and grounds of conviction beyond the sphere of the speculative understanding [it is significant that Marsh is here using 'understanding' with the Kantian, not the Coleridge-Transcendental connotation] in the voice of the conscience [and] the perishing *need* of a spirit fully awakened to a sense of what it needs; [and] for the other a system, that, confiding in speculative conclusions, explains away in the last resort the authority of conscience [and] terminates in a *consistent pantheism.* I very much fear that those, who talk of spiritual philosophy among you, mean nothing more than the opposite of sensualism, and still have a wide space between them [and] the spiritualism of St. Paul." (Marsh to Richard H. Dana, August 21, 1832; quoted by Wells, p. 161.) Again: "The whole of Boston transcendentalism I take to be rather a superficial affair; and there is some force in the remark of a friend of mine that the 'Dial' indicates rather the place of the moon than of the sun. . . . They pretend to no system or unity, but each utters, it seems, the inspiration of the moment, assuming that it all comes from the universal heart, while ten to one it comes only from the stomach of the individual." (Marsh to Henry J. Raymond, March 1, 1841; quoted by Wells, p. 161.)

49. *Christian Examiner,* XXIII (1837), 371.

50. It was this arraignment which Brownson took as the springboard for a rejoinder in the *Boston Quarterly Review* (January 1838): "Philosophy and Common Sense."

51. Notably, Andrews Norton, *A Discourse on the Latest Form of Infidelity,* and the *Princeton Review,* XI (January 1839); XII (January 1840); XX (April 1848); XXVIII (April 1856). One must also remember the judgment of Marsh.

The alleged "infidelity" of the "new school" became an increasingly awkward issue in the internecine conflict between Unitarianism and Transcendentalism and was intimately related to the eventual resignation of

Emerson from the ministry and the "excommunication" of Parker. The stridency and extravagance of expression characteristic of the more vocal Transcendentalists placed Unitarianism in an embarrassing position. Calvinism had long since labeled an early Unitarianism "a half-way house" to infidelity and had predicted that by the dropping of one orthodox doctrine after another the infidelity would become complete. Stung by this reminder, Unitarianism might have been expected to have dealt with conscionable severity with its refractory minority. However, not only did its tradition of liberalism make such chastisement distasteful, but also its past remonstrances against Calvinism's "exclusive system" would emphasize the inconsistency of any attempt to discipline its own protestants. The subject is covered in C. H. Faust's "The Background of the Unitarian Opposition to Transcendentalism," *Modern Philology*, XXXV (1938), 297-324.

7

The Minor Transcendentalists
and German Philosophy

RENÉ WELLEK

THE RELATIONS BETWEEN NEW ENGLAND TRANSCENDENTALISM
and German philosophy have never been studied in any detail. Most discussions are content to assume the influence of German philosophy, referring in
general terms to Kant, Schelling and Fichte, or try to dismiss the influence
altogether.[1] There are many suggestive remarks in books and articles, but we
have no systematic study which would examine this relationship in the light
of all the evidence, on the background of a thorough knowledge of the
German philosophers. In this paper little more can be attempted than the first
outlines of such an investigation. As an excuse for presenting it, I shall only
plead that I have not met such a survey elsewhere and that possibly my earlier
studies in Kant and his influence in England[2] have given me a starting point
and some initial scheme of reference.

In approaching the question of the relations between New England Transcendentalism and German philosophy, it will be necessary to touch first on a
subordinate subject: the exact beginnings of this influence and the way in
which German thought was imported into this country. I touch on it only

because there are two widely held views on this point which seem to me mistaken. One theory ascribes the importation of German thought to the return of American students such as Ticknor and Bancroft from Germany; the other assumes that German philosophy reached America first, and only, through Coleridge and Carlyle.

It has been shown convincingly that intellectual relations between America and Germany were by no means nonexistent even in the seventeenth century, and that the general lack of German books or of the knowledge of the German language in America has been exaggerated.[3] Especially toward the end of the eighteenth century there was considerable interest in German *belles lettres:* John Quincy Adams, for instance, translated Wieland's *Oberon* into good verse, and the Reverend William Bentley, pastor at Salem, collected German books which included the works of Klopstock and Schiller and many others. In the periodical literature there appear even scattered mentions of the recent German philosophers. An issue of the Philadelphia *Monthly Magazine* for 1798 included a note on Kant based on a German source, which speaks of the *Criterion [sic] of Pure Reason;* and the *Boston Register* of 1801 contains quotations from Fichte refuting the charges of atheism.[4] In Samuel Miller's interesting *Retrospect of the Eighteenth Century* (1803) there is a hostile account of Kant which reproduces a review by William Taylor of Willich's *Elements of Critical Philosophy* (1798) from the London *Monthly Review* of January 1799.[5] Obviously not much can be made out of such scattered notices except to suggest that the names of Kant and Fichte had begun to reach America.

An actual motive for the study of German thought was supplied only by the New England theologians, who became interested in German Biblical scholarship long before the earliest migration of American students to German universities after the end of the Napoleonic wars. As early as 1806, the Reverend Joseph Stevens Buckminster, later pastor of the Brattle Street Church at Cambridge, brought a library of some three thousand German books from Europe and started to lecture on Biblical criticism at Harvard College. Buckminster died young and apparently left few traces of his interests.[6] But Moses Stuart, Professor of Sacred Literature at Andover Theological Seminary, must have been a far more influential figure. In 1812 he encouraged his young friend Edward Everett to translate Herder's *Letters on Theology;* and in 1814, when Everett went on a trip to New York, Stuart asked him to buy German books. He wanted him especially to get a "copy of Kant's philosophy," whatever that may mean, which "would be a great curiosity."[7] He used Rosenmüller and de Wette in his classroom and in 1822 translated from the Latin a book called *The Elements of Interpretation* by the German J. A. Ernesti. In 1825 he underwent investigation for his views by the trustees of his college. The Committee reported that "the unrestrained cultivation of German studies has evidently tended to chill the ardor of piety, to impair belief in the fundamentals of revealed religion, and even to induce, for the time, an approach to universal skepticism."[8] But Stuart continued with his work, and as late as 1841 sent a spirited defense of German Biblical scholarship to the *Christian Review*. The work done by other figures, such as Dr. Convers Francis and James Walker, both students of German theology, still needs exploring.

The strongest argument for the role of Coleridge in transmitting German thought is furnished by the work of James Marsh, President of the University of Vermont from 1826 to 1833. In 1829 he edited *Aids to Reflection* adding a long preliminary discourse expounding the distinctions of German philosophers (such as that between Reason and Understanding) in the interpretation of Coleridge. In a letter to Coleridge, Marsh acknowledged his debt on this point quite specifically: "The German philosophers," he wrote, "Kant and his followers are very little known in this country; and our young men who have visited Germany have paid little attention to that department of study while there. I cannot boast of being wiser than others in this respect; for though I have read a part of the works of Kant, it was under many disadvantages, so that I am indebted to your own writings for the ability to understand what I have read of his works, and am waiting with some impatience for that part of your works which will aid more directly in the study of those subjects of which he treats."[9]

But Marsh certainly extended his interest in German thought beyond a secondhand knowledge derived from Coleridge. He read the anthropological and scientific writings of Kant and planned a book on logic designed to follow the textbook of Johann Jacob Fries, who had given an extreme objectivist interpretation to Kant. Nor could Marsh have needed Coleridge's stimulus to translate Herder's *Spirit of Hebrew Poetry* in 1833, or two scholarly German books, the *Geography of the Scriptures* and the *Historical Chronology*. Marsh can be described as a belated Cambridge Platonist, whose interests were primarily theological and educational.[10] Thus, clergymen who studied German Biblical scholarship and Kant appear to have made the first contact with modern German thought.

The role of the American students who returned from Germany has been, it seems to me, extremely overrated, at least for our question. Edward Everett, who was to procure that copy of Kant's philosophy for Moses Stuart, studied classical philology in Göttingen. Everett was President of Harvard from 1846 to 1849, but no interest in German philosophy is recorded in his life except an abortive plan to give an address on "the influence of German thought on the contemporary literature of England and America," in 1837.[11] As early as 1816 George Ticknor came to the conclusion that the present "barrenness" of German literature was to be charged to the philosophy of

Kant, which "absorbed and perverted all the talents of the land." It was a vast "Serbonian bog where armies whole have sunk."[12] After his return to Harvard, Ticknor lectured on French and Spanish literature. George Bancroft, who kept up an interest in German *belles lettres* and later wrote several valuable studies, went to hear Hegel in Berlin, but thought the lectures merely a "display of unintelligible words." He admired Schleiermacher, however, whom he heard lecture on education, largely because "he has never suffered himself to be moved by any one of the many systems which have been gaining admirers and losing them successively for thirty years past."[13]

Neither Motley nor Longfellow showed any interest in German philosophy.[14] The one exception among these students was Frederick Henry Hedge, who was, however, in Germany as a boy and developed interest in German philosophy only much later. In 1833 he wrote a review of Coleridge for the *Christian Examiner* which gives a fairly detailed account of German philosophy.[15] Hedge there deplores the meager information on German philosophy in Coleridge and proceeds to explain his own views. They show a knowledge which is quite independent of Coleridge and a firsthand acquaintance with Fichte's *Wissenschaftslehre* and Schelling's *System des transzendentalen Idealismus.* Kant, according to Hedge, "did not himself create a system, but furnished the hints and materials from which all the systems of his followers have been framed." The transcendental point of view is described as that of "interior consciousness." "In the language of the school, it is a free intuition, and can only be attained by a vigorous effort of the will. The object is to discover in every form of finite existence, an infinite and unconditioned as the ground of its existence, or rather the ground of our knowledge of its existence, to refer all phenomena to certain *noumena,* or laws of cognition. It is not a *ratio essendi,* but a *ratio cognoscendi.*" This sounds like a description of Kant's procedure. Hedge, however, elaborates the point that the method is "synthetical, proceeding from a given point, the lowest that can be found in our consciousness, and deducing from that point 'the whole world of intelligences, with the whole system of their representations.'" Immediately afterwards this description, which might apply to Schelling, is modified, and an explanation of the "alternation of synthesis and antithesis" in Fichte is followed by a quite technical and literal reproduction of the beginnings of the *Wissenschaftslehre.* But Fichte is criticized as leaning toward skepticism and as "altogether too subjective." Schelling seems to Hedge the most satisfactory of all the Germans. "In him intellectual philosophy is more ripe, more substantial, more promising, and, if we may apply such a term to such speculations, more practical than in any of the others." Hedge describes briefly the main principle of Schelling's natural philosophy as an endeavor to show that "the outward world is of the same essence with the thinking mind, both being different manifestations of the same divine principle." Hedge alludes to Oken's development of Schelling's system and mentions him with Hegel and Fries, apologizing that "our information would not enable us to say much, and our limits forbid us to say anything" about them. Unfortunately Hedge never followed-up the promise held out by these few competent pages. He collaborated in the *Dial,* to which he contributed a translation of Schelling's inaugural lecture at Berlin, and published an anthology of the *Prose Writers of Germany* (1847) which contained translated extracts from Kant's *Critique of Judgment,* Schellings's oration on the fine arts and passages from Friedrich Schlegel's and Hegel's *Philosophies of History* and Fichte's *Destiny of Man.* Late in his life, Hedge became Professor of German at Harvard and wrote papers on Leibniz and Schopenhauer.[16] Hedge was no original thinker, but he had a really good knowledge of German from the time of his schooldays. He could talk on German philosophy with his elders and friends, Emerson and Alcott, and may serve as an indication that America was not confined to secondhand information on German philosophy through either Coleridge or the French eclectics.

The influence of the German immigrants belongs mostly to a later time. Carl Follen, the first instructor and later professor of German at Harvard, is the most important figure among these. He was an enthusiastic German *Corpsstudent,* an admirer of Jahn, the nationalistic gymnastics teacher, and of Theodor Körner, the poet of the Napoleonic wars. But he also studied theology under Channing and in 1830 gave a course on moral philosophy which shows firsthand knowledge of Kant.[17] In the course of a brief history of ethics which discusses the Greeks, the New Testament and Spinoza, we get a fairly full exposition of Kant's philosophy. The description of the *Critique of Pure Reason* is elementary and vitiated by Follen's repeated reference to time, space and categories as "innate ideas": he suspects Kant's system of leading to subjective idealism and skepticism, but then gives an exposition of the moral philosophy which shows far better insight and even critical acumen. Kant is criticized for his mistake of considering man "sometimes entirely as a rational and moral, and sometimes entirely as a sensual or phenomenal being," and some good points are scored against the categorical imperative, which to Follen appears vague and general and merely an advice to search the nature, particularly the rational and moral nature, of man. Kant's religion of reason seems to him "nothing less than an avowal of atheism." His attitude toward Kant is extremely unsympathetic: he criticizes him not from the point of view of later German idealism (which he apparently did not know though he alludes to Fichte), but with empirical arguments which he manages to combine with a philosophy of faith. Nevertheless, in the following year, Follen, in his inaugural discourse as professor of German at Harvard, included a defense of German philosophy. He argued that its "records, from Leibniz to Kant and his disciples, Fichte, Schelling, Jacobi, and Fries do not exhibit the name of a single materialist or absolute skeptic."[18] Though Follen, in spite of his premature death, did something to foster interest in things German, he can scarcely be described as a propagandist for German idealist philosophy.

The other Germans who wrote on philosophy came later and could not have been of decisive importance. Frederick A. Rauch became President of Marshall College in Pennsylvania and wrote a Hegelian *Psychology: or a View of the Human Soul* (1841). Johann Bernhard Stallo settled in Cincinnati and wrote *General Principles of the Philosophy of Nature* (1848), a book which attracted Emerson's interest sufficiently to warrant long extracts in his *Journals.*[19] The editor of the *Journals* printed so few quotations from Emerson's transcript that it is impossible to judge the nature of his interest in Stallo, but the book may very well have been a source of Emerson's knowledge of Schelling, Oken and Hegel. Since Stallo does little more than give abstracts, it is difficult to lay one's hand on any indebtedness which Emerson might not have incurred from the original texts or from other secondhand accounts.[20] Another German, Emmanuel Vitalis Scherb, tried to instruct Emerson on Hegel in 1849 and 1851, but since the *Journals* do not tell us precisely of what this instruction consisted, we might as well not even begin to guess.[21]

All this is strictly preliminary, by way of clearing the path to a direct examination of the main figures in the Transcendentalist group. But I cannot suppress a few reflections on the general problem presented by the contact of two great intellectual movements. I avoid the term "influence," which to be used safely needs some closer definition. In discussing such a relation, we must, I think, distinguish carefully several questions which are frequently not kept clearly apart by investigators. First, we must see what was the reputation of German philosophy, the vague secondhand or tenthhand information which was floating about, and distinguish it from actual knowledge of German philosophy, either in more detailed descriptive accounts by English or French writers or in a real firsthand acquaintance with the texts themselves, in translation or in the original. Only when this first problem of the actual knowledge has been settled can we profitably inquire what precisely was the attitude and the opinion that American writers had of the German philosophers. Only after this can we raise the question of actual influence. Even then we have to distinguish between the use of isolated quotations or ideas and a really basic similarity in philosophical outlook or mental evolution. Isolated parallels merely establish the fact of the relation; one can speak of real influence only if the whole system of one man is compared with the whole system of another. ("System," of course, need not imply any systematic exposition in any technical sense, but merely means a personal view of the world.) Even then we ought to know exactly the original features (or at least the peculiar combinations of ideas in the two systems we are comparing) before we can maintain with absolute certainty that we have defined a shaping and determining influence and not merely uncovered a spiritual kinship, possibly explainable by similar intellectual antecedents. In the case of American Transcendentalism, this problem becomes extremely complex, since the ancestry of Transcendentalism includes almost the whole intellectual history of mankind: Plato; the pre-Socratic philosophers known to Emerson and Alcott in fairly detailed accounts; Neo-Platonism, partly available in the recent translations of Thomas Taylor; the English Neo-Platonists of the seventeenth and eighteenth centuries; the great tradition of mysticism represented especially by Jacob Böhme and Swedenborg, not to speak of Swedenborg's disciples in America (Sampson Reed) and France (Oegger); the native tradition of Calvinist and Unitarian theology; the British "moral sense" philosophy of the eighteenth century represented by Bishop Butler, Price and others: Coleridge, Carlyle and a few other interpreters of Kant, writing in English; and the French eclectic philosophers and the early Utopian socialists, including Madame de Staël, Cousin, Jouffroy, Benjamin Constant, Leroux and Fourier. At a later period Oriental philosophies must be added, and finally, before we mention the actual German philosophers, the many German poets and novelists who, in one or another form, assimilated and transmitted the philosophical thought of the technical philosophers: Goethe, of course, Schiller, Jean Paul, the Schlegels and Novalis. Who has ever clearly defined which idea comes from where? The historian of ideas would almost need a dictionary similar to the *Oxford Dictionary* which would list the first occurrence (subject to correction) of thoughts, giving author and date. And even this would not solve our difficulties, since the history of thought is the history not merely of unit-ideas but of systems and interrelations, new combinations and syntheses. When we look at German philosophy itself, we are also confronted with a difficult problem of distinctions, trends and conflicts within the fold itself. There is Leibniz looming in the background; Kant, still steeped in eighteenth-century rationalism, open to at least three or four widely divergent interpretations, not to speak of the hundred misinterpretations; then Herder, Jacobi and Schleiermacher, who sought the intuitive evidence of religion; then the dialectical philosophy growing out of Kant: Fichte, the early Schelling and later Hegel, all three distinct in their approach and intellectual background—Fichte, a moralist and dualist, Schelling primarily a philosopher of nature with mystical leanings, Hegel a logician and philosopher of history. Lorenz Oken and Henrik Steffens (a Norwegian) are speculative scientists nearest to Schelling; Novalis and Friedrich Schlegel have the closest links with Fichte, Jean Paul with Jacobi, Schiller with Kant, Goethe with Herder and Neo-Platonism. The Transcendentalists knew them all, more or less intimately, without, of course, necessarily understanding their relationships but instinctively looking for congenial ideas in kindred minds. Here is, at least, the suggestion of a convenient and feasible approach. We may take up each important figure in the Transcendental movement and ask several questions. What did he know about German philosophy—what from hearsay and what secondhand and what from actual texts? What did he think of the German philosophers? Which of the German thinkers did he treat with greatest sympathy and understanding? Thus, by empirical methods, we may place every American thinker in the scheme of the much-studied and carefully analyzed development of German philosophy and determine his approximate historical position. We may then make distinctions and lay out at least the ground for a discussion of direct influences.

We may begin with Bronson Alcott, who not only was the oldest in the group, but in his mental make-up represented also the oldest tradition of thought among them. Alcott knew scarcely any German (though he bought books in German when he was in London in 1842, including the mysterious volume called *Vernunft* by Fichte),[22] but early found his way to what appealed to him in German thought, namely, Jacob Böhme, the seventeenth-century cobbler from Silesia who evolved an elaborate system of mystical theosophy that was widely read in English translations during both the seventeenth and the eighteenth centuries. In 1833, when Alcott was in Philadelphia, he read Okely's *Life of Behmen,* and he read and re-read much of Böhme at different times. As late as 1882 he founded a small Mystic Club for the express purpose of discussing and reading Böhme.[23] The few published writings of Alcott contain a little essay on Böhme (first published in *The Radical,* 1870; reprinted in *Concord Days,* 1872). In this Alcott praises his "teeming genius, the genuine mother of numberless theories since delivered."[24] Law, Leibniz, Oken, Schelling, Goethe, and Baader seem all derived from him. Alcott thinks of Böhme as "the subtilest thinker on Genesis since Moses,"[25] though he disagrees with him on the fall of man and the symbolism of the serpent, as mystics are apt to disagree on the details of their allegories and symbols.

In 1849, Alcott read Lorenz Oken, the speculative scientist, whose *Elements of Physiophilosophy* had been translated in England in 1847.[26] Soon afterwards, Alcott had his second "illumination," in which he saw the universe as "one vast spinal column";[27] and all his following speculations on Genesis and the meaning of nature seem to be full of Oken's ideas and terminology, though obviously Alcott drew also from many other sources in the same tradition. To illustrate this, I like to point out a passage in Emerson's essay on Swedenborg,[28] in which he speaks of "a poetic anatomist of our day," obviously referring to Alcott, and then proceeds to reproduce his ideas. These ideas represent a combination of two different authors from whom Alcott seems to have drawn. He speaks first of the mystical quadrant of man (the vertical) and the serpent (the horizontal), an idea derived from

Oegger's *True Messiah,* which Emerson had copied in his *Journals* more than twenty years before;[29] and then he paraphrases Oken's curious fancy that the skull is another spine, and that the hands have been transformed into the upper jaw, the feet into the lower.[30] Alcott's precise relations to the German scientists like Oken and von Schubert, and possibly to the theosophist Baader, are quite unexplored and cannot be solved definitely without access to the fifty manuscript volumes of his journals. For our purpose it is sufficient to say that he was strongly attracted by the speculations of the Schellingian philosophy of nature and combined it with Neo-Platonic and generally mystical elements.

But Alcott knew also something of the main German idealistic philosophers. As early as 1833, in Philadelphia, before he had met Emerson or settled at Boston, Alcott read two expositions of Kant written in English by Germans, late in the eighteenth century.[31] One was Willich's *Elements of Critical Philosophy* (1798), in Odell Shepard's life of Alcott ascribed to Wellick. From the other, Friedrich August Nitsch's *View of Kant's Principles* (1796), Alcott copied out some 57 pages, proof, by the way, that he did not need the mediation of either Coleridge or the French to learn something about Kant. But Alcott's own view of Kant was soon decidedly unfavorable: he classed him with Aristotle, Bacon and Locke, and thought that all had "narrowed the range of the human faculties, retarded the progress of discovery by insisting on the supremacy of the senses and shut the soul up in the cave of the Understanding."[32] Alcott here interprets Kant as a skeptic, as a critic of all metaphysics, and uses Kant's own distinction between Reason and Understanding in a Coleridgean sense to condemn Kant's philosophy as pedestrian and sensual.

Later in his life, Alcott was brought into personal contact with the St. Louis Hegelians. He visisted them in 1859 and again in 1866, and became the nominal head of the Concord School of Philosophy, where for years Hegelians like William Torrey Harris expounded their doctrines under Alcott's patronage.[33] At first he was flattered by their admiration and overwhelmed and puzzled by Hegel's *Philosophy of History* and James Hutchinson Stirling's *Secret of Hegel,* which his daughter Louisa had brought from Europe as a present.[34] In the *Tablets* (1868) and the *Concord Days* (1872) there are quotations from Harris and two little essays on speculative philosophy and dialectics.[35] For a time, at least, Alcott expected a new philosophy in New England, "to which the German Hegel shall give impulse and furtherance."[36] But he soon decided that Hegel is not only "dry and crabbed," "strange and unintelligible," but that his own thinking is "ideal, his method analogical rather than logical" and thus "of a subtler and more salient type" than Hegel's, since it "implies an active and sprightly imagination inflaming the reason and divining the truths it seeks."[37] Thus, Alcott defines his own position clearly as an adherent of an imaginative, "analogical" mysticism which rejects as irrelevant the epistemological and logical methods of both Kant and Hegel.

George Ripley and Theodore Parker present a striking contrast to Alcott in their attitude toward German philosophy. Both were Unitarian clergymen who found in German thought additional support for their liberal religious convictions. Ripley was the more timid and also the more orthodox of the two. His early writings praise Herder and Schleiermacher[38] —"the greatest thinker who ever undertook to fathom the philosophy of religion"[39] —and his own thought seems to agree in every way with this professed sympathy. But Ripley knew also something of Kant. As early as 1832 he defended him as a "writer and reasoner from whom the great questions . . . have received more light than from any uninspired person, since the brightest days of Grecian philosophy." He contrasts him sharply with Coleridge, describing Kant's "cool, far-reaching, and austere habits of thought," "the severe logic, the imperturbable patience, the mathematical precision, and the passionless exhibition of the results of pure reason."[40] But soon, in a detailed account of Herder's conflict with Kant, Ripley sides with Herder, praising him for having made the system "lower its pretensions, and assume a more modest rank," though he recognizes Herder's incompetence to "do justice to the great merits" of the Kantian system "as an analytical exposition of the grounds of human knowledge."[41] In a later article on Fichte (1846) Ripley criticizes him as having failed to solve "the mighty problems of Divine Providence and Human Destiny" and tries to find in him merely negative virtues. According to Ripley, Fichte has shown the fruitlessness of speculation and thrown man back into "the world of moral emotions," "the instinctive sense of justice," "the interior voice"[42] —that is, precisely the teachings of Herder and Schleiermacher, with whom the historical Fichte had only scant sympathy. Ripley even sees in the study of Fichte a preparation for the acceptance of the doctrines of Fourier, possibly because of Fichte's strong collectivist outlook on social questions.

Ripley's attitude toward German philosophy became more and more hostile. Reviewing Hedge's *Prose Writers,* he asks "to what does [German philosophy] amount";[43] and a review of Stallo's book *Philosophy of Nature* is completely negative. Ripley thinks that its thoughts "offer no points of contact with the American mind." To him now, the study of German philosophy has only historical interest, much as "studying the remains of the Later Platonists or the Oriental philosophers" would have. The German thinkers produce only "wonderful specimens of intellectual gymnastics." They try to "explain the universe or the human soul by the mere force of thought, without the scientific analysis of facts," which is "as absurd as the attempt to leap over one's own head."[44] Later, Ripley also attacked Strauss and Feuerbach and the mid-nineteenth-century materialists like Büchner, and he showed some interest in Eduard Hartmann's *Philosophy of the Uncon-scious.*[45] But evidence enough has been presented to show that Ripley stands with Herder and Schleiermacher as a philosopher of faith, that he welcomed the German idealists only as far as they seemed, in his interpretation, to make room for such a philosophy, and that later he roundly condemned what he considered their mistaken intellectualism and *a priori* ways of thinking. It would be difficult to say which ideas Ripley could have derived from Germany, because the idea of a "religious sense" could have been found in British and French philosophy too.

Theodore Parker was both a bolder mind and man and a greater scholar than Ripley; but in our context he is nearest to Ripley, though he drifted further from the moorings of the church. Parker early studied German Biblical criticism and theology and translated a two-volume *Introduction to the New Testament* by de Wette, a liberal German theologian who was a follower of Fries and thus remotely of Kant. Parker's learning in German scholarship, theological, historical and literary, was really imposing, though the long strings of indiscriminately jumbled names in an article in defense of the German literature in the *Dial*[46] arouse some suspicions whether his knowledge, at least at that time, was always so thorough and firsthand as it seems. In this long and able article, which is ostensibly a review of Menzel's *History of German Literature,* little is said of German philosophy, though Parker calls Menzel's views on Kant "exceedingly unjust" and recognizes the political bias of his attacks on Hegel.[47] The next year, 1843, Parker went to Germany, called on de Wette in Basel and other theologians, and heard Werder, a Hegelian, lecture on logic in Berlin. The performance seemed to him merely ridiculous, as did Schelling, whom he heard lecture on the philosophy of revelation.[48] After his return, Parker became immersed in German theology, jurisprudence, ecclesiastical history, and later, of course, the cause of abolitionism. He thus never returned to German philosophy proper. But in the fine confession of faith which he wrote to his parishioners from Santa Cruz when on his last voyage to Italy in 1859, he confessed his debt to Kant, "one of the profoundest thinkers in the world, though one of the worst writers, even of Germany." "He gave me the true method, and put me on the right road. I found certain primal intuitions of human nature, which depend on no logical process of demonstration, but are rather facts of consciousness given by the instinctive action of human nature itself: the instinctive intuition of the divine, the instinctive intuition of the just and right, the instinctive intuition of the immortal. Here, then, was the founda-tion of religion, laid in human nature itself."[49] There is little point in stressing that this is a false interpretation of Kant. It is more interesting to note that this interpretation is in perfect harmony with the intuitive philosophy of Jacobi or Schleiermacher, of the French eclectics, and even of the Scottish common-sense school. Parker stands with Ripley, but succeeds in interpreting the *Critique of Practical Reason* as support for a philosophy of faith as an instinctive intuition of the human mind.

Orestes Brownson, or rather the early Brownson before his conversion to Roman Catholicism in 1844, who alone can be called a Transcendentalist, is related in outlook and starting point to both Ripley and Parker. Early in life he became an intuitionist, who read, admired and propagated Cousin and the other French eclectics. But Brownson had a stronger philosophical bent than his friends and associates, and a genuine gift for speculation as well as an altogether unusual grasp, in his time and place, of philosophical technicalities. He alone of all the Transcendentalists seems to have been seriously disturbed by the problems of knowledge and truth, and he alone made a close examination of Kant's actual text. This was written down shortly after his conversion, but the point of view there expounded can be found already in the scattered and unsympathetic pronouncements of his preconversion writings. The remarkable consistency and uniformity of his criticism of Kant and Hegel, which extends over a period of some thirty-five years of indefatigable writing, seems to point to a greater coherence and consistency in Brownson's philosophical outlook than is usually allowed by those who see only the shiftings and changes of his religious associations.

As to German philosophy, there is only one marked change of attitude. Brownson had learned to read German in 1834; and in a little book, *New Views of Christianity* (1836), he recommended the German theological movement starting with Herder and culminating in Schleiermacher. Brownson commended the "meeting of inspiration and philosophy" in Schleiermacher and praised him as a man for "remarkable warmth of feeling and coolness of thought," hinting at the similarity between him and Saint-Simon.[50] After the conversion, Brownson condemned Schleiermacher's views, since he makes religion purely subjective and "resolves the church into general society." He even went out of his way to brand Schleiermacher's "pantheistic spiritualism" as worse than rationalism, deism, and even the atheism of D'Holbach.[51]

But no such marked change can be discerned in his relations to Kant, Fichte, Schelling and Hegel. His attitude toward Kant seems to have been defined very early. Brownson had a great admiration precisely for the technical side of Kant's analysis of judgment and categories. In all his writings he was again and again to repeat the view that "Kant has with masterly skill and wonderful exactness, drawn up a complete list of the categories of Reason. His analysis of Reason may be regarded as complete and final."[52] This analysis, Brownson thought, was purely empirical and correct as far as it went. Very early he defended Kant against the charge of transcendentalism. Kant's method, he argued, "was as truly experimental as Bacon's or Locke's."

Even when Kant professed to describe *a priori* knowledge, he did so "by experience, by experiment, by a careful analysis of the facts of consciousness, as they actually present themselves to the eye of the psychological observer." If Kant is to be criticized, he should not be charged with leaving the "path of experience" or "rushing off into speculation." Rather, Brownson suggested, Kant fails in a thoroughgoing application of his method because he conceives of experience too narrowly as merely experience of the senses.[53]

But in spite of these frequent acknowledgements of Kant's power as an analyst of thought, Brownson seems never to have been in doubt as to his objections to the main epistemological position of Kant. In a review dating from 1842, Brownson rejected philosophical idealism as clearly and forcefully as he was to reject it for the rest of his life: "The refutation of Kant and Fichte, and therefore of all idealism, egoism, and skepticism, whether atheistic or pantheistic, is in a simple fact . . . that the objective element of thought is always *not me*. The error of Kant, and the error which led astray his whole school and all others, is the assumption that the *me* does or may develop as pure subject, or, in other words, be its own object, and therefore at once subject and object. Kant assumes that the *me* develops itself, without a foreign object, in cognition; hence he infers that all knowledge is purely subjective, and asserts the impotency of reason to carry us out of the sphere of the *me*." In a note, Brownson recognizes that this was not all of Kant's teaching: "We know very well that this was not the real doctrine of Kant, that it was only demonstrated by him to be the result, to which all philosophy must come, that *is based on pure reason*. He himself relied on practical reason, that is to say, on plain common sense, and his purpose of writing critques of pure reason, was to demonstrate the unsatisfactory character of all purely metaphysical speculations. A wise man, after all, was that same Emanuel Kant."[54] But this partial retraction, which seems to point to some knowledge of the *Critique of Practical Reason,* did not remain in Brownson's mind. He dismissed Kant's practical reason as nothing else than the common sense of Hume[55] and later was to write his criticisms of Kant without regard to other books than the *Critique of Pure Reason.*

When Brownson, immediately after the conversion, in the "Introduction" to *Brownson's Quarterly,* surveyed his own intellectual development, he could, it seems to me, with reason minimize the importance of German philosophy for his own development and define his attitude toward Kant in terms substantially in agreement with the earlier pronouncements. "The German philosophers," he says, "have afforded me very little satisfaction. It is true, that I have made no profound study of them; but, so far as I know them, I claim no affinity with them. I feel and own, the eminent analytic ability of Kant, but I am forced to regard his philosophy as fundamentally false and mischievous. His *Critic der reinen Vernunft,* if taken in any other light than that of a protest, under the most rigid forms of analysis, against all modern philosophy, is sure to mislead, and to involve the reader in an inextricable maze of error."[56] Strangely enough, Brownson thought it worth-while to make a careful study of the *Critique of Pure Reason,* apparently in the original, shortly afterwards and to write three closely reasoned essays on it for the first volume of his new quarterly.[57] There we find his fullest discussion of Kant, which is, however, in its approach and conclusion, completely identical with the preconversion pronouncements. Brownson criti-cizes Kant's fundamental question. It is "absurd to ask if the human mind be capable of science; for we have only the human mind with which to answer the question." Kant's phenomenalism is completely mistaken. One cannot find the object in the subject. "This simple truism, which is nothing but saying what *is,* is, completely refutes the whole critical philosophy." Brown-son drives home this main point with considerable dialectical power. Kant is thus interpreted as the arch-skeptic, who denied the very possibility of knowledge, as the "most masterly defender of Hume." With a flourish of Carlylean rhetoric Brownson depicts the dire consequences of this supposed universal skepticism. "So all science vanishes, all certainty disappears, the sun goes out, the bright stars are extinguished, and we are afloat in the darkness, on the wild and tempest-roused ocean of Universal Doubt and Nescience."[58] Kant, according to Brownson, turned out to be fundamentally a "sensist" and a "materialist." Brownson dismisses Kant's own development of his teachings in the other *Critiques* far too lightly;[59] but he has come, at least, to actual grips with the text of Kant, with his dialectics and logic, as no contemporary in America did. All the many later pronouncements of Brownson on Kant are merely variations on this point of view. He reiterates again and again his admiration for Kant's analysis of mind, his table of the categories and his negative conclusion which seems to Brownson to have established that "man's own subjective reason alone does not suffice for science."[60] But he also condemns his subjectivism, the views that the categories are mere forms of our mind, the denial of the objectivity of knowledge, and hence the skepti-cism which seems to him the "hardly disguised" result of Kant's philosophy. Kant thus was a philosopher who asked questions and who gave acute technical discussion of logical and epistemological questions; but his main position was entirely repugnant to Brownson, who early in his life had become an objectivist, an enemy of Cartesianism and all its forms.[61]

It is almost needless to expound Brownson's attitude toward Fichte. He appeared to him early as the *reductio ad absurdum* of idealism. Fichte, he says in an article written before the conversion, "asserted the power of the *me* to be his own object and sought the proof of it in the fact of volition. Hence he fell into the absurdity of representing all ideas as the products of the *me,* and even went so far as to tell his disciples how it is that man makes

God." But again, as in the case of Kant, Brownson was aware of the existence of Fichte's later views, which corrected some of his speculative errors.[62] Later, Brownson was to repeat several times that the "egoistic philosophy, so energetically asserted by Fichte, that God and the external world are only the soul projecting itself, is only a logical deduction from the Kantian premises," and that Cartesianism leads to Fichtean egoism.[63]

Toward Schelling and his disciples Brownson had at first, during the Emersonian stage of his development, shown some vague though cautious sympathy. He thought that "they give us a magnificent poem, which we believe to be mainly true, but which nevertheless is no philosophy and can in no degree solve the difficulty stated by Hume."[64] But later, Schelling was neglected or put down as an atheist and Spinozist. He "maintains the identity of subject and object, and thus asserts, from the subjective point of view, the Egoism of Fichte and, under the objective point of view, the Pantheism of Spinoza, while under both he denies intuition and even the possibility of science."[65]

From these pronouncements, we can already guess at Brownson's attitude toward Hegel. It was again defined long before the conversion. Brownson first rejects the whole deductive method. He cannot believe that "the system of the universe is only a system of logic," that the "ideal and essential, idea and being," are identical. Hegel's method "claims for man confessedly finite, absolute knowledge, which would imply that he himself is absolute and therefore not finite, but infinite." But "the boast is also in vain, for in the order of knowledge we are obliged to reverse the order of existence. We rise through nature up to nature's God, instead of descending from God through man to nature. None but God himself can know according to the order of existence, for none but he can know being in itself, and from the absolute knowledge of the cause, have a perfect *a priori* knowledge of the effect." While rejecting the pretensions of Hegel's philosophy to absolute knowledge, the American democrat Brownson cannot help smiling at Hegel's view that "the infinite God and all his works through all the past have been engaged expressly in preparing and founding the Prussian monarchy" and that "his gracious majesty Frederick William" could be "the last word of creation and progress."[66] After the conversion the tone of the objections against Hegel becomes more strident. Hegel's system appears to him, under other forms, "nothing but a reproduction of old French Atheism," his principles appear "unreal and worthless," and his philosophy "really less genuine, less profound, and infinitely less worthy of confidence" than that of Reid.[67] In detail, Brownson pays some attention to Hegel's first triad, in which he sees a false attempt to derive the real from the possible, existence from nothing.[68] He does not admit that Hegel is an ontologist. To Brownson he is a pure psychologist, who only ostensibly attempts to identify the psychological process with the ontological. Hegel is a subjective idealist who ends in pantheism and atheism, like all the other followers of Kant.[69]

Brownson's criticisms of German philosophy cannot always be justified: he surely overstressed the purely negative critical side of Kant and misunderstood the Hegelian dialectics; but within limits he presented the case against German philosophy forcefully and consistently from the point of view of an objective intuitivism which deplored the whole turn modern philosophy had taken since Descartes. He could even write that "Germany has produced no philosophical system not already exploded and no philosophers to compare with Vico, Galluppi, Rosmini, Gioberti and Balmes."[70] Thus, from his own point of view, Brownson rightly thought Leibniz to have been the "greatest of all modern philosophers" not in the Catholic communion. He could praise his refutation of the Cartesian doctrine that the essence of substance is extension and his rejection of the atomic in favor of a dynamic theory of matter. But even Leibniz is criticized as "the veritable father of German rationalism," and as a believer in the ontological argument and the priority of the possible before the real.[71] Brownson's lifelong sympathies were with an intuitivism and realism which managed finally to reconcile Reid and Gioberti, Catholicism and common-sense philosophy. In spite of his interest in some of the arguments of Kant, German philosophy stood for everything Brownson rejected all his life—subjectivism and pantheism, skepticism and atheism.[72]

Margaret Fuller stands apart from the other Transcendentalists. Her interests were obviously not primarily philosophical and theological, but rather aesthetic and later political. Her study of German led her to Goethe, Jean Paul, Bettina Brentano and, rather incongruously, the sentimental Theodor Körner and the spiritualist Justinus Kerner. Her direct contacts with German philosophy seem rare and not too happy. In Cambridge (presumably some time before 1833) she obtained books by Fichte and Jacobi, and she tells us: "I was much interrupted, but some time and earnest thought I devoted. Fichte I could not understand at all; though the treatise which I read was intended to be popular, and which he says must compel (*bezwingen*) to conviction."[73] She must refer to Fichte's *Sonnenklarer Bericht* (1801), which in its subtitle is called "Ein Versuch, die Leser zum Verstehen zu zwingen."[74] "Jacobi," she continues, "I could understand in details, but not in system. It seemed to me that his mind must have been moulded by some other mind, with which I ought to be acquainted, in order to know him well—perhaps Spinoza's." Later, in the *Dial,* when she wrote a review criticizing Menzel's view of Goethe, she referred to Jacobi as having written "the heart into philosophy as well as he could."[75] Reading the life of Sir James Mackintosh, she was pleased, "after my late chagrin, to find Sir James, with all his metaphysical turn, and ardent desire to penetrate it, puzzling so over the German philosophy, and particularly what I was myself troubled about, at Cambridge,—Jacobi's *Letters to Fichte.*"[76] In Groton, when she was planning her abortive "Life of Goethe," she came to the conclusion that she ought to get "some idea of the history of philosophical opinion in Germany" in order to understand its influence on Goethe. She consulted Buhle's and Tennemann's *Histories of Philosophy,* and dipped into Brown, Stewart and "that class of books."[77] In the winter 1836-37 she went one evening every week to Dr. Channing and translated for him German theological writings, mainly de Wette and Herder.[78] In 1841, apparently in connection with her "conversations," she translated Schelling's famous lecture "Über das Verhält- niss der bildenden Künste zu der Natur," a labor she might have saved had she noticed that Coleridge had paraphrased the very same oration very closely. [79] (The translation by Margaret Fuller has remained in manuscript.) Later, after her arrival in New York, she drifted more and more away from Transcen- dental contacts and interests. In the last year of her reviewing for the New York *Daily Tribune* (1846), she wrote a report on William Smith's *Memoirs of J. G. Fichte,* which consists largely of quotations. Still, it shows her obvious pleasure that William Smith brought out "the sunny side" of Fichte's character and gave a "charming account of the sincere, equal, generous and tender relation between him and his wife."[80] In a review of Charles Brockden Brown's *Ormond* and *Wieland,* she interestingly reveals her (and the Transcen- dentalists') weird conception of Hegelianism. She calls Brown and Godwin "born Hegelians, without the pretensions of science" as "they sought God in their consciousness and found him. The heart, because it saw itself so fearfully and wonderfully made, did not disown its Maker."[81] Sometimes she protests against all analytical philosophy, alluding particularly to Fichte. "I do not wish to *reflect* always, if reflecting must be always about one's identity, whether *'ich'* am the true *'ich'* etc. I wish to arrive at that point where I can trust myself."[82] On the whole, if one can combine these meager and scattered statements, they seem to show that Margaret Fuller cared nothing for what she thought were German technicalities and had only vaguely understood that German philosophy from Jacobi to Hegel justified the religion of the heart. Her point of view therefore seems to be nearest to Ripley's.

Thus, the minor Transcendentalists show only slight contacts with German philosophy proper. Alcott neglected the great German philosophers and found solace and support in the fanciful speculations of Jacob Böhme and Lorenz Oken. Ripley and Parker looked for a religion of the heart, a justification of intuitive faith, and found it either in Schleiermacher or in a misinterpreted Kant. Margaret Fuller faintly echoes this view in her writings. In Brownson, the Germans had a formidable critic of their subjectivism and pantheism. But only a full discussion of Emerson's relations to German philosophy will make these distinctions stand out more clearly and allow us to draw general conclusions.

NOTES

1. There are no discussions of the relations of Alcott, Parker, Brownson, Miss Fuller, Follen or Hedge to the German thinkers, except references in biographies and general studies of Transcendentalism (Frothingham, Goddard, Riley, Girard, Muirhead, Townsend). There is, however, a recent paper, "George Ripley: Unitarian, Transcendentalist or Infidel?" by Arthur R. Schultz and Henry A. Pochmann, in *American Literature*, XIV (1942), 1-19, which discusses Ripley's relations to German philosophy.

2. *Immanuel Kant in England, 1793-1838* (Princeton, 1931).

3. Harold S. Jantz, "German Thought and Literature in New England, 1620-1820," *Journal of English and Germanic Philology*, XLI (1942), 1-45.

4. I. W. Riley, *American Thought from Puritanism to Pragmatism and Beyond* (New York, 1923), pp. 232-35; Jantz, "German Thought and Literature in New England," p. 41.

5. Cf. *Immanuel Kant in England*, pp. 13 and 268. Harold S. Jantz, "Samuel Miller's Survey of German Literature, 1803," *Germanic Review*, XVI (1941), 267-77, notes that Miller owes this section to a "British literary journal," but does not identify the source.

6. *The Dictionary of American Biography*.

7. O. W. Long, *Literary Pioneers* (Cambridge, Mass., 1935; hereinafter, "Long"), p. 237, note 6.

8. Daniel Day Williams, *The Andover Liberals* (New York, 1941), p. 17.

9. Majorie Hope Nicolson, "James Marsh and the Vermont Transcendentalists," *Philosophical Review*, XXXIV (1925), 33.

10. Ibid., p. 49. Cf. also John Dewey, "James Marsh and American Philosophy," *Journal of the History of Ideas*, II (1941), 131-50.

11. Long, p. 75.

12. Ibid., p. 16; letter of February 29, 1816.

13. Ibid., p. 248, note 53; letter of December 28, 1820; and p. 133, letter of November 13, 1820.

14. Long on Motley. On Longfellow, see James Taft Hatfield, *New Light on Longfellow* (Boston, 1933). In 1844 Longfellow read Fichte's *Nature of the Scholar* (Hatfield, p. 110) and in 1848 he read Schelling's essay on Dante, which he translated for *Graham's Magazine* (Hatfield, p. 118).

15. *The Christian Examiner*, New Series, IX (1833), 108-29.

16. O. W. Long, *F. H. Hedge: A Cosmopolitan Scholar* (Portland, Me., 1940).

17. In Follen's *Works*, 5 vols. (Boston, 1841), vol. III. The "Life" by his widow in vol. I gives date of delivery of the lectures, p. 290.

18. "Inaugural Discourse" (September 3, 1831) in Follen's *Works*, vol. V. See especially p. 136.

19. Emerson, *Journals* (Boston, 1909-14), December 1849, VIII, 77.

20. Two possibilities will be suggested in the paper on Emerson.

21. Emerson, *Journals*, VIII, 69. See also VIII, 246.

22. Odell Shepard, *Pedlar's Progress* (Boston, 1937), p. 341.

23. Ibid., pp. 160, 341, 350, and 416; also *The Journals*, ed. Odell Shepard (Boston, 1938), pp. 34, 109, 332, and 530.

24. *Concord Days* (Boston, 1872), p. 238.

25. *Tablets* (Boston, 1868), p. 189.

26. Translated by Alfred Tulk, member of the Royal College of Surgeons of England; printed for the Ray Society (London, 1847). Cf. Alcott's *Journals*, pp. 211 and 212.

27. Shepard, *Pedlar's Progress*, p. 439.

28. Emerson, *Representative Men*, in *Complete Works*, Centenary Edition (Boston, 1903-04), IV, 107-08.

29. Emerson, *Journals*, III, 515, from Oegger, *Le Vrai Messie* (Paris, 1829). A partial translation by Elizabeth Peabody was published in Boston in 1835.

30. Oken, *Elements of Physiophilosophy* (London, 1847): "The Mouth is the stomach in the head, the nose the lung, the jaws the arms and feet" (364).

31. Shepard, *Pedlar's Progress*, p. 160. Willich and Nitsch are discussed in *Immanuel Kant in England*, pp. 7-15.

32. Alcott, *Journals*, pp. 38-39.

33. Shepard, *Pedlar's Progress*, pp. 474-76, 480-84, and 507 ff. Cf. Austin Warren, "The Concord School of Philosophy," *New England Quarterly*, II (1929), 199-233.

34. Alcott, *Journals*, pp. 340 and 383; August 1861 and July 1866.

35. Alcott, *Tablets*, pp. 164-65; *Concord Days*, pp. 73-74; "Speculative Philosophy," pp. 143 ff.; and "The Dialectic," pp. 156 ff.

36. *Concord Days*, p. 145.

37. *Journals*, p. 497, July 1879; and p. 536, August 1882.

38. Review of James Marsh's translation of Herder's *Spirit of Hebrew Poetry*, in the *Christian Examiner*, XVII (1835), 167-221; "Herder's Theological Opinions and Services," *ibid.*, XIX (1835), 172-204; and "Schleiermacher as a Theologian," *ibid.*, XX (1836), 1-46. Also Ripley's "Letters to a Theological Student" (written in December 1836) in the *Dial*, I (1840), recommends Herder highly (p. 187).

39. O. B. Frothingham, *George Ripley* (Boston, 1882), p. 229.

40. Review of Carl Follen's "Inaugural Discourse," *Christian Examiner*, XI (1832), 375.

41. Review of Marsh's *Spirit of Hebrew Poetry*, in the *Christian Examiner*, XVIII (1835), 209.

42. *Harbinger*, II (1846), 297 ff.

43. *Ibid.*, VI (1848), 107.

44. *Ibid.*, p. 110.

45. Frothingham, pp. 230 and 286.

46. *Dial*, I (1841), 315-39. Reprinted in Parker's *Critical and Miscellaneous Writings*, 2nd ed. (New York, 1864), pp. 28-60.

47. *Dial*, I (1841), 335-36; reprinted as above, pp. 54-55.

48. H. S. Commager, *Theodore Parker* (Boston, 1936), pp. 95-96.

49. J. Weiss, *The Life and Correspondence of Theodore Parker* (Boston, 1864), II, 454-55.

50. *Collected Works*, ed. H. F. Brownson (Detroit, 1882-1907), IV, 44-45.

51. *Ibid.*, III, 45; IV, 519; VIII, 424; and IX, 480; quotations dating from 1850, 1844, 1872 and 1873 respectively.

52. "Synthetic Philosophy," *Democratic Review* (1842), reprinted in *Works*, I, 165; see also I, 222; II, 299; V, 507; and IX, 263.

53. "Eclectic Philosophy," *Boston Quarterly* (1839), in *Works*, II, 536-38.

54. "Charles Elwood Reviewed," *Boston Quarterly* (1842), in *Works*, IV, 355.

55. "The Philosophy of History," *Democratic Review* (1843), in *Works*, IV, 391.

56. "Introduction," *Brownson's Quarterly Review*, I (1844), 8.

57. "Kant's Critic of Pure Reason" (1844), pp. 137-74, 181-309, and 417-99; also in *Works*, I, 130-213.

58. "Kant's Critic of Pure Reason," pp. 282, 284, 308, and 309; *Works*, I, 162, 163, 184, and 185.

59. "Kant's Critic of Pure Reason," p. 309; *Works*, I, 185-86. Here Brownson quotes Heine, in the French translation, ridiculing the *Critique of Practical Reason* as prompted by "fear of the police."

60. "An Old Quarrel," *Catholic World* (1867), in *Works*, II, 299.

61. Later passages on Kant, in *Works*, I, 222 and 244-45; II, 47, 295, and 520; V, 507; VI, 106; X, 263, and XIX, 384.

62. "Charles Elwood Reviewed," *Boston Quarterly* (1842), in *Works*, IV, 355.

63. "The Giobertian Philosophy," *Brownson's Quarterly* (1864), in *Works*, II, 250; and "The Cartesian Doubt," *Catholic World* (1867), in *Works*, II, 373.

64. *Christian Examiner*, XXI (1836), 46.

65. "The Giobertian Philosophy," *Brownson's Quarterly* (1864), in *Works*, II, 251.

66. "The Philosophy of History," *Democratic Review* (1843), in *Works*, IV, 369 and 384.

67. "Introduction," *Brownson's Quarterly Review* I (1844), 8. See also a passage containing the astonishing assertion that Hegel reproduces Holbach's *Systéme de la Nature* in "Transcendentalism," *Brownson's Quarterly* (1846), in *Works*, VI, 97; "The Refutation of Atheism," in *Brownson's Quarterly* (1873), in *Works*, II, 76; and "The Giobertian Philosophy," in *Brownson's Quarterly* (1864), in *Works*, II, 251.

68. Repeated frequently, e.g. *Works*, I, 401; II, 38, 71, and 268; VI, 97; VIII, 384; IX, 273; and XI, 229. Brownson refers several times to Hegel's *das Ideen*, a mistake for *Das Ideele*, which does not inspire confidence in his

reading of Hegel or close knowledge of German (cf. *Works,* VIII, 384; and III, 502).

69. *Works,* I, 401; II, 268; III, 502 and 504; and XI, 229.

70. "Spiritual Despotism," *Brownson's Quarterly* (1857), in *Works,* VII, 486.

71. "Catholicity and Naturalism" (1865), in *Works,* VIII, 352; "Holy Communion—Transubstantiation," *Brownson's Quarterly* (1874), in *Works,* VIII, 268; and "Refutation of Atheism," *Brownson's Quarterly* (1873), in *Works* II, 38.

72. A fuller discussion of Brownson's intellectual development, with stress on social and political questions, is given in Arthur M. Schlesinger, Jr., *Orestes A. Brownson: A Pilgrim's Progress* (Boston, 1939).

73. *Memoirs of Margaret Fuller Ossoli,* by R. W. Emerson, W. H. Channing, and J. F. Clarke (Boston, 1881), I, 127.

74. J. G. Fichte, *Werke* (Berlin, 1843), II, 323. "Bezwingen" in the text of the *Memoirs* is certainly an error, either of the transcriber or printer, for "zu zwingen."

75. *Life Without and Life Within* (Boston, 1859), p. 15. First appeared in the *Dial,* I (1841), 342.

76. *Memoirs,* I, 165.

77. See note 73.

78. *Memoirs,* I, 175.

79. Coleridge's lecture "On Poesy or Art" was first printed in *Literary Remains* (vol. I, 1836). Sara Coleridge's edition in *Notes and Lectures* (1849) gives a list of the parallels to Schelling's lecture.

80. New York *Daily Tribune,* July 9, 1846. Listed in Mason Wade's bibliography, *M. Fuller, Writings* (New York, 1941), p. 600.

81. *Art, Literature and the Drama* (Boston, 1875), p. 323; originally appeared in the New York *Daily Tribune* of July 25, 1846.

82. *Memoirs,* I, 123.

8

Victor Cousin and American Transcendentalism

GEORGES J. JOYAUX

IN THE INTELLECTUAL HISTORY OF FRANCE, VICTOR COUSIN (1792-1867) marks the idealistic reaction of the nineteenth century against the materialism of the eighteenth. His Eclecticism attempted to synthetize into a new unity all that was best in the various philosophical systems. Though Cousin never presented a complete *exposé* of his theory in a single work, his philosophical speculations achieved wide popularity in the first half of the nineteenth century, first through his well-attended lectures—at the Sorbonne and later at the Ecole Normale Supérieure—and through his numerous publications.

The material for this paper was gathered in a study of American periodicals published in the first half of the nineteenth century.[1] Its objective is to examine the reception of Victor Cousin and his Eclecticism by the contemporary American periodical press, and to throw some light on the much-debated question of the relations between American Transcendentalism and French Eclecticism.

Transcendentalism and Eclecticism are the two chief philosophical systems which colored American and French intellectual history respectively during the first half of the nineteenth century. Since the high point of Eclecticism

From *The French Review*, 29 (1955), 117-30. Reprinted by permission.

preceded that of American Transcendentalism by about a decade, the question of the latter's debt to the former has long elicited discussion. The answers tend to fall into two categories. Some, as William Girard, "would like to depreciate the whole German influence and substitute in first place that of Cousin, Maine de Biran, Jouffroy and Madame de Staël." Others, such as Walter Leighton or Octavius Frothingham, feel that "the influence of French philosophy was not particularly predominant" on American transcendentalism and that "the German idealists apparently appealed more strongly to the young idealistic philosophers of New England, than did the more rational, urbane, compromise philosophy of the French Eclectics."[2]

Certainly, a clear and definite answer to the question of Eclectic-Transcendentalist influences is hard to give when one keeps in mind that the two systems are both philosophically eclectic in nature, and that, furthermore, both represented a phase of idealistic reaction. Idealism was in the air, and what the two systems have in common might not necessarily be the result of the influence of one on the other, but might rather be the reflection of the climate of opinion of the epoch.

The statistics found in this study are eloquent: in the first half of the nineteenth century there appeared eighty references to French philosophy in the files of American magazines. Only fourteen of them appeared during the first twenty five years, while the rest, sixty-six, were published from 1828 to 1848, coinciding with the years of Cousin's success and the triumph of Eclecticism in France. Of these sixty-six references, all but fifteen deal with Eclecticism and its leader.[3]

The first reference to Cousin appeared in 1829, in the *North American Review.* In the fifty-six pages devoted to a review of four of Cousin's earlier works, the reviewer shows a very high opinion of Cousin and his works:

> Mr. Cousin unites, in a superior degree, most of the qualifications necessary for complete success in his writings . . . He combines the vivacity and fine taste that are in some degree natural to his countrymen, with the indefatigable industry, the wide research and patient meditation which, in these degenerate days, have been considered as almost peculiar to the Germans.

As to Eclecticism, the reviewer was rather cautious:

> We have already taken the liberty to express our doubts of the correctness of the peculiar theories of this writer; but we would not be understood to speak with confidence on the subject because we have not yet the means of ascertaining with precision what his views really are . . .[4]

The books reviewed were Cousin's first writings, some preceding Cousin's trip to Germany where he studied German philosophy at first hand. Also, it should be noted that the review came only a year after the publication—in French—of many of the books reviewed. A firm stand on the part of the reviewer would have been surprising, and it was to be expected that this first contact with French eclecticism would be cautious. At any rate, this first article clearly showed America's interest in France's intellectual life. This is confirmed by the comments made by Charles J. Ingersoll, in his 1823 oration before the American Philosophical Society, and reprinted in the *Christian Examiner*; Ingersoll, speaking in favor of a national literature, and for a greater intellectual independence from England declared:

> We fear that at the present moment English books want much which we need. . . . In England there is a great want of philosophy in the true sense of the word . . . , and although we have little respect for the rash generalizations of the bold and eloquent Cousin, yet, the interest which his metaphysics awaken in Paris is, in our estimation a better presage than the lethargy which prevails on such topics in England.[5]

More important is the informative essay published in the *American Quarterly Review* (December, 1831), in which the writer gives a very detailed outline of Cousin's philosophical system, displaying throughout a thorough acquaintance with the subject. "Cousin," the reviewer remarks, ". . . is no disciple of any of the schools which are commonly thought to include all ... o convey within ... nd aim of his ... lenies the right- ... various truths ... dmixture, and ... ed into a new ... th which is to ... ation and give ... e, the author ... s and for the ... ers and upon ... the reviewer ... beginning to ... we have no doubt that his lectures will be of great and wide use in imparting to thinking minds a sympathetic activity and freedom." However, the reviewer did not show much enthusiasm for the system itself, adding that the lectures were not ". . . in any way positively instructive."[7]

The impetus given by Cousin to philosophical speculation in America formed the main topic of the next reference to Cousin in the *North American Review.* "Cousin's genius," the reviewer wrote, "alike brilliant and profound, has given an attraction to the subject of metaphysics, altogether unprecedented in the annals of philosophy." He concluded that though Cousin's system could not be regarded as the ultimatum of intellectual philosophy, "yet the Science [was] deeply indebted to him for the new light bestowed by his genius, and the attraction with which he has clothed a subject often unjustly and ignorantly depreciated."[8]

In 1834 Caleb Sprague Henry, professor of philosophy at New York University, and a Christian Transcendentalist,[9] published his translation of Cousin's *Elements of Psychology.* The same year the first reviewer of Henry's translation took advantage of the occasion to praise Cousin for his stylistic facility, in contrast to that "dry and frigid abstractness which [one] expects in metaphysical writers." On the whole, the reviewer felt that Cousin's work was "particularly adapted to the taste of the English world," because there was in it "less of that misty vagueness of conception, and repulsive technicality of style, which have been complained of in the philosophers of the ideal school."[10]

After the publication of Henry's translation, references in the journals to Cousin and Eclecticism increased considerably, and no reviewer of Henry's *Elements of Psychology* failed to devote a large part of his comments to a discussion of Eclecticism.

In 1835, in a review of Cousin's works on education—he wrote reports on the educational systems in Prussia and Holland—we find the following remarks:

> The name and character of Mr. Cousin are already familiar to our readers. We have, on more than one occasion, been led to notice his labors in the great field of intellectual philosophy, and if we have not been able to give our unqualified concurrence to all his theories upon that subject, we have never risen from the perusal of any of his works without fresh admiration of his learning, eloquence and indefatigable industry.

Here again, the founder of Eclecticism is compared to the German philosophers, and he is praised for the clarity of his expression as opposed to the abstruseness of German philosophical writings. Furthermore, the reviewer added, Cousin combines "the vivacity and brilliancy of the French school of Literature, with the immense erudition and dogged perseverance in study [of the German scholars]."[11]

In 1836 there appeared an interesting review of three of Cousin's works— two in their American editions—by Orestes A. Brownson, an early member of the transcendentalist group. In his introduction Brownson wrote: "These works have attracted already considerable attention among us, and are beginning to exert no little influence on our philosophical speculations." Suprisingly enough, Brownson felt that Cousin's works would afford "important aid in rescuing the church and religious matters in general from their present lamentable condition." Though later, on religious grounds, he reversed his attitude and he attacked both Eclecticism and Cousin, here he viewed Eclecticism as a reaction against the skepticism and materialism of the eighteenth century. Therefore, he welcomed it as a possible way to end the war between Religion and Philosophy:

> Everybody knows that our Religion and our Philosophy are at war. Instead of quarreling . . . , we should re-examine our philosophy and inquire if there be not a philosophy true to human nature, and able to explain and verify instead of destroying the religious beliefs of mankind . . . We evidently need such a philosophy; such a philosophy we believe there is and we know of no works so well fitted to assist us in finding it as those of Mr. Cousin.

On the whole, Brownson felt that not only had Cousin brought about the downfall of materialism, but also he had broken ground for a new philosophy, "which shall include them all, and yet be itself unlike any of them."[12]

The next year, in a review of Theodore Jouffroy's *Cours de Droit Naturel,* Brownson devoted several pages to Cousin, Jouffroy's master.[13] For the first time, in many reviews, Eclecticism and Transcendentalism were joined. Comparing French Eclecticism with German and American Transcendentalism, Brownson distinguished between those men "who deem themselves competent to construct a new philosophy of man and universe by means of speculation alone," and those "who will attach no scientific value to any metaphysical system which is not a legitimate induction from facts patiently collected, scrupulously analyzed, and accurately classed." Turning on the critics of French Eclecticism, he added:

> If it be meant that the French Eclectics are transcendental in the sense these last are, we have no objection . . . , but this is not the case. They who call them Transcendentalists with the feeling that Transcendentalism is an accusation, mean to identify them with the other class, the speculators, the systematizers . . . But in this sense, the Eclectics are not transcendentalist. Cousin, their acknowledged chief, bases his whole system on psychology.

Brownson then endeavors to demonstrate that French Eclecticism is strictly scientific and experimental. To quote Cousin, adds Brownson, "there is and there can be no sound philosophy which does not begin with the observation or analysis of the facts of consciousness . . . , and Cousin "does not begin with what ought to be in the consciousness . . . , [but] what is." The observation of facts is then completed by the inductive method: "We cannot remain in the observation of facts, we are compelled to add facts together and find their sum total . . . These two methods of activity of the Reason, observation and induction, constitute Cousin's method." In conclusion, Brownson again emphasizes that French Eclecticism is not of German origin: "It received its impulse, its method, and its direction from Royer-Collard, who was, as everybody knows, the founder of the Scotch school."[14]

In 1838, George Ripley, an important member of the Transcendentalist group and the founder of Brook Farm, included large excerpts from the philosophical writings of Cousin, Constant and Jouffroy, in the first volumes of his new *Specimens of Foreign Standard Literature.* As Gohdes points out, "some significance may be attached to the fact that Ripley chose, as the first of his *Specimens,* not German idealism, but the spiritual philosophy of France."[15] These volumes were very well received. An article published in the *Boston Quarterly Review* praised Ripley for his project, since the reviewer felt that Americans had "much to learn in the department of philosophy, theology and history, from the literatures of France and Germany." French writings in general, and in particular the philosophical writings of the Eclectics were praised for their underlying democratic ideals: "(Their) writings breathe altogether more of a democratic spirit than do those of the English. Those of the French are altogether more democratic than the writings of American scholars themselves." In conclusion the reviewer declared that Cousin, Constant, Jouffroy were three authors who are an honor to France and mankind, while Cousin, "the chief of the new French school," was "if not the first, at least one of the first philosophers of the age."[16]

The *Christian Examiner* raised a dissenting voice, giving forty pages to a well documented discussion of Eclecticism. The attitude of the author of the article was summed up in his conclusion:

> Eclecticism cannot, strictly speaking, be applied to mental philosophy. It may be employed in matters of taste or utility, but in an affair of argument it is entirely inapplicable . . . He that carries in his own hand the measuring rod by which the truth of the system can be tested, must have first constructed a true system of his own. Eclecticism, therefore, is below the dignity of a true philosopher; and if we trace its history, we shall find that it has always originated from ignorance of the true method of philosophysing, from the darkness and perplexity of the human race with reference to difficult subjects, or from a timid disposition to sacrifice truth, in order to tranquillize the minds of heated partisans.[17]

Again in 1838 Rufus Dawes hurled another blast at Cousin in *The Hesperian.* Comparing Swedenborg to Cousin, the author declared: "The writings of that illustrious man [Swedenborg] contain all that is valuable in the French philosophy of the day, and infinitely more, in which the severest analysis and the closest logic cannot detect a fault."[18]

The second edition of Henry's translation from Cousin (1838), also received very favorable reviews. In the words of a contributor to *The Biblical Repository,* a conservative Presbyterian journal, the work "was a splendid production." Quoting from other magazines, he called it "the most important work on Locke since the *Nouveaux Essais* of Leibnitz," and "perhaps the greatest masterpiece of philosophical criticism ever exhibited to the public." In the reviewer's opinion, Cousin's American reputation was growing rapidly, and Henry's translation "had been introduced into a number of our most respectable universities and colleges."[19]

Likewise in the *Boston Quarterly Review* there appeared another essay in defense of Cousin:

> [He] is thought by many in this country to be merely a philosophical dreamer, a fanciful framer of hypotheses, a bold generalizer without solid judgment or true science . . . But nothing is more unjust than this impression. Mr. Cousin is the farthest in the world from being a mere theorizer, or from founding his philosophy, as some allege, on mere "a priori" reasoning.

The author, Brownson perhaps, insisted that "Cousin has very little in common with those [we] are in the habit of calling Transcendentalists." The latter, the reviewer felt, were of German origin; as to Cousin, "he cannot be classed with Kant, nor with any of the Germans. He has all that Germany can give, which is worth having, and much that Germany cannot give." Though Cousin had much in common with the Scotch school, the reviewer continued, "he leaves that school at an immeasurable distance behind him." And, after quoting at great length from the work reviewed, he concluded: "Cousin's method is the experimental method of modern philosophy itself, the only method philosophy has been permitted to follow since Bacon and Descartes."[20]

The same year, 1839, Ripley's *Specimens of Foreign Standard Literature*—the translations from Cousin, Constant and Jouffroy—again received laudatory reviews. A short notice published in the *Knickerbocker* declared that the three authors selected ". . . are the brightest stars in the philosophical constellation of France." Though mindful that Cousin "had been censured as an eclectic and as advocating a characterless philosophy," the reviewer expressed his gratitude "to him, who has by turns, interpreted ancient and modern doctrines, and revealed to us the sublimity of Plato, the casuistry of Descartes, and juxtaposition with the sensualism and transcendentalism of Locke and Kant."[21]

Quite different, however, was the judgment of a contributer to the *Princeton Review* who devoted seventy pages to a discussion of Cousin's Eclecticism and German Transcendentalism. America's need for a "new and

American-born philosophy," the writer felt, will not be fulfilled "so long as we received our philosophemata by a double transportation, from Germany via France, in parcels to suit the importers." In an attempt to create an American philosophy, some young philosophers were busily learning French and German, while those who could not were striving ".... to gather into one the Sibylline oracles and abortive scraps of the gifted but indolent Coleridge, and his gaping imitators, or in default of this sit at the urn of dilute wisdom, and sip the thrice-drawn influsion of English from French and French from German."[22]

To the author of this article, Cousin's Eclecticism was "a conduit from the stream of German transcendentalism at the most corrupt part of its current," and the writer expressed hope that the progress made by "this system of abomination among us,"[23] could be checked.

The irreconcilable opposition which he saw between Eclecticism and Christianity was the basis for the *Princeton Review's* bitter assault on Cousin's speculations. Likewise German transcendentalism came in for rebuke: "In the French imitation, no less than in the German original, there is a perpetual self-delusion practised by the philosopher who plays with words as a child with lettered cards, and combines what ought to be the symbols of thought into expressions unmeaning and self-contradictory."[24]

Naturally, American transcendentalism itself was tarred with the same brush, and the reviewer singled out Ralph Waldo Emerson, the flag-bearer of the movement, as the chief American legatee of Cousin. In Emerson's famous Divinity Address at Harvard he saw "an alarming symptom of the progress among us of [Cousin's] system," and after reading the address he "wanted words with which to express [his] sense of the nonsense and impiety which pervade it."[25]

The following year, 1840, a contributor to the *Boston Quarterly Review* undertook to answer these and similar charges against American transcendentalism. In defense of the movement, he wrote:

> It is really of American origin, and the prominent actors in it were carried away by it even before they formed an acquaintance with French or German metaphysics; and their attachment to the literatures of France and Germany is not the effect of their connexion with the movement, but the cause.[26]

Also, in 1840 William Henry Channing, one of the earliest advocates of socialism in the United States, published his translation of Jouffroy's *Introduction to Ethics* as the volumes V and VI of Ripley's *Specimens*. This naturally increased the number of references to Cousin, as the commentators of Jouffroy—Cousin's most important disciple—could not avoid referring to his master. In a review of these volumes in the *Christian Examiner,* Samuel

Osgood expressed what seems to be a fair view of the part played by Cousin in the intellectual development of America: "German and English philosophers are indebted to the French for the clearest exhibitions of their various systems. . . . We are indebted to Cousin for our clearest idea of German philosophy." Altogether this seems to have been Cousin's greatest contribution to the transcendentalist movement, for as the reviewer puts it, German philosophical thought "must first pass through the French mint, [to] take the form and beauty that fit it for practical purposes."[27]

In the next few years nothing of importance is added to the list of references to Cousin, except for several laudatory reviews which emphasized his importance as the link between America and Germany. Thus, in the *American Eclectic,* a reprint of Cousin's article on "Kant and his Philosophy" was introduced with these words:

> It is now sixty years since the *Critical Philosophy* was first submitted to the judgment of a restless and inquiring age. Its merits are still undetermined, but its success has been much less complete than the sanguine author anticipated. In Germany, indeed, the new system gained the ascendancy, but elsewhere its progress was slow . . .[28]

Explaining this partial failure, the writer added: "The deep thinking German [Kant] has been seldom understood except by his reflective and speculative countrymen." Cousin's labors, the reviewer felt, "will contribute something to the removal of these doubts," and help in making Kant and his philosophy better understood in America. Indeed, the reviewer concluded, "we can think of no living writer . . . better qualified to become the faithful interpreter of the *Critical Philosophy*," adding furthermore, that "if he [Cousin] shall fail to render Kant intelligible, we may well conclude that the cause is hopeless."[29]

Even such a magazine as *The Ladies' Repository* urged "its most intelligent female readers to skip the next popular novel, and read instead the *Philosophical Miscellanies* of Cousin, Constant and Jouffroy. However, a few paragraphs later the reviewer tempered his enthusiasm with a warning against Cousin's errors in religion: "We do not, of course, recommend the theological opinions of these men to the approval of our readers. They are often far enough from the true light."[30]

The same year, a contributor to the *Methodist Quarterly* declared that Cousin's great success was caused by "the boldness and originality of his ideas, (and) the eloquence and effectiveness with which they are urged upon his immense auditory." Though writing in a conservative magazine, the reviewer was evidently not aware of the theological implications of Cousin's philosophy. Unlike his colleague of *The Ladies' Repository,* he declared: "Though [Cousin] is a most absolute free-thinker in philosophy, he is also a

Christian, a believer in religion and revolution; and his philosophy, instead of being infidel in its character or tendency, is essentially Christian throughout."[31]

In 1841 the *North American Review* published a forty page essay on Eclecticism. In the subtitle, the reviewer, who later explained that Cousin's doctrine must be pieced together from prefaces, lectures, and scraps of criticism, listed three of Cousin's works in translation. In the reviewer's words, "Cousin's success in this country is well attested by the appearance of these three translations . . . , one of which has passed on to a second edition and has been prepared as a text-book for use in some of our principal colleges." This reviewer, too, contrasted Cousin's clarity with the abstrusities of German metaphysicians, feeling that Cousin's great success resulted from his ability to express doctrines admittedly borrowed from the Scotch and Germans "with greater force and clearness . . . freed from objectionable peculiarities, and thus brought within the reach of a wider circle of readers."[32]

In 1842 Cousin's *An Epitome of the History of Philosophy,* in Henry's translation, was published in Boston. The work was hailed immediately as excellent and a contributor to *The Ladies' Repository* advocated its "immediate introduction as a text-book in all our schools."[33] The same year, the *Methodist Quarterly Review* devoted a long essay to Cousin's philosophy. The "tardy" acceptance of Eclecticism in America, the writer declared, was not surprising when one reflected "with what suspicion every metaphysical system, originating in France, is received on this side of the Atlantic," a suspicion normally extended by Americans to any kind of writing coming from France. Concluding his study, the author declared: "The works of Cousin, we have no doubt, will have a tendency to excite a spirit of philosophical inquiry in this country."[34]

By 1842, Cousin had reached the peak of his success in America. In the following years, the number of references to his philosophy and favorable reactions to it decreased considerably. In 1844, Orestes Brownson, who so far had contributed many interesting articles on Cousin and his Eclecticism, launched his own *Quarterly Review* on its brief career. Introducing the first issue, he declared:

[In] the *Boston Quarterly Review* in 1839, I was still under the influence of the French school of philosophy founded by Mr. Cousin. That school took fast hold of me—completely subjecting me. It was long before I could master it and recover the free action and development of my own mind. I think I have finally mastered it; but I must not be understood as having rejected it. I am still a disciple of that school, though a free disciple, not a slave . . . I have obtained a clear, consistent, well-defined system of philosophy, satisfactory to my own mind; but, in obtaining it, I have assimilated no small share of the teachings of that school, and I cannot but feel myself largely its debtor.

But though he still held a high opinion of the Eclectic school and ranked its founder "along-side Abelard, Descartes, Locke, Leibnitz, and Schelling," [35] Brownson's conversion to Catholicism brought a complete change in his attitude. Reviewing Jouffroy's *Cours de Droit Naturel,* he firmly stated that he had repudiated his former allegiance to Eclecticism, and undertook to "assign some of the reasons which have finally operated to change [his] views, and to induce [him] to reject its principal doctrines as insufficient, false or mischevious." In essence, Brownson felt that the Eclectics committed "one fatal error—that of assuming that religion and philosophy do not differ as to their matter, but only as to their form." This was true not only of Eclecticism, but of contemporary philosophy as a whole, which was at war with religion:

> The Eclectic school, the modern German school, and even our liberal Christians . . . , really reject all supernatural revelation in believing themselves able to explain its mysteries. To explain, in the sense these understand it, is to make intrinsically evident to natural reason. A supernatural revelation must necessarily contain some mysteries. A mystery is something whose intrinsic truth is inevident to natural reason. The pretended explanation of a real mystery is never its explanation, but always its rejection.[36]

By the late forties Cousin's influence in American thinking was fast disappearing. Eclecticism in its turn was overthrown by the Positivism of Auguste Comte (the first reference to Comte dates from 1846), and references to Cousin and his school gradually disappear.

The last important reference to Cousin appeared in 1848, when *De Bow's Review* published five articles dealing with the Eclectic school. Feeling that much of the opposition to Eclecticism arose from its name, the critic endeavored to give a better presentation of the doctrine:

> Eclecticism does not attempt to admit as both true, such opposites as sensualism and spiritualism. After each has developed in its own way, Eclecticism sets about to reunite them . . . In Eclecticism, sensualism and spiritualism meet to reconcile their differences, to explain, illustrate and verify each other.[37]

Tracing the development of philosophical ideas in France during the last century, he concluded: "Cousin and Eclecticism may be said to be the last word, the last grand product and the highest and most perfect expression, not only of the philosophy of the eighteenth and nineteenth centuries, but also of all the antecedent times." Also, he regretted that not all of Cousin's works were translated into English, for "he is undoubtedly the greatest dialectician, the ablest master of his language, and the most erudite scholar that has lived in modern times."[38]

From this survey of American reception of Cousin and French Eclecticism, it appears that Cousin's doctrine was widely known in America and generally well received, lending support to Howard Mumford Jones's assertion that "no French thinker in the nineteenth century was more vigorously debated and discussed in the United States in our epoch (1750-1848)."[39] Much of the interest devoted to Cousin originated in the transcendentalist *milieu,* most of it paralleled closely the rise and development of transcendentalism.[40]

It would be wrong, of course, to assign a single source to American trancendentalism, and still more incorrect to find it in Eclecticism. However, if as Jones says, "Cousin was not the European foster-father of Transcendentalism—and he was not—"[41] it seems only fair to add that he was nevertheless an important contributor to the philosophical evolution of America, and certainly a collateral contribution to the development of American transcendentalism. Acting as a catalyst, Cousin assisted Americans in assimilation of German thought: "If Germany is known as the land of speculators, scholars, philosophers, France seems to have been appointed to state the results of German speculation in clear, distinct propositions and practical rules." [42] Finally and not the least, Cousin had a significant role in stimulating metaphysical speculations among young American philosophers.

NOTES

1. Unpublished dissertation (Michigan State College, 1951), by Georges J. Joyaux.

2. Howard Mumford Jones, *America and French Culture, 1750-1848* (Chapel Hill, 1927), pp. 461-62.

3. These figures confirm Clarence Gohdes' opinion that "the influence of French Eclecticism upon the development of American transcendentalism deserves a special study." See Clarence Gohdes, *The Periodicals of American Transcendentalism* (Durham, 1931), p. 54.

4. *North American Review,* XXIX (July 1829), 67-69. The four works reviewed were: *Oeuvres de Platon* (1822-28), *Fragments philosophiques* (1826), *Cours de philosophie* (1828), and *Nouveaux Fragments philosophiques* (1828). It is interesting to notice that here, as in many other cases, Cousin's works were reviewed in their French dress, which speaks highly of American intellectual leaders' acquaintance with the French language.

5. *Christian Examiner,* VII (January 1830), 292.

6. *American Quarterly Review,* X (December 1831), 291-93.

7. *Ibid.,* pp. 301-04.

8. *North American Review,* XXXV (July 1832), 19, 23.

9. Ronald V. Wells, *Three Christian Transcendentalists: James Marsh, Caleb Sprague Henry, Frederic Henry Hedge* (New York, 1943).

10. *Literary and Theological Review,* I (December 1834), 691-92.

11. *North American Review,* XL (April 1835), 512.

12. *Christian Examiner,* XXI (September 1836), 34-38.

13. Again Brownson expressed his faith in the new paths of investigation opened by Cousin's speculations: ". . . We believe an acquaintance with the researches [of the French Eclectics] . . . , a very important acquisition in the work of elaborating a better philosophy than any which has hitherto prevailed among us." See *Christian Examiner,* XXII (May 1837), 185.

14. *Ibid.,* pp. 187-93.

15. Gohdes, p. 54.

16. *Boston Quarterly Review,* I (October 1838), 438-43.

17. *Christian Examiner,* IV (March 1839), 35.

18. *The Hesperian,* II (1838), 482.

19. *The Biblical Repository,* I (January 1839), 247.

20. *Boston Quarterly Review,* III (January 1839), 27, 35.

21. *Knickerbocker Magazine,* XIII (March 1839), 353.

22. *The Princeton Review,* XI (January 1839), 42-43.

23. *Ibid.,* pp. 56, 92.

24. *Ibid.,* p. 88.

25. *Ibid.,* pp. 92, 95.

26. *Boston Quarterly Review,* III (July 1840), 271. On the whole, this position is not unlike that reached by more recent students of the transcendental revolution. See Professor René Wellek's study of "Emerson and German Transcendentalism," *New England Quarterly,* XVI (March 1943).

27. *Christian Examiner,* XXVIII (March 1840), 137-38.

28. *American Eclectic,* I (March 1841), 276. The article originally appeared in *La Revue des Deux Mondes.*

29. *American Eclectic,* I, 277-78.

30. *The Ladies' Repository,* I (March 1841), 159.

31. *The Methodist Quarterly Review,* I (July 1841), 336-37.

32. *North American Review,* LIII (July 1841), 1, 3.

33. *The Ladies Repository,* II (April 1842), 127.

34. *The Methodist Quarterly Review,* II (April 1842), 165, 192.

35. *Brownson's Quarterly Review,* I (January 1844), 6-7.

36. *Ibid.,* II (January 1845), 54-57. It is clear, however, that despite this reversal of opinion during the later years of the movement, Brownson who was influential in spreading the gospel of transcendentalism, had a large share in introducing and popularizing Cousin's theories in America. For the past ten years Brownson had been an "avowed disciple of the foreign master [Cousin]," and many of the latter's ideas found their way into transcendental circles through Brownson's articles in leading New England magazines. See Gohdes, p. 54.

37. *De Bow's Review,* V (January 1848), 62-63.

38. *Ibid.,* (March 1848), 216.

39. Jones, p. 463. His works, in translation, went through several American editions during his lifetime, and were even chosen as text books for use in colleges.

40. Though most of the material discussed in this paper originated in New England, we should point out that Cousin's influence spread as well throughout the country. Thus, Henry P. Tappan, President of the University of Michigan, had an almost complete collection of Cousin's works—most of them in the original—and "offered a course in the History of Philosophy which included as one of three topics 'Cousin and Eclecticism.' " *Michigan History,* XXXVI (September 1952), 301.

41. Jones, p. 471.

42. *United States Magazine and Democratic Review,* XV (July 1844), 22.

9

Transcendentalism and Jacksonian Democracy

ARTHUR M. SCHLESINGER, JR.

1

THE TRANSCENDENTALISTS OF MASSACHUSETTS CONSTITUTED the one important literary group never much impressed by Jacksonian democracy. This immunity was all the more singular because for two occasional members, George Bancroft and Orestes A. Brownson, the relations between transcendentalism and democracy seemed close and vital. The Jacksonians, in the minds of Bancroft and Brownson, were carrying on the same revolt against the dead hand of John Locke in politics which the transcendentalists were carrying on in religion. Both Democrat and transcendentalist agreed in asserting the rights of the free mind against the pretensions of precedents or institutions. Both shared a living faith in the integrity and perfectibility of man. Both proclaimed self-reliance. Both detested special groups claiming authority to mediate between the common man and the truth. Both aimed to plant the individual squarely on his instincts, responsible only to himself and to God. "The soul must and will assert its rightful ascendancy," exclaimed the *Bay State Democrat*, "over all those arbitrary and conventional forms which a false state of things has riveted upon society." "Democracy," cried Bancroft, "has given to conscience absolute liberty"[1]

But transcendentalism in its Concord form was infinitely individualistic, providing no means for reconciling the diverse intuitions of different men and deciding which was better and which worse. This did not worry most transcendentalists, who would allow Nicholas Biddle the authority of his inner voice and asked only to be allowed equally the authority of their own. The obligations of politics were not so flexible. Bancroft's great modification of transcendentalism was to add that the collective sense of the people provided the indispensable check on the anarchy of individual intuitions. "If reason is a universal faculty, the decision of the common mind is the nearest criterion of truth." Democracy thus perfected the insights of transcendentalism. "Individuals make proclamation of their own fancies; the spirit of God breathes through the combined intelligence of the people. . . . It is, when the multitude give council, that right purposes find safety; theirs is the fixedness that cannot be shaken; theirs is the understanding which exceeds in wisdom."[2]

For Bancroft and Brownson the battle against the past was indivisible, involving politics as much as philosophy. In his brilliant chapter on the Quakers in the second volume of his *History* (1837), Bancroft set forth in luminous prose his conception of the relations between the liberation of the soul of man and of his body. For Brownson conservatism in religion and in society were so nearly identical that he could observe of Victor Cousin, the French philosopher, "His works have made many young men among us Democrats." To Cousin himself he proudly declared, "We are combining philosophy with politics," adding that the Democratic party would soon adopt the views of the new school.[3] When Bancroft reviewed George Ripley's *Philosophical Miscellanies,* an anthology of French and German metaphysics, for the *Washington Globe,* he called it "a sort of manifesto of philosophical Democracy," and described how the glory of Jefferson had found new witnesses in the work of Cousin, Jouffroy and Constant.[4] An anonymous essayist in a Democratic paper even admonished the young men, in oddly Emersonian phrases, to *"Trust to Yourself"* and hymned the virtues of *"self-dependence."*[5]

Yet, for all the inspiration some Democrats found in transcendentalism, the transcendentalists remained singularly unmoved by the exertions of the Democrats. From their book-lined studies or their shady walks in cool Concord woods, they found the hullabaloo of party politics unedifying and vulgar. The rebuke of Nature was crushing: "So hot? my little Sir." Life was short, and much better to contemplate verities and vibrate to that iron spring than to make commitments to practicality. A political party, like society itself, was a joint-stock company, in which the members agreed, for the better securing of bread to each shareholder, to surrender the liberty and culture of the eater. "The virtue in most request is conformity. Self-reliance is its aversion."

But for the typical transcendentalist the flinching from politics perhaps expressed a failure they were seeking to erect into a virtue. The exigencies of responsibility were exhausting: much better to demand perfection and indignantly reject the half loaf, than wear out body and spirit in vain grapplings with overmastering reality. The headlong escape into perfection left responsibility far behind for a magic domain where mystic sentiment and gnomic utterance exorcised the rude intrusions of the world. But it was easier to rule the state from Concord than from Washington. And the state had to be ruled, it was the implacable vacuum: if Bronson Alcott preferred Fruitlands, he was not to complain when James K. Polk preferred the White House.

Yet these were the worst, the pure transcendentalists, incapable of effective human relations, terrified of responsibility, given to transforming evasion into a moral triumph. The tougher-minded men on the transcendental margin recognized that certain obligations could not be shaken. The existence of society depended on a mutuality of confidence, the maintenance of which required that the demands of hunger, want and insecurity be met, lest desperation shatter the social chain. These basic agonies were not to be dissolved in the maternal embrace of the oversoul. George Ripley, unlike Bronson Alcott, did not despise those who held the ordinary affairs of life to be important. Whiggery in politics persuaded him as little as Whiggery in religion, and the energy of his friends Bancroft and Brownson stimulated him to work with transcendental insights on the ills of society. "He has fairly philosophized himself into Democracy," wrote Brownson in 1836. Ripley himself bravely declared to Bancroft a year later that "almost to a man, those who shew any marks of genius or intellectual enterprise are philosophical democrats." (The date was September 20, but he had no observations on the independent treasury.) The intellectual ferment of Boston was heady. "There is a great feeding on the mulberry leaves, and it will be hard if silken robes are not woven for the shining ones.... I almost hope to see the time, when religion, philosophy and politics will be united in a holy Trinity, for the redemption and blessedness of our social institutions."[6]

But Ripley's gestures toward the Democratic party were those of a pure young man engaged in audacious coquetry with an experienced woman of shady reputation. He smiled, inclined, almost yielded, then snatched away with an air of indignation, his head flushed with the pleasing excitement and his virtue intact. When Bancroft allowed some of Ripley's remarks to fill an anonymous paragraph in the *Boston Post*, Ripley wrote with alarm, "I insist on the distinction between the philosophical principles of democracy, and the democratic party in this country." (His timid advances were being taken with undue seriousness; almost he was invited to meet the family.) ". . . So it is with my young men. They have little faith in parties, but a great zeal for principles. They love nothing about the Whigs but the personal worth which they possess; but they are inclined to doubt whether the opponents of the Whigs are after all true democrats. It is certain, I must confess, that some of the warmest advocates of democratical principles, some who cherish the loftiest faith in the progress of humanity, are found in the Whig ranks."[7] The notes were revealing, for Ripley was not the most innocent of the transcendentalists. Yet he seemed to have no conception at all of, say, the role of measures and policies in underwriting "democratical principles." The diet of mulberry leaves might weave robes for the shining ones, but it gave small nourishment to a realistic view of society.

Ripley had escaped, but his conscience continued peremptory. Then, in 1840, a fairer and more chaste maiden appeared in the vision of Brook Farm, and he was saved from the worldly life of Politics. For him, and for the other transcendentalists who shared his inability to explain away suffering, Brook Farm appeared as a serious solution of the conditions which had driven Bancroft and Brownson into the arms of Party. Their faith was a variant of Utopianism, and Brook Farm appropriately ended up as a Fourierite phalanx.

2

The Oversoul thus comforted the tender transcendentalists, while the tough mowed the hay and raked the dirt at Brook Farm. But beyond the transcendentalists, accepting their inspiration but safe from their illusions, was Emerson, the wisest man of the day. He was too concretely aware of the complexities of experience to be altogether consoled by vagueness and reverie. The doctrine of compensation had its limits, and he was not deceived by Ripley's community. "At Education Farm, the noblest theory of life sat on the noblest figures of young men and maidens, quite powerless and melancholy. It would not rake or pitch a ton of hay; it would not rub down a horse; and the men and maidens it left pale and hungry."[8] Yet politics represent his greatest failure. He would not succumb to verbal panaceas, neither would he make the ultimate moral effort of Thoreau and cast off all obligation to society. Instead he lingered indecisively, accepting without enthusiasm certain relations to government but never confronting directly the implications of acceptance.

He acknowledged the claims of the Democratic party expounded so ardently by Bancroft and Brownson. "The philosopher, the poet, or the religious man, will, of course, wish to cast his vote with the democrat, for free-trade, for wide suffrage, for the abolition of legal cruelties in the penal code, and for facilitating in every manner the access of the young and the poor to the sources of wealth and power."[9] He recognized, too, the inevitable drift of transcendentalism toward the democratic position. The first lecture of his series in 1839 on the "Present Age" was reported by Theodore Parker as "*Democratic-locofoco* throughout, and very much in the spirit of Brownson's article on Democracy and Reform in the last *Quarterly*." Bancroft left "in ecstasies . . . rapt beyond vision at the *locofocoism*," and one Boston conservative could only growl that Emerson must be angling for a place in the Custom House.[10]

Yet Emerson would go no farther. "Of the two great parties, which, at this hour, almost share the nation between them," he would lamely conclude, "I should say, that one has the best cause, and the other contains the best men."[11] This would have provided no excuse for inaction, even if it were true, for a man of Emersonian principle should follow his principle; but it was not even true.

Fear of institutions kept him cautious. A party seemed a form of church, and Emerson, a burnt child, shunned the fire. "Bancroft and Bryant," he said, "are historical democrats who are interested in dead or organized, but not in organizing, liberty."[12] He liked the *Washington Globe's* motto—"The world is governed too much"—though it appalled him that so many people read the paper. But in an imperfect world, should he not settle for "historical democrats" and *Washington Globes,* or at least remark on the alternative? Emerson was well aware of the discipline of choice. Yet here he failed himself, and ignored the responsibilities of his own moral position.

Fundamentally he did not care, and thus he was betrayed, almost without struggle, into the clichés of conservatism which had surrounded him from birth. In a flash of insight he could see that "banks and tariffs, the newspaper and caucus" were "flat and dull to dull people, but rest on the same foundations of wonder as the town of Troy, and the temple of Delphos." [13] Yet, in life at Concord, day in, day out, banks and tariffs were flat and dull to him. As he glanced at party contests, he was most impressed by "the meanness of our politics."[14]

He had little idea of the significance of the struggles of the eighteen-thirties. His ejaculation to Carlyle in 1834—"a most unfit man in the Presidency has been doing the worst things"—about exhausted his conception of the Jackson administration.[15] His reluctance to break with the Whigs was increased by his invention of a statesman named Daniel Webster to whom he gave profound devotion and whom he carelessly confused with the popular Whig politician of the same name. "That great forehead which I followed about all my young days, from court-house to senate chamber, from caucus to street" cast a hypnotic spell over a man otherwise hard to fool.[16] His comments, scattered over two decades of loyalty, show a literary fascination with the massiveness of personality, the stately rhetoric, the marble brow and face black as thunder: but little concern for his views on practical policy. This Webster was a mirage peculiar to Emerson. For Bryant, Bancroft, Cooper, Whitman and Hawthorne, Webster was the most vulnerable celebrity of the day.[17] But for Emerson he remained a great statesman—until Webster finally ran up against an issue which really excited Emerson's imagination and commanded his full attention, and the speech on the Compromise of 1850 disclosed to Emerson what he should have known for years. The steady wisdom of the sage of Concord faltered, in this one field, into sentimentality.

NOTES

1. *Bay State Democrat,* May 3, 1839; Bancroft, "Address to the Democratic Electors of Massachusetts," *Boston Post,* October 16, 1835.

2. Bancroft, "On the Progress of Civilization, or Reasons Why the Natural Association of Men of Letters Is with the Democracy," *Boston Quarterly Review,* I, 395 (October 1838); Bancroft, "Address to the Democratic Electors of Massachusetts," *Boston Post,* October 16, 1835.

3. Brownson to Bancroft, September 24, 1836, Bancroft Papers; Brownson to Cousin, June 23, 1838, Brownson Papers. The Bancroft Papers are in the possession of the Massachusetts Historical Society, while the Brownson papers are in the University of Notre Dame Library.

4. *Washington Globe,* March 9, 1838.

5. "To the Young Men," by "H. P.," *Bay State Democrat,* August 16, 1839.

6. Brownson to Bancroft, September 24, 1836, Ripley to Bancroft, September 20, 1837, Bancroft Papers.

7. Ripley to Bancroft, November 6, 1837, Bancroft Papers.

8. Emerson, *Essays* (World's Classics), p. 300.

9. *Ibid.,* pp. 407-08.

10. Parker to Convers Francis, December 6, 1839; J. E. Cabot, *Memoir of Ralph Waldo Emerson* (Boston, 1887), pp. 400-01.

11. *Essays,* p. 407.

12. *The Journals of Ralph Waldo Emerson,* ed. Edward Waldo Emerson and Waldo Emerson Forbes, 10 vols. (Boston, 1909-14), VI, 315.

13. *Essays,* p. 285.

14. *Ibid.,* p. 185.

15. Emerson to Carlyle, May 14, 1834, *Correspondence of Thomas Carlyle and Ralph Waldo Emerson, 1834-1872,* ed. C. E. Norton, 2 vols. (Boston, 1888), I, 16.

16. Emerson to Carlyle, August 8, 1839, *Correspondence,* I, 255.

17. Webster was the butt of the Democratic literary men, as his peculiar combination of cynicism and external moral grandeur made inevitable. Hawthorne's sketch of Webster as "Old Stony Phiz" in "The Great Stone Face" is well-known and penetrating, presenting him as "a man of mighty faculties and little aims, whose life, with all its high performances, was vague and empty, because no high purpose has endowed it with reality." Hawthorne, *Writings* (Boston, 1900), III, 51. For Bancroft's ribald running comment on Webster, see his correspondence with Van Buren. Bryant's famous editorial on Webster's humor in the New York *Evening Post* of November 20, 1837, is to be found in Bryant, *Prose Writings,* ed. Parke Godwin, (New York, 1884), II, 383-85. A typical Cooper reference is in *The Monikins,* Darley-Townsend

Edition (New York, 1860), p. 414. Whitman summed them all up with his brief remark that Webster was "overrated more than any other public man ever prominent in America." Brooklyn *Eagle,* April 11, 1846, *Gathering of the Forces,* ed. Cleveland Rodgers and John Black (New York, 1920), II, 182.

10

"This Unnatural Union of Phalansteries and Transcendentalists"

CHARLES R. CROWE

ONE OF THE MOST INTERESTING IDEOLOGICAL AND SOCIAL EX-periments in nineteenth-century America was the attempt by leaders of the Brook Farm community to reconcile Transcendentalism and Fourierist social-ism. The New England Transcendentalists who came to intellectual maturity between 1834 and 1838, emphasized individualism, non-conformity, and spontaneous living. Yet even before the movement had fully matured, the Jacksonian drive for equality, the coming of the industrial revolution, and the hardships brought about by the panic of 1837, combined to lead George Ripley, John S. Dwight, and other Transcendentalists away from ultra-indi-vidualism and toward the advocacy of collectivistic reform ideas.[1] In 1841 Ripley led a small group to West Roxbury, Massachusetts and began his celebrated socialist experiment. The conversion of Brook Farm leaders to the doctrines of Charles Fourier in January 1844[2] resulted in an even more intense collectivism, and made the community a powerful influence in the New England labor movement; it constituted the heart and mind of American Fourierism. Neither the early plans for Brook Farm nor the later commitment to Fourierism were made from any conscious desire to abandon Emersonian

From *Journal of the History of Ideas,* 20 (1959), 495-502. Reprinted by permission.

individualism. On the contrary, the Brook Farmers hoped to apply Transcendentalist ideas in a socialist context.[3]

Many Transcendentalists and some Fourierists thought that the two ideologies were incompatible. Emerson, Margaret Fuller, Bronson Alcott, and other Transcendentalists were basically sympathetic toward Brook Farm but refused to join the community, largely because of its collectivism. After the coming of Fourierism, the suspicion that Brook Farm was an exchange of Emersonian individualism for communal solace became a certainty.[4] G. W. Curtis, a young Emersonian, who had spent several years at Brook Farm, expressed a common response in his rejection of all collective approaches to reform:

> What we call union seems to me only a phrase of individual action. I live only for myself; and in proportion to my growth, so I benefit others. . . . Besides I feel that our evils are entirely individual. What is society but the shadow of the single men behind it?[5]

Hawthorne, sceptical from the beginning, left the community partly for practical reasons and partly because he felt that the artist was buried in the mass at Brook Farm.[6] Other Transcendentalists thought that spontaneity, the community's greatest asset, had been destroyed by Fourierist organization.[7] Even before the coming of Fourierism, Ripley began to place a greater emphasis on socialist ideology, and as a result some of the Transcendentalists who had not made a total commitment to reform left the community.[8]

By 1845 several Fourierists had added their criticisms to those of the Transcendentalists in protest against the effort to combine ideologies so diverse. When Brook Farm was on the verge of collapse in 1846, James Kay, Jr., the President of the Philadelphia Fourierist Union, argued vehemently that "the Jonathan Butterfields and the John Orvises" (i.e., the Transcendentalists) should "stay in the classroom where they belong," and not meddle in "practical" affairs. Kay insisted that the "indolent" and the "ethereal" no longer be defended by "this unnatural union of Phalansteries and (I dare not say Transcendentalists) the Spiritualists." Kay's implied meaning was clear enough: since Transcendentalism and Fourierism were contradictory, the Transcendentalists should resign positions of leadership in favor of the "practical" socialists.[9]

Even Ripley sometimes spoke as if the two ideologies could not be reconciled and individualism had to be abandoned:

> Much was said of the suffering . . . and Mr. Ripley said we had best own it, meet it strongly and care nothing about it,—our individualities must be forgotten; or rather, as unity itself without individualism would be tame, we must put up with the evil and suffering attendant upon this transition state and keep alive our faith, and hope that it will be temporary.[10]

This pessimistic thought, however, was the product of a despairing moment in which Ripley spoke carelessly about ideals that seemed to be slipping away. As a matter of fact, his entire life was committed to the belief that the two ideologies were compatible, and Brook Farm was essentially an attempt to demonstrate the practicality of this belief.

Emerson and Thoreau often complained about the fragmentation of the whole man by the specialized requirements of modern society, but it was Ripley who proposed to do something about this problem. At Brook Farm he wished to combine the thinker and the worker because he believed that the separation of manual labor and intellectual activity cheated the worker of a natural right to cultural goods and deprived the literate classes of work which was needed to give their lives unity and completeness.[11] When perfected, the Brook Farm Phalanx would provide hundreds of different occupations and each man might engage in as many of them as the complexity of his nature demanded. Thus, all aspects of the modern divided personality would be combined in the context of a society which would always make work, play, and education intrinsically satisfying.[12]

Socialist society, Ripley promised, would bring the freedom and the fulfillment that had always been Transcendentalist goals. The Emersonians thought of liberty as the freedom to develop creatively, and Fourier provided the blueprint for a society which would make possible the fullest self-development for all men. Most of the Transcendentalists had long believed that under optimum circumstances society might breed a race of Miltons and Shakespeares. When Ripley first came to Brook Farm he defined his ultimate goal as an attempt to substitute "a race of free, noble, and holy men and women" for the existing "dwarfish and mutilated specimens," and Fourierist ideology assured the Brook Farmers that "science" demonstrated the feasibility of this project. Poverty, vice, crime, aesthetic indifference, and lack of intellectual development, were the products of disorganized social relations. In socialist society, human nature was infinitely perfectible.[13]

According to Fourier, every human "passion" (instinct, emotion, or interest) was given by God for a specific reason. Ripley confidently asserted that "the desires of man" were "the promises of God," and insisted that if every passion were gratified, the end result would be harmonious personalities and the good society rather than crime and chaos. Evil acts were the result of conflicting passions arising from the stresses of competitive society.[14] Emerson had declared that "If I am the devil's child, then I shall live from the devil," but neither Fourier nor Ripley was willing to make this admission, and Ripley believed that a Phalanx would inevitably create a Transcendentalist paradise with social relations

> which are in perfect unison with the nature of man; to which every chord
> in his sensitive and finely vibrated frame will respond; which will call forth

as from a well tuned instrument, all those exquisite modulations of feeling and intellect, which were aptly termed by Plato, the 'music of his being.'[15]

Harmony with nature, God, and man as well as inner harmony was the product of self-development. According to Fourier, man was the only exception to the otherwise universal harmony that God had created. The universe was very much like a musical composition dominated and unified by a single thematic thread. From stellar nebulae to the surface of the globe, everything fell into series resembling measures of music with constituent parts similar to musical notes. When all men lived in socialist society, the universal harmony would be perfectly realized. Until the time when the harmonious personality was universal, freedom, as the irresponsible individualist imagined it, was impossible.

Accepting Fourier completely on this point, Ripley argued that those who accused the Brook Farmers of sacrificing individual freedom, did not realize the multitudinous ways in which competitive society enslaved men.[16] For example, "civilizees" were in bondage to class hatred. Ripley could point with pride to the harmony and ease of freely mingling mechanics and intellectuals at Brook Farm as evidence of "genuine" social freedom. When conflicts did arise, Ripley argued that Brook Farm was only a limited attempt to achieve socialism. Presumably these conflicts would disappear in a Phalanx of two thousand persons and a full schedule of occupations.

In competitive society, men were also in bondage to exploitative emotions toward nature and the feelings of guilt which were created. Again Brook Farm would be produced as evidence of another kind of freedom—that of forming harmonious relations with nature, and here the evidence is impressive. In spite of bitter struggles with sandy soil, Brook Farmers displayed an unusual gentleness toward physical nature. No hunting was ever permitted on community grounds. Wild animals came boldly to the Hive door, and not even the birds who pillaged the newly planted grain were begrudged the seeds they took. When the Brook Farmers discovered that the birds were apt to eat as much as three or four rows of grain in each field, they planted extra rows and good humoredly dismissed the problem.

Capitalist society, Ripley believed, also enslaved man by making of him a thing rather than a person, an instrument of work and ends alien to his nature. Nowhere did human slavery seem more complete to Brook Farmers than in the case of the screw turner, the lever puller, or the clerk who spent his days in recording meaningless figures. Awareness of these problems brought Ripley all the more enthusiastically to Fourier's doctrine of attractive labor. If men were given a sense of participation, ownership, and fruitful labor; if they were assigned the proper quality, quantity, and variety of labor in correspondence with human nature and the individual personality, then harmony and freedom rather than "passional" frustration and soul-destroy-ing, mechanical drudgery would be the end products of modern society.

The Brook Farmers ardently believed that socialist organization was the key to freedom. How could a man be free when he was at war with himself: when he had strong drives toward both brotherly co-operation and unscrupu-lous competition? In moderate quantities neither emotion was evil, and both would be recognized in socialist society where all human passions would be harmonized and balanced.

Moreover, social unity did not necessarily mean rigid conformity. The Fourierist structure of authority, Ripley asserted, demonstrated that freedom and regulation, variety and unity, could be reconciled. Brook Farm supported Ripley's beliefs in many respects.[17] An amazing variety of men and women lived in the community and each one chose his leader as well as his occupa-tion. A group leader was elected every week and the series chiefs were chosen by the workers with the advice and consent of the community council, itself an elective body. Never was an individual compelled to perform a task against his will. There was absolute freedom to join any group and a worker might change groups as often as he liked. In the course of a single day, a man might change not only from hoeing to a milking group, but even from the agricul-tural to the industrial or the educational series. The most disagreeable tasks were performed by a special group, the "Sacred Legion," which had a high morale and more volunteers than it could use. Apparently a sense of self-sacri-fice and high community prestige more than compensated for the unpleasant nature of many tasks.[18]

If, in spite of all this freedom, individualists still chose to complain about regimentation, Ripley was prepared to reply that when sufficient financial and human materials were available for a Phalanx, very few rules and regulations would be needed. In Ripley's mind the perfected Phalanx was an anarchistic society in which "everything would be regulated with spontaneous precision by the pervading common sense of the Phalanx, and the law written on the heart, the great and holy law of attraction, would supersede all others."[19] Marx was not the first to suggest that the establishment of socialism would be followed by a withering away of the state.

Thus, if the protestations of Ripley, Dwight, and others can be believed, there was no conflict between Transcendentalism and Fourierism. The Tran-scendentalists who came to Brook Farm had always defined freedom as the right to be one's self, to develop into a mature and distinctive personality, and this, they now believed, was possible only in a socialist society which would guarantee self-development for all men. To preach the salvation of isolated individuals was to mock both man and God. Communal values and individual liberty were combined in the Phalanx, which would secure and increase human variety rather than destroy it. Through the meditation of

Fourier's law of universal harmony, distinctive personalities could become members of a vast organic body without losing their individuality. The Brook Farmers insisted that the maximum self-development led to a soul motivated by love, an emotion which was the very essence of the human personality. John S. Dwight carried the collectivist spirit to an apex by insisting that the truest way for a man to realize himself was to blend his individual love into the universal love, to merge his life with the life of humanity:

> No man is himself, *alone*. Part of me is in you, in every fellow being. We "live and move and have our being" in one another, as well as in God. An individual is nothing in himself. . . . We are real *persons* only entering into true relations with all other beings; we enter into our lives and find ourselves just in proportion as we realize and make good those relations. Only so far as the electric chain of sympathies which God threw around us all, in sign that we are one . . . is kept entire and unobstructed . . . can we be said to live; and most men live, like old trees that are dying, only in a few branches, an incoherent, fragmentary, partial life; nothing continuous, fresh, and whole about it. It takes the life of all mankind to make our single life happy. . . . there is one life, one destiny in all humanity; . . . all men make up the one perfect man, and . . . only all men sharing each other's life, co-operating with and completing one another, can ever realize and bring out the full meaning of the idea of man. So far as each lives not in the whole, does he lack life; so far as he is indifferent to any, does he miss a portion of himself.[20]

Dwight's near mystical approach to the problem of the individual and the community helped to sustain the Brook Farmers, and most of them would have accepted his ideological position. In the actual life of the community, however, there were some conflicts between those who had been recruited as Transcendentalists and those who had come to the community because of Fourierist convictions. A few of the working-class members regarded the education group as an "aristocratic" element, even though all of the teachers worked in industrial and agricultural groups. Some craftsmen, led by the carpenter W. H. Cheswell, repeatedly expressed resentment and caused several stormy debates over the expansion of the school in 1844 and 1845. Their hostility was repaid by a little middle-class snobbery from some of the bluestockings in the community. From time to time there were also complaints that cliques had been formed on the basis of common residence in the same building. "Cabalism" was one of the twelve basic passions in Fourier's psychology, but the community leaders felt that these cliques represented an over-emphasis on a single emotion. Several reports were also made of discord within the work groups. In 1845 Christopher List and William Reynolds were expelled by the carpenter's group as "discordant elements."[21] On the whole, however, middle-class intellectuals and workers got along very well and supported Ripley's attempt to combine the two ideologies and apply the synthesis concretely to community life.

Brook Farm as an attempt to embody Transcendentalist ideas in a socialist context cannot be labeled either a total success or a total failure. Criticism enough can be made. Apparently some individual personalities found communal life stifling. There was some social conflict, and Ripley's glib explanation that all of this would completely vanish in a "true Phalanx" is no more satisfactory than similar statements from modern Russia explaining away the shortcomings of "socialist" society. Moreover, there is reason to believe that even the perfectly organized Phalanx might breed non-conformists for whom the society had no place. The sterile completeness of Fourier's system and the naiveté of Ripley's beliefs about human nature and social organization may also be criticized.

If Ripley does not convince us that the one and the many can be reconciled so easily and if Fourier does not persuade us that the socialist millennium will literally transform the seas into lemonade, we must still admit that Brook Farm was an interesting and significant attempt to retain some of the virtues of individualism in a collectivist society, and that Fourier had enough social realism to grapple with urgent human problems which Marx overlooked. Ripley and his followers were successful in combining co-operative living with much color, variety, and individualism. For all of their shortcomings, the Brook Farmers made an important effort to solve some of the most pressing cultural problems of the nineteenth century: how shall industrial labor be made "attractive"; how shall the problem of personality alienation among those in routine industrial and clerical occupations be overcome; how can the social isolation of so many in an impersonal industrial society be alleviated; how shall men and women be given a sense of participation, ownership, and interest in their occupations, communities and nations; how can a social climate be created which makes it possible for individualists to thrive in a mass society? These problems persist and the Brook Farm effort to reconcile Transcendentalism and Fourierism has as much significance for the twentieth century as it had for the nineteenth century.[22]

NOTES

1. The emergence of Transcendentalism is skillfully presented by Perry Miller in *The Transcendentalists* (Cambridge, Mass., 1950). Professor Miller's anthology contains a brief general bibliography which lists many of the relevant sources and secondary accounts and which is useful to both the general reader and the student of the period. Octavius B. Frothingham's *Transcendentalism in New England* (New York, 1876), with all its obvious flaws, is still the only book which gives a detailed and systematic account of Transcendentalist ideologies. F. O. Matthiessen's *American Renaissance* (New York, 1941) contains many valuable insights. The drift of Ripley's group toward political radicalism is discussed more fully in Charles R. Crowe, "George Ripley, Transcendentalist and Utopian Socialist" (Ph.D. thesis, Brown University, 1955). The writer is aware of the complexity of this intellectual movement and realizes that in a very true sense there were almost as many Transcendentalisms as there were Transcendentalists. However, some beliefs were held by all who accepted the label. No serious student of the movement would deny that all of those who called themselves Transcendentalists believed in personal liberty, spontaneous and creative living, and intuitive knowledge. Only those aspects of the movement will be dealt with here.

2. On this conversion to Fourierism see *The Present* (New York), January 15, 1844; and *The Phalanx* (New York), February 5, 1844.

3. See Ripley to R.W. Emerson, Boston, November 6, 1840, in O. B. Frothingham, *A Life of George Ripley* (Boston, 1882), pp. 306-10.

4. Emerson's changing attitudes, which were fairly representative of the most ardent individualists among the Transcendentalists, can be followed in his *Journals,* ed. E. W. Emerson and W. E. Forbes, 10 vols. (New York, 1909-11).

5. *Early Letters of G. W. Curtis to J. S. Dwight,* ed. G. W. Cooke (New York, 1898), p. 96.

6. Hawthorne, *The American Notebooks,* ed. Randall Stewart (New Haven, 1932), pp. 75-89.

7. For examples, see Amelia Russell, *Home Life of the Brook Farm Association* (Boston, 1900), p. 85.

8. Although he was also worried about community morals, George P. Bradford was in most respects a good example of this group. On Bradford's leaving Brook Farm see Emerson's *Journals,* VI, 391.

9. James Kay to J. S. Dwight, Philadelphia, March 12, 1846; Dwight Papers, Boston Public Library.

10. Marianne Dwight, *Letters from Brook Farm, 1844-1847,* ed. Amy L. Reed (Poughkeepsie, 1928), p. 91.

11. See Ripley's letter to Emerson in Frothingham, *Ripley,* pp. 306-10.

12. Ripley, "Tendencies of Modern Civilization," *The Harbinger* (Brook Farm), I (1845), 33; "Association," *The Harbinger,* I (1845), 48.

13. Frothingham, *Ripley,* p. 308. Also see "Association in this country," *The Harbinger,* I (1846), 189-90.

14. Fourier's significant writings are in *Oeuvres Complètes,* 6 vols. (Paris, 1841-48), but Albert Brisbane's *The Social Destiny of Man* (New York, 1840) is the key work for the movement in America.

15. Ripley, "Association," *The Harbinger,* V (1847), 137.

16. This "discussion" has been synthesized by the writer from numerous articles and letters. See, for example, Editor's Statement, *The Harbinger,* I (1845), 16; "Signs of Progress," *The Harbinger,* I (1845), 47-48; and Ripley's letters from 1843 to 1848 in the Boston Public Library and the Massachusetts Historical Society.

17. *Constitution of the Brook Farm Phalanx* (Boston, 1845); and the Brook Farm Minutes and Resolutions Book, Massachusetts Historical Society.

18. For the best accounts of Brook Farm during the Fourierist phase, see Marianne Dwight, *Letters, The Harbinger,* and J. T. Codman, *Brook Farm: Historic and Personal Memoirs* (Boston, 1894). The letters of George and Sophia Ripley, John S. Dwight, Albert Brisbane, John Allen, and W. H. Channing in the Boston Public Library and Massachusetts Historical Society are also useful.

19. Ripley, "Association," *The Harbinger,* I (1845), 160.

20. J. S. Dwight, "Association," *The Harbinger,* VI (1848), 170. Also see "Individuality in Association," *The Harbinger,* I (1845), 264-65.

21. On social conflicts at Brook Farm, see Marianne Dwight's *Letters,* pp. 38-39, 40-42, 61-63, 159-66.

22. On the relevance of utopian socialism to twentieth-century life, see Erich Fromm, *The Sane Society* (New York, 1955).

PART III
Theological Perspectives

11

Unitarianism and Transcendentalism

H. C. GODDARD

WHAT WAS THE NATURE OF THE TRANSCENDENTAL MOVEMENT IN New England? The critics can hardly be said to have reached a final answer to this question. There has been a good deal of innocent merriment. There has been a still larger amount of foolish scoffing and silly laughter—harmless, however, in the main. There have been knowing and indulgent smiles, telling, even better than condescending words, how deeply the pity of certain persons has been stirred at the sad vagaries of the transcendentalists. On the other hand there have been eulogies and esoteric utterances; or, where words have failed, there has been a bowing of heads in silent veneration. Between these two extremes, however, have appeared, fortunately, many saner and more critical estimates. But entire agreement, even here, has not by any means emerged; and there seem to be some reasons for believing that the word *transcendental* is itself responsible for much of the confusion.

The word *transcendental,* as applied to this movement, has been used in at least two distinct senses—one popular, the other more or less technically philosophical. The latter usage is to be traced of course to Kant and the

From *Studies in New England Transcendentalism* by Harold C. Goddard (New York: Columbia University Press, 1908), pp. 1-5, 18-40. The present editor has made a few deletions which are indicated by ellipses.

Critique of Pure Reason. For a full understanding of the philosophical side of New England transcendentalism it is necessary to know somewhat of this technical meaning of *transcendental;*[1] to have sojourned for a time in the kingdoms of the *Transcendental Aesthetic,* the *Transcendental Analytic,* and the *Transcendental Dialectic;* to have at least a bowing acquaintance with such formidable inhabitants of these realms as the *A Priori Synthetic Cognition* and the *Transcendental Ego of Apperception;* to recognize, for instance, what Schelling means by a *System of Transcendental Idealism;* and to understand somewhat of the nature of the German and other transcendental seeds that Coleridge sowed and tried to bring to flower in English soil. But fortunately for our present study, we may escape many of these difficulties that seemingly confront us; nor shall we have to excuse ourselves by saying that these matters belong to the professional metaphysicians, reasonable, perhaps, as such a plea might be; for the fact is that the question, What was the philosophy of the New England transcendentalists? is about the least mooted point in the whole discussion, and, if this alone were the question to be answered, such an essay as the present one would hardly be in order.

Transcendental, in its philosophical sense, was used in connection with this New England movement in a broad and often very elastic way; yet, after all, it had a quite definite and unmistakable meaning, nor can that meaning be said to have undergone any development or change. Emerson, at the beginning of his lecture, *The Transcendentalist,* tells us plainly what that usage was:

> It is well known to most of my audience, that the Idealism of the present day acquired the name Transcendental, from the use of that term by Immanuel Kant of Königsberg, who replied to the sceptical philosophy of Locke, which insisted that there was nothing in the intellect which was not previously in the experience of the senses, by showing that there was a very important class of ideas, or imperative forms, which did not come by experience, but through which experience was acquired; that these were intuitions of the mind itself; and he denominated them *Transcendental* forms. The extraordinary profoundness and precision of that man's thinking have given vogue to his nomenclature, in Europe and America, to that extent, that whatever belongs to the class of intuitive thought is popularly called at the present day *Transcendental.*

Theodore Parker's lecture *Transcendentalism* is an extended amplification of the same definition, and shows, with especial clearness, how the term was then employed.

Kant had taught that time and space are not external realities or even concepts derived from external experience, but *ways* in which the mind "constitutes" its world of sense. In terms of the familiar illustration, they are the mental spectacles through which we look. Again, cause and effect, he says, and all the other "categories" are forms or methods in accord with which the mental content is arranged. The ideas of God, furthermore, of freedom, and of immortality, are inevitable intuitions of the practical nature of man; and these intuitions, since man *is* essentially a practical and moral being, have therefore not a merely sentimental but a real validity. Now from these and other Kantian conceptions a broad generalization was made (as the passage from Emerson just quoted renders clear), and the word *transcendental* came to be applied—by the New England transcendentalists and others—to whatever in man's mental and spiritual nature is conceived of as "above" experience and independent of it. Whatever transcends (sensational) experience is transcendental. Innate, original, universal, *a priori,* intuitive—these are words all of which convey a part of the thought swept under the larger meaning of the term. To the transcendentalists the name John Locke stood for the denial of innate ideas. "Sensationalism" was the prevalent description of the doctrine of his Essay. Transcendentalism and sensationalism!—these were the poles of the philosophy of mind, and among the elect of the new movement to call a man a sensationalist was a polite way of informing him that he was an intellectual and spiritual dullard.

Transcendentalism was, then, first and foremost, a doctrine concerning the mind, its ways of acting and methods of getting knowledge. Upon this doctrine the New England transcendental philosophy as a whole was built. What the nature of that philosophy was, as has been said, is a matter of general agreement, and in setting down, briefly, its most important elements one is certain only to be repeating what has been often and well said before. Of course on minor points there is still plenty of room for controversy. One may discuss endlessly, for instance, how far Emerson's God was a personal being. It may be pointed out wherein in one respect Theodore Parker contradicts Bronson Alcott, or how in another Emerson differs from Margaret Fuller; and indeed in this connection it should not be forgotten that these transcendentalists were variously adapted, by both nature and training, for pure metaphysical thinking. But after everything has been said, there remains no possible doubt that in its large outlines they all held an identical philosophy. This philosophy teaches the unity of the world in God and the immanence of God in the world. Because of this indwelling of divinity, every part of the world, however small, is a microcosm, comprehending within itself, like Tennyson's flower in the crannied wall, all the laws and meaning of existence. The soul of each individual is identical with the soul of the world, and contains, latently, all which it contains. The normal life of man is a life of continuous expansion, the making actual of the potential elements of his being. This may occur in two ways: either directly, in states which vary from the ordinary perception of truth to moments of mystical rapture in which there is a conscious influx of the divine into the human; or indirectly, through the instrumentality of nature. Nature is the embodiment of spirit in the world of sense—it is a great picture to be appreciated; a great book to be read; a great task to be performed. Through the beauty, truth, and goodness incarnate in the natural world, the individual soul comes in contact with and appropriates to itself the spirit and being of God. From these beliefs as a center radiate all those others, which, however differently emphasized and variously blended, are constantly met with among the transcendentalists, as, for example, the doctrine of self-reliance and individualism, the identity of moral and physical laws, the essential unity of all religions, complete toler- ance, the negative nature of evil, absolute optimism, a disregard for all "external" authority and for tradition, even, indeed, some conceptions not wholly typical of New England transcendentalism, like Alcott's doctrine of creation by "lapse." But always, beneath the rest, is the fundamental belief in the identity of the individual soul with God, and—at the same time the source and the corollary of this belief—an unshakable faith in the divine authority of the intuitions of the soul. Insight, instinct, impulse, intuition—the trust of the transcendentalists in these was complete, and whenever they employ these words they must be understood not in the ordinary but in a highly technical sense. Through a failure to observe this point, and on the supposition that the word "instinct"—in the phrase "Trust your instincts"—has its usual meaning, scores of persons have completely misunderstood and grossly misrepresented the teaching of Emerson and his associates. Intuition—that is the method of the transcendental philosophy; no truth worth the knowing is susceptible of logical demonstration. Herein is seen the predominance, in the Kantian influence on this movement, of the *Critique of Practical* over the *Critique of Pure Reason.* . . .

. . . The history of American thought is, in its largest outlines, identical with that of Europe, though generally, save in politics, America lagged several decades, sometimes nearer a whole century, behind. Just as the various movements of the revolutionary age in Europe were both culminations of the eighteenth century and revolts against it, so New England transcendental- ism—whatever else it may have been—was both a culmination of that typically eighteenth century movement, early American Unitarianism, and at the same time a revolt against it. Transcendentalism, furthermore, was just such a union of thought and feeling as those we have been describing. And just as there emerged in Europe with the passing of the age of reason the longing for a new and deeper standard of truth, so transcendentalism was, in part, a search for some such profounder and more comprehensive way of grasping the nature of man and of the world.

New England took no plunge, as England did, from the moral heights of

Puritanism into the abyss of Restoration licentiousness. But there was a descent, which, if more gradual, was not on that account less real. Extreme Puritanism held within itself the germ of its own disintegration. As a mere matter of psychology, the intensity of Massachusetts Puritanism of the first generation could not be indefinitely continued, and some decline from earlier religious fervor was even more inevitable in a pioneer community where material development and protection from the Indians were crying necessities. Already, by the second generation, the falling off in piety was conspicuous, and at the time when Increase Mather was instrumental in calling the "Reforming Synod" of 1679 there was sad evidence, he believed, of "decay of godliness in the land; of the increase of pride; neglect of worship; sabbath breaking; lack of family government; censurings, intemperance, falsehood, and love of the world."[2] Though the widespread belief in witchcraft and the frequent occurrence of witchcraft delusions throughout the seventeenth century may make one hesitate to say so, it seems difficult not to regard Salem Witchcraft, from some points of view at least, as the *reductio ad absurdum* of the extreme religious spirit. It showed, apparently, that the old Puritanism had passed its prime, and it surely hastened the advent of more rational and common-sense ideas; while, to make the reaction stronger, all through the eighteenth century, especially in the neighborhood of Boston, the commercial and political questions of the day were sufficient to render impossible any exclusive absorption of the community's attention in things religious.

But the causes of these changes in the spiritual atmosphere were not wholly indigenous. English rationalistic and free-thinking tendencies penetrated to the colonies—and not always so slowly as might be imagined—and they had, particularly in the accessible region about Boston, their immediate effect. "Heresies" began to creep into the religious world. Reflecting the contemporary English interest in questions of morality, Arminianism appeared in Massachusetts, giving an unorthodox importance to matters of conduct, and attacking, though insidiously, the Calvinistic doctrine of election. The early Arminians in America, though they still believed that man was saved by the sovereign grace and mercy of God, held nevertheless that man could aid the operation of that grace by putting himself in a proper attitude for its reception, by attending, as it were, to what were called the "means" of grace; and gradually more and more efficiency was attributed to these "means." Arianism, too, appeared, subtly undermining the doctrine of the Trinity.

Nothing could show more clearly the religious condition of New England during the first half of the eighteenth century than the career of Jonathan Edwards and the story of the Great Awakening. The apprehensions of Edwards were aroused by two causes, and the Great Awakening was designed to remedy two evils—the spiritual deadness and the doctrinal heresies of the time. It need hardly be added that to Edwards these were aspects of one thing. The great wave of enthusiasm that swept over the colony was the protest against the decline of piety, the treatise on *The Freedom of the Will* the most famous part of the protest against the doctrinal Arminianism of the day. But what could better prove that New England, too, was living in the same eighteenth century with Europe, and that she was even less ready than England for any high manifestation of feeling, than the rapidity with which the emotional wave subsided and the completeness with which the old apathy returned? While the religious views of Jonathan Edwards were too spiritually lofty and too intellectually original and profound to be properly termed retrogressive in any age, and while in him and in his remarkable wife we find many anticipations of transcendentalism itself, it cannot be denied that, historically, his influence proved on the whole reactionary. Put Edwards beside any one of his Boston Arminian opponents. Can there be a moment's hesitation as to which was the greater man, the greater genius? But on the other hand, can there be any more question as to which was in closer touch with the dominant spirit of the time? The Great Awakening is the American analog of the Methodist movement—emotionally prophetic, theologically, in the main, reactionary.

The New England revival did not close the opening gulf in the religious world. It widened it rather. The efforts of Edwards had increased and consolidated the enemies he sought to slay; and the adherents of the opposing views continued in constantly diverging paths. The New Calvinists, as the followers of Edwards were called, went on to develop an American theology, uninfluenced essentially by European thought, and the large product of doctrinal discussion that resulted is the orthodox contribution to the age of reason. The liberal school, on the other hand, confirmed by the excesses of the Great Awakening in their dislike of enthusiasm, and constantly closer in touch with various forms of English thinking, grew more and more liberal, until, as the differences between their own and the New Calvinist views became wider and wider, the term Unitarian was finally applied to them.

It must not be forgotten that this movement had little direct connection with the English Unitarianism of Priestley and that it exhibited practically none of his materialistic and Socinian tendencies. This is only one reason why the term Unitarian is in some ways unfortunate, in some ways apt to prove misleading. It must be made to cover—if names are to correspond with realities—the whole early movement for freedom of thought and release from tradition within the New England religious world, and of that movement, discussions of the Trinity and of the nature of Christ were manifestly but single aspects. Unitarianism was something more than a passing agitation over a few theological doctrines. It was the product within this New England religious world of the combined rational and questioning tendencies of the age. It was contributed to not merely directly, from within, by writers or thought-currents of a religious sort; but it was contributed to also indirectly, from without, by whatever struck at tradition. Skeptical opinions that were in the air, the turmoil that accompanied the Revolutionary War,[3] speculations from France that preceded 1789 and echoes that followed it[4]—these things had various effects in various spheres of New England life, but within the religious sphere they tended, for the time, to strengthen the Unitarian position. Early American Unitarianism was eminently typical of the *critical* century in which it appeared. It seems, in many ways, much more a negative than a positive movement, or—if the term negative be objectionable—much more preparatory than final. Its essence consists more than in anything else in this: that it was a reaction from Calvinism. Its most immediate positive product was, perhaps, the atmosphere of tolerance it created.

If we have characterized the movement correctly, its continuity, then, cannot be insisted on too strongly. In 1785 King's Chapel became Unitarian by the revision of its liturgy—the first open denial of the doctrine of the Trinity by a New England church organization. This year is accordingly frequently chosen to mark the beginning of the movement. But the singling out of any one initial date is useless and confusing. The King's Chapel event was but one incident in a long development, and its real significance is that of an unmistakable sign that toward the end of the century the struggle between the liberals and the orthodox was approaching a critical stage. In this sense only it was a beginning.

In 1801, because their new pastor (Rev. James Kendall) exhibited, they thought, too advanced views, half the members of the original Pilgrim Church at Plymouth withdrew, founding a new organization that kept to the old faith. In 1805 Harvard College, which from the first had been a stronghold of the more radical thought, passed into the complete control of the Unitarians by the appointment of Rev. Henry Ware as Hollis Professor of Divinity—an event which soon caused the establishment of Andover Theological Seminary by the opposition. Another influence toward liberalism was the *Monthly Anthology*. This publication was begun (but soon abandoned) by a young graduate of Harvard. It was then assumed and continued through ten volumes by Emerson's father, the Rev. William Emerson, and the friends whom he gathered round him. This group was known as The Anthology Club, and their organ, though dedicated to the service of literature and general culture, discussed theology to some extent. In 1815 the whole controversy reached a climax, for then began—and continued for a quarter of a century—the open division of the Congregational churches into the Unitarian and the Trinitarian, a division accelerated, and on the orthodox side embittered, by the decision of the Massachusetts Supreme Court in the famous Dedham Case.

When we remember the varied tides of emotion that during these years were sweeping over Europe, the condition of New England life in the earlier decades of the nineteenth century seems, at first sight at least, somewhat inexplicable. It is clear that there had come no general invasion of European enthusiasm. Beginning about 1790—and lasting for two generations—a new series of revivals took place in the Trinitarian churches, and it is impossible to believe that these had no connection with the wider emotional currents of the day, though such a relationship it might be somewhat difficult to establish. It is obvious, too, that of the controversial sort there was no lack in the religious world of most intense and bitter feeling. But, after all, it seems plain that the spirit of the earlier eighteenth century, with all its lethargy and lack of fire, had lasted over, widely, in New England. Much of the community was still emotionally starved, and the young people especially must have looked about them in vain for that which could offer any lasting satisfaction to their deeper feelings.

The prevalent philosophy was the common-sense philosophy of Locke; the prevalent literature was still that of the uninspiring "classical" school. The educational world, conspicuously, within which the feelings of the young would naturally be fed, was infected with apathy. There is no reason to doubt that the descriptions given, for instance, by George Ticknor and James Freeman Clarke,[5] of conditions prevailing at Harvard, are just and characteristic. Of Professor John Farrar, who lectured in philosophy and the sciences, Clarke says, "He was a true teacher, but almost the only one in the whole corps of the professors." And then, as an example, is given an account of the Greek teacher, who never displayed any enthusiasm or the slightest appreciation of the poetry of *The Iliad*. The result was that the students began seeking emotional satisfaction outside the curriculum. . . .[6]

But this lack of enthusiasm, so widespread, was hardly anywhere more noticeable than in the Unitarian world. The Unitarians were, indeed, in a peculiarly untenable position. Their eighteenth century spirit had survived its usefulness—yet they clung to it tenaciously. The eighteenth century was an age of transition—and they were seeking to make its views and temper permanent. The eighteenth century was an age of compromise—and they would render its position final. The eighteenth century was an age of preparation—and they remained unwilling to advance. They had no philosophy to give their views consistency, and indeed no philosophy can be conceived that could have performed, even superficially, a task so hopelessly gigantic. With the orthodox and their "superstitions" on the one side and the kindly abyss that Hume with his logic had prepared for the reception of all rationalism on the other, the Unitarians were, most veritably, between the devil and the deep sea. And their enemies perceived their dilemma better, probably, than they did themselves. They were charged with lack of boldness in defending their position, even with cowardice and duplicity. Emerson's phrase "the pale negations of Boston Unitarianism" had, beyond doubt, justification, while Theodore Parker summed up their spiritual coldness in words that, at the same time, reveal how among the Unitarian preachers the eighteenth century interest in morality had still survived: "I felt early that the 'liberal' ministers did not do justice to simple religious feeling; to me their preaching seemed to relate too much to outward things, not enough to the inward pious life; their prayers felt cold; but certainly they preached the importance and religious value of morality as no sect, I think, had done before. . . . The defect of the Unitarians was a profound one. . . . It is a dismal fault in a religious party, this lack of Piety, and dismally have the Unitarians answered it; yet let their great merits and services be not forgot." It is indeed important that the merits of the Unitarians—in spite of the fact that their present position was a prosaic and in some respects a ridiculous one—should be remembered, for ·many and high those merits surely were. The typical Unitarian of the time, as far as there was any such, was a man of tolerance, of intellect, of cultured tastes, of unexceptionable private morality and notable civic virtue, as well as of many other admirable qualities, but not—let it be repeated—either metaphysical or emotionally spiritual in his temperament. Philosophy and enthusiasm he did not have; yet philosophy and enthusiasm were exactly the things of which his religion stood most lamentably in need.

Now the time was bound to come when the intense fervor and the new ideals of Europe should make their way to New England. And at that hour there were bound to be young people there ready to welcome and receive them. In so far as the new spirit was to enter the religious world—and it must not be forgotten that New England was still pre-eminently a religious community—it was natural, if like conditions were to produce the same or similar effects, that it should appeal most strongly to the Unitarians. Why? Precisely because the Unitarians, having taken their course in the (rational) spirit of the eighteenth century, were ready for that of the nineteenth, ready for it in a way in which the orthodox were not and could not be. If the Unitarians had carried over into the nineteenth the temper of the eighteenth century, it may almost be said—if the statement is not taken too literally—that the orthodox had carried over into the nineteenth the temper of the seventeenth century. Significant changes might first be expected then within the ranks of the "liberals," and signs were not completely lacking that changes were at work.

A man who early showed symptoms of appreciating the religious needs of the time, and who, had not early death cut short a career of exceptional promise, would inevitably have played an even more important part than he did in the development we are discussing, was the Rev. Joseph Stevens Buckminster (1784-1812). He was a preacher of great scholarship and eloquence, and of considerable literary power. The letters between the father, Rev. Joseph Buckminster (1751-1812), the stern old Calvinist, and his Unitarian son, throw much light on the times. In his sermons the latter opposed the doctrinal in favor of the spiritual and practical, and in Biblical scholarship, with the critical material and tools gained in Europe, accomplished so much that he was appointed the first lecturer in Biblical criticism at Harvard, and George Ticknor wrote of him, "It has, in our opinion, hardly been permitted to any other man to render so considerable a service as this to Christianity in the western world."

But there was another man who, more than anyone else in the religious world, showed himself open to the influence of the *Zeitgeist,* and who, largely because of this, became a power in the land whose effect is not likely to be overrated. This man, it need scarcely be added, was William Ellery Channing (1780-1842). Channing is usually spoken of as the great Unitarian, and his famous sermon on "Unitarian Christianity," preached at the ordination of Jared Sparks at Baltimore in 1819, is generally looked on as being in a sense the formulation of the denomination's creed. But if Channing was a Unitarian, he was one of an entirely new type; and with him—if we are to give him that name—the continuity of Unitarian development seems almost broken. Indeed the more one studies his character and beliefs in relation to his time, the more one must feel that he was scarcely a Unitarian at all, but rather the first of the transcendentalists. He had precisely what the Unitarians of the day had not—enthusiasm, a deeply spiritual character, and a liking for philosophy. His true position is seen in his own declaration that Unitarianism is "only the vestibule" of truth. This claim, to be sure, must not be pressed too far. In his theology and philosophy Channing appears not infrequently about half way between the Unitarian and the transcendental position. In such a sermon as his *Likeness to God* he is almost completely transcendental; but when he discourses on miracles or the future state he seems very far from Emerson and Parker. The point is, however, that he shows a development in the transcendental direction, and that all those distinctive doctrines which gave his preaching uniqueness and significance in his own day and which give him historical importance now, flowed from the transcendental elements in his belief. An example will make this clear. The Calvinists believed that human nature is totally depraved; the Unitarians denied this, their denial carrying with it the positive implication that human nature is essentially good; the transcendentalists believed that human nature is divine. What could show more clearly where Channing really stood than the fact that his "one sublime idea" was no other than this of the divinity of human nature? And further than this his temper and general spirit were singularly like those of the transcendentalists. He was, to be sure, much more conservative, but his conservatism was the inevitable outcome, among other things, of the earlier date of his birth. That his influence on the transcendentalists was so powerful and their sympathy for him so great—Emerson called him "our Bishop"—is the surest proof of the transcendentalism of his own nature. . . .

. . . He wrote in 1820:

> I have before told you how much I think Unitarianism has suffered from union with a heart-withering philosophy. I will now add, that it has suffered also from a too exclusive application of its advocates to biblical criticism and theological controversy, in other words, from a too partial culture of the mind. I fear that we must look to other schools for the thoughts which thrill us, which touch the most inward springs, and disclose to us the depths of our own souls. [7]

And these words were spoken in 1824:

> Now, religion ought to be dispensed in accommodation to this spirit and character of our age. Men desire excitement, and religion must be communicated in a more exciting form. . . . Men will not now be trifled with. . . . They want a religion which will take a strong hold upon them . . . . Much as the age requires intellectual culture in a minister, it requires still more, that his acquisitions of truth should be instinct with life and feeling. [8]

But it was not merely a new religious spirit to which Channing was awake; he appreciated as well the significance of the romantic note in the new fiction and poetry:

> The poetry of the age . . . has a deeper and more impressive tone than comes to us from what has been called the Augustan age of English literature. The regular, elaborate, harmonious strains, which delighted a former generation, are now accused, I say not how justly, of playing too much on the surface of nature and of the heart. Men want and demand a more thrilling note, a poetry which pierces beneath the exterior of life to the depths of the soul, and which lays open its mysterious workings, borrowing from the whole outward creation fresh images and correspondences, with which to illuminate the secrets of the world within us. So keen is this appetite, that extravagances of imagination, and gross violations both of taste and moral sentiment, are forgiven, when conjoined with what awakens strong emotion. [9]

Such words as these show plainly what was taking place—especially the references to "other schools" that must be looked to for "the thoughts which thrill us." That very phrase, "the thoughts which thrill us," tells it all. At last within the New England religious world was happening what had long since been happening across the water: radical ideas were being kindled with emotion. The theological and spiritual revolution that long had threatened now had come. There had been reasons for its delay. Revolutionary Europe had indeed already wrought some confusion by battering harshly on the outside of the conservative New England meeting-house; but even revolutionary Europe could cause a vitally transforming change inside only as it was the author of some new and larger ideal of truth, of some influence that could operate from within, some *positive* influence that could touch and move the very hearts of those that worshipped. The words of Channing show that such influences were now at work. German idealistic thought (especially that aspect of it which asserted new validity for the moral and religious instincts of man) and the new romantic literature—these things could operate from within, these things could appeal to the heart; and they supplied, moreover, exactly what the current Unitarianism needed most—philosophy and feeling. Their effect—as obvious reasons led us to predict—was strongest upon certain emotionally starved young people of the time and most conspicuous within the Unitarian world.

One result of this influx of radical speculation and fresh feeling was an inevitable division in the Unitarian church between those who welcomed and assimilated the new thought and spirit, and those who opposed them as dangerous and revolutionary, between the transcendentalists, that is, and the conservative Unitarians. In connection with this division it is important to notice, in passing, that the significant question is not one—for us at least—of approximation toward the truth, but one rather of adjustment to the spirit of the age; and just as there is no doubt that a hundred years before Charles Chauncy was nearer that spirit than was Jonathan Edwards, so there is no doubt that now Channing and Emerson were nearer it than—let us say—Professor Andrews Norton.

The history of this whole development may be represented roughly in some such way as this:

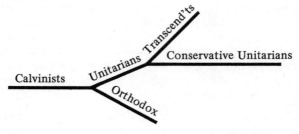

Of course such a diagram is far enough from explaining what transcendentalism—that complex product of most varied forces—really was. But it does, we think, fairly well represent its New England religious ancestry. It shows that the later division was not less real than the earlier; and it indicates in a way also that analogy with the development of European thought, on which we cannot, again, too strenuously insist. Just as the critical age succeeded the Puritan age in England, so "liberalism" came with the waning of the earlier New England spirit; and just as revolutionary Europe both repudiated the eighteenth century and at the same time accepted and transformed it, so the New England transcendentalists both repudiated and transformed with new life "the pale negations of Boston Unitarianism." They rejected its compromises; they rejected its cold spirit; but they accepted and carried further its rational method, so informing it with feeling, however, that it passed over into something quite unlike itself, the method of spiritual intuition. The diagram illustrates, too, why—though not impossible—it was hard for others than Unitarians to become transcendentalists. Individuals might and did pass rapidly over from the orthodox to the transcendental view. But after all, however unconscious of it they might be, it was Unitarianism that had made that easy transit possible. The rational spirit is the logical predecessor of the transcendental spirit. The enthusiasm of the opening sentences of Emerson's *Nature* and their easy disregard for all tradition are so spontaneous and sincere that they seem purely original. And purely original, in a sense, they are. But behind them, in another sense, are all the doubts and questionings of the age of reason, and in them the feeling of an entire epoch of European life.

It must not be understood, when we speak of a division within the Unitarian church, that there was an open schism or even, in every case, a definite taking of sides on the new issues. No; like the "liberal" movement of the previous century this movement was a gradual development, and it is impossible to put one's finger on any point and call it a beginning. Such an event, however, as Emerson's withdrawal from the ministry in 1832—owing mainly to a feeling that he could not conscientiously administer the communion—is comparable to the King's Chapel occurrence of 1785, already mentioned, and shows clearly the direction in which things were moving.

But it is especially in various publications and addresses of the fourth decade of the century that the progress of the "new" thought is most easily traced; and in confirmation of what we have said of the gradual growth of the transcendental spirit it is significant to remark that a number of these publications reached their readers through the columns of the *Christian Examiner,* the official organ of the Unitarian church. One of the most influential of them, probably, was an article on Coleridge—and incidentally on German philosophy—by Rev. Frederick Henry Hedge, which appeared in the *Examiner* for March, 1833. Hedge, who had been a pupil of George Bancroft, knew the German language well, was a man of ripe and sound scholarship, and would have played—had he lived nearer to Boston, and had his nature been a little more aggressive—a far more prominent part than he did in the movement. As it is, he must be reckoned one of the earliest and most influential of transcendentalists. There were other radical articles in the

Examiner. George Ripley, between 1830 and 1837, wrote ten such papers, "all either stating or foreshadowing his later conclusions." One of these, that on Martineau's *Rationale of Religious Inquiry* (November, 1836), caused somewhat of a sensation in conservative Unitarian circles. It elicited a reprimand for Ripley from Professor Andrews Norton in the *Boston Advertiser.*

In 1836 Emerson published *Nature*—a little work which comes nearer perhaps than anything else to being the philosophical "constitution" of transcendentalism. It was a call on the author's part to the world around him to realize that "the sun shines today also," and hence to cast aside conformity and live lives in touch with nature—"nature" in the sense of the natural constitution of things. He followed this up the next year with his Phi Beta Kappa oration, *The American Scholar,* simply an application of the conceptions of *Nature* to the world of literature and scholarship in the widest sense, a plea for originality and individualism in the realm of letters. Though in this address Emerson was careful not to let his philosophy obtrude itself, transcendental thought, nevertheless, forms the real essence of the essay. In 1838 came the *Divinity School Address,* another specific application of Emersonian philosophy, this time to the world of theology and religion. This utterance was widely considered the most radically dangerous declaration of the new school which had appeared up to that time, and called forth an immediate answer in behalf of the conservatives from Professor Andrews Norton. This, under the title, *The Latest Form of Infidelity,* was a vigorous attack on the intuitional philosophy, and elicited, in its turn, from George Ripley, a spirited rejoinder, *"The Latest Form of Infidelity" Examined.* Theodore Parker's declaration of war, his South Boston sermon on *The Transient and Permanent in Christianity,* was delivered in 1841. In connection with these various publications and addresses, here is perhaps the best place to note that the year 1838 was marked by the appearance of the first two of a significant and influential series of fourteen volumes, *Specimens of Foreign Standard Literature* (reprinted in Edinburgh in 1857), of which Ripley was the main editor. The opening volumes were called *Philosophical Miscellanies,* and contained among other things, translations from Cousin and Jouffroy. The same year saw the appearance of Emerson's collection of some of Carlyle's "Review" articles, under the title of *Critical and Miscellaneous Essays.* The American edition of *Sartor Resartus* had been issued two years earlier.

But meanwhile, long before the latest of the events we have just been chronicling, something approaching a transcendental organization had been effected. It is characteristic of the extreme individualism of the movement that it never attained a really formal organization. The dissenters did not withdraw from Unitarianism and form a new church. It was natural however, that kindred spirits who, in the words of Emerson, "perhaps . . . only agreed in having fallen upon Coleridge and Wordsworth and Goethe, then on Carlyle, with pleasure and sympathy,"[10] should find one another out. This they had done many months before any regular transcendental gatherings seem to have been contemplated. It was not until 1836 that these were begun, when on September 19—after a still smaller preliminary conference—Ralph Waldo Emerson, Frederick Henry Hedge, Convers Francis, James Freeman Clarke, and Amos Bronson Alcott, met with George Ripley at the latter's house and formed the germ of an organization to aid an exchange of thought among those interested in the "new views" in philosophy, theology, and literature. How far the later meetings were simply informal gatherings of sympathetic souls and how far there was a real distinction between members and non-members is a question concerning which there is little evidence. We may be perfectly certain, however, on *a priori* grounds, that they found it possible to dispense with all such mundane things as by-laws, minutes, and membership rolls. It was in connection with these meetings, probably, that the popular, satirical use of "transcendental" first arose. At any rate to the outside world those who attended them made up the Transcendental Club. To the initiated the group was known as the Symposium or the Hedge Club—the latter name being due to the fact that meetings of the Club were frequently called when Dr. Hedge, whose home was in Bangor, made a trip to Boston. From 1836 the Club continued to come together occasionally for a number of years—how occasionally or for how many years we do not know, for only the most meagre reports and records of the gatherings now exist.

Among those who were not at the first but who joined the group at later meetings, or were present now and then, were: Theodore Parker, Margaret Fuller, Orestes A. Brownson, Cyrus A. Bartol, Caleb Stetson, Elizabeth and Sophia Peabody, Thoreau, Hawthorne, Jones Very, Christopher P. Cranch, Charles T. Follen, and William Henry Channing. Dr. Channing and George Bancroft seem to have been present on one occasion. Of the men just mentioned to whom we shall not make further extended reference, there are two to whom, partly from their eccentricities, there attaches a peculiar interest—Jones Very and Orestes A. Brownson. We may pause here, then, long enough to remark that Very was a clergyman and poet of an extreme mystical tendency, whose capacity for soaring above terrestrial conditions of time and space gave rise to many amusing anecdotes of varying degrees of authenticity. Of Brownson and his erratic career we may note that, having passed through successive stages of Presbyteriansim, Universalism, Socialism, and Unitarianism, and having coquetted with transcendentalism (and, it might be added, with politics), he completed the cycle of his intellectual and religious experiences by emerging in 1844 as a full-fledged Roman Catholic. He spent much of the rest of his long life in administering ferocious chastisement to Protestantism—and incidentally to transcendentalism—in the columns of *Brownson's Quarterly Review.* The militant element in his nature is hinted at in Dr.

Hedge's remark *apropos* of the Transcendental Club: "Brownson met with us once or twice, but became unbearable, and was not afterward invited." Yet there is no doubt that Brownson was a man of exceptional ability.

For some time before anything definite came of the desire, it was felt by the aspostles of the new movement that they ought to have a literary organ, and in 1840, with the appearance of the first number of the *Dial,* this long-projected transcendental magazine became—to use a phrase which in different senses will satisfy all—a realized dream, with Margaret Fuller for editor and George Ripley as assistant editor. It never even approached financial success, and it was only through real devotion and sacrifice on the part of its editor and Miss Elizabeth Peabody that it was continued as long as it was. Miss Fuller resigned the editorship after two years and Emerson assumed it for a like period, after which the magazine was discontinued. Whatever defects the *Dial* may have had—and it obviously had many—a comparison of its pages with the dusty contemporary numbers of, let us say, the *North American Review,* is enough to convince one that the claim of its main contributors that they were dealing with subjects whose interest in a measure transcends time, is not entirely without foundation. The journal discussed questions of theology and philosophy; it contained—besides many other things—papers on art, music, and literature, especially German literature; translations from ancient "Oriental Scriptures"; original modern "scriptures" in the form of Alcott's *Orphic Sayings;* and finally, a good deal of verse. In this latter connection, one of the most interesting aspects of the *Dial* today is the opportunity and encouragement it afforded to the genius of Thoreau. Besides his and Emerson's, there were, among others, metrical contributions from Lowell, Ellery Channing, and Christopher P. Cranch—the latter one of the most picturesque figures of the period (an ex-minister who gave up preaching to study art abroad), poet, painter, musician, and ventriloquist. The *Dial,* it is needless to remark, did not satisfy the public. Hundreds of parodies, especially of the *Orphic Sayings,* were forthcoming, and "epithets, too, were showered about as freely as imitations; the Philadelphia 'Gazette,' for instance, calling the editors of the new journal 'zanies,' 'Bedlamites,' and 'considerably madder than the Mormons.'" Nor did it even fulfil the hopes of the transcendentalists themselves. Alcott thought it tame and compromising: "It satisfies me not, nor Emerson. It measures not the meridian but the morning ray; the nations wait for the gnomon that shall mark the broad noon." On the other hand Theodore Parker's declaration that his own *Massachusetts Quarterly Review* (1848-1850) was to be the *Dial* "with a beard" indicates that he thought the earlier periodical had offended in quite an opposite direction. On the whole, however, whatever our judgment of its intrinsic merit may be—and the mere fact that it contains some of Emerson's best known poems and essays is enough to establish a degree of such merit—we shall not be likely to overrate its significance in the history of American literature or the importance of the part it played in our literary emancipation.

Much more remotely connected with the Transcendental Club than the *Dial* was the Brook Farm enterprise. . . .

George Ripley, its head, was a graduate of Harvard and a Unitarian minister. As we have already seen, the nature of his beliefs was too radical for the Unitarian audience that listened to him, a fact which, together with his wide studies of European writers, led him gradually to see his duty more and more along the line of social reform. He accordingly left the pulpit; and in 1841 he and his enthusiastic wife gathered around them a number of supporters, subscriptions were received at $500 a share for the "Brook Farm Institute of Agriculture and Education," and the enterprise was begun with ten signers of the "Articles of Association" and by the purchase of a farm at West Roxbury, nine miles from Boston. While Brook Farm must not be considered an attempt at socialism, it was nevertheless collectivistic and communistic in its tendency. The hope was to make it a self-supporting group of men and women, where all should share in the manual labor, the leisure, and the educational and cultural advantages, and life be lived under something approaching ideal conditions. There has been ample testimony from the members that the attempt was far from being entirely unsuccessful. The adoption in 1844, with some modifications, of the principles of Fourier, seems, however, to have put an end to some of the more Arcadian features of Brook Farm; and this, together with the fact that the efforts of inexperienced farmers on a rather poor farm yielded insufficient financial return, was enough to doom the experiment to ultimate failure. The disbanding of the members was immediately occasioned by the burning in 1847 of the new "phalanstery," erected at a cost of ten thousand dollars, and—by an appropriate "transcendental" irony, some will be inclined to comment—uninsured. We must not forget to remark that for a time the Brook Farmers had a literary organ, *The Harbinger*.

There were other attempts during the transcendental period at ideal living. Of Bronson Alcott's communal experiment, "Fruitlands," which with his family and two English friends he undertood on a farm in Harvard, Massachusetts, and which cold weather brought to a speedy and disastrous conclusion, we shall have occasion to say something later on. Of Thoreau's two years at Walden Pond (1845-1847) almost everyone has heard. There, with a small cabin for headquarters, he practised an extreme form of the "simple life," studying the phenomena of nature, communing with her spirit, and noting down his observations and reflections in voluminous diaries. Both these enterprises—Alcott's and Thoreau's—were in most respects strikingly different in intent from Brook Farm. Especially was the Walden Pond episode, in its individualism the most completely transcendental of any of these experiments.

Mention should not be omitted of one other feature of the period—we mean the well-known "conversations." These seem on the whole to have been of the nature of informal lectures, the audience generally being small and the speaker willing to be interrupted by questions or comments. Sometimes the "talk" was more evenly distributed among those present, and the leader acted more as the chairman of a conference who had also the privilege of the floor. The conversations of Alcott and Miss Fuller have attained much notoriety and some fame. Alcott made use of the conversational method in his school teaching, but it was not till after the failure of his Temple School in 1839 that he ventured a trial of his theory in public. From that time, off and on, for a good many years he gave lectures of the conversational type. Miss Fuller's conversations began in November, 1839, and were held consecutively for five winters. The subjects dealt with were Greek Mythology, Fine Arts, Ethics, Education, the Influence of Woman. The conversations were held as a rule at the end of the morning, twenty-five or thirty being the average number present. "Ten or a dozen, besides Miss Fuller," says Mr. Higginson, "usually took actual part in the talk. Her method was to begin each subject with a short introduction, giving the outline of the subject, and suggesting the most effective points of view. This done, she invited questions or criticisms: if these lagged, she put questions herself, using persuasion for the timid, kindly raillery for the indifferent. There was always a theme and a thread."

The consideration of a further important aspect of transcendentalism, its relation to the anti-slavery agitation, may best be reserved for a later part of the discussion. Meanwhile, one question, suggested by this reference to slavery, belongs to the present chapter, the question: When did the transcendental period close? There can surely be little dissent from the proposition that the movement was at its height during the years 1835-1845; but to choose a date to mark its conclusion is just as impossible as to select one to designate its beginning. The results of a movement are often not less significant than its causes in explaining its real nature, and to obtain a true conception of transcendentalism it is as necessary in some cases to follow the lives of the transcendentalists even beyond the middle of the century, as it is to trace the early development of Unitarianism, or . . . to examine the intellectual and literary influences that moulded the thinking of these men.

NOTES

1. "I call all knowledge *transcendental* which is occupied not so much with objects, as with our *a priori* concepts of objects. A system of such concepts might be called Transcendental Philosophy. . . . Transcendental Philosophy . . . is a system of all principles of pure reason. . . . Transcendental philosophy is the wisdom of pure speculative reason." Introduction to the *Critique of Pure Reason* (pp. 9, 11, 12, translation of F. Max Müller, Macmillan, 1896).

2. Quoted from Williston Walker, *A History of the Congregational Churches in the United States* (New York, 1894), p. 187.

3. See "Life in Boston in the Revolutionary Period," by Horace E. Scudder, being chapter 4 of volume III of *The Memorial History of Boston*, ed. Justin Winsor (Boston, 1881).

4. William Ellery Channing's account of conditions at Harvard at the time he entered college (1794) gives an idea of the feeling of unrest that pervaded the country. "College was never in a worse state than when I entered it. Society was passing through a most critical stage. The French Revolution had diseased the imagination and unsettled the understanding of men everywhere. The old foundations of social order, loyalty, tradition, habit, reverence for antiquity, were everywhere shaken, if not subverted. The authority of the past was gone. The old forms were outgrown, and new ones had not taken their place. The tone of books and conversation was presumptuous and daring. The tendency of all classes was to skepticism." W. H. Channing, *The Life of William Ellery Channing, D.D.* (Boston, 1899), p. 30.

5. James Freeman Clarke, *Autobiography, Diary, and Correspondence,* ed. E. E. Hale (Boston, 1891), pp. 36-39; *Life, Letters, and Journals of George Ticknor,* 2 vols. (Boston, 1877), I, chap. 18.

6. "They did not read Thucydides and Xenophon, but Macaulay and Carlyle. . . . Our real professors of rhetoric were Charles Lamb and Coleridge, Walter Scott and Wordsworth."—a statement which shows that the condition of emotional indifference still survived at the time when the writings of Macaulay and Carlyle were becoming known.

7. W. H. Channing, *Life,* p. 276.

8. *The Works of William Ellery Channing, D.D.,* 14th ed., 6 vols. in 3 (Boston, 1855), III, 146.

9. *Ibid.,*

10. *The Complete Works of Ralph Waldo Emerson,* Riverside Edition, 12 vols. (Boston, 1884), X, 323.

12

Ripley, Emerson, and the Miracles Question

WILLIAM R. HUTCHISON

CORNELIUS FELTON, ELIOT PROFESSOR OF GREEK AT HARVARD, admitted to his friend Andrews Norton in 1840 that he had a somewhat personal reason for disliking Transcendentalist ideas. "German metaphysics and philosophical religion," he said, "make me feel like a mouse under an air pump."[1] Norton himself, who led the Unitarian opposition to Transcendentalism in the 1830's, had no similar feelings of helplessness; or if he had, he was not the kind to acknowledge them. As James Walker was later to say, Norton was a man who not only disliked groping in the dark, but who also made it a policy to keep his own counsel about such uncertainties as did beset him. When he announced scholarly findings and doctrinal interpretations, he invariably spoke with the self-assurance of one who has found the only possible answer. As a teacher in the Divinity School, he gained a reputation that was the exact reverse of the one Convers Francis was later to acquire. While Francis' students were annoyed by his insistence on considering all sides of all questions, Norton's complained of their teacher's impatient refusal to sympathize with their doubtings. Norton, as Walker recalled, "never put

From *The Transcendentalist Ministers: Church Reform in the New England Renaissance* by William R. Hutchison. Copyright © 1959 by Yale University Press.

himself to much trouble to comprehend the ignorance or the errors of other people." If students appeared unconvinced by a conclusion which to him was clear and unarguable, he simply gave them up.[2]

In the Transcendentalist controversy which first broke out in November 1836, Norton applied these lecture-hall methods in the larger arena of public dispute, where they aroused enough indignation to make his name a lasting symbol of dogmatism and utter illiberality. Indeed, historians have sometimes given the impression that Norton's name stood for little else in the public mind of his own day. But contemporaries found Norton personally admirable, as well as formidable in the field of scholarship. In ordinary intercourse, if not always in the classroom, he was known to be amiable and generous, "modest even to diffidence." "Few men have ever lived," Walker said, "who had less of ill-will or unkindness."[3] And George Ripley, Norton's foremost opponent among the Transcendentalists, in later years paid tribute to the man's "thorough scholarship . . . refined and exquisite taste . . . hatred of pretension [and] devotion to truth."[4] Norton's excellence as a scholar was well known to his contemporaries, and so was his early record as a champion of liberality in opposition to Calvinist dogmas. The public estimate rested as much upon his *Genuineness of the Gospels* and his *Statement of Reasons* as upon the *Discourse on the Latest Form of Infidelity,* which is now commonly treated as his chief claim to attention. Norton exercised a degree of influence which would not have been possible to such an unreasoning pedant as the usual caricature presents.

His attitude toward the European philosophies and biblical studies of his time was, however, an illustration of the positiveness for which Norton has been remembered most widely. If he ever experienced Felton's sense of being tossed about intellectually by those powerful Germanic currents, he had no intention of admitting it. He was perfectly confident that he knew which of the foreign speculations had validity and which had not.

As a biblical scholar, Norton stood firmly in the tradition of literary and historical analysis in which the names of Simon, Bentley, John Mill, Wettstein, and Griesbach were most prominent. The general tendency of these critics, whose work spanned the period from the end of the seventeenth to the end of the eighteenth century, had been toward a rejection of the theory of verbal inspiration. Their researches, which led at first to a recognition of the internal contradictions of Scripture, by the beginning of the nineteenth century had influenced such scholars as Norton to take historical circumstances, peculiarities of idiom, and the prepossessions of writer and audience into account when interpreting a scriptural passage or inquiring into its authorship.[5]

Among the types of speculation which Norton opposed were, first of all, those which presupposed a suprasensory mode of receiving religious truth,

and which therefore tended to minimize the importance of such manifestations as the biblical miracles. Locke and the Scottish realist philosophy
formed the basis for his thought, and for his opposition to romantic intuitionism. He criticized Schleiermacher, along with Spinoza before him and such
later theologians as DeWette, Paulus, and Strauss, for their alleged reduction
of Divine Personality to a pantheistic omnipresence in the soul and in
Nature.[6] He also rejected the conclusions reached by German biblical scholars
in the "quest for the historical Jesus" which Schleiermacher's *Reden über die
Religion* (1799) had initiated. Belief in both the personality of God and the
divinity of Christ was being undermined, Norton believed, by the interpretations of Eichhorn, who doubted the traditional authorship of the Gospels; of
DeWette, who advanced a theory of "complements and interpolations" to
account for the inconsistencies of Scripture; of Baur and the "Tübingen
School," advocates of an Hegelian explanation of the emergence of early
Christian doctrine; and of Strauss, whose *Leben Jesu* (1835) denied scriptural
authority and treated the New Testament narratives as chiefly mythical.
Norton's work on the *Genuineness of the Gospels* was a defense of the Bible's
claim to divine inspiration against the incursions made by these critics.[7]

In the fall of 1836 George Ripley in Boston and William Furness in
Philadelphia both became open advocates of theories of biblical interpretation which Norton had rejected. Both of them made the argument, among
others, that the miracles of Jesus, though perfectly authentic, were not
performed for the purpose of confirming the truth of Christ's teachings.
Norton reacted violently to Ripley's article, in a letter to the *Boston Daily
Advertiser,* but oddly enough offered no public objection to the speculations
of Furness.

Furness, to be sure, had given a more conservative appearance to his
thought by expatiating on the beauty of Christ's character and the absolute
reliability of the Gospel accounts; but the differences between Furness' ideas
and Ripley's were not sufficient to explain the variance between Norton's
reactions to the two writings. The real reason for that variance grew out of
the respective circumstances of publication.

All of Norton's protests in this and later stages of the "miracles" controversy showed a marked concern not only about dangerous opinions but also
about the auspices under which the opinions were expressed. His usual
justification for entering a dispute of this nature was that he believed the
Unitarian reputation (and indirectly his own) was at stake. In the dispute of
1836, Norton was protesting against Ripley's ideas, but almost equally against
the bad judgment of the editor of the *Examiner* in allowing such heresies to
appear in an official Unitarian organ.

This interpretation is confirmed in the correspondence which took place
between Furness and Norton before and after publication of the *Four*

Gospels. Furness, too cautious a man to plunge boldly into controversy, had shown his manuscript to several friends in Philadelphia during the summer of 1836; and when some of these persons were doubtful whether he ought to publish it, he had written asking Norton to read the work and give his opinion. Norton apparently sent a polite refusal, explaining that although he could not agree with the thesis which Furness had outlined to him, he did not believe an authoritative stamp of approval was necessary for a manuscript published on the author's own responsibility. Furness accordingly sent the work to the press in mid-August, and it was on sale in Boston by November 12.[8] By December, Norton had read the *Four Gospels,* and he told Furness that his views were mistaken but not especially dangerous. Since, by that time, Norton's denunciation of Ripley had already appeared in the Boston papers, Furness was understandably gratified that his book had escaped censure.[9]

The importance of the question of "auspices" is further underlined by the fact that the opinions to which Norton took such violent exception in Ripley's article not only were similar to those of Furness' book but were announced in a much less formidable way. They appeared somewhat incidentally in the last seven pages of a thirty-page review.

The work reviewed, James Martineau's *Rationale of Religious Inquiry,* was an attempt to find the "seat of certainty" in Christianity by critical analysis of both Catholic and Protestant doctrines, and by application of the inductive method to religious practices. Ripley applauded this attempt to promote a scientific approach to the study of theology. Where he took exception to Martineau's ideas, he did so, ironically enough, more from a conservative than from a radical point of view: his complaint was that Martineau seemed to deny the divine inspiration of the writers of Scripture. He thought that this denial marked a peculiar inconsistency in an author who appeared to rest almost the entire case for Christianity on the authenticity of the miracles of Jesus.[10]

It was in his remarks on the second half of this alleged inconsistency that Ripley ventured into dangerous territory. Although miracles are important and are entirely credible, he argued, acceptance of them had never in the past been demanded of all who call themselves Christian, and ought not to be now. He admitted that Jesus may sometimes have used miraculous displays to help in confirming the source of his authority, but thought that neither divine authority nor moral teachings could have been authenticated by miracles alone, since in the time of Jesus miracle-workers were everywhere. If Christ's doctrines had not been true and convincing in themselves, no one would have believed that he came from God, nor would they have obeyed his teachings.[11] Ripley thus brought into public discussion, through the medium of a representative Unitarian publication, the view he had been preaching since 1834 that Christ was simply the enunciator of religious truths which would have been equally valid had he never come.

The young theologian was not unmindful of the opposition which his doctrine of miracles would arouse among orthodox Unitarians. Despite the apparently casual manner in which he had broached the subject, the move had been a deliberate one. He had discussed his intention with Theodore Parker, who had warned him that "the first one who lifted a hand in this work would have to suffer," and had advised him to "push some old veteran German to the forefront of the battle, who would not care for a few blows."[12]

The vehemence of Andrews Norton's reaction justified such apprehensions as those of Parker. Norton's first impulse on reading the article expressed itself in a letter which he drafted, but evidently did not send, to James Walker, editor of the *Examiner*. He asked Walker to announce in the next issue that Andrews Norton had severed his connection with the journal.[13] He regretted, he said, that the managing editors had not seen fit to consult him "before anyone was allowed to take such grounds" in the *Examiner*. Since the mischief was now irremediable, he said, he had no course but to disassociate himself from the magazine. "Every individual has some influence," he added modestly; and he was unwilling that his own should be perverted to "the publication of such doctrines in a work of popular instruction."[14]

Whether or not this letter was ever dispatched, Norton shortly decided upon a somewhat different course. Instead of announcing withdrawal of his support from the *Examiner*, he contented himself with a public letter expressing his disapproval of Ripley's position. Sidney Willard, editor of the weekly *Christian Register*, declined "from personal considerations" to print this missive,[15] and it appeared instead in the *Daily Advertiser* of November 5.

Norton's letter began by expressing the "surprise and sorrow" which he felt on reading the concluding passages of Ripley's review. The theory outlined there was not only wrong, he said, but also capable of doing infinite damage, since it tended to destroy faith in "the only evidence on which the truth of Christianity *as a revelation* must ultimately rest." He had no wish, he said, to interfere with "the rights of free discussion," but it seemed to him that those rights were too often misunderstood. Certain limits must be fixed for the good of the community.

Norton then suggested, in what was by far the most objectionable part of his communication, that two rules should in future be followed by writers attempting to controvert doctrines which those "who have thought most concerning them" consider true and important. The first rule was that such innovators must be perfectly certain that they have "ability to discuss the subject." The second was that they should withhold their views from publication pending approval by "those who are capable of judging of their correctness."[16]

To Ripley, whose reputation for careful scholarship was not greatly inferior to that of his former teacher, and who had been a preacher and editor long enough to know something about his responsibilities to the public, it was not pleasant to receive a knuckle-rapping for neglecting to have his composition approved. His reply appeared in the *Advertiser* on November 9, and under the circumstances it showed admirable restraint. "I would have to forget the benefits I have received from the severity of your taste and the minuteness of your learning," he told Norton, ". . . before I can persuade myself to discuss any subject with you in a manner incompatible with your superiority in years and attainments to myself." He felt, however, that Norton's charge of "heresy" could only be called absurd; and he added, in a phrase that must have struck home for non-Unitarian readers, that "we are both too deeply laden with offences of that kind to make the spectacle of our flinging stones at each other anything but ludicrous." The public would be especially amused, he thought, to find Norton showing such outraged concern about a signed article in a periodical of which he was not the editor. They would be asking whether the writer were not "of age to assume his own responsibilities."

Aside from all this, he said, the charges of heresy had been put forward in an unfair manner. Norton, "with singular indefiniteness," and without deigning to discuss the issues, had pronounced Ripley's article injurious to the public good. Was it not rather late in the day, Ripley asked, for this kind of demagogic appeal "to the fears of the uninstructed?"

The younger man proposed to lay the whole case before the reading public, "to whose verdict, on such points, I attach more importance, than you think it deserves." To show that his understanding of the miracles had ample precedent, he cited the Scriptures, the Fathers of the early Church, the Protestant reformers, and several modern theologians. He trusted that these citations would at least indicate "that I did not utter my opinion without thought."[17]

The editor of the *Register,* despite his earlier refusal to publish Norton's letter, now, at Ripley's request, printed the whole exchange, though he was circumspect enough to ask his readers to observe that "we make no comments."[18] Few further contributions to the argument appeared in the *Register* for a month; but on the tenth of December an unsigned letter appeared which deserves to rank far above Norton's as a statement of conservative objections to Ripley's views.

Ripley's very justifiable complaint that Norton had tried to suppress his arguments instead of discussing them was fully recognized by this later correspondent. The writer decried Norton's alarmism and expressed his own appreciation of the desirable spiritual emphasis which the Transcendentalists were bringing into Unitarianism. Then, after making every concession to the spatial limitations under which Ripley's remarks had been set down, he proceeded to give a detailed reply from the conservative point of view.

The true issue, this correspondent said, was whether or not Christianity is merely a set of moral and ethical teachings. If it is nothing more than this, he argued, then the miracles are at most a kind of seal of approval used to inspire confidence in the authority of the teacher; but if, as Christians have always believed, the primary importance of Jesus was his announcement of a divine interposition in human affairs, then miracles confirm this special divine action. While it may be true, he said, that the mere ethical teachings of Christianity could have been conveyed by a natural process, God's sending of his Son to redeem the world constituted a supernatural intervention which could be confirmed only by supernatural occurrences.[19]

Although this balanced criticism represented the reaction of a considerable body of Unitarians, and in fact reflected the position of the *Register* itself, [20] Norton's stronger aspersions also found support. Professor George Noyes of Harvard Divinity School and Charles W. Upham, pastor of the First Church in Salem,[21] both wrote to Norton to express support of his stand. Upham stated that, while he regretted that his friend Ripley had been exposed to censure, he was relieved that someone of influence had spoken out against Transcendentalism, which he considered "absolutely and not remotely, of infidel tendency and import."[22]

Another Salem minister, eager to discipline the *Examiner* though singularly vague about its offenses, reported to Norton that, while he had not read Ripley's article, he could judge from Norton's letter in the *Advertiser* "what its import is," and he suggested, somewhat cabalistically, "a meeting of a few persons, at some convenient place," to take concerted measures for bringing the *Examiner's* editorial policy into line. He had recently written the *Examiner,* he said, to complain about certain articles on the Resurrection and "on Swedenborg (I believe it was)," but had received very unsatisfactory replies from the editor. He had also been disturbed by "some papers published by Mr. Brownson" in praise of Thomas Carlyle. He found it impossible, he said, to understand what Mr. Carlyle's opinions really were, but he did know "that his admirers belong to the class of persons" who were endangering the morals of the community.[23]

William Henry Furness, whose good fortune and observance of protocol had helped him to escape Norton's censure, was not entirely spared by other critics of Transcendentalism. An *Examiner* review of *Remarks on the Four Gospels* expressed "unqualified dissent" from Furness' naturalistic theory of miracles, and linked that heresy to Ripley's. "There is a class of writers among us," said this reviewer, "who are, consciously or unconsciously, *philosophizing* away the peculiarities of the Gospel, and reducing it to a level with mere naturalism." Although Furness might not consider himself one of this class, the reviewer added, it was undeniable that his theories tended in a harmful direction. "The arrow has been discharged from the bow; where it may fall, or whom it may wound, is not for him to determine." On the whole, despite a personal veneration for the ideal of free expression, the writer was "disposed to regret" the publication of the work.[24]

James Walker, as editor of the *Examiner,* apparently felt little concern about Furness' "dangerous tendencies"; for the latter was allowed to answer his critic in the next issue. In this article Furness re-affirmed his "naturalistic" explanation of the miracles, though he side-stepped the question of indispensability which had so aroused Norton against Ripley.[25]

This first stage of controversy had run its course by mid 1837, but the attack upon conventional religion which the *Examiner* had seen as merely a "tendency" was made explicit in Emerson's Divinity School Address of 1838, and the reaction this time was not so short-lived. Again, as in the disturbance of two years earlier, the question of sponsorship was prominent, for the speaker to this official gathering had been invited by vote of the graduating seniors.

Under such circumstances, even a vague statement of transcendental commonplaces might have caused something of a stir. It is not surprising, therefore that Emerson's premeditated and for him systematic attack upon the popular theology provoked a major controversy. The ideas in the Divinity School Address were not new.[26] The pronouncement achieved its status as epoch-making because it was the first Transcendentalist attack upon Unitarianism which left no avenue of escape from open conflict. If the reformers followed Emerson's prescription as given in this famous sermon, they would not attempt "to project and establish a Cultus with new rites and forms," but would concentrate instead upon breathing "the breath of new life . . . through the forms already existing."[27] Reforming energies were not to be siphoned off harmlessly into a new and eccentric religious sect, but were to be applied to the radical remaking of Unitarianism.

Emerson began his address by setting forth the philosophical basis for the reforms which he proposed. Reiterating the thesis of *Nature,* he pointed out the correspondence between the consummate beauties of the Earth "in this refulgent summer" and the perfection of those spiritual laws which "traverse the universe and make things what they are." He then carried the discussion immediately into the realm of morality by explaining a further correspondence: that between the "spiritual laws" of the universe and the moral law within the human mind. "The sentiment of virtue," he said, is nothing but the response of the receptive heart to "certain divine laws" which are perceived by introspection and are immediately recognized to be the laws of the universe as well as of the mind. The spiritual laws cannot be made into formulae, he explained, but their operations can be described: these laws oversee all moral activities, and with a "rapid intrinsic energy" execute rewards and punishments for each human deed at the very moment it is being carried out. The operations of the spiritual laws have always "suggested to man the sublime creed" that the world is the product "of one will, of one mind"; and it is this conviction, he said, which originally creates and shapes religious institutions.

The speaker's complaint against conventional Christianity was that this intuitive basis of religious institutions and creeds has been forgotten. In Christianity, as in some other religions, he said, men have lost their belief in direct inspiration. Having, nonetheless, a sort of nostalgia for their lost faith, they pretend that one man or a few men in all of history have been capable of receiving direct intuitions of truth, and they accordingly attribute to these favored individuals the "divinity" which rightly belongs to all men.

Jesus, Emerson explained, proclaimed not his own divinity, but that of the human soul. Though Christ spoke of miracles, he meant only that all of life is a miracle. And when the writers of Scripture claimed to be inspired of God, their meaning was simply that all men are inspired. It is, he claimed, only the later interpreters—the formulators of "historical Christianity"—who have imagined otherwise.

The Christian Church, Emerson thought, has not only fostered false and redundant doctrines, but also, conversely, has neglected to preach Christ's real message, namely man's direct access to the spiritual laws. Popular preaching, he said, is ineffectual because ministers of the Gospel are unaware even of the possibility of direct inspiration, and therefore have not attempted to attain that experience or lead others to it.

Emerson's basic prescription for remedying the ills of the Church was the replacing of "second-hand" formulae with spiritual insights gained at first hand. Opponents afterward liked to quote his declaration that "the remedy . . . is first, soul, and second, soul, and evermore, soul"; but he also stated the solution in more precise terms. He told the young graduates to "go alone," to eschew conformity, and to have higher than common standards of morality. Instead of attempting revolutionary departures from the existing institutional forms, they were to make use of the instruments which Christianity provides, especially those of preaching and the Sabbath. Above all, they were to communicate "a faith like Christ's in the infinitude of man."[28]

The phrasing of this last admonition suggests the most fundamental of the disagreements between Emerson and standard Unitarianism. The doctrine he advocated was "faith in man," a faith not "in Christ" but "like Christ's." This

implicit rejection of the usual Christian Confession was made more galling to
conservatives by Emerson's searing allusions to formalism and coldness in the
pulpit, and by his sometimes deprecatory phrasing. His remark, for example,
that "Miracle, as pronounced by Christian churches, is Monster," was regarded as irreverent. His call for "a new Teacher" seemed clearly to be a
denial that the religion of Jesus is God's final or even his most complete
revelation.[29]

The first manifestation of the bitter controversy stirred by this discourse
was not an argument about Emerson's opinions but rather a confused attempt
to fix responsibility. Emerson himself clearly had no wish to be looked on as
a spokesman for anyone else,[30] but he was, after all, a prominent alumnus of
the College and Divinity School, and one who had been preaching with some
regularity in Unitarian pulpits for over a decade. Cambridge theologians,
therefore, asked indignantly whether the Senior Class was willing to sponsor
Emerson's heresies; Unitarian clergymen asked the same about the faculty of
the Divinity School; and non-Unitarians queried and happily affirmed, by
turns, the responsibility of the whole denomination.[31]

The young seniors were in the least enviable position in this crossfire. They
wrote Emerson to say that although some of them disagreed with the ideas he
had expressed, all thanked him for speaking at their graduation. They were
uncertain, they said, whether under the circumstances the address should be
published or merely printed and circulated privately.[32]

Publication eventually was decided upon. After August 25, when the
Address was placed in the hands of the public, there was no longer any reason
for Unitarian conservatives to hold their fire, and within two days Norton had
expressed his reaction in the pages of the *Advertiser*. The vitriol in this
outburst made the attack upon Ripley two years earlier seem relatively mild.
Norton began by ridiculing the entire New School in the most abusive terms.
Their aberrations had arisen, he said, because of a "restless craving for
notoriety and excitement," which had recently been intensified by the praise
which "that foolish woman" Harriet Martineau had accorded the Transcendentalists in her work *Society in America*.[33] Transcendentalist ideas, he said,
were the outgrowth of "ill-understood notions, obtained by blundering
through the crabbed and disgusting obscurity of some of the worst German
speculatists." Most of the American Transcendentalists, Norton thought, had
not even bothered to read the Germans at first hand but had relied upon the
interpretations of Carlyle and Cousin—both of whom received suitably de-
rogatory epithets from Norton's angry pen. And he added a denunciation of
"the atheist Shelley," whose sole relevance to this discussion was that the
Transcendentalist *Western Messenger* had printed something favorable about
his poetry.

Norton then elaborated upon some of the less technical characteristics of the New School, its "extraordinary assumption . . . great ignorance . . . incapacity for reasoning . . . contempt for good taste . . . " and "buffoonery and affectation of manner." Ordinarily, he said, such absurd persons as the Transcendentalists would not merit notice of any kind; but Emerson's recent discourse had attacked principles basic to the good of society, and apparently some "silly" people were being persuaded to abandon Christianity for Transcendentalism. The situation therefore had become "disastrous and alarming."

As in his reprimand of Ripley, the author again disdained to examine the arguments he was condemning. "It is not necessary," he explained, "to remark particularly on this [Emerson's] composition. It will be sufficient to state generally, that the author professes to reject all belief in Christianity as a revelation," and "makes a general attack upon the Clergy, on the ground that they preach what he calls 'Historical Christianity.' " Emerson, so far as Norton could discern, did not believe in God in any "proper" sense of the term.

Having stated his adversary's views to his own satisfaction, Norton remarked that "what *his* opinions may be" was a matter of minor concern. Emerson might believe whatever he liked; and it could hardly be expected "that his vanity would suffer him long to keep his philosophy wholly to himself." A more serious question was how such a dangerous man had been permitted to speak before the Divinity School on an official occasion. The Senior Class, by inviting Emerson, had made themselves accessories, and Norton thought they owed an explanation to the public for their part in this "great offense."[34]

The denunciatory retort from Norton is the one that has been remembered by historians of the Transcendentalist Movement, but it was nonetheless unrepresentative of the general Unitarian reaction. Some members of the Boston Association raised the question whether Emerson should be called a Christian,[35] but most of the earliest conservative commentaries on the Divinity School Address show as much embarrassment and annoyance about Norton as disagreement with Emerson.

Theophilus Parsons, a prominent lawyer who later became a Professor in the Harvard Law School, wrote to the *Advertiser* on August 30 attempting to set the conservative argument on sound footing.[36] He first reprimanded Norton for his "outbreak of indignant contempt." While he agreed that Emerson and the new philosophy were dangerous, he could not believe that error would be defeated by "anger, derision, intolerance, and blind and fierce denunciation." The effect of Norton's arguments, he thought, had been to show that their author was afraid of new ideas merely because of their newness; certainly no more plausible objection to Emerson's philosophy had been stated. As for the letter's charges of "assumption," "ignorance," and "incapacity of reasoning," Parsons could only inquire incredulously: "Where sits the judge who passes such a sentence?"[37]

Even more critical of Norton's stand was another correspondent, writing to the Boston *Morning Post.*[38] Like Parsons, this conservative thought Emerson's opinions were wrong. The attitude of "the Cambridge Professors," however, seemed to him to verify the maxim "whom the gods will destroy they first deprive of reason." If it was true, he suggested, that young people were being led astray by Emerson, it might be that these young people had looked to the Cambridge professors for support in free inquiry, and had not received it. The followers of Emerson, as this writer remarked in words that remind one of a similar appraisal by Matthew Arnold, undoubtedly valued him less for his opinions than for his insistence upon spiritual freedom. "It is as the advocate of the rights of the mind, as the defender of personal independence in the spiritual world, not as the Idealist, the Pantheist, or the Atheist, that he is run after."[39]

Norton's tirade, far from placing the Unitarian conservatives in a less vulnerable position, had aggravated an already delicate problem in disentanglement. Some who would have joined immediately in a tactfully engineered disavowal of Emerson's ideas were now unwilling to associate their names with Norton's in such an effort. Of those who found themselves in this situation, none was more painfully tried than the Rev. Chandler Robbins, a young man twenty-eight years of age who a year earlier had been chosen editor of the *Register.*

Robbins, though staunchly orthodox, was Emerson's personal friend and his successor at the Second Church. For this reason, and also, perhaps, because the *Register* had always tried to remain neutral in intra-Unitarian disputes, the paper took no stand on the current controversy until it had raged a full month. Direct challenges from non-Unitarians, however, finally provoked Robbins into entering the fight.

Early in October the Rev. M. A. DeWolfe Howe,[40] an editor of the Episcopal *Christian Witness,* jabbed at the entire Unitarian party by telling his readers that in the absence of any official pronouncements to the contrary, it must be assumed that Transcendentalism had infected at least one entire wing of Unitarians. "Let it not be supposed . . . that the young saplings alone have bowed before this 'wind of doctrine:' No—some of the sturdiest cedars in their Lebanon have felt its influence."[41] When another outsider, two weeks later, addressed a letter directly to Robbins, asking him whether the *Register,* "as the organ of the Unitarian body," regarded Emerson as a "fair representative" of that Church, the detached attitude could no longer be maintained.

Robbins' answer to the challenge was that neither the Unitarian Church nor any of its members made themselves responsible for opinions expressed by one of their number. Speaking for himself, he said that he dissented from

Emerson's ideas but had a high regard for their expositor as a person, and disliked the "popular roar" which had arisen against him. "That liberal Christians are called upon to father and answer for all his peculiarities of opinion," Robbins said in summary, "this we stoutly deny . . . but, that he is a highly gifted, accomplished and holy man, and at heart and in life a Christian, we shall not cease to believe and to declare, until we see the best of reasons . . . "[42]

Norton, who had just finished explaining to the public that Emerson was not a Christian, of course found it unsettling to have the *Register* declare that he was. With characteristic impulsiveness he immediately drafted a public letter criticizing editor Robbins. Instead of sending this one immediately to the papers, however, he took the precaution of showing it first to his brother-in-law, Samuel A. Eliot,[43] who suggested some dozen changes "which, without altering the meaning or the force of the article, will qualify the manner." Eliot advised his relative to add "we conceive," or "it seems to us that . . . " to some of the stronger assertions. He also suggested that Norton's description of the Transcendentalists as "puffed up with mystical, irreligious speculations" would impress some readers as "slightly contemptuous."[44]

Norton did accept these modifications, and the letter in its final form somewhat restored his reputation as a polite controversialist. Transcendentalism was still branded as Atheism, but the arguments against it were now more reasoned and the angry epithets were missing. Norton argued that the *Register's* disclaimer of responsibility for Emerson's opinions was nugatory, since it could "be made equally of any individual," however damaging his heresies. The plain fact was, he said, that un-Christian doctrines were being preached by professedly Christian and Unitarian ministers. Robbins' assertion that Emerson was not an infidel amounted only to the use of words "in a new, arbitrary, false sense." As far as opinions (as distinguished from morals) were concerned, he could think of "no infidel who is not entitled to the name of Christian, if it be due to Mr. Emerson." The total effect, he thought, of Robbins' editorial had been to place a major Unitarian newspaper squarely behind infidelity.[45]

Robbins' hurt reply three days later accused Norton of having "ranked me with a class of men to which I do not belong," and thus of jeopardizing his standing with the public and his congregation. Norton, he complained, had chosen to overlook all of his distinct disavowals of Emersonian opinions. If he was to be censured for commending Emerson, he ought also to be commended for censuring him.[46]

In a *Register* editorial that same week, Robbins reiterated his personal distaste for the "popular roar" against Emerson, and with some bitterness asked his readers' forgiveness "for not always chiming with the prevailing tone of censure." Unfortunately, he said, he found himself "constitutionally prone to sympathize" with good men whose real and supposed faults have become "the fashionable quarry" among critics who "should hold their peace, and do penance in secret before God for their own unworthiness." He realized, he added sarcastically, that a penchant for noticing the good qualities of an unpopular figure "is almost an *intolerable* fault in the editor of a paper devoted to Christian Liberality." For this and other reasons, he declared, he would soon cease to impose himself upon the readers of the *Register.*[47]

At this juncture, Eliot interposed his good offices to end the increasingly personal dispute between his relative and Robbins. When Norton showed him another letter, a tedious defense of his dealings with the young editor, Eliot instead of suggesting revisions proposed a settlement out of the journalistic court. In a frank appeal to Norton's paternal instincts, Eliot assured him that Robbins was actually a lad of sound heart and good intentions, lacking only "a little force of character" to make him a man of thoroughly proper opinions.[48] Norton, who for all his assertiveness seems to have valued the advice of his peers, agreed to send the letter directly to Robbins instead of to the papers, and Robbins replied to this magnanimity in a deferential if not thoroughly chastened manner.[49]

In the sequel to this small drama, the *Register* continued its advocacy of fair treatment for Emerson; and when Robbins eventually carried out his earlier threat of resignation, he was able to state triumphantly that many readers had written supporting his position. The paper had gained more subscribers than it had lost. Robbins had discovered, in other words, that "the popular roar" was not so universal as it had appeared to be at first. His Parthian shot as he took leave of his critics was that he "would not now erase one sentiment to which they have objected" in his editorials.[50] Robbins had marshaled enough "force of character" to effect a successful holding action, if not an outright victory, for the party of tolerance.

If Emerson's successor at the Second Church was torn between personal loyalties and public responsibilities, the situation of his former colleague in that church was equally painful. Henry Ware, Jr., owed a heavy debt of gratitude to the young man who, in the earlier years of Ware's ill health, had assumed the heaviest burdens of the Second Church pastorate; and to Emerson, Ware had always been *le bon Henri.* Writers on Transcendentalism, nonetheless, have usually pictured Ware as hastening rather angrily to rebuke Emerson for the Divinity School Address, and of attempting to goad him into a public debate.[51] The facts of the episode do not entirely support this interpretation.

On the evening of July 15, 1838, Emerson and his wife, though declining

Ware's invitation to stay the night at his home, remained long enough to discuss the discourse which Emerson had just delivered at the Divinity School. In the course of their conversation, Emerson made some qualifying remarks which caused Ware to say that he might be able to assent to the ideas in the Address if such qualifications were added to them. On the following day, however, feeling that he had conceded too much, Ware wrote Emerson to say that the discourse had contained some statements which he could not accept even with modifications. Some of Waldo's ideas, he had decided, were "more than doubtful," and would "tend to overthrow the authority and influence of Christianity" if widely accepted. He added that he rejoiced in Emerson's "lofty ideas and beautiful images of spiritual life," and that he would never have mentioned the reservations which he felt if "a proper frankness" had not required it.[52]

Emerson, in reply, acknowledged that while he could not have withheld any part of his thought, he had been aware that his words would offend "dear friends and benefactors of mine." He promised Ware that the manuscript would be carefully revised before it was sent to the printer. "I heartily thank you," Emerson added, "for this renewed expression of your tried toleration and love."[53]

In September 1838 Ware put some of his objections to Transcendentalist ideas in a sermon called *The Personality of the Deity.* Christianity, he declared, asserts that God is a Person who wills and acts, who loves and exacts obedience. Attempts to reduce God to an abstract set of laws or moral relations are, therefore, essentially vicious. Some men, he acknowledged, may hold erroneous beliefs about God and yet live blameless lives, for "to the pure, all things are pure." But in general, a doctrine of Divine Impersonality robs morality of its sanctions and makes true piety impossible.[54]

Although Ware did not mention Emerson in this discourse, or specifically identify the theories he was opposing as "transcendental," it was clear that Emersonian ideas had been prominently in his mind as he wrote. Using some of the very words and phrases of Emerson's Divinity School Address, Ware denied that the laws of God are comparable to the law of gravitation, that reverence for the ordinances of Nature is what produces all forms of worship, or that laws which "execute themselves" can be the laws of God. He seemed clearly to be answering Emerson when he denied that a man's ultimate responsibility is to his own conscience. And his assertion that Christ cannot be ranked with "Plato or Mahomet . . . Luther or Confucius . . . Fénélon or Swedenborg," even reflected the cataloguing device which was a trademark of Emerson's prose style.[55]

These apparently obvious though inexplicit allusions to the controversial Address caused Ware's colleagues to seize upon his sermon as an authoritative and direct rebuke to Emerson. At their request he had the discourse published, and immediately felt under obligation to send a copy to Emerson with an explanatory word. He told Emerson that he had meant to controvert current errors of doctrine, including some which he believed were present in the Divinity School Address. The sermon, however, had been one of a series on the doctrine of God, and had been planned before Emerson's Address was given. "If I assail positions, or reply to arguments, which are none of yours," Ware wrote, "I am solicitous that nobody should persuade you that I suppose them to be yours." He was, he said, "particularly unhappy to be thus brought into a sort of public opposition to you."[56] Ware was perhaps less than candid in trying to minimize the degree to which his sermon had been directed against Emerson, but it would seem that he had little intention of drawing his former colleague into open debate.[57]

If Ware was unwilling to say precisely whom the shoe was supposed to fit, other conservatives were not so cautious. The *Christian Examiner,* by reviewing Emerson's discourse and Ware's sermon together, succeeded in confirming the impression which Ware himself—somewhat belatedly—had sought to avoid. Some of the "intolerant" suggestions in this brief and anonymous notice[58] were destined to be associated with Ware's name long after his own painstaking fairness had been forgotten. The reviewer began by assuring readers that he was taking note of Emerson's "strange notions" solely because the community desired to know whether or not Unitarians approved them. The answer, he said, was that most Unitarians considered Emerson's theories "so far as they are intelligible . . . to be neither good divinity nor good sense."

The reviewer was not equally certain about the reactions to Emerson among students in the Divinity School. He assumed that they had not been taken in; but he thought that in the future, measures should be taken to prevent student exposure to such doctrines: "The instructors of the School should hereafter guard themselves, by a right of veto . . . against the probability of hearing sentiments, on a public and most interesting occasion, and within their own walls, altogether repugnant to their feelings, and opposed to the whole tenor of their own teachings."[59]

This suggestion, both in content and in phrasing, was too reminiscent of classic illiberalism to be appreciably softened by anything else the reviewer might say. He did, however, attempt to reconcile it with the Unitarian pretensions to open-mindedness. "We beg to be understood," he said, "as not questioning the right of the author of this address to utter his own thoughts in his own way." The reviewer had no wish "to fetter the human mind by the bonds of prescription and antiquity"; but surely it was not persecution when Emerson had exercised his own right to speak "freely and boldly," for others to dissent with equal boldness.[60]

For the defenders of Emerson, this gesture in the direction of free inquiry hardly met the case. Denouncing heterodox opinions, they said, was one thing, but banning them from expression at Harvard was quite another. The Transcendentalist *Western Messenger* asked why there should be such solicitude for the "feelings" of certain professors. "Was the Cambridge Divinity School built up for the benefit of its instructors? Were its professorships endowed for the purpose of giving certain gentlemen the opportunity of disseminating *their* opinions?"[61] As for Norton's apparent desire for an official condemnation of Emerson, the *Messenger* reminded Unitarians that their church, having no synods or formal creeds, could have no use for the weapon of excommunication. The editors suggested that "if Mr. Emerson has taught anything very wrong," it would be found out, and he and other Unitarians would quietly part company.

Readers were also cautioned against Norton's ill-considered attempt to link the opinions of the New School to those of a miscellaneous list of foreign writers. The Transcendentalists, said the *Messenger,* had their unity not in common attachment to any set of foreign writers whatever, but simply in their desire for "more of LIFE, soul, energy, originality" in religion and letters.[62]

Orestes Brownson also came to the aid of his fellow Transcendentalists. Before Norton's intervention had raised the issue of free inquiry, Brownson had expressed serious reservations about the Divinity School Address. He had criticized Emerson's idea of "obedience to self" as tending toward "pure egotism." It amounted, he thought, to "deification of the soul with a vengeance." Such a position could hardly escape atheism, since "the soul's conception of God is not God, and if there be no God out of the soul, out of the *me*, to answer to the soul's conception, then is there no God." Brownson also had thought Emerson's thrusts against "historical Christianity" too extreme. The Church, he acknowledged, plainly has erred "by giving us only the historical Christ, but let us not now err, by preaching only a psychological Christ." In spite of all these reservations, Brownson brought the heavy ordnance of his argumentative powers to the support of Emerson once Norton's ill-tempered attack had given a new turn to the controversy. Norton's heresy-hunting, Brownson said, was inexcusable. "The brand of heresy is and long has been as deep on him as it can be on anyone else . . . " And Brownson suggested that the charge of skepticism was more clearly applicable to those who could believe nothing without the miracles than to others who could believe everything without them.[63]

Emerson himself had not spoken a controversial word since the Divinity School Address, and he was to be even less a participant in the next phase of the dispute. Oliver Wendell Holmes aptly likened Emerson's position at this time to that of Patroclus when the Greeks and Trojans fought over his body.[64] By late 1839 George Ripley had stepped into the role which

Emerson declined to fill—that of chief polemicist and champion of Transcendentalism against the conservative attack.

Ripley's former altercation with Norton, over the Martineau review of 1836, had had little apparent effect upon his high standing among Unitarians. His markedly transcendental *Discourses on the Philosophy of Religion,* published in Boston in late 1836, and the first volumes of *Specimens of Foreign Standard Literature,* issued under his editorship in 1838, had been praised by the Unitarian periodicals.[65]

Late in 1839 Ripley was drawn back into active controversy to answer Norton's *Discourse on the Latest Form of Infidelity.* Norton had delivered this in July at the behest of the newly formed "Association of the Alumni" of the Divinity School. Arguing clearly and without the denunciatory language of his newspaper appearances, the conservative champion had pointed out the difficulty of explaining the words and actions of Jesus if the place of miracles is depreciated. Christ, Norton said, indicated clearly that his miracles attested his mission. If we do not believe that they had this function, then we must believe Jesus either a fiend or a madman for having spoken as he did. What is more, said Norton, the absence of miracles would leave Christianity without any authentication whatever; for the transcendental "religious sentiment," despite all claims made for it, is ultimately less dependable than the testimony of the senses. Those who belittle sense experience because it is contingent and uncertain, Norton argued, are asking for a degree of metaphysical certainty which simply is not attainable. In religion, as in all other areas of human knowledge, we must be content to rest our belief upon the strongest probabilities, as these are determined by the wisest teachers.[66]

The Transcendentalists' objections to this argument were intensified by Norton's addition, in the published version, of appendices in which he analyzed the "infidel" speculations of Hume, Spinoza, Schleiermacher, Hegel, Strauss, and DeWette—and clearly implied that the New School in America were guilty of the same errors. This implication was bitterly resented, as was Norton's pompous assumption that ordinary persons must rely for their interpretation of Christian truth upon the findings of such learned persons as himself. Another major objection was that Norton, having placed the foregoing philosophers and their supposed American adherents under a common antimiracle rubric, denied the right of the Transcendentalists to appear before a credulous public as "Christian" teachers.[67]

George Ripley's rejoinder, published anonymously as *"The Latest Form of Infidelity" Examined,* recorded the Transcendentalists' demurrer to all of the foregoing assertions,[68] and, leaving the defensive, reproached Norton for pretending that his own peculiar views were universally accepted Christian doctrines. The "personal dogma" of which Ripley particularly complained was Norton's alleged insistence that miracles are the only possible proof of Christianity,[69] and he attempted to show, by lengthy citations of Christian writers of all periods, that this was a doctrine almost unique with Norton, and not even espoused by that theologian himself at an earlier time.[70]

Norton's reply to this charge was that Ripley had gone to great pains to prove something which had not in the least been denied. What he had meant, Norton said, was that miracles are the only means of authenticating a revelation and proving that it is actually from God, not that men are convinced of the truth of Christianity by no other evidence than the miraculous.[71] The distinction here would seem to be a small one, since Norton still held that miracles are the decisive form of evidence; that is, that without them no other proof of Christian doctrine would be convincing. But a certain amount of accommodation had been achieved between the two schools of opinion. Norton had implicitly made the concession, significant to the Transcendentalists, that men are sometimes persuaded of the truth of Christianity by other evidences than the purely empirical.

Except for his clarification on this point, Norton's second pamphlet was merely an attempt to vindicate the author's former aspersions against Spinoza, DeWette, and Schleiermacher, all of whom he had accused of denying the personality of the Deity.[72] And Ripley, the somewhat overconscientious scholar, unfortunately allowed himself to be lured into this irrelevant textual analysis. This was an especially grave tactical blunder, since it seemed to confirm what Norton had assumed from the beginning, that the Transcendentalists were committed to defend these writers. Ripley's last two pamphlets in the series[73] gave 218 pages in all to this scholarly analysis and only nine pages, at the end of the second pamphlet, to a treatment of the real issue.

In those final passages Ripley gave an able summary which might have attracted some notice if published separately. Norton's form of supernaturalism, he said, was a logical deduction from the Lockean philosophy, but both the doctrines and the philosophy are rejected by "the universal consciousness of man." "Does the body see, and is the spirit blind?" Ripley asked. If the spirit were "blind," then Norton would be right, and religious truths would be "a mere balance of probability, decided by intellectual researches." The certainty of faith would then have to proceed from "reliance on others; not from a spiritual witness in ourselves." But most men, he said, will never believe that this is so.[74]

Young Theodore Parker entered the controversy at this point, under the pseudonym of "Levi Blodgett." Parker's pamphlet served the purpose of publishing the Transcendentalist case in a form which the public would read. "Blodgett" declared that to unlearned persons like himself it certainly seemed that faith in Christ precedes and does not depend upon faith in miracles. The miracles, whose validity he cordially affirmed, are only added confirmations for an essentially intuitive belief.[75]

If Ripley allowed another person to give the final word on the Transcendentalist side, his adversary also stepped aside at this point, and the current stage of the Transcendentalist controversy was brought to a close with Norton's republication of *Two Articles from the "Princeton Review."* These articles constituted a systematic and hard-hitting criticism of the "impious temerity" of German philosophizing, and of its "hideous and godless" results. Though sympathetic to the need for a more spiritual philosophy in American religion, the authors deplored the fact that foreign imports, rather than native intelligence, had been appealed to for a corrective.[76]

It has been usual in accounts of the Transcendentalist controversy to accept a somewhat overcaricatured Andrews Norton as typical of the Unitarian conservatives. The truth is that Norton gave way to more even-tempered men after the first four years of a controversy which continued for seventeen years. It is also highly probable that one reason for Norton's complete abstention from debate after 1840 was the stubborn refusal of the denomination in the 1830's to support his program of exclusion. Whether from timidity or some better reason, the men most in agreement with Norton doggedly refused to come out publicly for his measures. Thus the almost reverential attitude which Norton's colleagues expressed toward his leadership has overtones of polite appeasement, and the bold champion of conservatism may well have felt that he was being humored. It is clear that he felt and deeply resented his isolation.

Typical of the encomiums heaped upon Norton through private correspondence was that contained in a letter from the Rev. Charles Upham. "We look to you alone in this exigency," Upham wrote.

> Dr. Channing favors the new views. . . . Dr. Walker has never lifted a finger against them. In point of fact he has favored them, and his appointment to Cambridge was hailed as the first step towards bringing the college and Unitarianism to Transcendentalism. My only hope is in you. May your life be spared to deliver us from a state of things which . . . could only issue in the destruction of the faith . . .[77]

A Philadelphia Unitarian wrote that he had been shocked to hear two of his fellow citizens, shortly after the Divinity School Address, discussing the "open and formal declaration of unbelief in Christianity" which had been made by Emerson on behalf of Harvard University. The writer had "speedily communicated this fact," he said, to Harvard authorities, but no official disclaimers had been forthcoming.[78]

Henry Ware, Jr., praised Norton for his "noble and astonishing forbearance," and another writer contrasted the "calmness and elevation of spirit" in Norton's pamphlets with Ripley's "bitterness and unkind feeling." This correspondent said he had been confident from the beginning that the Cambridge leader would answer *"triumphantly,"* and had found his arguments "perfectly satisfactory and convincing." Ezra Gannett thanked Norton for having put his mind at rest about German philosophy, which he said he had previously opposed without fully understanding.[79]

The profound deference felt for Norton is further evidenced in letters from two Unitarians whose support Ripley might have hoped to gain in this dispute. George R. Noyes, the biblical scholar who because of suspicions raised in 1834 about his orthodoxy has sometimes been cast as a sort of forerunner of Transcendentalism,[80] told Norton that while he had not read Ripley's pamphlets, he had known in advance "what his views are, and what his mode of defending them, viz. by the use of language which means one thing to the initiated, and another to common people." And the Transcendentalist William H. Furness again notified Norton that his own orthodoxy was intact despite his unusual theory of the miracles. "However peculiar my own views," Furness wrote, "I cannot endure that these important facts should be rejected, or thrown into the shade."[81]

The *Christian Register,* even under the new and "safer" editor who had replaced Chandler Robbins, tried to maintain a neutral position. "If this subject must be discussed," the Rev. Rufus Johnson pleaded, "let us do it in perfectly good humor." But the *Register* later devoted four long editorials to a good-humored defense of Norton. Waxing ecstatic and almost lyrical, Johnson assured readers that "he ever moves in light. Mists disperse as he advances ... It is really refreshing in the midst of those flitting phantoms, shadows and clouds which are lowering on the regions of theology, to hear a certain, decided, penetrating, calmly confident voice."[82]

But this kind of support, even in the public prints, was no substitute for a real participation in Norton's campaign by such men as the Wares, Channing, Walker, Gannett, Palfrey, and Noyes. What was worse, the two men who shared pre-eminence with Norton in Unitarian leadership, Walker and Channing, had flatly and openly rejected his view of the Transcendentalist danger. Walker in 1840, addressing the same group of Divinity School alumni who had heard *The Latest Form of Infidelity* the previous year, had the effrontery to call for a more balanced understanding of the foreign philosophies and less unreasoning alarm about them. After pointing out the valuable contributions of Schleiermacher, DeWette, Kant, Cousin, and others, Walker declared that though "men may put down Transcendentalism if they can ... they must first deign to comprehend its principles."[83] And Dr. Channing, who in 1838 had said he doubted whether Emerson meant to deny a personal Deity, greeted Walker's conciliatory speech of 1840 by saying he was "glad to learn that Dr. Walker understands the spirit of our alarmists." Opponents of Transcendentalism, he said, were showing "a want of faith in religion . . . more alarming than the infidelity which they condemn."[84]

As if this show of high-echelon complacency were not bad enough, it suddenly appeared that Norton's three-year campaign to control the Unitarian publications had been a labor of Sisyphus. The *Examiner* published an article by Andrew Peabody, the Unitarian minister in Portsmouth, New Hampshire, which agreed with the Transcendentalists that "a belief in miracles constitutes no part of a sanctifying faith in Christ." Peabody, aiming at conciliation, asserted that Norton's charge of "infidelity" had been leveled only against the German philosophers; and he innocently represented Norton as valuing miracles mainly because they bolster the faith of the unlearned masses. "The vast majority of the ignorant, the unspiritual, and the sinning," Peabody explained, must rely upon supernatural evidences; and the chief error of the Transcendentalists was that "in the retirement of their studies" they had simply forgotten "that all men were not as spiritual as themselves."[85]

Truly dismayed by this new evidence of the *Examiner's* waywardness, Norton wrote an angry private letter to the editor, William Ware.[86] With his usual tact he told Ware that "it is clear from the manner in which the *Christian Examiner* has been conducted that you have not thought and felt on this subject as I do, probably because you have known less about it." The *Examiner's* delinquency, he said, was symptomatic of a general attitude on the part of conservative leaders, whose course "with some honorable exceptions" has been "equally ruinous and discreditable."[87]

William Ware replied to these strictures with dignity and with even more firmness than Chandler Robbins had shown under a similar attack. He insisted that the *Examiner's* moderate course had been the correct one. He could not agree, he said, either that Unitarians had been negligent in combating the current heresies, or that any significant number of American Transcendentalists had accepted the skeptical conclusions of foreign philosophers. Four or five, he admitted, may have gone beyond the pale of Christian belief; but he knew of only two members of the Boston Association who had done so (a reference probably to Parker and Ripley); and the other members of the Association had made plain their rejection of the ideas of these two.

Ware, while acknowledging that Peabody's review had contained a lower estimate of miracles than Norton himself would agree to, contended that the article "was certainly a Christian one." The *Examiner,* in fact, had been exercising such caution about accepting radically transcendental pieces that the editors had been charged with "exclusiveness" by no less a Unitarian leader than Dr. Channing. "You will acknowledge the difficulty of my position," Ware ventured. But he added, after some thought about that doubtful proposition, "I cannot suppose that I have satisfied you."[88] Norton indeed was far from satisfied, and he wrote William Ware again to suggest that when the *Examiner* should get around to reviewing the whole Ripley-Norton controversy, he would be glad to "furnish the reviewer with some facts, that he might not else observe or be aware of."[89]

When this accommodating proposal produced nothing, Norton attempted to step around the editor and supply a reviewer as well as material. In April 1840 he asked Professor Palfrey to write an article refuting Ripley's second pamphlet. If Palfrey would undertake this work in the *Examiner,* it would, he said, "go far to settle the vacillating character of that publication," and would encourage those "who think rightly" to speak out. Norton explained that he hesitated to write the review himself, lest this be taken as "the pleading of an advocate in his own cause."

To forestall Palfrey from arguing lack of time, Norton assured him of "such assistance as would bring the labor within a narrow compass." He then added several pages of detailed instructions as to what ought to be in the review, and concluded by promising that "if you will give me any encouragement, I will go on with my comments."[90] Whether or not the good Doctor gave encouragement, the projected article did not appear, and the *Examiner* continued to represent a counsel of moderation.

While Norton was making these somewhat frenetic final efforts behind the scenes, George Ripley, too, was moving off the stage of controversy, and was issuing the last proposals of his career as a church reformer.

Ripley's final break with the Unitarian ministry was not lightly undertaken or rapidly effected. His first move was a letter to the "proprietors" of his church in May 1840, in which he spoke of the poor financial condition of the society and suggested his own resignation as a remedy.[91] The proprietors would not hear of his resigning on these grounds, but Ripley then expressed more basic reasons for his proposal. He felt, as he told the parish in October 1840, that the relationship between pastor and people had become strained. Some of his parishioners had been complaining about his liberal theological and social opinions. He had tried to minimize the friction by preaching on traditional, noncontroversial subjects, but this had become a burden to himself. He could continue to minister to them, he said, only if they would consent to reforms in pastoral duties and church organization.

The first of Ripley's demands was that the congregation must allow him to preach on all subjects of human concern. He proposed, secondly, that the pew-ownership system should be abolished, or should at least be modified in such a way that parishioners would no longer have reason to continue as members after they had ceased to sympathize with the views of the minister.[92]

Negotiations continued until the beginning of 1841, by which time Ripley had concluded that the society would not accept his reform proposals. On the first of January he tendered his resignation, and this was accepted with expressions of great and undoubtedly sincere regret.[93]

In Ripley's *Farewell Discourse,* which was filled with kindly sentiments toward the congregation as a whole, the one harsh note was a bitter commentary on the pressures which had been exerted upon him by some members of the society and by his critics in the recent public controversy. Ripley told his parishioners that their pastor would not have had to leave the ministry if he had been

> more inclined to conform to ancient usage; if he were willing to work in the yoke of popular customs, to take his views of truth from his elders . . . if he would acquiesce more readily in prevalent errors and abuses; if he would take the social standard of Boston at this moment as the everlasting standard of right . . . in short, if it were his aim to be more of a priest and less of a man.

He had always been, he said, and would continue to be "a peace man, a temperance man, an abolitionist, a transcendentalist, a friend of radical reform in our social institutions." If Unitarians could not bear to hear discussion of those subjects from their ministers, then he must cease to be a minister.[94]

Despite the acerbity of these remarks, neither the church nor the Unitarian community judged harshly of Ripley. The society's "farewell Resolutions" were warmly eulogistic. The *Register* praised Ripley's "Christian attainments." And Gannett's *Monthly Miscellany,* after expressing the regret of the community about Ripley's departure, wished him success in his projected "educational experiment" at Brook Farm which, as Gannett remarked acutely enough, did not sound at all "transcendental."[95] With the launching of the new utopian community on November 1, 1841, Ripley passed permanently from the role of church reformer.[96]

The first stage of the Transcendentalist controversy had ended in a stalemate which gave no clear indication of the direction which Unitarianism would take in dealing with the Transcendentalist challenge. The conservatives had achieved some unanimity in defining their stand on the miracles question. They had taken a position clearly favoring a supernatural interpretation of Christianity, an interpretation to which many of them thought belief in miracles was an essential corollary. But no significant amount of support had appeared as yet for Norton's proposal to anathematize transcendental speculations and deny the Christian name to those who doubted supernaturalist doctrines.

Despite the traditional conception of this early phase of the controversy as one in which intolerance and exclusiveness reigned on the conservative side, it is questionable whether more than two individuals could justly be accused of doing violence to Unitarian principles of free expression in their opposition to Emerson and Ripley. These two are Norton and the author of the proposed ban on nonconforming speakers at Harvard Divinity School. The School faculty did exercise their right to approve graduation speakers after 1838, and there were many whose personal attitude toward the Transcendentalists showed something bordering on exclusiveness. But official pronouncements, and also influential private opinion, leaned heavily on the side of moderation. The Unitarian tradition of liberality had not, as yet, given way to the exigencies of doctrinal defense.

Norton, whose efforts to bring a different result had put him in such an unfavorable light, must nonetheless be credited with having discerned the radical implications of Transcendentalism more acutely than either his hesitant colleagues or the Transcendentalists themselves. Leaders on both sides were sufficiently attuned to the movements of contemporary thought to know that a debate over Christian supernaturalism was no mere teapot tempest; and their repeated references to the foundations of "popular faith" showed a common awareness of the extent to which such questions as that of the miracles were the stuff of ordinary discourse in nineteenth-century New England. Neither party was quibbling over a few loaves and fishes. But Norton, in addition to recognizing the deeper issue, plotted a future course for Transcendentalist logic and found it ending not in the worship of Christ but, at most, in the veneration of Jesus. The later struggle over christology in liberal Protestantism showed the cogency of this projection.

Norton, however, was dealing with men as well as abstractions, and men have a right to their inconsistencies. There is real injustice, as well as futility, in assuming that one's opponents will be utterly logical, and in denouncing conclusions which they have not admitted. With the notable exception of Theodore Parker, the Transcendentalists were to stop short of an explicit rejection of revealed Christianity. In this perspective the failure of Norton's enterprise in the 1830's stemmed not merely from the infelicities of his debating methods but even more from the fact that he was combating Theodore Parker several years before the latter's appearance in the conflict.

NOTES

1. Felton to Norton, December 1840, in the Andrews Norton Collection, Harvard University Library. Hereafter, this collection will be designated NC.

2. Samuel A. Eliot, ed., *Heralds of a Liberal Faith,* 4 vols. (Boston, 1910-52), II, 197-98. Hereafter designated as Eliot.

3. Eliot, II, 195, 197.

4. In Justin Winsor, ed., *The Memorial History of Boston . . .* (Boston, 1880-81), IV, 299.

5. George A. Buttrick, et al., eds., *The Interpreter's Bible* (New York: Abingdon-Cokesbury, 1952-57), I, 128-32; Wright, in George H. Williams, ed., *The Harvard Divinity School: Its Place in Harvard University and in American Culture* (Boston, 1954), pp. 46-49. For Norton's acknowledgments to this group of biblical critics, see his *The Evidences of the Genuineness of the Gospels* (abridged ed., Boston, 1867), pp. 202, 417-25, 450-53.

6. Andrews Norton, *A Discourse on the Latest Form of Infidelity . . . 19th of July, 1839* (Cambridge, Mass., 1839), pp. 41-47; *Remarks on a Pamphlet Entitled " 'The Latest Form of Infidelity' Examined"* (Cambridge, Mass., 1839), pp. 11-70.

7. Buttrick, *Interpreter's Bible,* I, 132-34; Norton, *Genuineness of the Gospels,* pp. 24-27, 45-47, 180-82, and passim.

8. *Christian Register,* November 12, 1836.

9. Furness to Norton, July 15, August 14, December 12, 1836, NC.

10. *Christian Examiner,* XXI (1836), 225-45.

11. *Ibid.,* pp. 249-53.

12. O. B. Frothingham, *Theodore Parker: A Biography* (Boston, 1874), pp. 78-79.

13. Norton since 1835 had been one of the "sponsors" of the magazine. F. L. Mott, *History of American Magazines,* 4 vols. (Cambridge, Mass., 1938-57), I, 287.

14. Norton to Walker, November 1, 1836, NC.

15. It was characteristic of Willard to avoid controversy, but his motive in this case may have been a feeling of deference toward his predecessor Ripley. Willard was a former Hancock Professor of Hebrew and Oriental Languages in Harvard College. After 1830 he devoted his time to editing various periodicals, and to public office. He died in 1856. See his *Memories of Youth and Manhood* (Cambridge, Mass., 1855).

16. Boston *Daily Advertiser,* November 5, 1836.

17. *Ibid.,* November 9, 1836.

18. *Christian Register,* November 12. After a month of the controversy, Willard still found it impossible to disagree with either participant; see his editorial of December 10. Cf. letters from correspondents, *Register,* November 19, December 10.

19. *Christian Register,* December 10. The tone and logical preciseness of this composition suggest Gannett as the author.

20. *Ibid.*

21. An able Unitarian controversialist, Upham later attracted notice as a Whig politician, and gained literary immortality as the supposed prototype of Hawthorne's Judge Pyncheon. *Dictionary of American Biography.*

22. Noyes to Norton, July 25, 1837; Upham to Norton, November 5, 1836, NC.

23. John Brazer to Norton, November 7, 1836, NC. Brazer had been Professor of Latin in Harvard College 1817 to 1820; Merle E. Curti, in the *Dictionary of American Biography,* interprets Brazer's leanings toward natural religion as anticipations of Emersonian thought, but it appears that Brazer himself would have been scandalized by this suggestion.

24. *Christian Examiner,* XXII (1837), 104. The reviewer was M. L. Hurlbut, a teacher and Unitarian clergyman of Philadelphia. See H. H. Hurlbut, *The Hurlbut Genealogy . . .* (Albany, 1888).

25. "The Miracles of Jesus," *Christian Examiner,* XXII, 283-321.

26. See Clarence Gohdes, "Some Remarks on Emerson's 'Divinity School Address,' " *American Literature,* I (1929), 27-31.

27. *The Complete Works of Ralph Waldo Emerson,* Centenary Edition, 12 vols. (Boston, 1903-04), I, 149-50.

28. *Ibid.,* p. 144.

29. *Ibid.,* pp. 136-42, 129, 151.

30. Letter to Henry Ware, Jr., October 8, 1838, *The Letters of Ralph Waldo Emerson,* ed. R. L. Rusk, 6 vols. (New York, 1939), II, 166-67.

31. Theodore Parker penned an amusing account of this exchange of recriminations in a letter to George Ellis (August 7, 1838), in F. B. Sanborn and W. T. Harris, *A. Bronson Alcott, His Life and Philosophy,* 2 vols. (Boston, 1893), I, 279-81.

32. Emerson, *Letters,* II, 147. The seven members of the Class of 1838 were Benjamin Fiske Barrett, Harrison Gray Otis Blake, Theodore H. Dorr, Crawford Nightingale, George F. Simmons, Frederick A. Whitney, and William D. Wilson. *Harvard University Quinquennial Catalogue* (Cambridge, Mass., 1930), p. 1114. Robert C. Waterston, who studied at Cambridge "under the personal charge" of Drs. Ware and Palfrey, was co-signer of some of the group's communications with Emerson. Eliot, II; Emerson, *Letters,* II, 147.

33. 3 vols. (London, 1837), III, 284-85, 342-59.

34. Boston *Daily Advertiser,* August 27, 1838.

35. Frothingham, *Parker,* pp. 107-08.

36. Authorship of this letter is noted by Norton on his own clipping; NC.

37. Norton, answering the Parsons letter several days later, wrote that there had been no need to use reasoned arguments in answering Emerson, since the latter had himself used no arguments but had confined himself to "professions of infidelity and irreligion." *Daily Advertiser,* September 1, 1838. A rebuttal by Parsons appeared on September 3.

38. The writer, according to Norton's notation, was "G. T. Davis." Probably the reference is to George Thomas Davis, lawyer and editor of Greenfield who was then serving in the Massachusetts House of Representatives; he later became a Whig Congressman. NC; *Lamb's Biographical Dictionary.*

39. Boston *Morning Post,* August 31, 1838.

40. Howe (1808-95) became a bishop of the Episcopal Church, and was the father of the noted writer of the same name.

41. Quoted in the *Christian Register,* October 13, 1838.

42. *Ibid.,* September 29, 1838.

43. Eliot, who was mayor of Boston at this time, had married one of Norton's sisters; President Charles Eliot of Harvard was their son. *Dictionary of American Biography.*

44. Eliot to Norton, October 10, 1838, NC.

45. *Daily Advertiser,* October 15, 1838.

46. *Ibid.,* October 18, 1838.

47. *Christian Register,* October 20, 1838.

48. Eliot to Norton, October 21, 1838, NC.

49. Norton to Robbins, October 23; Robbins to Norton, n.d., NC.

50. *Christian Register,* January 26, February 2, March 30, 1839.

51. Perry Miller, ed., *The Transcendentalists: An Anthology* (Cambridge, Mass., 1950), p. 196; Henry Steele Commager, *Theodore Parker* (Boston, 1936), p. 67; Ralph L. Rusk, *The Life of Ralph Waldo Emerson* (New York, 1949), p. 271.

52. Ware to Emerson, July 16, 1838, in James E. Cabot, *A Memoir of Ralph Waldo Emerson,* 2 vols. (Boston, 1887), II, 689-90.

53. Emerson to Ware, July 28, in Cabot, *Memoir,* II, 690-91. Emerson subsequently decided against making any revisions, believing that to do so would be to take unfair advantage of his critics. Elizabeth P. Peabody, *Reminiscences of Rev. Wm. Ellery Channing, D.D.* (Boston, 1880), p. 373.

54. Henry Ware, Jr., *The Personality of the Deity* . . . (Boston, 1838), p. 22 and passim.

55. *Ibid.,* pp. 8, 13-14, 17, 20-21.

56. Ware to Emerson, October 3, 1838, in Cabot, *Memoir,* II, 691-92.

57. Ware issued no "challenge" to Emerson. He wrote as follows: "I am anxious to have it understood that, as I am not perfectly aware of the precise nature of your opinions . . . I do not therefore pretend especially to enter the lists with them . . . I do not know by what arguments the doctrine that 'the soul knows no persons' is justified to your mind." Emerson's reply, so often quoted without this context, was: "I could not give account of myself, if challenged. I could not possibly give you one of the 'arguments' you cruelly hint at, on which any doctrine of mine stands. For I do not know what arguments mean in reference to any expression of a thought." Cabot, *Memoir,* II, 691-93.

58. Presumably the writer was one of the new editors—F. W. P. Greenwood and William Ware—who had taken over from James Walker in 1838; but

Cushing apparently was uncertain about the authorship. William Cushing, *Index to the "Christian Examiner"* (Boston, 1879), p. 38.

59. *Christian Examiner,* XXV (1838), 266.

60. *Ibid.,* pp. 266-67.

61. *Western Messenger,* VI (1838), 118-21. The *Messenger* was a monthly theological and literary magazine published at Cincinnati from June 1835 to April 1841. The principal contributors were the Transcendentalists James Freeman Clarke, Christopher Cranch, Samuel Osgood, and W. H. Channing. See Gohdes, *Periodicals of American Transcendentalism* (Durham, N. C., 1931), chap. 2.

62. *Messenger,* VI, 37-47. See also the answers of Clarke and Osgood to Norton's taunts about "the atheist Shelley." *Daily Advertiser,* September 28, October 5, 16, 1838.

63. *Boston Quarterly Review,* I (1838), 504-12; II (1839), 87, 112.

64. Holmes, *Ralph Waldo Emerson* (Boston, 1885), p. 116.

65. The *Specimens* (14 vols. Boston, 1838-42) contained translations of works by Cousin, Jouffroy, Constant, Goethe, Schiller, DeWette, and others. For reviews of the *Discourses* see the *Christian Register,* December 3, 1836; *Messenger,* III (1837), 576-83; *Christian Examiner,* XXI (1837), 402-03.

66. Norton, *Latest Form of Infidelity,* pp. 21-35.

67. *Ibid.,* pp. 8-13, 37-39, 50-64.

68. *"The Latest Form of Infidelity" Examined: A Letter to Mr. Andrews Norton, Occasioned by His "Discourse before the Alumni of the Cambridge Theological School,"* by "An Alumnus of That School" (Boston, 1839), pp. 16-23, 154-60.

69. *Ibid.,* p. 31.

70. *Ibid.,* pp. 23-29, 43-95.

71. Norton, *Remarks on . . . " 'The Latest Form of Infidelity' Examined'* (see n. 6, above), pp. 4-8.

72. *Ibid.,* pp. 11-70.

73. *Defence of " 'The Latest Form of Infidelity' Examined," A Second Letter to Mr. Andrews Norton . . .* (Boston, 1840); *A Third Letter to Mr. Andrews Norton . . .* (Boston, 1840).

74. Ripley, *Third Letter,* pp. 148-53.

75. Theodore Parker, *The Previous Question between Mr. Andrews Norton and His Alumni, Moved and Handled in a Letter to All Those Gentlemen* (Boston, 1840).

76. *Two Articles from the "Princeton Review" Concerning the Transcendental Philosophy of the Germans and of Cousin, and Its Influence on Opinion in this Country* (Cambridge, Mass., 1840). The authors of the articles, one of which was a cooperative effort, were Professor Hodge of Princeton Seminary and Professors Dod and Alexander of Princeton College. Norton's sponsorship of this reprinting has been taken as indicating "to what straits" he had been reduced (Miller, *Transcendentalists,* p. 232). It should be noted, however, that the articles in question expressed sympathy with the

Unitarians of New England not only in their defense against German speculations but also in their dispute of long standing with the New England
Theology, which the Princetonians believed had become overly rigid in the
post-Edwardean period (*Two Articles*, pp. 7-10). Norton's action, in other
words, was not so desperate as it might appear. Hodge's letters to Norton at
this time indicate that both men felt their agreements—their common supernaturalist emphasis, their reliance upon Locke and the Scottish philosophers,
and their partial concurrence on the faults of New England Calvinism—were
stronger than their disagreements, making an alliance natural at this particular
juncture. They agreed to delete some mild criticisms of Norton from the
Boston reprinting of the *Two Articles*. Hodge to Norton, February 27 and
March 12, 1840, NC.

77. Upham to Norton, September 4 and December 21, 1839, NC.

78. James Taylor to Norton, September 10, 1839, NC.

79. Ware to Norton, December 7, Samuel K. Lothrop to Norton, Decem-
ber 16, Gannett to Norton, August 27, 1839, NC. Similar letters came from
Harm Jan Huidekoper, John Ware, George F. Simmons, and Alexander
Young, NC.

80. Henry Steele Commager, "Tempest in a Boston Tea Cup," *New
England Quarterly*, VI (1933), 651-52.

81. Noyes to Norton, February 21, 1840; Furness to Norton, September
13, 1839, NC.

82. *Christian Register*, July 27, October 26, November 2, 23, December
14, 1839; January 4, 1840.

83. Quoted in O. B. Frothingham, *Transcendentalism in New England: A
History* (New York, 1876), p. 122. See also *Christian Register*, July 25, 1840.

84. Peabody, *Reminiscences*, pp. 379-81, 416.

85. *Christian Examiner*, XXVII (1839), 223, 224, 226.

86. This brother of Henry Ware, Jr., had been the pioneer Unitarian
minister in New York City (1821-36), and was proprietor and editor of the
Examiner from 1838 to 1844. He died in 1852. Eliot, II, 250-58.

87. Norton to W. Ware, February 24, 1840, NC.

88. W. Ware to Norton, February 25, 1840, NC.

89. Norton to W. Ware, March 10, 1840, NC.

90. Norton to Palfrey, April 13, 1840, NC.

91. O. B. Frothingham, *George Ripley* (Boston, 1882), pp. 61-63.

92. George Ripley, *A Letter Addressed to the Congregational Church in
Purchase St. by Its Pastor* (Boston, 1840), pp. 3-10, 20-24.

93. Frothingham, *Ripley*, pp. 61-91.

94. Ripley, *A Farewell Discourse Delivered to the Congregational Church
in Purchase Street, March 28, 1841* (Boston, 1841), pp. 17-18.

95. Appendix to ibid., pp. 22-24; *Register*, April 3, 1841; *Monthly Miscellany*, IV (1840), 293-95. For accounts of Brook Farm see Lindsay Swift,
Brook Farm: Its Members, Scholars, and Visistors, New York, 1900; Frothingham, *Ripley*, pp. 108-98. Although Ripley, W. H. Channing, and others
occasionally led religious services at Brook Farm, no formal church organiza-

tion was attempted, and the famous agricultural experiment of the Transcendentalists is therefore not part of the story of Transcendental church reform. Brook Farmers attended services in Boston and at Theodore Parker's church in West Roxbury. Swift, pp. 55, 221; Frothingham, *Ripley*, p. 119.

96. Ripley's Purchase St. society moved to a new location in 1848, taking the name "Thirteenth Congregational Church." The latter expired in 1860. Frothingham, *Ripley*, p. 93.

13

The Theological Response of the Transcendentalists to the Civil War

ROBERT C. ALBRECHT

ALTHOUGH THE MOVEMENT OF TRANSCENDENTALISM ENDED some time before the firing on Fort Sumter, most of the people identified with it were still active in 1861. Since the 1840's many of them had changed their beliefs but most continued to be idealists, and for them the war was a time of crisis. The Transcendentalists had been preaching in their lectures and sermons the divinity of man, man's potential, the good society to come. The year 1861 brought man at war, man in hate, man destroying. Accustomed to finding meaning in Nature and Man, what meaning would they find in bloodshed? What rhetoric would they use? Could they provide a new rhetoric as they had tried to provide a new religion beyond Unitarianism? For most Transcendentalists the answer to these questions was their concept of the war as "a remission by blood."

Before the war many Transcendentalists had been leaders toward a more liberal religion. Though many of them had begun their lives in Calvinist homes, they moved into the Unitarian church in which many became ministers; some went beyond that to establish nondenominational churches of their own or to leave organized religion entirely. During the Civil War,

From *The New England Quarterly,* 38 (1965), 21-34. Reprinted by permission.

however, most of the Transcendentalists reverted to the religious concepts they had apparently rejected years before. Sin and salvation, the doctrines preached in Congregational and other orthodox churches, became their themes. They became religious nationalists in formulating their response to the crisis, preaching that the war was a remission by blood for the salvation of man and nation.

Rather than becoming an intellectual elite which could lead the nation around war or through the war on a rationalistic or humanistic basis, they reverted to earlier, perhaps more primitive, ideas which demanded blood sacrifice for the remission of sins. Intellect turned back upon emotion. To the Transcendentalists the war was not a legal controversy, a mere war for union, a sectional struggle, not even a war to end slavery. It was a cosmic battle which could be talked about only in the rhetoric of orthodoxy. While to the modern historian the Civil War is a concurrence of battles, generals, armies, and politics, for the Transcendentalists it took place on quite a different level of reality. The meaning of the war was theological, its significance, moral.

A typical theme of the Transcendentalists' response to the war was that of the millennium. Though it was not typical of their thought in the 1850's or the 1870's, this theme, so strong in conservative Protestant thought, appeared continually in their writings during the war. At that time the Transcendentalists put history in the hands of Providence and mitigated man's efforts to achieve salvation. Free will became less important. The movement toward the millennium was in God's hands. The Transcendentalists no longer believed in man's ability to construct a utopia.

The pattern of response was not universal among the Transcendentalists. For instance, Emerson's conception of the war, as evidenced by his rhetoric, was not the same as that of James Freeman Clarke or Cyrus A. Bartol. But the responses of most Transcendentalists whether they were Unitarians or religious radicals—the two groups whose writings I shall later discuss—were quite similar. Before an examination of the writings of the Transcendentalists, however, a brief look at doctrines preached by an orthodox clergyman may establish a basis for comparison.

George B. Cheever, an outspoken abolitionist, was a Congregational minister who had severely attacked the Unitarians in the 1830's. Just before the Civil War he published *The Guilt of Slavery* in which he warned, "If God's judgment is really revealed against slavery as sin, then we, as a people, are condemned and guilty beyond any other nation under heaven."[1] Having perceived this guilt of the whole nation, he was ready to say during the war, "The opportunity is granted to us of God, of saving ourselves by doing a commanded work of justice, mercy, deliverance for others." Though it was God's decision, and not man's, to bring the war upon the nation, the salvation of the nation depended upon its actions in the crisis. The meaning of the war was theological when Cheever described it: "It is God's judgment, and it calls us to repentance; and the work of giving freedom and salvation to four millions of human beings held as slaves, is a work of immediate benevolence, the opportunity of which, if we avail ourselves of it, converts the war itself into the greatest of our blessings, drawing from it indeed the salvation of our country, as well as the redemption of the enslaved."[2]

This interpretation of the war, one which emphasized the place of God's will, the nation as an instrument of God, the theological realities of sin and salvation, belonged no less to the Transcendentalists than to the orthodox. Though the Transcendentalists emphasized the place of atonement and sacrifice, the basic view of the reality of the war most of them shared with men like Cheever. This assertion can most clearly be substantiated by examining the writings of the conservative–Unitarian–Transcendentalists. However, if we then turn to the more liberal ministers, we will find their interpretation of the war to be along the same lines. Only in Emerson's writings can there be found the breath of a new rhetoric which comprehends the cataclysm of the war.

Four clergymen who represent the conservative Transcendentalists are Thomas Starr King, James Freeman Clarke, William Henry Channing, and Cyrus A. Bartol. All were Unitarian ministers during the war, though Clarke's Boston church, the Church of the Disciples, resembled a free church. These men—closer to Cheever's orthodoxy than the others discussed here—more often and more clearly expressed their ideas in the rhetoric to which most of the Transcendentalists reverted. It was in the concepts and language of orthodoxy that they were able to find and express the meaningful reality of the war.

Unlike his friends in the East, Thomas Starr King often spoke of the war as one for union rather than against slavery. But the imagery and metaphors in his sermons and letters reveal that his basic view was similar to theirs. In a letter of May 1, 1861, King wrote, ". . . I assure you, in these times of moral separation,—the political judgment-day in America,—that California is *true to the cause of civilization.*"[3] King did present the North's cause as that of civilization carried forward by democracy. But the use of the term "judgment-day" indicates that he thought of the conflict as primarily a religious one which would lead to salvation and millennium. The combination of the two types of rhetoric was not unusual among the Transcendentalists, and the use of both reveals at once an attempt to find a new rhetoric and a failure to do so.

Calling the war a trial, King prophesied in his sermons that in a hundred years historians would say, "Then God sat by the furnace, and smelted America till her crime was purged, and she became pure gold." (King's notion of the written history of 1960 is indicative of what he thought, or hoped, the nation would be.) The concept of purification is similar to the Transcendentalists' common themes of testing and atonement, as well as George Cheever's view of the war as an opportunity for salvation. King's conception of "pure gold" was that the nation would be "homogeneous,—sounder in its system of labor, nobler and more symmetrical in its civilization. . . ."[4] On the one hand, his interpretations transcend the concepts of orthodoxy; on the other, they remain firmly anchored in that faith. History, for example, was a moral tale. In "Secession in Palestine and Its Results," King said, "He [God, in the Bible] reveals to us the principles which we are to set as lights behind the moving panorama of events in all kingdoms, so that history may be translucent with Divine radiance, and preach to us always the moral rule of a Holy God."[5] History was a moral lesson to be read for man's instruction.

Since history was a moral tale to King, he readily linked patriotism and religion. In 1862 he delivered to college students a lecture called, "Intellectual Duties of Students in Their Academic Years." Two books he urged that all must read were the New Testament and a history of their country. "Religion and patriotism must stream into every fibre of his [the student's] brain, into every duct of his blood." The conjunction of ideas that King presented in that passage is a key to an idea held by many Transcendentalists, that of religious nationalism. The nation itself was an object of religious concern. King said, "If there had been a deeper study of the history of America in the last twenty years in the rebellion districts, and a baptism in the spirit which that study liberates, this war would not have been."[6] A study of history would have had a religious effect. Religion and patriotism were inseparable. For King, the war was part of the drama of religion and history, of religion in history.

Though King may have tried to employ a new rhetoric, other conservatives did not make this attempt. James Freeman Clarke, for example, employed the orthodox language and concepts to understand, interpret, and explain the war. He saw it as a remission by blood. The national sins of money-love and slaveholding required expiation—suffering by the sinner to expiate the sin— and atonement—suffering by innocent people which, when borne willingly, reconciles the sinner to God. When he reviewed Cyrus A. Bartol's sermon, *The Remission By Blood,* he assented to the doctrine "that suffering and death are necessary to expiate sin, and that this suffering may often fall on the innocent . . . and this truth is fully illustrated in the present war."[7] In a funeral sermon he used the following imagery to explain the doctrine: "Our Massachusetts mothers . . . bring their spotless lambs to the altar, expiatory victims for a nation's sins."[8] The symbols were those of orthodoxy, though the congregation to which he preached was nondenominational, a "free" church.

At the end of the war Clarke told his congregation that the North won by its ideas and its faith in God and human rights, while the South continued to sin and did not have God's support.[9] Expressing the optimistic faith which had led him on, he said in a letter to a friend, "Abolition of slavery, fall of Charleston, fall of Richmond,—when they arrive they are like things fore-ordained from the foundation of the world."[10] On the same day he asked in a sermon, "But who has not seen through all these glorious and terrible days, the visible arm of God's providence leading our nation on?"[11] These state-ments evidence more than a belief in the Christian interpretation of history; they suggest he believed in foreordination, if not predestination.

Another member of this group who asserted his beliefs in these doctrines was William Henry Channing. A Transcendentalist minister who had been a member of several utopian communities in the 1840's, Channing related the visions of the millennium he had in the earlier period to those he had in the 1860's. Writing to a friend in December, 1860, he said, ". . . all the glowing hopes which after the night of reaction in 1848-49 fell into a trance and were reverently laid in the tomb amid sweet spices, with an ever-burning lamp at head and foot, are now putting off their cerements, pushing aside the heavy stones, and rising glorified on this Easter morn of the Republic." In the central metaphor here the resurrection of the nation—the utopian dreams of heaven on earth—are substituted for the familiar resurrection of Christ, the very kernel of orthodoxy. Channing felt that he and his fellow Christian socialists had planted the seeds of the future in the 1840's. The fault, the delay, was not in their vision but in that of the people. "True, inasmuch as the nation would not choose the better way of peaceful transformation, God, in his infinite grace, compelled us to enter this flinty, trying way of destruc-tion."[12] Since the nation would not follow the right path twenty years before, God was forcing it to move towards the millennium in this fashion. Channing had joined the utopian dreams to the promise of the result of the war. The war was an instrument of purification, an impetus to salvation, a bridge to the millennium, and it was a direction not chosen by men but by God. Cheever, the Congregationalist, agreed.

In 1861, before the fighting had begun, Channing proclaimed the war as the "Providential method of National redemption." (It was, he said, "a *holy war.*") He explained, "Monstrous has been the Nation's crime; total let the repentance be, and costly the sacrifice of atonement."[13] In this almost barbaric prayer, this guilt-ridden plea, Channing asked for widespread death and destruction. It is a prayer for punishment; it is the martyr spirit calling for its suffering. By May of 1864 he was to cry, "Enough!" In a letter to James Freeman Clarke, he asked, "Ah! loving Heavenly Father, must there be all this hideous butchery ere our sins be washed white as wool?"[14] Working in the hospitals around Washington, Channing saw the butchery he could but imagine in his prayer of 1861. Yet this was the fire he thought God was leading the nation through to reach the utopia Channing expected. Here was no constitutional view of the war, no legal interpretation, no economic analysis; here was a theological view.

Though Clarke and Channing did preach the concept of the war as atonement, neither of them preached it as often or as long as Cyrus A. Bartol. During the war he emphasized sacrifice. In 1861, he told his Boston congregation, "It is the law of our life, that all earthly progress in every good cause starts in sacrifice, lives on sacrifice, and without ever-new sacrifice would faint and die."[15] Sacrifice was part of history, and history was a theological drama. Like Channing, he was sure of the results to come. In his sermon, *The Nation's Hour,* Bartol said, ". . . God is using our action with that of our rulers, the citizens, leaders, soldiers . . . as elements in the great result to come."[16] Bartol saw the theological-historical process as soon reaching a termination, a millennium.

The war which had come from God he welcomed as a penalty, since neither North nor South was "very good or holy anywhere." The war was from God, a "summons to a struggle against our own sins." But North and South were not equal foes, for ". . . the terrible North, as the fate and finger of God, moves to meet the tropical South." Bartol pointed out in this sermon that while the interference of gods in the affairs of mortals in Homer was often called "a fine fancy," it was but another example "that celestial strength is always pledged to righteous enterprise."[17] That the North was both agent and victim is not a theological paradox, only a secular one. Bartol, like Clarke and Channing, thought and said that God acted directly in the history of men.

It was in his sermon, *The Remission By Blood,* that Bartol set forth his central explanation of the war. He presented the death of Christ on the cross, that sacrifice of blood, as the "supreme token of the moral endurance by which atonement must be made for all transgression." But that was not enough; there was not enough blood shed. All who bore sacrifice for the sake of others completed that act. "Every martyr to the cause of truth and duty in the world mingles his blood . . . with that of the great Redeemer of mankind." He continued, "For the sins of our country there was no remission but by the shedding of blood."[18] Bartol had voiced the view held by most of the Transcendentalists. His language was not that of a freethinker, a rationalist, but of an orthodox clergyman, because in that he could best express his concepts. The war in this interpretation was not merely a civil war of the nineteenth century but a sacrificial battle in the theological drama of history.

Though it is not altogether surprising to find Bartol and other Unitarian Transcendentalists viewing the war in this way, it is more unexpected to find this view held by Transcendentalists who were leading religious radicals before and especially after the war. Three representatives of this group are Moncure Conway, Samuel Johnson, and David A. Wasson. Conway decided to stay in England in 1863 to become minister at the South Place Chapel, preaching a faith of "humanized theism," as he called it. Johnson was a contributor to the *Radical,* a supporter of the Free Religious Association, and a minister at the Free Church at Lynn, Massachusetts, for almost twenty years. Wasson was an essayist, poet, and minister who, in 1865, was asked to take Theodore Parker's old congregation, the Twenty-Eighth Congregational Society in Boston. None of these men could accurately be described as a Unitarian, since each had left that faith sometime before the war. The war, however, caused them to preach on themes of atonement for, or expiation of, sins, judgment and salvation. While seeing the issues of union and slavery, and responding to the personalities who led the nation, they preferred to find the reality of the war on a theological level.

In *The Rejected Stone,* his first book published during the war, Conway expressed his conceptions of the war in the rhetoric of orthodoxy. There he wrote, "The shame of repelling the fugitive from her [Liberty's] door has nerved her to the atonement she is now ready to make by shedding of blood. . . ."[19] The same sort of rhetoric he employed in *The Golden Hour.* "America is to-day in the wilderness of temptation, and beside her is the Tempter."[20] Similar examples can be found in his third book of the period, *Testimonies Concerning Slavery,* where he called the war, "the Day of judgment for our guilty land. . . ."[21] This was a common metaphor in the Transcendentalists' writings, since many of them believed the war would be followed by national salvation. In his *Autobiography* Conway wrote that he was happy in England where he had moved in 1863, "to have no further need to preach about slavery and dogma."[22] Had the American situation forced him to use a rhetoric from which he wished to escape?

Statements concerning the Day of Judgment and salvation can also be found in the writings of another minister who was to become a radical after the war, Samuel Johnson, minister of the Free Church at Lynn. Writing to George L. Stearns, the industrialist who had been a financial supporter of John Brown and a recruiter of Negro troops during the war, Johnson said, "We are borne on the saving tide towards issues which the whole nation, North and South . . . has resisted and still resists. A terrible Nemesis, a stern atonement, and then, the *'irresistible* Grace *of God!'*" Six months later he commented on the war as "this magnificent *sweep of purification.*"[23] He found the war most impressive in its theological aspect and could only express its significance in the rhetoric most meaningful to him.

The purification about which these Transcendentalists spoke was to be accomplished through atonement, the doctrine of the suffering of the innocent for the redemption of all. Wasson, social conservative and theological radical, wrote in 1863 that the bloodshed of the war was the price the nation was paying for its vice and for its virtue.[24] In his installation sermon in 1865, Wasson discussed the meaning of atonement, "that monostrous doctrine of vicarious atonement." Referring, perhaps, to Lincoln's death less than a month before, he said, "He who stands for the divine in humanity is most tasked at its dead weight, and to stretch a little wider its limitations." It was particularly "the noblest hearts," the "greatest," "the representative soul" who suffered for others.[25] The "monstrous doctrine" helped to explain not only Lincoln's death, but the deaths of all those virtuous men who died to atone for the sins of the nation.

Wasson's statement about "the representative soul" can be better understood with reference to the Transcendentalists' continual search for a hero during the war. Throughout the conflict many of them lamented the absence of a leader to take the nation through the crisis. They did not find a hero until 1865 and Lincoln's death. The comments on Lincoln at the time of his death as well as many of the complaints concerning the lack of a leader were made in language suggesting the orthodox conceptions of Christ or Moses, the chosen redeemer or leader. The notions of deliverance and salvation are not humanistic or deistic, but beliefs accepted by orthodox Protestants in the nineteenth century. The lamentations over the lack of a political leader in the 1850's became, during the war, faint prayers for a deliverer.

While most of the Transcendentalists employed a rhetoric which seemed more appropriate to the orthodoxy of men like Cheever, one man did manage to use a new rhetoric in describing and interpreting the war. Emerson himself seldom reverted to orthodox language and concepts as did other Transcendentalists. Only he was able to express an interpretation of the war in a contextual rhetoric which removed it from the realm of orthodox theology to the new level of religion which he had so long been advocating in his lectures. Only Emerson interpreted the war in the rhetoric which one might have expected from all of the Transcendentalists.

Although in 1861 he wrote, "If the abundance of heaven only sends us a fair share of light and conscience, we shall redeem America for all its sinful years since the century began," such rhetoric was not typical of Emerson. [26] Far more often he spoke of the moral problem: "We must get ourselves morally right. Nobody can help us."[27] While others spoke of religious salvation, Emerson spoke of moral triumph. He was certain of the increased importance of morals; "Certain it is that never before since I read newspapers, have the morals played so large a part in them as now."[28]

Emerson's employment of a rhetoric quite distinguishable from that of other Transcendentalists can easily be seen in statements such as this of 1863: "The war is an exceptional struggle, in which the first combatants are met,—the highest principles against the worst. What a teacher! what a field! what results!"[29] Other Transcendentalists would fall back upon the terminology of sin and righteousness to express a similar concept, but Emerson had gone beyond this. While he could describe the war to Carlyle as "the battle for Humanity," others would call it a battle for salvation.[30] While others could say the war saved the nation, Emerson wrote that the war had "*moralized* cities and states."[31] The Congregationalist, Cheever, would not employ such a term. Emerson had found a rhetoric in which to express a conception of the war not characterized by "a remission by blood." His view, like those of other Transcendentalists, was a religious one, but his rhetoric demonstrated radicalism in religion.

In the wartime writings of some of these Transcendentalists, especially the more radical, are the barest beginnings of a new religious rhetoric. But it is never primary, it is never whole, it is never developed. But even when the rhetoric is somehow new, it is still theological. Emerson's statement, "The evolution of a highly destined society must be moral; it must run in the grooves of the celestial wheels," is an excellent example. The key phrases—highly destined, moral, celestial wheels—all suggest a religion beyond orthodoxy but a religion, nevertheless.

The significance of the reversion to orthodoxy which commonly occurred among most Transcendentalists is primarily what is revealed about that group. Transcendentalism was primarily a religion. The reversion to orthodoxy suggests that most of the Transcendentalists were unsuccessful in their attempt to form a new body of religious thought signified by a new rhetoric distinguishable from that of an orthodox Congregationalist like Cheever. That they were driven back to orthodoxy and found there the rhetoric appropriate to explain the war indicates also the impress of the war upon them. They could treat it only as cataclysm, as Armageddon, as Judgment Day.

To the Transcendentalists the American Civil War was not a series of battles between armies over union, slaves, economic theories or the Constitution. It was a struggle of theological importance and meaning. They justified the bloodshed by raising the stakes: men died not only for a ground or law or loyalty; they died for the salvation not only of themselves but of the nation. The war had driven these idealists back to the bedrock of their ideas and their ideals. They asserted not the divinity in man, not his natural goodness, not the shallow optimism of which they have so often been accused; they asserted the justice of God and the essential optimism of that faith. This view of reality allowed them to accept the defeats and the carnage. It allowed them to hate not the South but the evil it represented. It allowed them to continue to ignore the political realities they had always overlooked. They need not concern themselves with elections, executives, and legislatures for these were not the instruments of bringing war or ending it. The war did not change the Transcendentalists; their theological response was not an escape to a refuge. Rather, it was the essence of that path they had always trod. They revealed themselves to be what they had always been—religious nationalists searching for the meaning of the existence of themselves and their nation and finding it in the traditional Christianity which they sought to interpret but never discard.

NOTES

1. (Boston, 1860), p. 21.

2. *The Salvation of the Country Secured by Immediate Emancipation* (New York, 1861), pp. 4, 24.

3. *Monthly Journal,* II (June 1861), 263.

4. *Christianity and Humanity...*, ed. Edwin P. Whipple, 3rd edition (Boston, 1878), p. 354.

5. Mss. sermon, 2. Boston Public Library. By courtesy of the Trustees of the Boston Public Library.

6. *Substance and Show, and Other Lectures,* ed. Edwin P. Whipple (Boston, 1881), pp. 428, 431.

7. "The Remission By Blood," *Monthly Journal,* III (August 1862), 369.

8. "From 'Lieut. William Lowell Putnam...,' " in John Gilmary Shea, ed., *The Fallen Brave...* (New York, 1861), p. 195.

9. Original quotation in Arthur S. Bolster, Jr., *James Freeman Clarke: Disciple to Advancing Truth* (Boston, 1954), p. 284.

10. *James Freeman Clarke: Autobiography, Diary and Correspondence,* ed. Edward Everett Hale (Boston, 1891), p. 290.

11. *Sermon preached before the delegates to the National Unitarian Convention* (Boston, 1865), p. 29.

12. O. B. Frothingham, *Memoir of William Henry Channing* (New York, 1886), p. 333.

13. *The Civil War in America...* (Liverpool, 1861), pp. 90-91, 93.

14. Frothingham, *Channing,* p. 326.

15. *Our Sacrifices* (Boston, 1861), p. 3.

16. (Boston, 1862), p. 5.

17. *The Duty of the Time* (Boston, 1861), pp. 6, 11-12.

18. (Boston, 1862), p. 5.

19. (Boston, 1861), p. 22.

20. (Boston, 1862), p. 110.

21. (London, 1865), p. 113.

22. *Autobiography, Memories and Experiences* (New York, 1904), I, 290.

23. *Samuel Johnson: Lectures, Essays and Sermons,* ed. Samuel May (Boston, 1883), p. 93.

24. "The Law of Costs," *Atlantic Monthly,* XI (February 1863), 241.

25. *The Radical Creed* (Boston, 1865), p. 23.

26. *The Letters of Ralph Waldo Emerson,* ed. Ralph L. Rusk (New York, 1939), V, 253.

27. *The Correspondence of Thomas Carlyle and Ralph Waldo Emerson, 1834-72,* ed. C. E. Norton (Boston, 1883) II, 281.

28. *Journals of Ralph Waldo Emerson...*, ed. Edward Waldo Emerson and Waldo Emerson Forbes (Boston, 1909-14) IX, 492.

29. Ibid., pp. 576-77.
30. *Correspondence*, II, 285.
31. *Journals of Ralph Waldo Emerson*, X, 105.

PART IV
The Central Man: Emerson

14

Emerson's Problem of Vocation: A Note on the American Scholar

HENRY NASH SMITH

1

AMONG THE MANY FINE PERCEPTIONS OF HENRY JAMES'S ESSAY on Emerson in the *Partial Portraits* is his allusion to the period of "movement, experiment and selection . . . of effort too and painful probation" through which Emerson had to pass before he could discover his true vocation as artist and thinker.[1] James, with his instinct for subjective values, saw clearly enough that Emerson's withdrawal from the ministry was less significant than the years of inner quest and adventure which followed. The plot was given: the hero was destined in the end to attain a luminous poise, "the equanimity of a result,"[2] with great power to nourish his disciples. Yet the heart of the drama was not its beginning or its end, but the perplexed motives of the rising action. Sympathizing with a fellow craftsman, James offered a technical statement of the problem: "Emerson had his message, but he was a good while looking for his form."[3] Yet this seems at once too purely aesthetic and too simple a way of explaining what happened; it suggests that the message was fully developed at the outset, and fails to allow for the all-important interaction between half-formed intuition and increasingly ade-

From *The New England Quarterly,* 12 (1939), 52-67. Reprinted by permission.

quate expression. If Emerson's message was eventually (to use a telegraphic abbreviation) self-reliance, it gained clarity and force only by virtue of the inner struggle preceding its utterance. The problem was very much more than stylistic; it was so nearly central in his early development that it calls for fuller exploration.

Emerson's effort to work out a satisfactory relation to society had two principal phases centering in two problems posed for him successively by the declining Puritan tradition in which he had been reared and by the new, industrial society which was rapidly taking shape about him during his young manhood. As an undergraduate he had accepted the conventional assumption that young men of unusual gifts should be dedicated to the ministry. This choice, made for him (as he later, perhaps unjustly, implied) "against his inclination," or, to speak more accurately, made by him "before he was acquainted with the character of his own mind,"[4] was the first serious obstacle he encountered in his effort to find his true vocation. But after he had abandoned the ministry he still had to come to terms with that astonishing Massachusetts of the 1830's whose Calvinistic soil had nourished Romantic and humanitarian seed to yield such an unprecedented harvest of reformers and improvers and plain cranks. Militant humanitarianism, closely related to the rapid urbanization and industrialization of eastern Massachusetts, replaced the clerical tradition as the most alarming threat of the outer world to impose restraint upon Emerson's career of self-realization. His earlier struggle had been against the established order; now, ironically, his most formidable adversaries were men even more hostile to the established order than he.[5] They, or the ethical ideal they represented, gave him little peace until he could make it plain to everyone, including himself, that even in dissent he could belong to no man's party but his own. A further complication was the difficulty of justifying an artist's apparent idleness in a strenous society unaccustomed to behold Man Thinking outside the pulpit or the college classroom.[6]

As was always his practice, Emerson set down his meditations concerning both phases of his inner struggle. His effort to throw off the clerical convention, for instance, underlies an early sermon, recently published which his editor calls "Find Your Calling."[7] The later struggle with the humanitarian ideal finds expression in the *Journals* and in several of the public discourses and essays. But the clearest single statement of all the issues as Emerson saw them is contained in the "Lecture on the Times," delivered in December of 1841.[8] Here, in dramatic form, appear the two phases of the problem of vocation as he had faced it during the previous decade. The first phase, related to the crisis of ten years before, when he had decided to withdraw from the ministry, appears in the address as a tension between the Party of the Past and that of the Future. It is the eternal conflict between "the dissenter, the theorist, the aspirant" and the established order of things: the ground-pattern of Transcendentalism, springing as the movement did from the whole Puritan past of New England, yet violently protesting against the society in which it grew. But the conflict between the Past and the Future, the World and the Newness, yields place almost at once to a debate between two groups within the party of the Future: the Actors, easily recognizable as the humanitarians of Emerson's day, who favor direct, tangible reforms in the structure of society; and the Students, who are likewise hostile to the Past, but who are withheld from action by a Romantic perplexity and ennui, a perception that their faculties are superior to any concrete task lying before them. In spite of Emerson's ironic realization that neither attitude represents the whole truth, he is obviously on the side of the Future against the Past, and of the Student against the Actor.

It does not take much reading between the lines to find in this address a condensed chapter of Emerson's autobiography, an imaginative statement of dominant issues in his ethical development. Expanded by reference to his other early writings, the symbolic shorthand can be interpreted as a gloss on Emerson's complex attitude toward humanitarianism, and even—if one reads quite closely—on that ultimate idiosyncrasy which the doctrine of self-reliance so cryptically expresses.

2

The decision to withdraw from the ministry in 1832 has been recognized as a significant event in the history of Transcendentalism. "The mind of the young preacher," says Emerson's most recent editor, "was the stage on which struggled for supremacy two theories of the universe. . . . His decision to abandon the profession of the ministry was his vote in favor of the new age."[9] Certainly a profound change in outlook was necessary before the descendant of generations of ministers could deliberately reject a vocation representing the noblest aspirations of the past in order to embark upon a quest for a new and higher calling that could not even be said to exist. But it would be unwise to conclude that Emerson's action was made inevitable by the logic of Transcendentalism. The doctrinal issue concerning the Lord's Supper was not fundamental, for he later declined a call from the congregation at New Bedford which, influenced by Hicksite Quakers, had accepted a view of the rite similar to his.[10] And Theodore Parker was to demonstrate even ten years later that an apostle of the Newness in its fully developed form might throw off the mild yoke of Unitarianism, yet continue pastoral functions at full blast. In fact, two contrasting theories of vocation could be derived from the Unitarian assertion of man's divinity. The most obvious development of the new faith led to an energetic humanitarianism and thus into the many vital or quaint proposals for reform characteristic of the thirties and forties. This was the vocation of the Transcendentalist as Actor, admirably illustrated by Parker. But on the other hand the exploration of the infinity within might lead far away from society to the highly individualistic and passive cult of self-reliance. This was the vocation of the Transcendentalist as Student, represented by Emerson and, with an even more uncompromising rigor, by Thoreau.

The intellectual forces impelling Emerson toward contemplation instead of action were quite various. Very early he expressed a Deistic confidence that "the everlasting progress of the universe" needs no tinkering from human hands, and certainly does not "hang upon the bye-laws of a Missionary Society or a Sunday School."[11] Later he developed the Neoplatonic argument that "facts and persons are grown unreal and phantastic by reason of the vice in them," so that the philosopher sacrifices his dignity in confronting evil on the phenomenal level.[12] Even more important was the belief, confirmed by the major voices of the Christian tradition, that no changes of outward circumstances can bring about "mental and moral improvement."[13] One must also take into account Emerson's temperamental dislike of association in any form. As R. M. Gay has pointed out, what Emerson objected to in Brook Farm was not communism but organization.[14] "At the name of a society," he wrote in 1840—significantly, to Margaret Fuller—"all my repulsions play, all my quills rise and sharpen."[15] Yet action, in the specific environment of time and place, almost inevitably meant for Emerson "movements," participation in the work of what would now be called "pressure groups," while contemplation seemed possible only through a complete withdrawal from the busy life of the community. Reform, like religion, was inherently institutional. Emerson was committed to the aims of both, but the same lack of the talent for coöperation and social living which unfitted him for the pastorate[16] made him chary of joining the new secular church of the philanthropists. One wonders, too, whether the precarious state of his health was not an important influence leading him to avoid the strenuous career of a reformer.

But the most interesting influence upon Emerson's cult of solitude and contemplation, and thus upon the doctrine of self-reliance, was English Romanticism. The Romantic cult of nature tended to ignore society altogether by placing the intuitive genius alone in the cosmos as Nature's Priest; and the Wordsworthian anti-urban primitivism, touching Emerson just when Boston was growing in population from 43,000 in 1820 to 100,000 in 1842, neatly coincided with the other forces that were leading him to the bucolic setting of Concord.

All these conflicting impulses, and many others, were involved in Emerson's problem of Action versus Contemplation. The issue was thoroughly real for him. "Elusive, irreducible, merely gustatory,"[17] and in a paradoxical sense even irresponsible, he was very reluctant to take up his trumpet and his pitcher with the other warriors of New England. Yet he could not easily escape from the sense of social responsibility that was important in his Puritan heritage, and he was hampered in his desire to reject both the clerical and the humanitarian conventions by the lack of a clearly defined ethical ideal to which he could turn. He had indeed abandoned a material profession, despairing no doubt of finding his true and unique vocation in a society which was not "fertile in variations";[18] but if the society was simple it was highly responsible, and Emerson could hardly avoid meeting the moral issue involved in the problem of vocation. If he found no profession already formed for him, he must create one for himself, even if only as an ideal; and the ideal must not only be defensible before the world, but also represent adequately all the forces of tradition, temperament, and literary contagion that were at work in him. Given such varied and conflicting stimuli, the task was to devise a response that would sacrifice as few as possible of the valid impulses. The test of any proposed response as an acceptable ideal of vocation was the extent to which, in Emerson's words, it could bring every power of his mind into freedom and action.[19]

This was the situation which gave rise, in the decade following Emerson's withdrawal from the ministry, to the various hero types which appear in the *Journals* and the published addresses. The best-known of these is of course the Scholar. But during the thirties Emerson created, tested, and abandoned a whole company of these somewhat ghostly characters, such as the Man of Genius, the Seer, the Contemplative Man, the Student, the Transcendentalist.[20] The terms are to some extent interchangeable; they fix points on the circumference of a circle at whose center is an undefined conception, the final cause of the others. All the characters are in some sense Emerson, and all of them are what Emerson strove toward as an ethical ideal; they resemble the hypotheses of a scientist which are continually being subjected to experimental verification and revision in the laboratory. Some of the fictions, in addition, seem intended as generic representations of recurrent types in the fermenting New England that Emerson knew; and occasionally the terms seem to become ironic designations for eccentricities which he wishes to avoid.[21] In fact, since the possible degrees of dramatic disengagement (or "plasticity" in the Aristotelean sense) are almost infinite, each occurrence of these terms presents a fresh problem. One seems to be studying a collection of embryos that might have developed eventually into characters of fiction, save for the fact that Emerson did not have a truly dramatic imagination. The pehnomenon resembles that quality in Wordsworth which Coleridge called "ventriloquism."[22] The Scholar is the hero of Emerson's unwritten *Prelude,* and belongs with all the Werthers and the Childe Harolds and the Teufelsdröckhs of the period. It will be readily understood that essays and addresses in which characters of this sort appear should be regarded as rudimentary narratives rather than as structures of discursive reasoning. Their form is that of the plot, not the syllogism, their force not demonstrative but dramatic.

3

The corpus of Emerson's work that shows his concern with the problem of vocation is extensive. In addition to one or two early sermons and many entries in the *Journals* during the thirties, it includes "The American Scholar" and the four important lectures on "The Times" delivered in the winter of 1841-1842, as well as two later addresses on "The Man of Letters" and "The Scholar." As a rule, one can detect in Emerson's writing on the subject an original tension or conflict of impulses arising from his inability to satisfy simultaneously the conventions of his youth, the demands of the humanitarians, his own temperamental inclination, and the ethical ideals of English Romanticism. Emerson the artist repeatedly responds to these mingled stimuli by projecting various imaginative forms of the contemplative ideal. As a result, the symbols have a curiously mixed character. The Scholar is the Genius, but is also a lineal descendent of the New England clergyman.[23] For a decade Emerson was unable either to merge the two ideals successfully, or to abandon one in favor of the other.

On occasion he tried to resolve the tension by the desperate procedure of equating the opposites—in "Man the Reformer" (1841), for instance, redefining reform as love with the declaration that "one day all men will be lovers; and every calamity will be dissolved in the universal sunshine."[24] But such an evasive solution could not satisfy him for long, and as a rule he recognized that a choice was necessary, that the alternatives before him were not identical, that something must be given up. It is this inner debate which explains the peculiar vehemence with which Emerson insisted upon poise and proclaimed the doctrine of self-reliance. Only by envisaging the Actor can one understand the strongly apologetic basis of Emerson's conception of the Scholar.

One of the earliest phases of Emerson's concern with vocation may be observed in the notion of "character" which appears in the *Journals* in 1828. Character stands at first for a confident acquiescence in God's perfect governance of the universe.[25] From another point of view character is interpreted as global integrity, self-sufficiency, self-reliance resulting from the soul's "absolute command of its desires," with a corresponding loss of solicitude concerning what other men do.[26] The idea lends itself, again, to a Neoplatonic declaration of the unreality of all action, concerned as it necessarily is with the realm of mere phenomena and of evil.[27] Yet character can also become—very significantly—the equivalent of lawless, irrational genius, a synonym of the German's *Daimonisches*;[28] and so desperate is Emerson's concern to defend his ideal of passivity against "carpenters, masons, and merchants" who "pounce on him" for his supposed idleness[29] that he can resort to an almost physiological determinism, maintaining that God "has given to each his calling in his ruling love, . . . has adapted the brain and the body of men to the work that is to be done in the world." If some men "have a contemplative turn, and voluntarily seek solitude and converse with themselves," in God's name, he exclaims with surprising heat, let them alone![30]

The famous address on "The American Scholar" is in large part but a summary of these and other ideas that had been recurring in the *Journals* for a decade.[31]   Character is recognized here as the special attribute of the Contemplative Man; and it is noteworthy that the address contains a long and confused discussion of the issue of Action versus Contemplation.[32] Emerson is still troubled by the popular conception of the Scholar as a recluse, realizing that such an interpretation makes contemplative inaction a species of valetudinarianism; and he seeks to redeem the Scholar from the implied charge of weakness and cowardice. Yet the passage on the value of manual labor in enriching a writer's vocabulary merely confuses the issue by using "action" in a new sense; and the praise of action because it is "pearls and rubies to [the Scholar's] discourse" seems almost *fin de siècle* in its subordination of life to art. Only by an extreme irony or a thoroughly artistic failure to distinguish the actual from the imagined can Emerson go on to exclaim, "I run eagerly into this resounding tumult [of the world]. I grasp the hands of those next to me, and take my place in the ring to suffer and to work. . . ." And the proposed end is still merely literary: the Scholar enters the world not in order to reform it, but in order that the dumb abyss of his inarticulate thought may become "vocal with speech." A deeper level of Emerson's meaning appears in the warning that the Scholar, in committing himself to action (here in its usual sense of humanitarian reform), runs the danger of forfeiting his self-reliance to the tyranny of "the popular judgments and modes of action." And at the end of the address the Contemplative Man's scrutiny is directed to "the perspective of [his] own infinite life"—that is, integrity, character—to be explored and developed by introspection. It hardly settles the issue to add to the Scholar's "study and . . . communication of principles" the further task of "making those instincts prevalent, the conversion of the world."[33] For the original problem was the choice of a means— active reform or passive mediation—for converting the world. Emerson's refusal to choose between these alternatives is highly significant. On the one hand it reveals again the essentially contemplative nature of his Scholar-ideal;

on the other it shows his curious reluctance to surrender the Scholar's claim to the contradictory virtues of the active reformer.

It has become customary to interpret "The American Scholar" as a statement of literary nationalism. But in the light of Emerson's prolonged struggle with the problem of vocation, the nationalistic phase of the address seems of diminished importance. Emerson was struggling to affirm a creed of self-reliance, and the fiction of the Scholar was a phase of the struggle. To the extent that the intellectual domination of Europe interferes with the Scholar's integrity, he must of course throw it off. But Europe is by no means the Scholar's worst enemy. His hardest struggles are civil and American: with vulgar prosperity; with the tyranny of the past; with "the popular cry," even though this be momentarily for some good thing—in short, with all the forces against which Emerson was striving to protect the inarticulate secrets of his own mind, the intuitive belief in his personal mission.

Impressive as the fiction of the Scholar was for Emerson's contemporaries, it did not bring about at this time a permanent equilibrium of conflicting impulses within the author himself. The address contains no coherent statement of the Scholar's positive functions. In many respects Emerson's situation in 1837 was the same as it had been five years before, when he withdrew from the pulpit: he had made concrete discoveries concerning what he must deny, but had not found a tangible alternative to the program of the reformers. He was still disturbed by his inability to renounce the ethical ideal of overt action.

It is not surprising, therefore, that the theme of apology for not fulfilling a supposed obligation to assist in "the philanthropic enterprises of Universal Temperance, Peace, Abolition of Slavery" soon reappears in the *Journals.*[34] The conflict which persisted is clearly illustrated by an incident in the spring of 1838—the famous letter, "hated of me"—which he consented to write to President Van Buren about "this tragic Cherokee business."[35] There had been a public meeting, and Emerson agreed that the persecution of the Indians by land-hungry Georgians was "like dead cats around one's neck," even for a peaceable resident of Massachusetts. He yielded to popular pressure and wrote his letter of protest, but afterwards experienced a revulsion from such "stirring in the philanthropic mud." The violence of Emerson's language concerning this relatively trivial act reveals how tense was his inner debate with regard to humanitarianism. The solicitation of his friends, the reformers, in alliance with his own impulse to make active war upon the evils of society, had momentarily overcome his intuition concerning his true vocation. He had failed in perfect self-reliance, for although he sympathized with the sentiments he had set down, the letter itself was not his own, not prompted from within. His resentment over outside interference leads him into an almost savage renunciation of philanthropic meetings and "holy hurrahs."[36] The whole response, in its morbid disproportion to the importance of the occurrence, shows how deep in Emerson originated both the impulse to accept and the stronger impulse to reject the humanitarian program.

During the following years the conception of the Scholar takes on an increasingly Romantic cast. In 1840, asserting that he has been working at his essays as "a sort of apology to my country for my apparent idleness," Emerson threatens to abandon even this form of the deed.[37] A later congener of the Scholar, the Youth, appearing in the lecture on "The Conservative" also as the Reformer and the Hero,[38] represents an almost fantastic extreme of Emerson's effort to explain how the Scholar-Sage can fulfill his supposed obligation to eradicate evil from the universe. The Hero's desire to descend as "a Redeemer into Nature" is, in its theological implications, even more startling then the Divinity School Address, for here the Transcendental merging of a divine *logos* with an apotheosized humanity is not so much affirmed as casually taken for granted: the idea seems to come straight from the subconscious. It is not easy to tell how seriously Emerson means this suggestion, which lends itself to almost every nuance of interpretation known to Christian theology. But some sort of magical version can hardly be avoided when one places beside the remark Emerson's later statement that "the path which the hero travels alone is the highway of health and benefit to mankind."[39] Here the extension to all mankind of the divinity reserved for Jesus in the Calvinistic scheme seems to have had its natural consequence in the rehabilitation of the whole myth of the man-god in a pre-Christian form, and we are led unexpectedly into the sphere of *The Golden Bough*. The Scholar makes the most impressive of all his appearances as the Priest-King, the uniquely endowed representative of the tribe, doomed endlessly to die and to live again that he may redeem humanity and nourish his people upon the life-force in nature. If such an interpretation reads too much anthropology into Emerson, it may at least serve as a reminder of the magical presuppositions underlying Romantic theories of communion between man and nature.

Whatever the final form of the Scholar-ideal may have been, the fiction apparently served its purpose, and Emerson's problem of vocation was solved in terms of self-reliance and contemplation. At the end of the lecture on "The Transcendentalist," the dialogues between opposed characters give way to a description of two opposed "states of thought." Although Emerson must still lead two lives, "of the understanding and of the soul," at any rate the conflict between opposed ideals is gone.[40] In its stead appears a simpler tension between the actual Emerson and an ideal which, to be sure, he sometimes betrays, but which is itself accepted without question. The passive life of the soul has been legislated into a norm; the fiction of the Transcendentalist is a relatively adequate and stable synthesis of the conflicting impulses; and the issue of Action versus Contemplation has disappeared along with the opposed fiction of the Actor.

After 1842 the ideal of the Scholar seems not to have undergone any significant evolution; the two later addresses on similar topics[41] are little more than repetitions of Emerson's earlier utterances. Possibly his growing realization of his influence as a writer and lecturer, and his countrymen's disposition to accept him as a man of letters exempt from the obligation to follow some obviously useful occupation, provided the support he needed in his inner debate.

The most discerning general comment that could be made regarding Emerson's attitude toward the problem of vocation is his own reminder that the Transcendentalists were the heirs of Puritanism.[42] But they no longer had a church to furnish a profession for them; they were "scholars out of the church."[43] By 1832 Emerson had in effect seceded from the state as well.[44] Having gone out from the shelter of the conventional cadres of society, he had to perform the intellectual and imaginative labor of conceiving a new vocation for himself, and almost a new society in which this vocation might have meaning.[45] He was fully aware that in place of the "ease and pleasure of treading the old road, accepting the fashions, the education, the religion of society," the Scholar had to take up "the cross of making his own, and, of course, the self-accusation, the faint heart, the frequent uncertainty and loss of time, which are the nettles and tangling vines in the way of the self-relying and self-directed. . . ."[46] In the face of this task, it is small wonder that Emerson found his "strength and spirits . . . wasted in rejection."[47] But like so many other artists before him, he discovered that the very tensions which drained his strength provided him with important themes for his art.

NOTES

1. *Partial Portraits* (London and New York, 1888), p. 6.

2. *Ibid.*, p. 5.

3. *Ibid.*, p. 6.

4. Arthur Cushman McGiffert, Jr., editor, *Young Emerson Speaks: Unpublished Discourses on Many Subjects by Ralph Waldo Emerson* (Boston, 1938), p. 251. The passage containing these words has been scratched out in the manuscript of a sermon delivered February 5, 1832—some four months before Emerson decided to resign his pastorate.

5. An illustration is the meeting with George and Sophia Ripley, Margaret Fuller, and Bronson Alcott in October of 1840 to discuss the "Social Plans" for Brook Farm, described in *Journals,* edited by E. W. Emerson and W. E. Forbes (Boston, 1909-14), V, 473-74. This entry contains the famous passage about the hen-coop and the siege of Babylon. On September 26, Emerson had written a passage later incorporated in "Man the Reformer" (*ibid.,* p. 466), and two days after the meeting occurs another entry used in the same essay (*ibid.,* p. 480). The meeting also yielded reflections for "Self-Reliance" (*ibid.,* p. 477). John T. Flanagan has documented Emerson's coolness toward various schemes of reform in "Emerson and Communism," *New England Quarterly,* X (1937), 243-61.

6. Cooper, in *Notions of the Americans . . .* (1828), had pointed out that the people of the United States had been too fully absorbed in securing the necessaries of everyday life to support a class of "learned idlers" (II, 124-25).

7. McGiffert, p. 250.

8. *Nature, Addresses, and Lectures* (revised edition, Boston, 1883), pp. 245-76.

9. McGiffert, p. 240.

10. *Ibid.,* p. 255.

11. *Journals,* II (1828), 240-41.

12. *Ibid.,* V (1840), 405. See also III (1834), 355; *Nature, Addresses, and Lectures* (1841), p. 219.

13. *Nature, Addresses, and Lectures* (1841), p. 267.

14. *Emerson: A Study of the Poet as Seer* (New York, 1928), p. 142.

15. Quoted by Gay from James Eliot Cabot, *A Memoir of Ralph Waldo Emerson* (Boston, 1887), II, 434.

16. McGiffert, p. xii.

17. *Partial Portraits,* p. 25.

18. *Ibid.,* p. 7.

19. McGiffert, p. 166.

20. Some of the more important terms in this class are: the contemplative man (*Journals,* III [1834], 349); the man of genius (*ibid.,* IV [1836], 131; V

[1840], 443); the scholar (*ibid.*, IV [1836], 6); the torch-bearer (*ibid.*, V [1838], 82); the seer (*Nature, Addresses, and Lectures* [1841], p. 230); the saint (*ibid.*, p. 223); the dissenter (*ibid.*, p. 255); the aspirant (*ibid.*); the radical (*ibid.*, p. 301); the spiritualist (*ibid.*, p. 271); the idealist (*Journals*, VI [1841], 65); the Transcendentalist (*Nature* . . . , p. 317); and the hero (*ibid.*, p. 337). Henry James says, somewhat hastily, that Emerson means by the Scholar "simply the cultivated man, the man who has had a liberal education" (*Partial Portraits*, p. 20). But the real complexity of the term's denotation is well indicated by James's very discerning statement that Thoreau "took upon himself to be, in the concrete, the sort of person Emerson's 'scholar' was in the abstract" (p. 24). This endeavor involved, among other things, non-payment of taxes, refusal to wear a necktie, and the preparation of one's own food: items in a program which, while one may agree with James that it is "not of the essence," requires more explanation than the mere endeavor to act like a man with a liberal education. The term Scholar, with its charming connotation of rustic awe before a man with a tincture of books which James so deftly fixes upon, is in Emerson's use sometimes made to serve other and quite surprising purposes.

21. James points out that when Emerson was bored by the literalness and eccentricity of people like Thoreau and Alcott, he could declare himself "guiltless" of the transcendental doctrine (*Partial Portraits*, p. 25).

22. *Biographia Literaria*, J. Shawcross, editor (Oxford, 1907), II, 109.

23. Emerson makes the clerical lineage of the Scholar quite explicit in *Journals*, V (1839), 337; and *Nature* . . . , p. 95.

24. *Nature* . . . , p. 242.

25. *Journals*, II (1828), 240-41.

26. *Ibid.*, II (1832), 527-28.

27. *Ibid.*, V (1840), 405. This idea is associated with both the Scholar and the problem of reform in "Man the Reformer" (*Nature* . . . , p. 219).

28. *Journals*, IV (1837), 224.

29. *Ibid.*, IV (1836), 6-7.

30. *Ibid.*, III (1834), 407.

31. Some of the more important ideas of "The American Scholar" concerning vocation which appear earlier in the *Journals* are the following: (1) The Scholar's task is to classify the facts to discover the spiritual laws which determine them (*Nature* . . . , p. 87; see *Journals*, IV, 7-8); (2) The Scholar is closely related to the man of genius (*Nature* . . . , pp. 91-92; see *Journals*, IV, 198, where Shelley's skylark-poet is mentioned, although the identity of the Scholar and the man of genius is not made explicit); (3) The Scholar is scorned by practical men because he is not active (*Nature* . . . , p. 95; see *Journals*, IV, 6-7); (4) The Scholar operates through the unconscious radiation of virtue upon his associates, and this power is associated with "character" (*Nature* . . . , pp. 99-100; see *Journals*, III, 403; IV, 105-06; and IV, 183); (5) The Scholar is in a state of "virtual hostility" to society (*Nature* . . . , p. 102; see *Journals*, IV, 6-7); (6) The Scholar must resist vulgar

prosperity and avarice (*Nature* . . . , pp. 102, 113; see *Journals*, IV, 89-90, where it is stated that the two most important handicaps upon American intellectual performances are "our devotion to property" and the "influence of Europe"); (7) The Scholar realizes the world is mere appearance and beholds absolute truth through contemplation (*Nature* . . . , pp. 91, 102; see *Journals*, III, 355); (8) The Scholar will leave government to clerks (*Nature* . . . , p. 107; see *Journals*, II, 527-28).

32. *Nature* . . . , pp. 95-100.

33. *Ibid.*, p. 114.

34. *Journals*, IV (1837), 301.

35. *Ibid.*, IV (1838), 426.

36. *Ibid.*, IV (1838), 430-31.

37. *Ibid.*, V (1840), 469. The order of ideas in this entry is revealing. Emerson begins with an allusion to critics who accuse him of sloth and invite him to participate in active reforms. The threat to abandon the act of composition is developed from a Neoplatonic theory of the Scholar's indifference not only to philanthropies but to all "mere circumstances."

38. *Nature* . . . , pp. 298, 305. In the introductory lecture the idea of reform had appeared as a function of the Students because they are in contact with "the spiritual principle"—another attempt to redefine reform so as to remove its actively humanitarian connotations (*ibid.*, pp. 269-71).

39. *Ibid.*, p. 337. The earlier proposal that the Scholar should "replenish nature" from "that most real world of Ideas within him" (*Journals*, V [1840], 405) is probably another version of the same idea, leading through Plotinus to a hint of the regeneration of sinful physical nature by the incarnation of the *logos* (as in the hymn in "On the Morning of Christ's Nativity").

40. *Nature* . . . , pp. 332-34.

41. "The Man of Letters" (1863) and "The Scholar" (1876), in *Lectures and Biographical Sketches* (Boston, 1884), pp. 229-46 and 247-74.

42. *Journals*, VI (1841), 53. See also *Nature* . . . , p. 258.

43. *Journals*, V (1840), 337.

44. One recalls Emerson's statement that the Scholar stands in a state of "virtual hostility" to society (*Nature* . . . , p. 102), his terming the Transcendentalists "unsocial" (*ibid.*, p. 323), and his insistence that they were "not good citizens, not good members of society" (*ibid.*, p. 328). The entry of similar import for 1827 is in *Journals*, II, 527-28. See also *ibid.*, V, 302.

45. Thoreau put the matter quite pointedly: "The society which I was made for is not here" (*The Writings of Henry David Thoreau: Journal*, Bradford Torrey, editor [Boston, 1906], II [1851], 317).

46. *Nature* . . . , pp. 101-02.

47. *Ibid.*, p. 336.

15

Brownson and Emerson: Nature and History

A. ROBERT CAPONIGRI

1

THE CAREER OF ORESTES BROWNSON POSSESSES A UNIQUE IN-terest for the student of American civilization. Alone of all the figures intimately associated with New England transcendentalism, he took the road to Rome which so many of his European contemporaries were taking. By what course of thought did he find himself compelled to take this step? The initial interest in this question is increased immensely by even a partial answer; for a cursory examination of his thought, in this connection, yields indubitable evidence that Brownson entered the Roman Catholic Church in the belief that it held the answer to the fundamental problem which he had found implicit in the whole Protestant tradition from which he came: the problem of nature and history.

That the problem of nature and history is the central problem of Transcen-dentalism is the axiom from which the thought of the most eminent Tran-scendentalists, and of Emerson in particular, proceeds. The history of western thought since the Reformation justifies this assumption. For this problem is dictated to Transcendentalism by its historical position at the close of the

From *The New England Quarterly,* 18 (1945), 368-90. Reprinted by permission.

second phase of the historical career of the Protestant principle, and of this historical moment the problem of nature and history was the dialectical imperative.

The historical career of Protestantism manifested itself in two large phases which, upon the surface, may appear antithetical but are, in fact, logically continuous moments in the history of a single principle. In its first phase, Protestantism appears as a force for historical rectification. Operating as it did within the institutional framework of western Christendom, its ostensible purpose was to restore the historically authentic Christian spirit and form. Its real effect, inevitably, was nothing like its ostensible purpose—inevitably, because this purpose was intrinsically unfeasible. Its actual effect was to dissolve the unity of mediaeval Christendom and to multiply credal and institutional forms, all of which were more or less mimetic of the parent form and all of which bore indelibly the marks of their historical origin. The Protestant principle clearly operated, not to "rectify," but, as does every authentic historical principle, simply to "create" history. For such historical rectification is essentially impossible. To this end the irreversibility of history demands that one have recourse to an ahistorical principle, such as Protestantism did possess in the principle of private judgment. When this ahistorical principle is actually applied to the task of rectifying history, its effect is not to rectify, but to abolish history. Any ahistorical principle so applied must end by ultimately questioning the reality of history.

Such was the ultimate effect of the Protestant principle of private judgment. To the question of the historically authentic form of Christianity, another question inevitably succeeded. What is the need of any historical form for the Christian life? This new question was inevitable because the principle of private judgment is essentially a counterprinciple and not a correlative to any principle of historical continuity. The second phase of the historical career of Protestantism is marked by the gradual emergence and dominance of this new question and reaches its logical terminus in the assertion that the spiritual life of man is intrinsically independent of history because it is orientated not toward history, but directly toward the absolute spiritual principles of the universe, which are above and beyond history.

With the ascendency of this question the issue becomes strictly one of philosophy; for the imperative need is a philosophical, or more strictly speaking, an ontological principle which will substantiate this assertion of historical independence by demonstrating the direct orientation of the spiritual life of man toward absolute, trans-historical principles. Historically, the principle was at hand in the conception of nature as it underlies, on the one hand, scientific, and on the other, sentimental, naturalism in the modern world. In the fabric of both these forms of naturalism the concept of nature is such as to render history, if not ontologically impossible, then essentially illusory. Scientific naturalism comes to this end through the development of its concept of the absolute fixed laws of nature, while sentimental naturalism arrives at the same goal by way of its cult of the individual, of inspiration, of genius, of the divine indwelling in human nature. There emerges, inevitably, the antithesis, nature *versus* history. By the appeal to nature, scientist and sentimentalist alike try to emancipate themselves from history.

American Transcendentalism, viewed in historical perspective, is a moment in this second phase of the historical career of Protestantism. This is demonstrated by its preoccupation and its doctrine. Its preoccupation is the re-orientation of the spiritual life of man away from history toward absolute principles. It seeks to effect this re-orientation by the exploration and expansion of the concept "nature," which it derived from the new naturalism. The truth of this interpretation of the historical and intrinsic character of Transcendentalism is best demonstrated by the thought of its foremost figure, Emerson.

2

The release of man's spiritual and moral life from history is the chief motive and objective of Emerson's thought. He reveals this preoccupation and purpose most clearly in the crucial discourse of his first efforts as an independent thinker. The *Divinity School Address* has as its main theme the excoriation of historical Christianity. All of Emerson's charges reduce themselves to one: the church, in all its historical forms, has sinned inexcusably against the individual soul by erecting, under the guise of a machinery of mediation, an impenetrable barrier between the soul and the absolute spiritual laws and reality toward which it is by nature oriented. By its exaltation of the historical person of Christ, by the machinery of the sacraments, by its dogmas of original sin, of vicarious justification, and of grace, historical Christianity has obscured, indeed almost obliterated, the profoundest truths of the spiritual life, namely, the indwelling of the divine in every soul, the universal Christhood of mankind, the natural and direct affinity of the soul with the divine and the good. To release the soul from this bondage by demonstrating the illusory character of the hold which history has upon its life, to re-direct its attention and its energies to the absolute spiritual reality which operates without mediation in the individual soul, is the apostolic work to which he sets himself.

Emerson perceives that such a re-orientation can be effected only on the basis of principles whose ultimate implication is the ahistorical character of Being, itself. History must be destroyed not merely as a religious and human force, but as a principle of Being. It must be shown that man's spiritual life is independent of history because reality itself is ultimately ahistorical. That this course of thought involves the reduction of history to an illusion and of experience to a pin-point present, and finally the obliteration of the distinction between contingent and absolute Being, Emerson is well aware; and nowhere in his thought does he shrink from these implications. The idea by which he hopes to effect this re-orientation in his doctrine of nature, and in his thought the dialectical[1] function of this concept is to nullify the concept of history in its ultimate, that is, its ontological dimension.

The development of the concept "nature" and of its ahistorical implications proceeds in Emerson's thought on three levels: that of Truth, that of the Good, and, ultimately, that of Being. By his doctrine of intuition as a principle of nature, Emerson tries to render the individual independent of history on the level of Truth; by the doctrine of spiritual laws, on the level of the Good; by his doctrine of causality, on that of Being.

Intuition is without doubt one of the most important concepts in Emerson's doctrine of nature, and he exploits it fully for his polemical purpose. The term antithetical to "intuition" in the masked dialectic of Emerson's thought is not reason but authority. The latter term involves essentially a historical dimension, for in the last analysis authority means historical authority; the derivation of certainty from a nonexperiential source involves a relationship which is in essence historical, the transference of experience in the form of dogma. Conversely, the strength of the hold which history possesses over the thoughtful is dogma: knowledge crystalized but removed from the domain of individual experience. If the individual is to be released from this hold of history, the concepts of dogma and authority must be dissolved, the absolute order toward which the soul is to be re-orientated must be shown to be immediately accessible in its fullness to the immediate experience of the individual.[2] The concept "intuition" is an instrument of this liberation because the faculty which it symbolizes is the most direct channel between man and the realm of absolute spiritual reality.[3]

Although he inherits the term "intuition" from a long tradition of philosophical usage, Emerson employs it without special concern for its historical associations, investing it with new significance directed always toward his polemical purpose. In its traditional employment the term has signified almost universally the direct apprehension of an existing object according to the complete conditions of its existence. From this signification the antihistorical thesis which Emerson has in mind cannot be drawn. The term of the activity of intuition in this sense is the principle of Being, according to which the radical potency of existence is actualized, *viz.*, particular substance. Particular substance alone completely realizes the conditions of actual existence, and particular substance is always historical, because the complete determination of existence involves at least causal and perhaps also temporal dependence and succession. Consequently, Emerson revises the historical and traditional import of the term, by redefining both the object and the condition of its activity.

The specific object of intuition, according to Emerson's use of the term, is the realm of spiritual laws; and the attributes which he ascribes to this realm put beyond question its transhistorical character. For the spiritual laws are "out of time, out of space, and not subject to circumstance."[4] They thus escape all the limiting conditions of actual, historical existence and cannot be conceived of as historical either in the sense of fulfilling or defining these conditions. Emerson is also at pains to warn against the illusion that the spiritual laws operate or manifest themselves directly through history. Their dynamic relation is directly to the present, within which they operate always with their full force; history never mediates their power. They appear in history only obliquely, or representatively, in Emerson's own term. This redefinition of the specific object of intuition is a step forward, consequently, in the emancipation of the spiritual life of the individual from history; Emerson proceeds further to assert that not only the object but the mode of operation of intuition is transhistorical.

The basis for this redefinition of the mode of operation of intuition is ultimately Emerson's doctrine of the identity of subject and object. Since the object of intuition has been defined as the absolute realm of spiritual laws, intuition is in reality a mode by which the soul realizes its identity with this object. Intuition involves, consequently, a discipline of withdrawal from the historical stream of conscious or reflective life. It comes in moments of vision, in which, for the instant, the whole clamor of the life of the senses and the understanding is stilled, in which the discursive stream of consciousness which constitutes the historical dimension of individual life is in abeyance. The strengthening of intuition moves toward the state of ecstasy or surrender to this identity. In the moment of intuition the individual's sense of selfhood transcends the discursive historical self; and such moments come to him, not through the historical organic processes of his life, but by visitation, not through the extension of life on this historical organic level, but through retreat (or ascent) from it to the level of primal identity of Being. Thus, the intuitional moment is transhistorical in the individual, that is, comes to him, not through the preparation of the organic processes, but by visitation; it withdraws him from the discursive stream of consciousness, and ultimately tends to re-unite him in moments of ecstasy with the transhistorical object.[5]

As a principle of nature, then, intuition is ahistorical and transhistorical in its object and in its mode of operation; on the level of truth, consequently, it makes for the emancipation of the individual from history, and re-orientates his life toward the absolute. The emancipation achieved on the level of Truth by intuition is achieved on the level of the Good by the doctrine of the mode of operation of the spiritual laws.

The point of departure for Emerson's development of the concept of nature on the ethical level is, as we might expect, the historical doctrines of imputed sin and imputed grace, the whole historical economy involved in Christianity as it has taken historical form in the west. His purpose is again very clear: it is to emancipate the moral life of the individual from history, to re-orientate it to absolute moral principles whose nature and operation are alike transhistorical in character. These principles are the spiritual laws.

The spiritual laws are transhistorical in their very nature, in their mode of operation, and in the theatre of their action. They define the absolute, unchanging forces of the universe, of Being itself; they are neither descriptive nor prescriptive, but constitutive. They absolve and execute themselves, depending on no mediate or historical agencies, in the instant of time, which is time's only reality. They look not from man to man, but to the individual wholly; his justice is never mediate, but consists wholly in the activity of these laws within himself. Morality in human life looks not from man to man, but directly from the individual to the absolute spiritual forces whose theatre he is. His justice is his, and his injustice. In his quest for the Good, he must look neither backward nor forward, but above; the spiritual laws directly define and constitute his moral state, so that through them he becomes identical with the absolute moral being of the universe.[6]

As all morality is, then, not from man to man, or from man to God through any mediation, but directly from the individual to the absolute moral principles of the universe itself; and since the whole theatre of the moral economy of the universe is each individual soul, the moral life has no historical dimension. Imputed justice and imputed injustice are alike without meaning. As no one's sin can be visited upon another, so no one's salvation can be wrought by another; but in each soul the entire drama is enacted. By this concept of the moral life Emerson is able to reject the entire historical theology of Christianity, to emancipate the individual wholly from history and again to direct his being on the moral level toward the absolute and the transhistorical. Intuition opens the soul to the realm of spiritual laws; the ethical life unites the soul to these laws, realizes them in itself. The spiritual laws define the absolute good; when these laws become the principle of the individual life, the individual lives with their reality; he does not do good so much as he becomes good.

This direct vertical relationship of the individual to the absolute truth and the absolute Good advance his historical emancipation; but it yet remains to be completed by demonstration that the relationship in the order of Being itself is equally direct between individual and absolute. Emerson's thought moved toward this complete emancipation through his development of the doctrine of causes. Writing in the eighteen-fifties, Brownson remarked that Emerson lacked completely any grasp of the doctrine of causes. Although the statement is extreme, and therefore unjust, it nevertheless indicates the correct point of departure for the consideration of the development of the ahistorical implications of Emerson's concept of nature on the level of Being; this question must center about Emerson's treatment of the doctrine of causes.

In the theistic tradition of the western world, history has been explained ontologically, in terms of Being, as an order of secondary causes whose operation, while essentially contingent, is hypothetically necessary; that is, on the assumption of the possibility and actuality of history. The order of these causes, their system or complexus, constitutes nature; and since their order is successive, nature and history seem clearly to derive from the same character of created Being, that is, its contingency. Indeed, the thesis that nature and history are, in principle of Being, one, appears almost as an axiom in much western thought. Brownson's charge would seem to imply that Emerson is unaware of this tradition which makes for the unity and identity in principle of nature and history through the doctrine of secondary causes; on the contrary, however, Emerson gives every evidence of being well aware of it, and indeed of having this tradition in mind in the development of his own doctrine.

Emerson is more urgently beset by the problem of contingency than are most thinkers, because of his peculiar philosophic preoccupation, the discrediting of history. History is generated by the contingency of Being, so that the denial of the one seems to imply that of the other. Emerson, is willing, nay, eager to dispense with history; but he is unwilling to do so at the price of the individual, the epitome of contingency. His problem is thus determined for him: to relate the individual directly to absolute Being, while preserving the individuality, the separateness intact. Two ways to this end seem possible: the reduction of the absolute to the individual, and the elevation of the individual to the absolute. Either way demands the development of a principle of identity which will unite while yet distinguishing the contingent and the absolute. This problem once brought Emerson to the very borders of Hegelianism; but, as Gray remarks,[7] this reach of thought was beyond him.

Emerson is frequently assumed to have fallen into one or another of the pitfalls which have in history beset this problem: emanationism, pantheism, evolutionism. In justice to him, however, it must be pointed out that none of these terms precisely and exhaustively characterizes his solution of the problem of contingency. His position may perhaps best be summarized in the saying that the entire force of the first and absolute cause is directed to the actuality of the individual, to every individual, and that every individual exists by the full influx of the first cause. There is here, on the level of Being, a strict analogy with the operation of the economy of the spiritual laws. The whole causative force of the first cause executes itself in every individual, just as the whole economy of good and evil completes itself in the individual soul. This conception does not in any way raise the question of the identity of the individual with the absolute cause, for the reply is apparent before the question takes form: the individual, by its individuality, cannot be equated with the Absolute; the Absolute by its infinity, cannot be exhausted, either by a single individual or by an infinity of individuals. And it is only the force of the ultimate and absolute cause which can adequately account for the existence of any individual; any other mediate causes or system of causes must reductively lead the mind back to the absolute. Emerson prefers to believe that what appear to us to be secondary causes in the historical order can better be explained by the doctrine of representation, which, he believes, adequately accounts for the relation of individuals and truly defines the nature of history. Every individual is the object of the causative force of the first cause; it stands to every other individual as a reminder of the absolute power which is poured out in it also.

Correlative to this doctrine is the disciplinary admonition, to open the soul to the consciousness of this direct influx of the first cause; for always the thought lies at the back of Emerson's mind that the conscious reflective life of man, of the individual man and of the race, has operated to obscure this truth; that man has been falsely made dependent upon the oblique sight, the mediated action.

By this doctrine the individual is freed from historical dependence and set up on the ultimate plane of Being itself. In the ultimate order of Being, his individual life has been orientated toward the absolute which he is admonished to recognize as his sole cause. And correlatively, history is assigned its true place in the perspective of human life, assigned its representative status and value. The emancipation of man from history and his re-orientation toward the absolute would seem thus to be complete and the historical drive of Emerson's thought to have reached its term.

3

Brownson's affinity to Transcendentalism is closest at the point of its ahistorical bias, and this affinity is the result of the movement of his own thought. In his early career, Brownson had recapitulated in his own experience the historical phases of Protestantism. His errancy among the available Protestant sects was dictated by the stupendous task which he had set himself and which was none other than the ostensible task of historical Protestantism itself: to ascertain, upon the principle of private judgment, the historically and doctrinally authentic form of Christianity. Disillusionment in the task was as inevitable for him as, historically, it has been for Protestantism, and disillusionment brought both to the same term, the questioning of history itself. It was at this moment, when in the depression of his first disillusion-ment he was prepared to challenge the meaning of history itself, that Brownson found himself in sympathy with Transcendentalism. Certain state-ments made by him at this time condemning the cult of the historical Jesus, asserting the universality of the Incarnation in all men, charging the historical church with obstructing the immediate communion of human nature with the eternal and absolute springs of goodness and divinity, might almost with indifference be ascribed to Emerson or Channing. Witness the words in which he arraigns the historical church:

> When she [the historical church] asserted the incarnation of the ideal in Jesus, she asserted the truth; when she asserted that it was and could be incarnated in him alone, she erred.

And again:

> The Church of the future will be based on two great principles . . . the generalization of the incarnation. . . ."[8]

At this very point of greatest affinity, however, a marked difference—a fundamental difference of intuition—between Brownson and Transcendental-ism makes its appearance, and this difference first indicates to us the princi-ples upon which Brownson will reconstruct, in constant dialectic with the ideas of Transcendentalism, his doctrine of nature and history. While assert-ing, on the one hand, the universal divinity of man and the human spirit's independence of history, Brownson nevertheless draws back from the ex-treme individualism and subjectivism to which these assertions appear to lead in Emerson. The crucial question is that of the immediacy of the relationship of the individual to the divine. To Emerson the doctrine of the divinity of man could mean but one thing, the divinity of every individual and, conse-quently, the immediate access of every individual to the plenitude of the divine in his own experience. Brownson, on the contrary, maintained from the beginning that the ascription of divinity must be made not in the first instance to the individual but to humanity. It is humanity which in the first instance is divine and the individual through his unity with humanity. This term, humanity, becomes a key term in his reconstruction of the doctrine of history.

And here it may be remarked, somewhat parenthetically, that Brownson's condemnation of individualism is not limited to this idea as it appears in Transcendentalism; he objects as strenously to what appears to him to be the extreme and hampering individualism of the historical church.[9] The basis for this rejection of individualism is the same in both cases: Brownson's sense of the solidarity of the individual with the group, and ultimately with the whole of mankind in all its dimensions.

Brownson's intuition of the solidarity of the individual and the race—it is an intuition, similar to that "sense of dependence" which he employs in his theology and which allies him with the school of Schleiermacher—finds expression or formulation on several levels of human experience. It is this intuition, formulated and expressed on the level of truth and knowledge, which precipitates Brownson's attack upon the principle of private judgment and inspires his partial rehabilitation of the doctrine of tradition and universal consent as a criterion of certitude. In the act of knowing, he asserts, in direct opposition and with obvious reference to Emerson, the mind apprehends its object not in virtue of a radical identity but of an ultimate polarity. This polarity he conceives dynamically, as the actualization of the latent power of the individual to know by contact with an object which defines and realizes that power. The polarity, subject-object, is irreducible, while the actuality of knowledge is a synthesis in being of these polar elements. The principle of private judgment, consequently, in as far as it appears to involve an identity of the subject and object, is repugnant to experience.[10]

Although the act of knowledge is realized in the individual, yet the individual mind neither constitutes its object nor apprehends it in virtue of a radical identity. Its object is the common world, which it shares with other minds. From this it appears clear to Brownson that the proper object of the mind is not addressed to the individual mind but to the intelligent faculty of the human nature in which the individual participates; concretely, to humanity. The testimony of universal assent, consequently, gains precedence in his mind over individual experience. Although he never examines either the structure or the implications of this doctrine with anything like the thoroughness of Lamennais or Newman, its influence upon him is great and he tries to employ it in his own thought; he was also able to comprehend immediately its temporal dimension, so that without further concern he speaks interchangeably of universal consent and of tradition. His philosophy of history leads him later to refine considerably on the concept of tradition.[11]

In his epistemological discussions Brownson employs the concept of human nature as a real principle of Being, transcending the individual and defining his character. It becomes increasingly clear that the solidarity of the race depends upon the truth of this conception of human nature and the adequate explanation it can be given. Reviewing the work of the Saint-Simonian, Pierre Leroux, he writes with warm approval of the general line of that movement:

> Humanity is not an aggregate of individuals . . . humanity precedes individuals and is their origin and support. It is human nature, that is the human species, which makes individual men and women.[12]

His method of exploring the empirical evidence for this principle follows the pattern set by his treatment of the problem of knowledge. Experience establishes that not only in respect to knowledge, but in regard to feeling and action, as well, the individual needs the "objective" in order to complete [or] actualize, his being.

> Leroux holds (and in this we coincide with him) that man taken alone is never competent to the task of his own manifestation. He remains in a latent virtual state till assisted to actualize himself by that which is not himself. . . . His whole life, whether intellectual, sentient, or sentimental is jointly in himself and in that which is not himself. His life is then at once subjective and objective.[13]

Nature and society afford the individual the object elements of life; and since, without the objective element, his life and nature remain latent, in potency, in a state of non-being with respect to that which it might and should be, the dependence upon nature and society cannot be looked upon as accidental, but only as constitutive and essential.

> As he has need of living, so has he need of this communion, the indispensable condition of his life.[14]

Since the solidarity of the individual with nature and society is so fundamental a principle. Brownson is led to examine its dimensions in full, and this inquiry leads him directly to the question of the reality of history as a principle of Being. So long as the relationship of the individual to the objective elements of his life is stated in general and abstract terms, such as nature and humanity, there might seem to be no particular occasion for the problem of history to arise. The actual orientation of the individual, Brownson warns, however, is not in the abstract, not toward mankind in general, nor toward nature as a vague concept or sentiment, but toward the concrete. The conditions under which solidarity, and the actuality of his life, are achieved by the individual are concrete, and he defines them as three: family, nation, and property. All these are fundamentally historical terms. The family most obviously, but the nation and property also quite clearly, define relationships with essential historical dimensions. The concrete conditions of life and actuality in the individual would seem therefore to be historical relations. The relevancy of the problem of history for Brownson is thus clear; he must face the question of the character of history as a principle of Being. He has been led inexorably to this point by the initial drive of his intuition of the solidarity of the individual and the group. Brownson formulates his answer to the problem of history in his doctrine of creation, by which he believes that he establishes the ultimate historical character of contingent Being itself.

Like Emerson's use of "nature," Brownson's term "creation" is one heavy with historical associations, which his own interpretation alters. Traditionally, the term "creation" has been used within the framework of the theistic position, which assumes the absolute transhistorical character of the first cause. As a consequence of this assumption, the theistic position had been beset by the problem of contingency, and in a form which to many has appeared critical. For if a first cause be assumed or proved to be absolutely outside history, the question cannot fail to arise, why historical and contingent Being exists at all and by what mode it comes into being. Brownson, in his doctrine of creation, following Gioberti and, more remotely, Malebranche, is concerned with preserving the fundamentals of the theistic position; but is also concerned to escape the traditional embarrassments of the problem of contingency. And his point of departure is still the first intuition which has led him to this point: that of dependence, the sense of solidarity of the forms of Being.

Brownson's doctrine of creation is really the metaphysical or ontological projection or extension of his perception of the objective-subjective character of the life of individual man. The individual man, he has observed, is not autonomous, but needs the objective to actualize his latent humanity. The same is true of Being as a whole. Every form of Being needs its objective complement, the principle outside itself which will reduce its latent or potential power to actuality. The objective complement of the universe is its creative principle, the Creator. Creation is then the term which designates the objective-subjective character of Being in its ultimate terms, in terms of the universe and of God; it is the name of that real relation of dependency which defines the antecedent conditions of the actuality of the world which is given us in experience. In the light of this conception of the term, the problem of contingency in its traditional formulation appears spurious. The question, why does the Creator create, can never, in the true state of the problem, arise. For the first cause is known to us only as it manifests itself, that is only as creator, as the ultimate objective ground of the being of the universe. The actuality of the world postulates this objective principle as actual; it is inconceivable that the ultimate objective principle should not be that ultimate objective principle. There is no basis in reason or experience for the fantastic question whether the universe might not be, or its correlative, whether God is necessarily Creator. He is necessarily Creator in as far as it is given us to know him, i.e., as the objective principle of the universe; he is, further, necessarily Creator, if his nature be of that absolute character, which it is, that demands that all his relations be necessary and objective. In a word, creation is nothing else but the ultimate creative principle manifesting itself, God expressing himself, by an unquestionable necessity of his being.[15]

The term *creation* is not the designation of a static relationship, but of a process which is essentially historical. For its end or term is the actually existent, which, Brownson holds, is always the concrete individual. But the Being of the creative principle can be imparted to the concrete individual only through the mediation of secondary causal principles, whose character it is to assure the concrete conditions for the actualization of the individual and whose mode of operation necessarily is successive, or progressive. For the end of creation is the expression of God's nature according to the conditions of actual concrete individual existence; but as the nature to be expressed is infinite, and the medium finite, succession or infinite progression interposes itself between the finite and the infinite as the only mode by which the expression of the one in terms of the others is possible. The complexus of secondary causes which mediate the expression of the infinite and absolute creative principle according to the conditions of individual concrete existence, constitute the order of nature, which is of necessity, historical.[16]

Brownson illustrates this doctrine by his conception of species. The immediate object of the creative force is not the individual, he holds, but the humanity. Secondary causes operate historically, that is, in a causal sequence which induces temporal sequence. Human nature, for example, is precedent to the individual man not only logically, or conceptually, but actually, as a creative principle operating historically. The ultimate object of this activity is the actual individual, and the concrete historical form of the operation of the principle is, in this instance of man, the family.[17] Nature, therefore, being itself in as far as given in nature, is essentially historical and history enters as a real principle of Being into the actuality of every individual substance.[18]

What is the significance of this conclusion for Brownson's special problem, that of the access possessed by the individual to the divine? The complete denial of any immediate natural access and the quite unconditional assertion that the individual soul, in the nature of things, approaches the divine mediately, through the channels of history and tradition, just as it approaches the very well springs of Being through the mediation of historical natural causal forces.[19]

At this point the severance of his affinity for the ahistorical element in Transcendentalism is completed. He has established in complete antithesis to Emerson, the concept of nature as essentially historical, or the individual life as fundamentally dependent upon history in all its actuality, of the spiritual life of man as mediated by history. He is still far, however, from the acceptance of the historical claims of any form of Christianity to be the historical channel. The steps by which he comes to this further term continue the process by which he has reached his rehabilitation of the doctrine of history, and the first step toward this ultimate goal is the formulation of the doctrine of the supernatural.

Brownson's treatment of the problem of the supernatural falls into two phases, the first prior to, the second succeeding, his conversion. With this second phase, in which he is concerned primarily with establishing the ontology of the supernatural and in which he ventures, without great success, into the labyrinth of scholastic metaphysics, we are not here concerned. In the first phase the supernatural appears as a principle of the philosophy of history, and Brownson's preoccupation is with the establishment of the supernatural as a fact of history. This preoccupation accords with his principle (formulated clearly only much later, but implicit in all his thought on the matter) that it is only from the fact of the supernatural that one can proceed to its rational explanation. It is in the light of this principle that he later, as a Catholic, attacks the traditional methodology of the treatise "On The True Religion" in which the procedure is to establish antecedently the possibility of the supernatural. The providential view of the philosophy of history which he expounds appears to him to have the merit of establishing the fact of the supernatural, as the basis for all speculation concerning its ontological character and mode of operation.

The providential theory of history, as Brownson conceives and expounds it, is a continuation of his doctrine of creation. Creation, it will be recalled, he has defined as the real nexus between absolute objective being and contingent subjective being. This nexus is necessarily historical and progressive, i.e., creation is a historical principle of Being, a continuous process.

The operation of the creative principle in history cannot be defined or limited by the fixed laws of nature alone, either analytically or empirically. For from the nature of the creative principle, infinite and absolute, fixed laws of its activity cannot be deduced. If fixed laws can be formulated for the operation of the creative principle in nature and history, their formulation must be inductive and empirical. Experience, however, as emphatically as analysis, forbids the description of fixed laws which preclude any special intervention of the creative principle. On the contrary it compels the postulation of such special intervention as the only rational explanation of indisputable facts of history.

> For ourselves, we confess our utter inability to explain the past history of the race on the theory of natural development or even on that of the supernatural inspiration which we believe to be common to all men. That history is all bristling with prodigies which are inexplicable save on the hypothesis of the constant intervention in a special manner of the ever-watchful father.[20]

The special intervention of the creative force appears most clearly in providential men. These appear at every crisis in human affairs, and their powers and characters are such as to render impossible any account of them in the terms of ordinary human activity. The attempt to dissolve these semi-mythical personages into legendary embodiments of men's experience appears to him unsound. They can be accounted for only in terms of a specially intervening creative power and providence.

Providence itself he defines empirically as the order or *ratio* of this special intervention, and as such it constitutes the supernatural order whose actuality in history is empirical fact. This conception of the supernatural also affords the basis for at least a descriptive definition of it: it is nothing more or less than the divine creative force itself, immediately active at a point in time and history. It is God and what he does immediately.[21]

This theory of the supernatural defines the basis upon which he is prepared to accept and finally does accept the historical claims of Catholicism: that there is a providential and supernatural intervention and agency in history, directed to some extraordinary and crucial historical end. The end toward which this supernatural agency and intervention is directed he recognizes as the healing of the rupture of original sin; and the succeeding steps in his movement toward the acceptance of the historical faith is his reconstruction of this doctrine and also that of the special mission of Christ and the historical necessity of its continuation through a historical principle or institution.

The reconstruction of the doctrine of original sin follows easily upon the sequence of Brownson's thought up to this point:—the doctrine of creation, of the historical character of nature and being, of the solidarity of the human race, the ontological character of the principle of mediation. These all conspire to establish the antecedent possibility of the doctrine because they demonstrate the reasonableness of its fundamental element: the transference of guilt. The unity of the race in Adam constitutes the ultimate ontological ground for this transference of guilt, while the doctrine of the unity of the race in Adam is itself a conclusion to be derived from the theory of creation and the mediated and historical character of Being.

The fact of original sin Brownson believes that he establishes by a trinity of arguments, from tradition, from scripture, and from experience. The doctrine of human depravity is universally held in one form or another by all mankind, he asserts; but such universal credence is an argument, at least a presumptive argument, for the truth of the idea, in accordance with the precedence which tradition has been shown to possess over the evidence of individual reason and experience.[22] To the argument from Scripture he accords, at this point, an authority but little surpassing that of an element in the universal tradition. The experience of depravity he believes to be individual, immediate, and universal; and his description of this experience he derives from the dualism of the Pauline tradition.

The intrinsic character of this depravity is made clear to him by the opinion he has already reached. It is not individual, but generic, inhering in the common human nature, and pertaining to the individual only in the sense and to the extent to which he shares the common human nature as the basis for his own actuality. Further, it cannot be conceived of as a fall from original perfection, for such a fall appears to him intrinsically impossible. Man was created in the first instance imperfect, sharing thus the general imperfection of created nature, which itself derives from the impossibility of a finite realization of the infinite nature of God. In its innermost essence this original depravity of man can consist only in the deviation of the human race, as one dimension of creation, from the purpose of the whole creation, the progressive actualization or external realization of the perfection of God.[23]

The fact of original sin established the necessity of redemption, the purpose and conditions of which are defined, on the one hand by the historical character of Being, and on the other by the intrinsic character of the original depravity. The latter indicates that the purpose of redemption must be the reintegration of the life of the human race with the primitive end of creation. This end of redemption can be actualized only by a special intervention of God himself, a historical incursion of his special activity, in the character of a providential agent, a mediator.

This historical mediator is Christ. Entirely reversing his previous position, namely, that Christ is to be looked upon as no more than one instance of the divine indwelling which is the natural gift of every man, Brownson now contends unreservedly for his special character and divine mission.

> It is impossible then to press Jesus into the category of ordinary men; he stands out as distinct, peculiar.[24]

The unique historical incursion of the Mediator will not suffice, however, to the work of redemption. It must be historically perpetuated by an institution or principle which will continue and actualize its work on the historically successive planes of individual being. This historical perpetuation of the work of the mediator and redeemer is demanded by the historical character of nature itself. For, if the Redeemer is to impart to the human race a new life, that life must possess a historical dimension and principle. The church is the natural and inescapable principle perpetuating the Messianic or mediatorial work, and toward it the spiritual life of the individual must be orientated as toward that objective principle which alone can actualize it.

With this conclusion, the circle of Brownson's thought is complete. From his initial denial of the historical orientation of the spiritual life of man he has passed through the full cycle of reconstruction to its inescapable conclusion: the acceptance of the historical principle of the perpetual mediatorial work of Jesus as the imperative of the religious and moral life. And, with this complete revision of his position, his affinity to Transcendentalism is completely dissolved. Now he stands upon the threshold of the ancient church, over which he did not hesitate to pass.

NOTES

1. Or as Brownson calls it, the "political" and "practical". Henry F. Brownson, editor, *The Works of Orestes A. Brownson* (Detroit, 1882-1907), III, 424.

2. "All history becomes subjective; in other words there is properly no history. Every mind must know the whole lesson for itself—must go over the whole ground. What it does not see, what it does not live, it will not know. . . . " R. W. Emerson, *Essays, Second Series* (Boston, 1884), pp. 14-15 and passim.

3. *The Complete Works of Ralph Waldo Emerson* (Boston, 1903), I, 126-27.

4. *Ibid.*, p. 122.

5. *Ibid.*, I, 9, 10; II, 64, 65, 285, 304; III, 69, 176; IV, 16; X, 75, 78, 178; XII, 32, 33.

6. *Ibid.*, I, 122; II, 131ff.

7. Henry David Gray, *Emerson* (Palo Alto, 1917), p. 43.

8. *The Works of Orestes A. Brownson*, IV, 63, 71.

9. *Ibid.*, pp. 104-05.

10. *Ibid.*, I, 35; III, 488; IV, 355; V, 128.

11. *Ibid.*, II, 98, 129; III, 193; XVIII, 52; and passim.

12. *Ibid.*, IV, 134.

13. *Ibid.*, pp. 115ff.

14. *Ibid.*

15. *Ibid.*, p. 421.

16. *Ibid.*, p. 413: "Nature is not only active, but progressive. This is demonstrable from the very conception which we have and cannot but have of God, if we conceive of him at all. Our only conception of God is of him as cause, creator, but as an infinitely wise, powerful and good cause. He is essentially cause, not merely a potential cause, but actually eternally and universally a cause. In causing and creating he is realizing his own infinite ideal in space and time. But space and time are limited and can contain only the finite. Creation, therefore, or the universe, viewed either as a whole or in detail must be incomplete, can only be a finite realization of the infinite: consequently only an imperfect realization of the infinite.

It must be now and always an imperfect, that is, incomplete, realization of the divine ideal, because, if it were not, the ideal being infinite, the creation would be infinite. An infinite creation is an absurdity. . . . But God is essentially creator, always and everywhere a creator. His ideal is infinite and he never relaxes, so to say, the creative effort to attain it. Consequently, the realization must be forever coming nearer and nearer to the complete; which implies, through the continuous creative energy of the creator, a continuous progress of the universe towards the full and perfect realization of the infinite ideal. Hence the progressiveness of nature herself."

17. *Ibid.*, p. 105.

18. *Ibid.*, p. 81.

19. *Ibid.*, pp. 151, 153.

20. *Ibid.*, p. 94; see also p. 399: "This theory of the non-intervention of Providence, save through the fixed and permanent laws of nature, will not suffice to explain and account for the facts of human history."

21. *Ibid.*, IX, 335.

22. Parenthetically, the inconclusive character of his doctrine of tradition and of universal consent is shown by his assertion (IV, 152) that "the individual must determine what is tradition,"—a manifest impossibility and inconsistency.

23. *The Works of Orestes A. Brownson,* IV, 152, 153, 421.

24. *Ibid.*, p. 149.

16

Emerson

HENRY JAMES

MR. ELLIOT CABOT HAS MADE A VERY INTERESTING CONTRIBU-
tion to a class of books of which our literature, more than any other, offers
admirable examples: he has given us a biography[1] intelligently and carefully
composed. These two volumes are a model of responsible editing—I use that
term because they consist largely of letters and extracts from letters: nothing
could resemble less the manner in which the mere bookmaker strings together
his frequently questionable pearls and shovels the heap into the presence of
the public. Mr. Cabot has selected, compared, discriminated, steered an even
course between meagreness and redundancy, and managed to be constantly
and happily illustrative. And his work, moreover, strikes us as the better done
from the fact that it stands for one of the two things that make an absorbing
memoir a good deal more than for the other. If these two things be the
conscience of the writer and the career of his hero, it is not difficult to see on
which side the biographer of Emerson has found himself strongest. Ralph
Waldo Emerson was a man of genius, but he led for nearly eighty years a life
in which the sequence of events had little of the rapidity, or the complexity,
that a spectator loves. There is something we miss very much as we turn these
pages—something that has a kind of accidental, inevitable presence in almost

From *Partial Portraits* by Henry James. London: Macmillan, 1888.

any personal record—something that may be most definitely indicated under the name of colour. We lay down the book with a singular impression of paleness—an impression that comes partly from the tone of the biographer and partly from the moral complexion of his subject, but mainly from the vacancy of the page itself. That of Emerson's personal history is condensed into the single word Concord, and all the condensation in the world will not make it look rich. It presents a most continuous surface. Mr. Matthew Arnold, in his *Discourses in America,* contests Emerson's complete right to the title of a man of letters; yet letters surely were the very texture of his history. Passions, alternations, affairs, adventures had absolutely no part in it. It stretched itself out in enviable quiet—a quiet in which we hear the jotting of the pencil in the notebook. It is the very life for literature (I mean for one's own, not that of another): fifty years of residence in the home of one's forefathers, pervaded by reading, by walking in the woods and the daily addition of sentence to sentence.

If the interest of Mr. Cabot's pencilled portrait is incontestable and yet does not spring from variety, it owes nothing either to a source from which it might have borrowed much and which it is impossible not to regret a little that he has so completely neglected: I mean a greater reference to the social conditions in which Emerson moved, the company he lived in, the moral air he breathed. If his biographer had allowed himself a little more of the ironic touch, had put himself once in a way under the protection of Sainte-Beuve and had attempted something of a general picture, we should have felt that he only went with the occasion. I may overestimate the latent treasures of the field, but it seems to me there was distinctly an opportunity—an opportunity to make up moreover in some degree for the white tint of Emerson's career considered simply in itself. We know a man imperfectly until we know his society, and we but half know a society until we know its manners. This is especially true of a man of letters, for manners lie very close to literature. From those of the New England world in which Emerson's character formed itself Mr. Cabot almost averts his lantern, though we feel sure that there would have been delightful glimpses to be had and that he would have been in a position—that is that he has all the knowledge that would enable him—to help us to them. It is as if he could not trust himself, knowing the subject only too well. This adds to the effect of extreme discretion that we find in his volumes, but it is the cause of our not finding certain things, certain figures and scenes, evoked. What is evoked is Emerson's pure spirit, by a copious, sifted series of citations and comments. But we must read as much as possible between the lines, and the picture of the transcendental time (to mention simply one corner) has yet to be painted—the lines have yet to be bitten in. Meanwhile we are held and charmed by the image of Emerson's mind and the extreme appeal which his physiognomy makes to our art of discrimination. It is so fair, so uniform and impersonal, that its features are simply fine shades, the gradations of tone of a surface whose proper quality was of the smoothest and on which nothing was reflected with violence. It is a pleasure of the critical sense to find, with Mr. Cabot's extremely intelligent help, a notation for such delicacies.

We seem to see the circumstances of our author's origin, immediate and remote, in a kind of high, vertical moral light, the brightness of a society at once very simple and very responsible. The rare singleness that was in his nature (so that he was *all* the warning moral voice, without distraction or counter-solicitation), was also in the stock he sprang from, clerical for generations, on both sides, and clerical in the Puritan sense. His ancestors had lived long (for nearly two centuries) in the same corner of New England, and during that period had preached and studied and prayed and practised. It is impossible to imagine a spirit better prepared in advance to be exactly what it was—better educated for its office in its far-away unconscious beginnings. There is an inner satisfaction in seeing so straight, although so patient, a connection between the stem and the flower, and such a proof that when life wishes to produce something exquisite in quality she takes her measures many years in advance. A conscience like Emerson's could not have been turned off, as it were, from one generation to another: a succession of attempts, a long process of refining, was required. His perfection, in his own line, comes largely from the non-interruption of the process.

As most of us are made up of ill-assorted pieces, his reader, and Mr. Cabot's, envies him this transmitted unity, in which there was no mutual hustling or crowding of elements. It must have been a kind of luxury to be—that is to feel—so homogeneous, and it helps to account for his serenity, his power of acceptance, and that absence of personal passion which makes his private correspondence read like a series of beautiful circulars or expanded cards *pour prendre congé*. He had the equanimity of a result; nature had taken care of him and he had only to speak. He accepted himself as he accepted others, accepted everything; and his absence of eagerness, or in other words his modesty, was that of a man with whom it is not a question of success, who has nothing invested or at stake. The investment, the stake, was that of the race, of all the past Emersons and Bulkeleys and Waldos. There is much that makes us smile, to-day, in the commotion produced by his secession from the mild Unitarian pulpit: we wonder at a condition of opinion in which any utterance of his should appear to be wanting in superior piety—in the essence of good instruction. All that is changed: the great difference has become the infinitely small, and we admire a state of society in which scandal and schism took on no darker hue; but there is even yet a sort of drollery in the spectacle of a body of people among whom the author of *The American Scholar* and of the Address of 1838 at the Harvard Divinity College passed for profane, and who failed to see that he only gave his plea for the spiritual life the advantage of a brilliant expression. They were so provincial as to think that brilliancy came ill-recommended, and they were shocked at his ceasing to care for the prayer and the sermon. They might have perceived that he *was* the prayer and the sermon: not in the least a seculariser, but in his own subtle insinuating way a sanctifier.

Of the three periods into which his life divides itself, the first was (as in the case of most men) that of movement, experiment and selection—that of effort too and painful probation. Emerson had his message, but he was a good while looking for his form—the form which, as he himself would have said, he never completely found and of which it was rather characteristic of him that his later years (with their growing refusal to give him the *word*), wishing to attack him in his most vulnerable point, where his tenure was least complete, had in some degree the effect of despoiling him. It all sounds rather bare and stern, Mr. Cabot's account of his youth and early manhood, and we get an impression of a terrible paucity of alternatives. If he would be neither a farmer nor a trader he could "teach school"; that was the main resource and a part of the general educative process of the young New Englander who proposed to devote himself to the things of the mind. There was an advantage in the nudity, however, which was that, in Emerson's case at least, the things of the mind did get themselves admirably well considered. If it be his great distinction and his special sign that he had a more vivid conception of the moral life than any one else, it is probably not fanciful to say that he owed it in part to the limited way in which he saw our capacity for living illustrated. The plain, God-fearing, practical society which surrounded him was not fertile in variations: it had great intelligence and energy, but it moved altogether in the straightforward direction. On three occasions later—three journeys to Europe—he was introduced to a more complicated world; but his spirit, his moral taste, as it were, abode always within the undecorated walls of his youth. There he could dwell with that ripe unconsciousness of evil which is one of the most beautiful signs by which we know him. His early writings are full of quaint animadversion upon the vices of the place and time, but there is something charmingly vague, light and general in the arraignment. Almost the worst he can say is that these vices are negative and that his fellow-townsmen are not heroic. We feel that his first impressions were gathered in a community from which misery and extravagance, and either extreme, of any sort, were equally absent. What the life of New England fifty years ago offered to the observer was the common lot, in a kind of achromatic picture, without particular intensifications. It was from this table of the usual, the merely typical joys and sorrows that he proceeded to generalise—a fact that accounts in some degree for a certain inadequacy and thinness in his enumerations. But it helps to account also for his direct, intimate vision of the soul itself—not in its emotions, its contortions and perversions, but in its passive, exposed, yet healthy form. He knows the nature of man and the long tradition of its dangers; but we feel that whereas he can put his finger on the remedies, lying for the most part, as they do, in the deep recesses of virtue, of the spirit, he has only a kind of hearsay, uninformed acquaintance with the disorders. It would require some ingenuity, the reader may say too much, to trace closely this correspondence between his genius and the frugal, dutiful, happy but decidedly lean Boston of the past, where there was a great deal of will but very little fulcrum—like a ministry without an opposition.

The genius itself it seems to me impossible to contest—I mean the genius for seeing character as a real and supreme thing. Other writers have arrived at a more complete expression: Wordsworth and Goethe, for instance, give one a sense of having found their form, whereas with Emerson we never lose the sense that he is still seeking it. But no one has had so steady and constant, and above all so natural, a vision of what we require and what we are capable of in the way of aspiration and independence. With Emerson it is ever the special capacity for moral experience—always that and only that. We have the impression, somehow, that life had never bribed him to look at anything but the soul; and indeed in the world in which he grew up and lived the bribes and lures, the beguilements and prizes, were few. He was in an admirable position for showing, what he constantly endeavoured to show, that the prize was within. Any one who in New England at that time could do that was sure of success, of listeners and sympathy: most of all, of course, when it was a question of doing it with such a divine persuasiveness. Moreover, the way in which Emerson did it added to the charm—by word of mouth, face to face, with a rare, irresistible voice and a beautiful mild, modest authority. If Mr. Arnold is struck with the limited degree in which he was a man of letters I suppose it is because he is more struck with his having been, as it were, a man of lectures. But the lecture surely was never more purged of its grossness—the quality in it that suggests a strong light and a big brush—than as it issued from Emerson's lips; so far from being a vulgarisation, it was simply the esoteric made audible, and instead of treating the few as the many, after the usual fashion of gentlemen on platforms, he treated the many as the few. There was probably no other society at that time in which he would have got so many persons to understand that; for we think the better of his audience as we read him, and wonder where else people would have had so much moral attention to give. It is to be remembered however that during the winter of 1847-48, on the occasion of his second visit to England, he found many listeners in London and in provincial cities. Mr. Cabot's volumes are full of evidence of the satisfactions he offered, the delights and revelations he may be said to have promised, to a race which had to seek its entertainment, its rewards and consolations, almost exclusively in the moral world. But his own writings are fuller still; we find an instance almost wherever we open them.

> All these great and transcendent properties are ours. . . . Let us find room for this great guest in our small houses. . . . Where the heart is, there the muses, there the gods sojourn, and not in any geography of fame. Massachusetts, Connecticut River, and Boston Bay, you think paltry places, and the ear loves names of foreign and classic topography. But here we are, and if we will tarry a little we may come to learn that here is best. . . . The Jerseys were handsome enough ground for Washington to tread, and London streets for the feet of Milton. . . . That country is fairest which is inhabited by the noblest minds.

We feel, or suspect, that Milton is thrown in as a hint that the London streets are no such great place, and it all sounds like a sort of pleading consolation against bleakness.

The beauty of a hundred passages of this kind in Emerson's pages is that they are effective, that they do come home, that they rest upon insight and not upon ingenuity, and that if they are sometimes obscure it is never with the obscurity of paradox. We seem to see the people turning out into the snow after hearing them, glowing with a finer glow than even the climate could give and fortified for a struggle with overshoes and the east wind.

> Look to it first and only, that fashion, custom, authority, pleasure, and money, are nothing to you, are not as bandages over your eyes, that you cannot see; but live with the privilege of the immeasurable mind. Not too anxious to visit periodically all families and each family in your parish connection, when you meet one of these men or women be to them a divine man; be to them thought and virtue; let their timid aspirations find in you a friend; let their trampled instincts be genially tempted out in your atmosphere; let their doubts know that you have doubted, and their wonder feel that you have wondered.

When we set against an exquisite passage like that, or like the familiar sentences that open the essay on History ("He that is admitted to the right of reason is made freeman of the whole estate. What Plato has thought, he may think; what a saint has felt, he may feel; what at any time has befallen any man, he can understand"); when we compare the letters, cited by Mr. Cabot, to his wife from Springfield, Illinois (January 1853) we feel that his spiritual tact needed to be very just, but that if it was so it must have brought a blessing.

> Here I am in the deep mud of the prairies, misled I fear into this bog, not by a will-of-the-wisp, such as shine in bogs, but by a young New Hampshire editor, who over-estimated the strength of both of us, and

fancied I should glitter in the prairie and draw the prairie birds and waders. It rains and thaws incessantly, and if we step off the short street we go up to the shoulders, perhaps, in mud. My chamber is a cabin; my fellow-boarders are legislators. . . . Two or three governors or ex-governors live in the house. . . . I cannot command daylight and solitude for study or for more than a scrawl. . . .

And another extract: —

A cold, raw country this, and plenty of night-travelling and arriving at four in the morning to take the last and worst bed in the tavern. Advancing day brings mercy and favour to me, but not the sleep. . . . Mercury 15° below zero. . . . I find well-disposed, kindly people among these sinewy farmers of the North, but in all that is called cultivation they are only ten years old.

He says in another letter (in 1860), "I saw Michigan and its forests and the Wolverines pretty thoroughly;" and on another page Mr. Cabot shows him as speaking of his engagements to lecture in the West as the obligation to "wade, and freeze, and ride, and run, and suffer all manner of indignities." This was not New England, but as regards the country districts throughout, at that time, it was a question of degree. Certainly never was the fine wine of philosophy carried to remoter or queerer corners: never was a more delicate diet offered to "two or three governors, or ex-governors," living in a cabin. It was Mercury, shivering in a mackintosh, bearing nectar and ambrosia to the gods whom he wished those who lived in cabins to endeavour to feel that they might be.

I have hinted that the will, in the old New England society, was a clue without a labyrinth; but it had its use, nevertheless, in helping the young talent to find its mould. There were few or none ready-made: tradition was certainly not so oppressive as might have been inferred from the fact that the air swarmed with reformers and improvers. Of the patient, philosophic manner in which Emerson groped and waited, through teaching the young and preaching to the adult, for his particular vocation, Mr. Cabot's first volume gives a full and orderly account. His passage from the Unitarian pulpit to the lecture-desk was a step which at this distance of time can hardly help appearing to us short, though he was long in making it, for even after ceasing to have a parish of his own he freely confounded the two, or willingly, at least, treated the pulpit as a platform. "The young people and the mature hint at odium and the aversion of faces, to be presently encountered in society," he writes in his journal in 1838; but in point of fact the quiet drama of his abdication was not to include the note of suffering. The Boston world might feel disapproval, but it was far too kindly to make this sentiment felt as a weight: every element of martyrdom was there but the important ones of

the cause and the persecutors. Mr. Cabot marks the lightness of the penalties
of dissent; if they were light in somewhat later years for the transcendentalists and fruit-eaters they could press but little on a man of Emerson's
distinction, to whom, all his life, people went not to carry but to ask the right
word. There was no consideration to give up, he could not have been one of
the dingy if he had tried; but what he did renounce in 1838 was a material
profession. He was "settled," and his indisposition to administer the communion unsettled him. He calls the whole business, in writing to Carlyle, "a
tempest in our washbowl"; but it had the effect of forcing him to seek a new
source of income. His wants were few and his view of life severe, and this
came to him, little by little, as he was able to extend the field in which he
read his discourses. In 1835, upon his second marriage, he took up his
habitation at Concord, and his life fell into the shape it was, in a general way,
to keep for the next half-century. It is here that we cannot help regretting
that Mr. Cabot had not found it possible to treat his career a little more
pictorially. Those fifty years of Concord—at least the earlier part of them—
would have been a subject bringing into play many odd figures, many human
incongruities: they would have abounded in illustrations of the primitive New
England character, especially during the time of its queer search for something to expend itself upon. Objects and occupations have multiplied since
then, and now there is no lack; but fifty years ago the expanse was wide and
free, and we get the impression of a conscience gasping in the void, panting
for sensations, with something of the movement of the gills of a landed fish.
It would take a very fine point to sketch Emerson's benignant, patient,
inscrutable countenance during the various phases of this democratic communion; but the picture, when complete, would be one of the portraits, half a
revelation and half an enigma, that suggest and fascinate. Such a striking
personage as old Miss Mary Emerson, our author's aunt, whose high intelligence and temper were much of an influence in his earlier years, has a kind of
tormenting representative value: we want to see her from head to foot, with
her frame and her background; having (for we happen to have it), an
impression that she was a very remarkable specimen of the transatlantic
Puritan stock, a spirit that would have dared the devil. We miss a more liberal
handling, are tempted to add touches of our own, and end by convincing
ourselves that Miss Mary Moody Emerson, grim intellectual virgin and daughter of a hundred ministers, with her local traditions and her combined love of
empire and of speculation, would have been an inspiration for a novelist.
Hardly less so the charming Mrs. Ripley, Emerson's life-long friend and
neighbour, most delicate and accomplished of women, devoted to Greek and
to her house, studious, simple and dainty—an admirable example of the
old-fashioned New England lady. It was a freak of Miss Emerson's somewhat
sardonic humour to give her once a broomstick to carry across Boston

Common (under the pretext of a "moving"), a task accepted with docility but making of the victim the most benignant witch ever equipped with that utensil.

These ladies, however, were very private persons and not in the least of the reforming tribe: there are others who would have peopled Mr. Cabot's page to whom he gives no more than a mention. We must add that it is open to him to say that their features have become faint and indistinguishable to-day without more research than the question is apt to be worth: they are embalmed—in a collective way—the apprehensible part of them, in Mr. Frothingham's clever *History of Transcendentalism in New England*. This must be admitted to be true of even so lively a "factor," as we say nowadays, as the imaginative, talkative, intelligent and finally Italianised and shipwrecked Margaret Fuller: she is now one of the dim, one of Carlyle's "then-celebrated" at most. It seemed indeed as if Mr. Cabot rather grudged her a due place in the record of the company that Emerson kept, until we came across the delightful letter he quotes toward the end of his first volume—a letter interesting both as a specimen of inimitable, imperceptible edging away, and as an illustration of the curiously generalised way, as if with an implicit protest against personalities, in which his intercourse, epistolary and other, with his friends was conducted. There is an extract from a letter to his aunt on the occasion of the death of a deeply-loved brother (his own) which reads like a passage from some fine old chastened essay on the vanity of earthly hopes: strangely unfamiliar, considering the circumstances. Courteous and humane to the furthest possible point, to the point of an almost profligate surrender of his attention, there was no familiarity in him, no personal avidity. Even his letters to his wife are courtesies, they are not familiarities. He had only one style, one manner, and he had it for everything—even for himself, in his notes, in his journals. But he had it in perfection for Miss Fuller; he retreats, smiling and flattering, on tiptoe, as if he were advancing. "She ever seems to crave," he says in his journal, "something which I have not, or have not for her." What he had was doubtless not what she craved, but the letter in question should be read to see how the modicum was administered. It is only between the lines of such a production that we read that a part of her effect upon him was to bore him; for his system was to practise a kind of universal passive hospitality—he aimed at nothing less. It was only because he was so deferential that he could be so detached; he had polished his aloofness till it reflected the image of his solicitor. And this was not because he was an "uncommunicating egotist," though he amuses himself with saying so to Miss Fuller: egotism is the strongest of passions, and he was altogether passionless. It was because he had no personal, just as he had almost no physical wants. "Yet I plead not guilty to the malice prepense. 'Tis imbecility, not contumacy, though perhaps somewhat more odious. It seems very just, the irony with which you ask whether you may not be trusted and promise such docility. Alas, we will all promise, but the prophet loiters." He would not say even to himself that she bored him; he had denied himself the luxury of such easy and obvious short cuts. There is a passage in the lecture (1844) called "Man the Reformer," in which he hovers round and round the idea that the practice of trade, in certain conditions likely to beget an underhand competition, does not draw forth the nobler parts of character, till the reader is tempted to interrupt him with, "Say at once that it is impossible for a gentleman!"

So he remained always, reading his lectures in the winter, writing them in the summer, and at all seasons taking wood-walks and looking for hints in old books.

> Delicious summer stroll through the pastures. . . . On the steep park of Conantum I have the old regret—is all this beauty to perish? Shall none re-make this sun and wind; the sky-blue river; the river-blue sky; the yellow meadow, spotted with sacks and sheets of cranberry-gatherers; the red bushes; the iron-gray house, just the colour of the granite rocks; the wild orchard?

His observation of Nature was exquisite—always the direct, irresistible impression.

> The hawking of the wild geese flying by night; the thin note of the companionable titmouse in the winter day; the fall of swarms of flies in autumn, from combats high in the air, pattering down on the leaves like rain; the angry hiss of the wood-birds; the pine throwing out its pollen for the benefit of the next century. . . . (*Literary Ethics.*)

I have said there was no familiarity in him, but he was familiar with woodland creatures and sounds. Certainly, too, he was on terms of free association with his books, which were numerous and dear to him; though Mr. Cabot says, doubtless with justice, that his dependence on them was slight and that he was not "intimate" with his authors. They did not feed him but they stimulated; they were not his meat but his wine—he took them in sips. But he needed them and liked them; he had volumes of notes from his reading, and he could not have produced his lectures without them. He liked literature as a thing to refer to, liked the very names of which it is full, and used them, especially in his later writings, for purposes of ornament, to dress the dish, sometimes with an unmeasured profusion. I open *The Conduct of Life* and find a dozen on the page. He mentions more authorities than is the fashion to-day. He can easily say, of course, that he follows a better one—that of his well-loved and irrepressibly allusive Montaigne. In his own bookishness there is a certain contradiction, just as there is a latent incompleteness in his whole literary side. Independence, the return to nature, the finding out and doing for one's self, was ever what he most highly recommended; and yet he is constantly reminding his readers of the conventional signs and consecrations—of what other men have done. This was partly because the independence that he had in his eye was an independence without ill-nature, without rudeness (though he likes that word), and full of gentle amiabilities, curiosities and tolerances; and partly it is a simple matter of form, a literary expedient, confessing its character—on the part of one who had never really mastered the art of composition—of continuous expression. Charming to many a reader, charming yet ever slightly droll, will remain Emerson's frequent invocation of the "scholar": there is such a friendly vagueness and convenience in it. It is of the scholar that he expects all the heroic and uncomfortable things, the concentrations and relinquishments, that make up the noble life. We fancy this personage looking up from his book and arm-chair a little ruefully and saying, "Ah, but why *me* always and only? Why so much of me, and is there no one else to share the responsibility?" "Neither years nor books have yet availed to extirpate a prejudice then rooted in me [when as a boy he first saw the graduates of his college assembled at their anniversay], that a scholar is the favourite of heaven and earth, the excellency of his country, the happiest of men."

In truth, by this term he means simply the cultivated man, the man who has had a liberal education, and there is a voluntary plainness in his use of it—speaking of such people as the rustic, or the vulgar, speak of those who have a tincture of books. This is characteristic of his humility—that humility which was nine-tenths a plain fact (for it is easy for persons who have at bottom a great fund of indifference to be humble), and the remaining tenth a literary habit. Moreover an American reader may be excused for finding in it a pleasant sign of that prestige, often so quaintly and indeed so extravagantly acknowledged, which a connection with literature carries with it among the people of the United States. There is no country in which it is more freely admitted to be a distinction—*the* distinction; or in which so many persons have become eminent for showing it even in a slight degree. Gentlemen and ladies are celebrated there on this ground who would not on the same ground, though they might on another, be celebrated anywhere else. Emerson's own tone is an echo of that, when he speaks of the scholar—not of the banker, the great merchant, the legislator, the artist—as the most distinguished figure in the society about him. It is because he has most to give up that he is appealed to for efforts and sacrifices. "Meantime I know that a very different estimate of the scholar's profession prevails in this country," he goes on to say in the address from which I last quoted (the *Literary Ethics*), "and the importunity with which society presses its claim upon young men tends to pervert the views of the youth in respect to the culture of the intellect." The manner in which that is said represents, surely, a serious mistake: with the estimate of the scholar's profession which then prevailed in New England Emerson could have had no quarrel; the ground of his lamentation was another side of the matter. It was not a question of estimate, but of accidental practice. In 1838 there were still so many things of prime material necessity to be done that reading was driven to the wall; but the reader was still thought the cleverest, for he found time as well as intelligence. Emerson's own situation sufficiently indicates it. In what other country, on sleety winter nights, would provincial and bucolic populations have gone forth in hundreds for the cold comfort of a literary discourse? The distillation anywhere else would certainly have appeared too thin, the appeal too special. But for many years the American people of the middle regions, outside of a few cities, had in the most rigorous seasons no other recreation. A gentleman, grave or gay, in a bare room, with a manuscript, before a desk, offered the reward of toil, the refreshment of pleasure, to the young, the middle-aged and the old of both sexes. The hour was brightest, doubtless, when the gentleman was gay, like Doctor Oliver Wendell Holmes. But Emerson's gravity never sapped his career, any more than it chilled the regard in which he was held among those who were particularly his own people. It was impossible to be more honoured and cherished, far and near, than he was during his long residence in Concord, or more looked upon as the principal gentleman in the place. This was conspicuous to the writer of these remarks on the occasion of the curious, sociable, cheerful public funeral made for him in 1883 by all the countryside, arriving, as for the last honours to the first citizen, in trains in waggons, on foot, in multitudes. It was a popular manifestation, the most striking I have ever seen provoked by the death of a man of letters.

If a picture of that singular and very illustrative institution the old American lecture-system would have constituted a part of the filling-in of the ideal memoir of Emerson, I may further say, returning to the matter for a moment, that such a memoir would also have had a chapter for some of those Concord-haunting figures which are not so much interesting in themselves as interesting because for a season Emerson thought them so. And the pleasure of that would be partly that it would push us to inquire how interesting he did really think them. That is, it would bring up the question of his inner reserves and scepticisms, his secret ennuis and ironies, the way he sympathised for courtesy and then, with his delicacy and generosity, in a world after all given much to the literal, let his courtesy pass for adhesion—a question particularly attractive to those for whom he has, in general, a fascination. Many entertaining problems of that sort present themselves for such readers: there is something indefinable for them in the mixture of which he was made—his fidelity as an interpreter of the so-called transcendental spirit and his freedom from all wish for any personal share in the effect of his ideas. He drops them, sheds them, diffuses them, and we feel as if there would be a grossness in holding him to anything so temporal as a responsibility. He had the advantage, for many years, of having the question of application assumed for him by Thoreau, who took upon himself to be, in the concrete, the sort of person that Emerson's "scholar" was in the abstract, and who paid for it by having a shorter life than that fine adumbration. The application, with Thoreau, was violent and limited (it became a matter of prosaic detail, the non-payment of taxes, the non-wearing of a necktie, the preparation of one's food one's self, the practice of a rude sincerity—all things not of the essence), so that, though he wrote some beautiful pages, which read like a translation of Emerson into the sounds of the field and forest and which no one who has ever loved nature in New England, or indeed anywhere, can fail to love, he suffers something of the *amoindrissement* of eccentricity. His master escapes that reduction altogether. I call it an advantage to have had such a pupil as Thoreau; because for a mind so much made up of reflection as Emerson's everything comes under that head which prolongs and reanimates the process—produces the return, again and yet again, on one's impressions. Thoreau must have had this moderating and even chastening effect. It did not rest, moreover, with him alone; the advantage of which I speak was not confined to Thoreau's case. In 1837 Emerson (in his journal) pronounced Mr. Bronson Alcott the most extraordinary man and the highest genius of his time: the sequence of which was that for more than forty years after that he had the gentleman living but half a mile away. The opportunity for the return, as I have called it, was not wanting.

His detachment is shown in his whole attitude toward the transcendental movement—that remarkable outburst of Romanticism on Puritan ground, as Mr. Cabot very well names it. Nothing can be more ingenious, more sympathetic and charming, than Emerson's account and definition of the matter in his lecture (of 1842) called "The Transcendentalist"; and yet nothing is more apparent from his letters and journals than that he regarded any such label or banner as a mere tiresome flutter. He liked to taste but not to drink—least of all to become intoxicated. He liked to explain the transcendentalists but did not care at all to be explained by them: a doctrine "whereof you know I am wholly guiltless," he says to his wife in 1842, "and which is spoken of as a known and fixed element, like salt or meal. So that I have to begin with endless disclaimers and explanations: 'I am not the man you take me for.'" He was never the man any one took him for, for the simple reason that no one could possibly take him for the elusive, irreducible, merely gustatory spirit for which he took himself.

It is a sort of maxim with me never to harp on the omnipotence of limitations. Least of all do we need any suggestion of checks and measures; as if New England were anything else. . . . Of so many fine people it is true that being so much they ought to be a little more, and missing that are naught. It is a sort of King René period; there is no doing, but rare thrilling prophecy from bands of competing minstrels.

That is his private expression about a large part of a ferment in regard to which his public judgment was that

> That indeed constitutes a new feature in their portrait that they are the most exacting and extortionate critics. . . . These exacting children advertise us of our wants. There is no compliment, no smooth speech with them; they pay you only this one compliment of insatiable expectation; they aspire, they severely exact, and if they only stand fast in this watch-tower, and stand fast unto the end, and without end, then they are terrible friends, whereof poet and priest cannot but stand in awe; and what if they eat clouds and drink wind, they have not been without service to the race of man.

That was saying the best for them, as he always said it for everything; but it was the sense of their being "bands of competing minstrels" and their camp being only a "measure and check," in a society too sparse for a synthesis, that kept him from wishing to don their uniform. This was after all but a misfitting imitation of his natural wear, and what he would have liked was to put that off—he did not wish to button it tighter. He said the best for his friends of the Dial, of Fruitlands and Brook Farm, in saying that they were fastidious and critical; but he was conscious in the next breath that what there was around them to be criticised was mainly a negative. Nothing is more perceptible to-day than that their criticism produced no fruit—that it was little else than a very decent and innocent recreation—a kind of Puritan carnival. The New England world was for much the most part very busy, but the Dial and Fruitlands and Brook Farm were the amusement of the leisure-class. Extremes meet, and as in older societies that class is known principally by its connection with castles and carriages, so at Concord it came, with Thoreau and Mr. W. H. Channing, out of the cabin and the wood-lot.

Emerson was not moved to believe in their fastidiousness as a productive principle even when they directed it upon abuses which he abundantly recognised. Mr. Cabot shows that he was by no means one of the professional abolitionists or philanthropists—never an enrolled "humanitarian."

> We talk frigidly of Reform until the walls mock us. It is that of which a man should never speak, but if he have cherished it in his bosom he should steal to it in darkness, as an Indian to his bride. . . . Does he not do more to abolish slavery who works all day steadily in his own garden, than he who goes to the abolition meeting and makes a speech? He who does his own work frees a slave.

I must add that even while I transcribe these words there comes to me the recollection of the great meeting in the Boston Music Hall, on the first day of

1863, to celebrate the signing by Mr. Lincoln of the proclamation freeing the Southern slaves—of the momentousness of the occasion, the vast excited multitude, the crowded platform and the tall, spare figure of Emerson, in the midst, reading out the stanzas that were published under the name of the Boston Hymn. They are not the happiest he produced for an occasion—they do not compare with the verses on the "embattled farmers," read at Concord in 1837, and there is a certain awkwardness in some of them. But I well remember the immense effect with which his beautiful voice pronounced the lines—

> Pay ransom to the owner
> And fill the bag to the brim.
> Who is the owner? The slave is owner,
> And ever was. Pay *him!*

And Mr. Cabot chronicles the fact that the *gran' rifiuto*—the great backsliding of Mr. Webster when he cast his vote in Congress for the Fugitive Slave Law of 1850—was the one thing that ever moved him to heated denunciation. He felt Webster's apostasy as strongly as he had admired his genius. "Who has not helped to praise him? Simply he was the one American of our time whom we could produce as a finished work of nature." There is a passage in his journal (not a rough jotting, but, like most of the entries in it, a finished piece of writing), which is admirable descriptive of the wonderful orator and is moreover one of the very few portraits, or even personal sketches, yielded by Mr. Cabot's selections. It shows that he could observe the human figure and "render" it to good purpose.

> His splendid wrath, when his eyes become fire, is good to see, so intellectual it is—the wrath of the fact and the cause he espouses, and not at all personal to himself. . . . These village parties must be dish-water to him, yet he shows himself just good-natured, just nonchalant enough; and he has his own way, without offending any one or losing any ground. . . . His expensiveness seems necessary to him; were he too prudent a Yankee it would be a sad deduction from his magnificence. I only wish he would not truckle [to the slave-holders]. I do not care how much he spends.

I doubtless appear to have said more than enough, yet I have passed by many of the passages I had marked for transcription from Mr. Cabot's volumes. There is one, in the first, that makes us stare as we come upon it, to the effect that Emerson "could see nothing in Shelley, Aristophanes, Don Quixote, Miss Austen, Dickens." Mr. Cabot adds that he rarely read a novel, even the famous ones (he has a point of contact here as well as, strangely enough, on two or three other sides with that distinguished moralist M. Ernest Renan, who, like Emerson, was originally a dissident priest and cannot imagine why people should write works of fiction); and thought Dante "a man to put into a museum, but not into your house; another Zerah Colburn; a prodigy of imaginative function, executive rather than contemplative or wise." The confession of an insensibility ranging from Shelley to Dickens and from Dante to Miss Austen and taking Don Quixote and Aristophanes on the way, is a large allowance to have to make for a man of letters, and may appear to confirm but slightly any claim of intellectual hospitality and general curiosity put forth for him. The truth was that, sparely constructed as he was and formed not wastefully, not with material left over, as it were, for a special function, there were certain chords in Emerson that did not vibrate at all. I well remember my impression of this on walking with him in the autumn of 1872 through the galleries of the Louvre and, later that winter, through those of the Vatican: his perception of the objects contained in these collections was of the most general order. I was struck with the anomaly of a man so refined and intelligent being so little spoken to by works of art. It would be more exact to say that certain chords were wholly absent; the tune was played, the tune of life and literature, altogether on those that remained. They had every wish to be equal to their office, but one feels that the number was short—that some notes could not be given. Mr. Cabot makes use of a singular phrase when he says, in speaking of Hawthorne, for several years our author's neighbour at Concord and a little—a very little we gather—his companion, that Emerson was unable to read his novels—he thought them "not worthy of him." This is a judgment odd almost to fascination—we circle round it and turn it over and over; it contains so elusive an ambiguity. How highly he must have esteemed the man of whose genius *The House of the Seven Gables* and *The Scarlet Letter* gave imperfectly the measure, and how strange that he should not have been eager to read almost anything that such a gifted being might have let fall! It was a rare accident that made them live almost side by side so long in the same small New England town, each a fruit of a long Puritan stem, yet with such a difference of taste. Hawthorne's vision was all for the evil and sin of the world; a side of life as to which Emerson's eyes were thickly bandaged. There were points as to which the latter's conception of right could be violated, but he had no great sense of wrong—a strangely limited one, indeed, for a moralist—no sense of the dark, the foul, the base. There were certain complications in life which he never suspected. One asks one's self whether that is why he did not care for Dante and Shelley and Aristophanes and Dickens, their works containing a considerable reflection of human perversity. But that still leaves the indifference to Cervantes and Miss Austen unaccounted for.

It has not, however, been the ambition of these remarks to account for everything, and I have arrived at the end without even pointing to the grounds on which Emerson justifies the honours of biography, discussion and illustration. I have assumed his importance and continuance, and shall probably not be gainsaid by those who read him. Those who do not will hardly rub him out. Such a book as Mr. Cabot's subjects a reputation to a test—leads people to look it over and hold it up to the light, to see whether it is worth keeping in use or even putting away in a cabinet. Such a revision of Emerson has no relegating consequences. The result of it is once more the impression that he serves and will not wear out, and that indeed we cannot afford to drop him. His instrument makes him precious. He did something better than any one else; he had a particular faculty, which has not been surpassed, for speaking to the soul in a voice of direction and authority. There have been many spiritual voices appealing, consoling, reassuring, exhorting, or even denouncing and terrifying, but none has had just that firmness and just that purity. It penetrates further, it seems to go back to the roots of our feelings, to where conduct and manhood begin; and moreover, to us to-day, there is something in it that says that it is connected somehow with the virtue of the world, has wrought and achieved, lived in thousands of minds, produced a mass of character and life. And there is this further sign of Emerson's singular power, that he is a striking exception to the general rule that writings live in the last resort by their form; that they owe a large part of their fortune to the art with which they have been composed. It is hardly too much, or too little, to say of Emerson's writings in general that they were not composed at all. Many and many things are beautifully said; he had felicities, inspirations, unforgettable phrases; he had frequently an exquisite eloquence.

> O my friends, there are resources in us on which we have not yet drawn. There are men who rise refreshed on hearing a threat; men to whom a crisis which intimidates and paralyses the majority—demanding not the faculties of prudence and thrift, but comprehension, immovableness, the readiness of sacrifice, comes graceful and beloved as a bride. . . . But these are heights that we can scarce look up to and remember without contrition and shame. Let us thank God that such things exist.

None the less we have the impression that that search for a fashion and a manner on which he was always engaged never really came to a conclusion; it draws itself out through his later writings—it drew itself out through his later lectures, like a sort of renunciation of success. It is not on these, however, but on their predecessors, that his reputation will rest. Of course the way he spoke was the way that was on the whole most convenient to him; but he differs from most men of letters of the same degree of credit in failing to strike us as having achieved a style. This achievement is, as I say, usually the bribe or toll-money on the journey to posterity; and if Emerson goes his way, as he clearly appears to be doing, on the strength of his message alone, the case will be rare, the exception striking, and the honour great.

NOTES

1. *A Memoir of Ralph Waldo Emerson,* 2 vols. (London: Macmillan, 1887).

PART V
Dissent

17

The Significance of
The Bridge, by Hart Crane,

or What Are We to Think of Professor X?

YVOR WINTERS

IN SPEAKING OF THE "SIGNIFICANCE" OF *THE BRIDGE,* I AM USING the word "significance" in both of its common meanings: I refer to the content which the author apparently wished to communicate and also to the "moral," so to speak, that we as observers and as members of his society may deduce from his effort and from the qualities of its success or failure. It is the second sense of the word that I should like to emphasize if I had time, but before I can begin on it I must deal somehow with the first: What is *The Bridge* about? What did Crane think he was getting at?

Most of Crane's thought, and this is especially true of *The Bridge,* was derived from Whitman. This fact is generally recognized. It is my personal impression likewise, and my personal impression is derived not only from a study of the works of Crane and of Whitman, but also from about four years of frequent and regular correspondence with Crane and from about four long evenings of uninterrupted conversation with him. Crane and I began publishing poems in the same magazines about 1919; I started quarreling with Harriet Monroe about 1925 of 1926 to get Crane's poems into *Poetry: A Magazine of Verse;* Crane and I started corresponding shortly thereafter; I

From Yvor Winters, *In Defense of Reason* © 1937, 1947. Excerpts reprinted by permission of The Swallow Press, Chicago. The present selection includes only the first half of the original essay.

spent a few evenings talking to Crane during the Christmas holidays of 1927; our correspondence ended as a result of my review of *The Bridge* in 1930; and about two or two and a half years later Crane committed suicide.

Most of Crane's thought was, as I say, derived from Whitman. In turn, nearly all of Whitman's thought was derived from Emerson, or could easily have been. Whitman professed himself Emerson's disciple, and Emerson offered Whitman his professorial blessing. But Emerson in turn was in no wise original, at least as regards the bare formulae of his thought: his ideas are the commonplace ideas of the romantic movement, from the time of the third Earl of Shaftesbury to the present. In the restating of these ideas, however, Emerson did something which was important, at least in the American context. What were these ideas, and what did Emerson do to them?

The ideas were, briefly, these:

God and his creation are one. God is good. Man, as part of the creation, is part of God, and so is good. Man may therefore trust his impulses, which are the voice of God; through trusting them absolutely and acting upon them without reserve, he becomes one with God. Impulse is thus equated with the protestant concept of conscience, as a divine and supra-rational directive; and surrender to impulse, which unites one with God, becomes equivalent in a sense to the traditional and Catholic concept of the mystical experience. We are confronted here with an illogicality, for our first principles tell us that man is a part of God whether he trusts his impulses or not; but this is merely a part of the illogicality which denies the validity of Reason. For Emerson, as for other Romantics, Reason is the source of all evil, is the adversary of Impulse, and is that which has no part in God in a universe in which everything is a part of God and in which everything is good. In life and in art the automatic man, the unreflective creature of impulse, is the ideal; he is one with God and will achieve the good life and great art.*

Let me quote from Emerson on these subjects:

As to the pantheistic doctrine, he writes, for example, in *Nature:*

> The knowledge that we traverse the whole scale of being from the center to the poles of nature, and have some stake in every possibility, lends that sublime luster to death, which philosophy and religion have too outwardly striven to express in the popular doctrine of the immortality of the soul. The reality is more excellent than the report. Here is no ruin, no discontinuity, no spent ball. The divine circulations never rest nor linger. Nature is the incarnation of a thought, and turns to a thought again, as ice becomes water and gas. The world is mind precipitated, and the volatile essence is forever escaping again into the state of free thought. Hence the virtue and pungency of the influence on the mind of natural objects,

---

*Despite the capital letters, Winters is here referring to the rational faculty, not Transcendental Reason.—Ed.

whether inorganic or organized. Man imprisoned, man crystallized, man vegetative, speaks to man impersonated.

In the last sentence, "man imprisoned" is in apposition with "man crystallized" and with "man vegetative," terms which may be translated respectively as "God in the form of a crystal" and as "God in the form of a cabbage"; the expression "man impersonated" may be translated as "God in the form of man," or more simply, as "man." The passage, like many others in Emerson, indicates that man in death remains immortal while losing his identity. The concept is doubtless comprehensible to those who understand it. I once argued this issue with Crane, and when he could not convert me by reason, he said: "Well, if we can't believe it, we'll have to kid ourselves into believing it." Something of the same attitude seems to be implied in a passage in his poem *The Dance* (that section of *The Bridge* which deals most explicitly with this notion) in which he begs his Indian medicine man to "Lie to us! Dance us back the tribal morn!"

There are innumerable passages in Emerson on the divine origin of impulse and on its trustworthiness. In *The Poet* he writes as follows (here as elsewhere the italics are mine):

> It is a secret which every intellectual man quickly learns, that beyond the energy of his possessed and conscious intellect he is capable of a new energy (as of an intellect doubled on itself), *by abandonment to the nature of things;* that beside his privacy of power as an individual man, there is a great public power on which he can draw, *by unlocking at all risks his human doors* and suffering the ethereal tides to roll through him. . . .

In *Spiritual Laws* he writes:

> A little consideration of what takes place around us every day would show us that a higher law than that of our will regulates events; that our painful labors are very unnecessary and altogether fruitless; that *only in our easy, simple, spontaneous action we are strong, and by contenting ourselves with obedience we become divine.* . . . We need only obey. There is guidance for each of us, and by lowly listening we shall hear the right word. *Why need you choose* so painfully your place, and occupation, and associates, and modes of action, and of entertainment? Certainly there is a possible right for you *that precludes the need of balance and of willful election.* For you there is a fit place and congenial duties. Place yourself in the middle of the stream of power and wisdom which flows into you as life, place yourself in the full center of that flood, then you are *without effort* impelled to truth, to right, and to perfect contentment.

And in *The Oversoul:*

> Ineffable is the union of man and God in every act of the soul. The simplest person who in his integrity worships God becomes God. . . . He

believes that he cannot escape from his good. The things that are really for thee gravitate to thee. You are running to meet your friend. *Let your feet run, but your mind need not.* If you do not find him, will you not acquiesce that it is best you should not find him? for there is a power, which, as it is in you, is in him also, and could therefore very well bring you together, if it were for the best.

The last three passages all point unmistakably to Emerson's concept of automatism as the equivalent of the mystical experience; and in the last passage quoted the concept is very dramatically expressed—one could hardly ask for anything more explicit. Closely related to this notion is the familiar romantic notion of the beatitude of ignorance and of mediocrity, to say nothing of the beatitude of infancy. We are familiar with Gray's mute inglorious Miltons and with Wordsworth's young child who was a mighty prophet, seer blest. Similarly Emerson writes in *Spiritual Laws:*

> The intellectual life may be kept clean and healthful, if man will live the life of nature, and not import into his mind difficulties which are none of his. *No man need be perplexed in his speculations.* Let him do and say what strictly belongs to him, and *though very ignorant of books,* his nature shall not yield him any intellectual obstructions and doubts.

A passage such as this one makes very short work of our universities. In *Self-Reliance* Emerson writes:

> What pretty oracles nature yields us on this text in the face and behavior of children, babes, and even brutes! That divided and rebel mind, that distrust of a sentiment because our arithmetic has computed the strength and means opposed to our purpose, these have not. Their mind being whole, their eye is as yet unconquered, and when we look in their faces we are disconcerted. Infancy conforms to nobody; all conform to it; so that one babe commonly makes four or five out of the adults who prattle and play to it.

This passage is offered as a kind of vision of social beatitude. Unfortunately for those of us whose curiosity is insatiable, Emerson does not take the next step in his argument: although he tells us what happens when we have one babe (conforming to nobody) and four or five adults (conforming to the babe), he does not say what happens when we have five or six babes (all conforming to nobody): therein lies the crux of the matter.

Emerson was not wholly unaware of the theoretical objections which could be made to his position, but unless we are to assume that he personally was a corrupt and vicious man, which I think we can scarcely do, we are forced to admit that he simply did not know what the objections meant. In *Self-Reliance* he wrote:

I remember an answer which when quite young I was prompted to make to a valued adviser, who was wont to importune me with the dear old doctrines of the church. On my saying, "What have I to do with the sacredness of traditions, if I live wholly from within?" my friend suggested,—"But these impulses may be from below, not from above." I replied, "They do not seem to me to be such; but if I am the Devil's child, I will live then from the Devil." No law can be sacred to me but that of my nature. Good and bad are but names very readily transferable to that or this; the only right is what is after my constitution; the only wrong what is against it.

Emerson's friend, in this passage, offers the traditional objection of the Roman Church to the quietistic schismatic; and Emerson appears to be ignorant of the traditional functions of the Devil and of the viscera. But in the last few statements in this passage we see clearly another consequence of the Emersonian position: its thoroughgoing relativism. That is right for me which is after my constitution; that is right for you which is after yours; the Oversoul will guide us both in the ways which best befit us, if we will both only follow our impulses. My impulse to commit incest may horrify you; your impulse to commit murder and arson may horrify me; but we should ignore each other and proceed.

In *Circles,* Emerson writes to the same purpose, at the same time suggesting a new difficulty, with which, however, he is not impressed. He says:

And thus, O circular philosopher, I hear some reader exclaim, you have arrived at a fine Pyrrhonism, at an equivalence and indifferency of all actions, and would fain teach us that, if we are true, forsooth, our crimes may be lively stones out of which we shall construct the temple of the true God!

I am not careful to justify myself. . . . But lest I should mislead any when I have my own head and obey my whims, let me remind the reader that I am only an experimenter. Do not set the least value on what I do, or the least discredit on what I do not, as if I pretended to settle anything as true or false. I unsettle all things. No facts are to me sacred; nor are profane; I simply experiment, an endless seeker, with no past at my back.

Here Emerson suggests the difficulty that he has eliminated values: in teaching that everything is good, he has merely arrived at the conclusion that everything is equal to everything else, for nothing is either good or bad unless there are grounds for distinction. Emerson has arrived at a doctrine of equivalence, a doctrine to the effect that there are no grounds for choice; and he hopes to save himself only through not having to make a choice, through leaving choice wholly to God and to performing, himself, as an automaton. And in the last expression, in which he describes himself as an "endless seeker, with no Past at my back," we see his glorification of change as change;

we can find this elsewhere in Emerson; we can find it likewise in Whitman; it is one of the most important ideas of *The Bridge*. It should be observed that the glorification of change as change is a necessary part of a system in which every act is good, in which there is no way to choose between courses of action, in which there is no principle of consistency, and in which there is no conception of a goal other than to be automatically controlled from moment to moment.

It is not surprising that Emerson should regard that art as the best which is the most nearly extemporaneous. He wrote in *Art:*

> But true art is never fixed, but always flowing. The sweetest music is not in the oratorio, but in the human voice when it speaks from its instant life tones of tenderness, truth, or courage. The oratorio has already lost its relation to the morning, to the sun, and to the earth, but that persuading voice is in tune with these. All works of art should not be detached, but extempore performances. A great man is a new statue in every attitude and action. A beautiful woman is a picture which drives all beholders nobly mad. Life may be lyric or epic, as well as a poem or a romance.

This view of art rests on the assumption that man should express what he is at any given moment; not that he should try by all the means at his disposal to arrive at a true understanding of a given subject or to improve his powers of understanding in general. Related to this notion is the principle that if we will only express what we are at any given moment, if we will only record our casual impressions, we may be sure to equal Shakespeare. This is from *Self-Reliance:*

> In every work of genius we recognize our own rejected thoughts; they come back to us with a certain alienated majesty. Great works of art have no more affecting lesson for us than this. They teach us to *abide by our spontaneous impression* with good-humored inflexibility then most when the whole cry of voices is on the other side. Else tomorrow a stranger will say with masterly good sense precisely what we have thought and felt all the time, and we shall be forced to take with shame our own opinion from another.

And this is from *The Oversoul:*

> The great poet makes us feel our own wealth, and then we think less of his compositions. . . . Shakespeare carries us to such a lofty strain of intelligent activity, as to suggest a wealth which beggars his own. . . . The inspiration which uttered itself in *Hamlet* and *Lear* could utter things as good from day to day forever. Why, then, should I make account of *Hamlet* and *Lear*, as if we had not the soul from which they fell as syllables from the tongue?

The natural conclusion from these speculations would be that the most effective writing is automatic writing. In the poem entitled *Merlin,* in which *Merlin* is viewed as the bard, Emerson writes:

> Great is the art,
> Great be the manners, of the bard.
> He shall not his brain encumber
> With the coil of rhythm and number;
> But leaving rule and pale forethought,
> He shall aye climb
> For his rime.
> 'Pass in, pass in,' the angels say,
> 'In to the upper doors,
> Nor count compartments of the floors,
> But mount to Paradise
> By the stairway of surprise.'

In Whitman and his close followers there is occasionally a momentary approach to the kind of automatic writing here suggested; but this ideal was most nearly fulfilled by another line of Romantic writers, and probably reached Crane by way of them, in the main: the line starting with Poe, and proceeding through Verlaine, Mallarmé, Rimbaud, and the lesser Symbolists to such Americans as Pound, Eliot, and Stevens. The concept of automatic writing is an inevitable development from the initial Romantic ideas, and it is bound to appear whenever the ideas long govern literary practice. Crane had almost no French—I spent a couple of hours one evening taking him through various poems by Rimbaud—but his friends had doubtless translated the French poets for him and described them, and he knew the later Americans very thoroughly. He told me once that he often did not understand his poems till after they were written; and I am fairly confident that this kind of experimentation was common in Crane's generation and earlier, and in fact that it is still common in certain quarters. I know that I myself engaged in it with great fascination when I was young, and I know that certain other persons did so. The result is likely to be a poetry which frequently and sometimes wholly eludes paraphrase by at least a margin, but which appears constantly to be suggesting a precise meaning.

Many poets engage in the practice only semi-consciously; in general, one may say that wherever the poet's sensibility to the connotation of language overbalances his awareness of the importance of denotation, something of the kind is beginning: it is this unbalance which distinguishes the Shakespeare of the sonnets, for example, most sharply from his great contemporaries, such as Jonson, Greville, Donne, and even Sidney. But beginning with the notion of organic form, the notion that the subject, or the language, or the oversoul, or something else operates freely through the poet, who is merely a passive medium, the doctrine begins to be explicit. The beginnings, in theory, may be traced perhaps as far back as Edward Young, certainly as far as Coleridge; and *Kubla Khan* is perhaps the first ambitious experiment in actual practice. Emerson states the theory with an explicitness which verges on violence, but does not appear seriously to have practiced it. Poe's concept of poetry as something which deals with certain materials of this life only incidentally, in the hopes that meanings otherwise unattainable may be suggested, begins to describe the kind of poetry which will result when automatic writing is practiced by men of talent: a poetry which appears always to be escaping the comprehension, yet which is always perceptible; a poetry which deals with the fact of nature *dans sa presque disparition vibratoire,* to use a phrase from Mallarmé, "in its vibratory almost-disappearance."

Mallarmé employs this phrase in an essay called *Relativement au vers:* in English, *On the Subject of the Poetic Line.* In this essay he describes the kind of "pure" poetry in which he is interested, the poetry in which feeling is as nearly as possible isolated from all denotation, and near the end he writes the following passage, which I shall render as nearly verbatim as possible, in spite of any awkwardness which may seem to result:

> The pure work implies the elocutory disappearance of the poet, who cedes the initiative to the words, mobilized through the shock of their inequality; they light each other with reciprocal reflections like a virtual train of fires upon jewels, replacing the respiration perceptible in the lyric inspiration of former times or the enthusiastic personal direction of the phrase.

And Rimbaud, in his poem *Bonheur,* states that the charm of which he has made a magic study has taken possession of him body and soul, with the result that his language is no longer to be understood, but takes wing and escapes. Verlaine offers a somewhat more cautious statement of the same doctrine in his poem entitled *Art Poétique,* in which he praises the "drunken song," the word exhibiting a content of "error," in which the indecisive is joined to the precise. Rimbaud's poem might easily have been written by Emerson: in fact Rimbaud's *Fêtes de la Faim* resembles Emerson's *Mithridates* very closely in imagery and in symbolism, though it resembles the stylistic quality of Emerson's best verse less closely than does *Bonheur.* And the passage from Mallarmé, if we make allowances for certain personal mannerisms, might well have been written by Emerson. But Rimbaud and Mallarmé put the doctrine into practice, not occasionally but systematically, and the result was a revolution in style, both in verse and in prose. One of the most eminent practitioners of the semi-automatic method in more recent times was the late W. B. Yeats, with his notions of demonic possession and dictation.

The ideas of Emerson were, as I have said, merely the commonplaces of the Romantic movement; but his language was that of the Calvinistic pulpit. He was able to present the anarchic and anti-moral doctrines of European Romancism in a language which for two hundred years had been capable of arousing the most intense and the most obscure emotions of the American people. He could speak of matter as if it were God; of the flesh as if it were spirit; of emotion as if it were Divine Grace; of impulse as if it were conscience; and of automatism as if it were the mystical experience. And he was addressing an audience which, like himself, had been so conditioned by two hundred years of Calvinistic discipline, that the doctrines confused nothing, at the outset, except the mind: Emerson and his contemporaries, in surrendering to what they took for impulse, were governed by New England habit; they mistook second nature for nature. They were moral parasites upon a Christian doctrine which they were endeavoring to destroy. The same may be said of Whitman, Emerson's most influential disciple, except that Whitman came closer to putting the doctrine into practice in the matter of literary form: whereas Emerson, as a poet, imitated the poets of the early 17th century, whose style had been formed in congruence with the doctrines of Aristotle, Aquinas, and Hooker.

I cannot summarize the opinions of Whitman in this essay as fully as I have summarized those of Emerson. I must ask my readers to accept on faith, until they find it convenient to check the matter, the generally accepted view that the main ideas of Whitman are identical with those of Emerson. Whitman believed this; Emerson believed it; and scholarly specialists in both men believe it. I wish to quote a part—only a small part—of Professor Floyd Stovall's summary of Whitman's views.[1] Professor Stovall is a reputable scholar. Every detail which he gives is referred by a footnote to its source in Whitman. I believe that his summary, purely as a summary, is accurate. He writes:

> He saw that creation is a continuous organic growth, not a work that is begun or finished, and the creative force is the procreative impulse in nature. *Progress is the infallible consequence* of this creative force in nature, *and though the universe is perfect at any given moment, it is growing constantly toward higher orders of perfection.* If new forms are needed they are produced as surely as if designed from the beginning. "When the materials are all prepared and ready, the architects shall appear." Every moment is a consummation developed from endless past consummations and preparing for endless consummations in the future. . . .
>
> Nature is not only perfect but also divine. Indeed it is perfect because it is divine. There is no division in nature . . . no separate deity looking down from some detached heaven upon a temporal world that his hand created and may destroy at pleasure. That which is at all is of God. . . . *Whatever is*

is well, and whatever will be will be well. . . . God is in every object,
because every object has an eternal soul and passes eventually into spiritual
results. . . .

. . . The seed of perfection is in each person, but *no matter how far he*
advances, his desire for further advancement remains insatiable.

The final purpose of this restlessness of spirit in man and nature is the
continuity of life. Nothing is real or valid, not even God, except in relation
to this purpose. . . . Something, Whitman perceives, drives man forward
along the way to perfection, which passes through birth, life, death, and
burial; he does not fully understand what it is, but he knows that it is
form, union, plan—that it is happiness and eternal life.

Whitman calls it soul, this mysterious something, strangely linked with
the procreative impulse, that gives form and continuity to the life of
nature and impels man toward happiness and immortality. . . .

The ignorance both of philosophy and theology exhibited in such ideas as
these is sufficient to strike one with terror. But I must limit myself to only a
few comments at the present moment. I wish to call attention especially to
the passages which I have italicized: (1) "Progress is the infallible consequence," or to put it more briefly, progress is infallible; (2) "though the
universe is perfect at any given moment, it is growing constantly toward
higher orders of perfection"; (3) "Whatever is is well, and whatever will be
will be well"; and (4) "No matter how far man advances, his desire for further
advancement remains insatiable."

I wish to insist on this: that it is impossible to speak of higher orders of
perfection unless one can define what one means by the highest order and by
the lowest order, and this Whitman does not venture to do. Higher and lower,
better and worse, have no meaning except in relation to highest and lowest,
best and worst. Since Whitman has identified God with the evolving (that is,
with the changing) universe, he is unable to locate a concept of best or
highest, toward which evolution is moving, for that concept would then be
outside of God and would supersede God; it would be, in theological
language, God's final cause; and such a concept would be nonsense. Whitman
tells us that whatever happens to exist is perfect, but that any change is
necessarily toward a "higher" order of perfection. The practical effect of
these notions is merely to deify change: change becomes good of necessity.
We have no way of determing where we are going, but we should keep moving
at all costs and as fast as possible; we have faith in progress. It seems to me
unnecessary to dwell upon the dangers of such a concept.

Hart Crane was not born into the New England of Emerson, nor even into
the New York of Whitman; he was born in 1899 in Cleveland, Ohio. The
social restraints, the products of generations of religious discipline, which
operated to minimize the influence of Romantic philosophy in the personal

lives of Emerson and of Whitman, were at most only slightly operative in Crane's career. He was unfortunate in having a somewhat violent emotional constitution: his behavior on the whole would seem to indicate a more or less manic-depressive make-up, although this diagnosis is the post-mortem guess of an amateur, and is based on evidence which is largely hearsay. He was certainly homosexual, however, and he became a chronic and extreme alcoholic. I should judge that he cultivated these weaknesses on principle; in any event, it is well known that he cultivated them assiduously; and as an avowed Whitmanian, he would have been justified by his principles in cultivating all of his impulses. I saw Crane during the Christmas week of 1927, when he was approximately 29 years old; his hair was graying, his skin had the dull red color with reticulated grayish traceries which so often goes with advanced alcoholism and his ears and knuckles were beginning to look a little like those of a pugilist. About a year later he was deported from France as a result of his starting an exceptionally violent commotion in a bar-room and perhaps as a result of other activities. In 1932 he committed suicide by leaping from a steamer into the Caribbean Sea.

The doctrine of Emerson and Whitman, if really put into practice, should naturally lead to suicide: in the first place, if the impulses are indulged systematically and passionately, they can lead only to madness; in the second place, death, according to the doctrine, is not only a release from suffering but is also and inevitably the way to beatitude. There is no question, according to the doctrine, of moral preparation for salvation; death leads automatically to salvation. During the last year and a half of Crane's life, to judge from the accounts of those who were with him in Mexico, he must have been insane or drunk or both almost without interruption; but before this time he must have contemplated the possibilities of suicide. When his friend Harry Crosby leapt from a high window in one of the eastern cities, I wrote Crane a note of condolence and asked him to express my sympathy to Mrs. Crosby. Crane replied somewhat casually that I need not feel disturbed about the affair, that he was fairly sure Crosby had regarded it as a great adventure.

In the course of my correspondence with Crane, I must somewhere have made a moralizing remark which I have now forgotten but of which Crane disapproved. I remember Crane's answer: he said that he had never in his life done anything of which he had been ashamed, and he said this not in anger but in simple philosophical seriousness. This would be a sufficiently surprising remark from any son of Adam, but as one thinks of it and of Crane in retrospect, one can understand it, I believe, only in one way, as an assertion of religious faith, neither more nor less.

NOTES

1. Floyd Stovall, ed., *Walt Whitman: Representative Selections, with Introduction, Bibliography, and Notes* (American Book Company, 1934), p. xxxvii.

Selected Bibliography

THE PRINCIPLES ON WHICH I HAVE COMPILED THIS BIBLIOGRAPHY
need to be made clear. To list everything relevant to the subject would mean
bibliographing nearly the whole of nineteenth-century American literature,
philosophy, and theology. Prescinding from that, I have made a list that
complements the intention of the text: included are those items which assist
towards a basic definition of the movement. Like the essays, these items all
help us to see the object as in itself it is.

The student should be aware of other sources available to him. The
Bibliography volume of *The Literary History of the United States*, 3rd ed.
(New York: Macmillan, 1963) is a basic tool, though few items on Transcendentalism are listed. Clarence Gohdes, *Bibliographical Guide to the Study of
the Literature of the U.S.A.*, 3rd ed. rev. (Durham: Duke Univ. Press, 1970) is
indispensable. Lewis Leary, *Articles on American Literature, 1900-1950*
(Durham: Duke Univ. Press, 1954), and *Articles on American Literature,
1950-1967* (Durham: Duke, 1970) are both fairly thorough for the learned
journals. For history there is Oscar Handlin, et al., *The Harvard Guide to
American History* (Cambridge: Harvard Univ. Press, 1954); for religion,
Nelson R. Burr, *A Critical Bibliography of Religion in America*, 2 vols.
(Princeton: Princeton Univ. Press, 1961); for philosophy perhaps the most
useful start is the extensive bibliography in Herbert W. Schneider, *A History
of American Philosophy*, 2nd ed. (New York: Columbia Univ. Press, 1963),
pp. 527-81. Five learned journals are devoted, in whole or part, to the

subject: *American Literature,* 1929—; *American Quarterly,* 1949—; *American Transcendental Quarterly,* 1969—; *Emerson Society Quarterly,* 1955—; *New England Quarterly,* 1928—. The *Thoreau Society Bulletin,* 1941—, is also useful. Since 1963, the American Literature section of the Modern Language Association has published annual volumes reviewing the year's work. These bibliographical essays are entitled *American Literary Scholarship: An Annual,* and each contains an essay, "Emerson, Thoreau, and Transcendentalism." James L. Woodress was senior editor through 1967; since 1968 J. Albert Robbins has filled that role; Duke University Press is the publisher. Woodress has also edited *Dissertations On American Literature,* 1891-1966 (Durham: Duke Univ. Press, 1968).

Except for a handful of things which forward the effort at critical definition, I have not tried to list the huge volume of work done on Emerson and Thoreau. The student is referred to Floyd Stovall, ed., *Eight American Authors: A Review of Research and Criticism,* 2nd ed. (New York: Norton, 1971) for the appropriate essays. He should be warned, however, that the second edition is difficult to use and does not entirely replace the first.

I have also abstained from listing items from the *American Transcendental Quarterly* and the *Emerson Society Quarterly.* It seemed foolish to reproduce their contents practically *en masse,* so the student is referred to the journals themselves. Kenneth W. Cameron founded both and all students of the period are in his debt. The most readily available collections of primary literature are the anthologies edited by George Hochfield and Perry Miller listed below.

Items reproduced in this book, whether in whole or part, are marked with an asterisk *. Books available in paperback are annotated Pb. Where an item contains a particularly useful bibliography, I have annotated it Biblio. The following abbreviations have been used:

> *AL* — *American Literature*
> *JHI* — *Journal of the History of Ideas*
> *NEQ* — *New England Quarterly*

*Albrecht, Robert C. "The Theological Response of the Transcendentalists to the Civil War." *NEQ,* 38 (1965), 21-34.

Alcott, Amos Bronson. *The Journals of Bronson Alcott,* edited by Odell Shepard. Boston: Little, Brown, 1938.

Anderson, Quentin. *The Imperial Self.* New York: Knopf, 1971. Pb.

Bier, Jesse. "Weberism, Franklin, and the Transcendental Style." *NEQ,* 43 (1970), 179-92.

Boas, George, ed. *Romanticism in America.* Baltimore: Johns Hopkins Univ. Press, 1940.

Bolster, Arthur S. *James Freeman Clarke: Disciple to Advancing Truth.* Boston: Beacon, 1954.

*Bowers, David. "Democratic Vistas." In *The Literary History of the United States,* edited by Robert E. Spiller, et al. 3rd ed. rev. New York: Macmillan, 1963.

Branch, Edgar. *The Sentimental Years*. New York: Appleton, 1934. Pb.

Bridges, William E. "Transcendentalism and Psychotherapy: Another Look at Emerson." *AL*, 41 (1969), 157-77.

Brooks, Van Wyck. *The Flowering of New England*. New York: Dutton, 1936. Pb.

Brown, Arthur W. *Always Young For Liberty: A Biography of William Ellery Channing*. Syracuse: Syracuse Univ. Press, 1956.

Brownson, Henry F. *Orestes A. Brownson's Early Life, Middle Life, Later Life*. 3 vols. Detroit, 1898-1900.

Brownson, Orestes A. *The Works of Orestes A. Brownson*. Edited by Henry F. Brownson. 20 vols. Detroit: Thorndike, Nourse, 1882-1902.

Buell, Lawrence. "Transcendental Catalogue Rhetoric: Vision Versus Form." *AL*, 40 (1968), 325-39.

Cameron, Kenneth W. *Transcendental Climate: New Sources for the Study of Emerson, Thoreau, and Their Contemporaries*. 3 vols. Hartford: Transcendental Books, 1963.

—————. *The Transcendental Workbook*. Hartford: Transcendental Books, 1957.

—————. *The Transcendentalists and Minerva*. 3 vols. Hartford: Transcendental Books, 1958.

Canby, Henry Seidel. *Thoreau*. Boston: Houghton-Mifflin, 1939.

*Caponigri, A. Robert. "Brownson and Emerson: Nature and History." *NEQ*, 18 (1945), 368-90.

Carpenter, Frederick Ives. *American Literature and the Dream*. New York: Philosophical Library, 1955.

*—————. *Emerson Handbook*. New York: Hendricks House, 1953.

Channing, William Ellery. *The Works of William Ellery Channing, D.D.* 6 vols. Boston: J. Munroe, 1841-43.

Channing, William Henry. *The Life of William Ellery Channing, D.D.* Boston: American Unitarian Association, 1880.

Christy, Arthur E. *The Orient in American Transcendentalism*. New York: Columbia Univ. Press, 1932.

Clarke, James Freeman. *Autobiography, Diary and Correspondence*. Edited by E. E. Hale. Boston: Houghton, Mifflin, 1891.

Coleridge, Samuel T. *Aids to Reflection, With a Preliminary Essay by James Marsh*. Burlington, Vt., 1829. Rpt. New York: Kennikat, 1971.

Commager, Henry Steele. *Theodore Parker*. Boston: Little, Brown, 1936.

Cooke, George W. *An Historical and Biographical Introduction to Accompany "The Dial."* Cleveland: The Rowfant Club, 1902.

—————. ed. *The Poets of Transcendentalism: An Anthology*. Boston: Houghton, Mifflin, 1903.

—————. *Unitarianism in America: A History of Its Origin and Development*. Boston: American Unitarian Association, 1902.

Copleston, Frederick, S.J. *A History of Philosophy, vol. 8: Modern Philosophy: Bentham to Russell*. Garden City, N.Y.: Image Books, 1967. Pb.

Cronkhite, G. F. "The Transcendental Railroad." *NEQ*, 24 (1951), 306-28.

Crowe, Charles R. *George Ripley: Transcendentalist and Utopian.* Athens: Univ. of Georgia Press, 1967.

*—————. " 'This Unnatural Union of Phalansteries and Transcendentalists.' " *JHI,* 20 (1959), 495-502.

—————. "Transcendentalist Support of Brook Farm: A Paradox?" *Historian,* 21 (1959), 281-95.

Culver, Donald. "New England Culture." *Scrutiny,* 6 (1937), 109-15.

Curti, Merle. "The Great Mr. Locke: America's Philosopher, 1783-1861." *Huntington Library Bulletin,* 11 (1937), 107-55.

—————. *The Growth of American Thought.* New York: Harper, 1943. Biblio.

Davis, M. R. "Emerson's 'Reason' and the Scottish Philosophers." *NEQ,* 17 (1944), 209-28.

Dewey, John. "James Marsh and American Philosophy." *JHI,* 2 (1940), 131-50.

Duffy, J. J. "Problems in Publishing Coleridge: James Marsh's First American Edition of *Aids to Reflection.*" *NEQ,* 43 (1970), 193-208.

Edgell, D. P. "A Note on Channing's Transcendentalism." *NEQ,* 22 (1949), 394-97.

Ekirch, Arthur A., Jr. *The Idea of Progress in America, 1815-1860.* New York: Columbia Univ. Press, 1944.

Elder, Marjorie. *Nathaniel Hawthorne: Transcendental Symbolist.* Athens: Ohio Univ. Press, 1969.

Eliot, Samuel A., ed. *Heralds of a Liberal Faith.* 3 vols. Boston: American Unitarian Association, 1910.

Ellis, Charles M. *An Essay on Transcendentalism.* Boston, 1842. Rpt. Westport: Greenwood Press, 1970.

Emerson, Edward W. *The Early Years of The Saturday Club.* Boston: Houghton Mifflin, 1918.

Emerson, Ralph Waldo. *The Complete Works of Ralph Waldo Emerson.* Centenary Edition. 12 vols. Boston: Houghton, Mifflin, 1903-04.

—————. *The Journals of Ralph Waldo Emerson.* Edited by Edward Waldo Emerson and Waldo Emerson Forbes. 10 vols. Boston: Houghton Mifflin, 1909-14.

—————. *The Letters of Ralph Waldo Emerson.* Edited by Ralph L. Rusk. 6 vols. New York: Columbia Univ. Press, 1939.

Faust, Clarence H. "The Background of the Unitarian Opposition to Transcendentalism." *Modern Philology,* 35 (1938), 297-324.

Feidelson, Charles, Jr. *Symbolism and American Literature.* Chicago: Univ. of Chicago Press, 1953. Pb.

Feuer, Lewis S. "James Marsh and the Conservative Transcendentalist Philosophy: A Political Interpretation." *NEQ,* 31 (1958), 3-31.

Fridén, Georg. "Transcendental Idealism in New England." *Neuphilologische Mitteilungen,* 69 (1968), 256-71.

Frothingham, Octavius B. *Boston Unitarianism, 1820-1850.* New York: Putnam's, 1890.

—————. *George Ripley.* Boston: Houghton, Mifflin, 1882.

—————. *Theodore Parker: A Biography.* Boston: J. R. Osgood, 1874.

—————. *Transcendentalism in New England: A History.* New York: Putnam's, 1876. Pb.

Gilley, Leonard. "Transcendentalism in *Walden." Prairie Schooner,* 42 (1968), 204-07.

Girard, William. "Du Transcendentalisme consideré essentiellement dans sa definition et ses origines françaises." *University of California Publications in Modern Philology* 4 (1916), 353-498.

*Goddard, Harold C. *Studies in New England Transcendentalism.* New York: Columbia Univ. Press, 1908. Biblio.

Gohdes, Clarence F. "Alcott's 'Conversation' on the Transcendental Club and *The Dial." AL,* 3 (1931), 14-27.

—————. *The Periodicals of American Transcendentalism.* Durham: Duke Univ. Press, 1931.

Gray, Henry D. *Emerson: A Statement of New England Transcendentalism as Expressed in the Philosophy of Its Chief Exponent.* Palo Alto: Stanford Univ. Press, 1917.

Hazard, Lucy L. *The Frontier in American Literature.* New York: Crowell, 1927.

Higginson, Thomas Wentworth. "The Sunny Side of the Transcendental Period." *Atlantic,* 93 (January 1904), 6-14.

*Hochfield, George. "Introduction." *Selected Writings of the American Transcendentalists.* New York: Signet Classics, 1966. Pb. Biblio.

Horton, Rod W., and Edwards, Herbert. *Backgrounds of American Literary Thought.* 2nd ed. New York: Appleton, 1967. Pb. Biblio.

Hutchison, William R. "To Heaven in a Swing: The Transcendentalism of Cyrus Bartoll." *Harvard Theological Review,* 56 (1963), 275-95.

*—————. *The Transcendentalist Ministers: Church Reform in the New England Renaissance.* New Haven: Yale Univ. Press, 1959. Rpt. Boston: Beacon, 1965. Pb. Biblio.

Isely, Jeter A. and Elizabeth. "A Note on George Ripley and the Beginnings of New England Transcendentalism." *Proceedings of the Unitarian Historical Society,* 13 (1961), 75-85.

Jackson, Sidney L., trans. "A Soviet View of Emerson." *NEQ,* 19 (1946), 236-43.

*James, Henry. "Emerson," *Partial Portraits.* London: Macmillan, 1888. Rpt. in various collections of James's criticism.

James, William. *The Varieties of Religious Experience.* New York and London: Longmans, Green, 1902.

*Joyaux, Georges. "Victor Cousin and American Transcendentalism." *French Review,* 29 (1955), 117-30.

Kern, Alexander. "The Rise of Transcendentalism." In *Transitions in American Literary History,* edited by Harry Hayden Clark. Durham: Duke Univ. Press, 1954.

Ladu, Arthur I. "Channing and Transcendentalism." *AL,* 11 (1939), 129-37.

–––––. "The Political Ideas of Orestes A. Brownson, Transcendentalist." *Philological Quarterly,* 12 (1933), 280-89.

Leighton, Walter. *French Philosophers and American Transcendentalism.* Charlottesville: Univ. of Virginia Press, 1908.

Lewis, R. W. B. *The American Adam: Innocence, Tragedy and Tradition in the Nineteenth Century.* Chicago: Univ. of Chicago Press, 1955. Pb.

Liebman, Sheldon W. "Emerson's Transformation in the 1820's." *AL,* 40 (1968), 133-54.

Madison, C. A. "Margaret Fuller: Transcendental Rebel." *Antioch Review,* 2 (1942), 422-38.

Marx, Leo. *The Machine in the Garden: Technology and the Pastoral Ideal in America.* New York: Oxford Univ. Press, 1964. Pb.

Matthiessen, F. O. *American Renaissance: Art and Experience in the Age of Emerson and Whitman.* New York: Oxford Univ. Press, 1941. Pb.

Maynard, Theodore. *Orestes Brownson: Yankee, Radical, Catholic.* New York: Macmillan, 1943.

Michaud, Régis. "Emerson's Transcendentalism." *American Journal of Psychology,* 30 (1919), 73-82.

Miller, F. DeWolfe. *Christoper Pearse Cranch and His Caricatures of New England Transcendentalism.* Cambridge, Mass.: Harvard Univ. Press, 1951.

Miller, Perry, ed. *The American Transcendentalists: Their Prose and Poetry.* New York: Doubleday, Anchor, 1957. Pb. Biblio.

–––––. ed. *Consciousness in Concord: The Text of Thoreau's Hitherto "Lost Journal" (1840-41) Together With Notes and a Commentary.* Boston: Houghton-Mifflin, 1958.

–––––. *Errand into the Wilderness.* Cambridge, Mass.: Harvard Univ. Press, 1956. Pb. Contains "From Edwards to Emerson."

*–––––. "From Edwards to Emerson." *NEQ,* 13 (1940), 589-617.

–––––. *Nature's Nation.* Cambridge. Mass.: Harvard Univ. Press, 1967. Contains "Emersonian Genius and the American Democracy," "The Location of American Religious Freedom," "Melville and Transcendentalism," "Theodore Parker: Apostasy Within Liberalism," and "Thoreau in the Context of International Romanticism."

–––––. "New England's Transcendentalism: Native or Imported." In *Literary Views: Critical and Historical Essays,* edited by Carroll Camden. Chicago: Univ. of Chicago Press, 1964.

–––––, ed. *The Transcendentalists: An Anthology.* Cambridge, Mass.: Harvard Univ. Press, 1950. Pb. Biblio.

Mumford, Lewis. *The Golden Day.* New York: Boni and Liverwright, 1926.

Myerson, Joel. "A Calendar of Transcendental Club Meetings." *AL,* 44 (1972), 197-207.

Newbrough, G. F. " 'Reason' and 'Understanding' in the Works of Theodore Parker." *South Atlantic Quarterly,* 47 (1948), 64-75.

Nichols, Charles H., S. J. "Theodore Parker and the Transcendental Rhetoric: The Liberal Tradition and America's Debate on the Eve of Secession (1832-1861)." *Jahrbuch für Amerikastudien,* 13 (1968), 69-83.

Nicolson, Marjorie Hope. "James Marsh and the Vermont Transcendentalists." *Philosophical Review*, 34 (1925), 28-50.

Niebuhr, H. Richard. *The Kingdom of God in America*. New York: Harper, 1937. Pb.

Parker, Theodore. *The Works of Theodore Parker*. 15 vols. Boston, 1907-13.

Parrington, Vernon L. *Main Currents in American Thought: Volume Two: The Romantic Revolution*. New York: Harcourt, 1927. Pb. Biblio.

Paul, Sherman. *Emerson's Angle of Vision*. Cambriage, Mass.: Harvard Univ. Press, 1952.

—————. *The Shores of America: Thoreau's Inward Exploration*. Urbana: Univ. of Illinois Press, 1958. Pb.

—————. "The Wise Silence: Sound as the Agency of Correspondence in Thoreau." *NEQ*, 22 (1949), 511-27.

Peabody, Elizabeth P. *Reminiscences of Rev. William Ellery Channing, D.D.* Boston: Roberts Brothers, 1880.

Pochmann, Henry A. *German Culture in America: Philosophical and Literary Influences, 1600-1900*. Madison: Univ. of Wisconsin Press, 1957.

—————. *New England Transcendentalism and St. Louis Hegelianism*. Philadelphia: Carl Schurz Foundation, 1948.

Pollock, Robert C. "Ralph Waldo Emerson: The Single Vision." In *American Classics Reconsidered*, edited by Harold C. Gardiner. New York: Scribner's, 1958.

Porte, Joel. *Emerson and Thoreau: Transcendentalists in Conflict*. Middletown, Conn.: Wesleyan Univ. Press, 1966.

—————. "Transcendental Antics." In *Veins of Humor*, edited by Harry Levin, Harvard English Studies, 3. Cambridge, Mass.: Harvard Univ. Press, 1972.

Porter, L. C. "Transcendentalism: A Self-Portrait." *NEQ*, 35 (1962), 27-47.

Riley, I. Woodbridge. *American Thought From Puritanism to Pragmatism*. New York: Holt, 1923.

—————. "Two Types of Transcendentalism in America." *Journal of Philosophy*, 15 (May 23, 1918), 281-92.

Ripley, George, ed. *"The Dial": A Magazine for Literature, Philosophy, and Religion*. 4 vols, rpt. New York: Russell & Russell, 1961.

Rosenthal, Bernard. *"The Dial*, Transcendentalism, and Margaret Fuller." *English Language Notes*, 8 (1970), 28-36.

Rusk, Ralph L. *The Life of Ralph Waldo Emerson*. New York: Scribner's, 1949.

Sanborn, Franklin B., and Harris, William T. *A. Bronson Alcott: His Life and Philosophy*. 2 vols. Boston: Roberts Brothers, 1893.

Santayana, George. *The Genteel Tradition*. Edited by D. L. Wilson, Cambridge, Mass.: Harvard Univ. Press, 1967. Pb.

*Schlesinger, Arthur M., Jr. *The Age of Jackson*. Boston: Little, Brown, 1946. Pb. Biblio.

—————. *Orestes Brownson: A Pilgrim's Progress*. Boston: Little, Brown, 1939. Pb. Biblio.

Schneider, Herbert W. *A History of American Philosophy.* 2nd ed. New York: Columbia Univ. Press, 1963. Pb. Biblio.

Schultz, Arthur, and Pochmann, Henry. "George Ripley: Unitarian, Transcendentalist, or Infidel?" *AL,* 14 (1942), 1-19.

Scott, Leonora Cranch. *The Life and Letters of Christopher Pearse Cranch.* Boston, 1917.

Shepard, Odell. *Pedlar's Progress: The Life of Bronson Alcott.* Boston: Little, Brown, 1937.

Shivers, F. R. "A Western Chapter in the History of American Transcendentalism." *Bulletin of the Historical and Philosophical Society of Ohio,* 15 (1957), 117-30.

Simon, Myron, and Parsons, T. H., eds. *Transcendentalism and Its Legacy.* Ann Arbor: Univ. of Michigan Press, 1966. Pb.

*Smith, Henry Nash. "Emerson's Problem of Vocation." *NEQ,* 12 (1939), 52-67.

Smith, H. Shelton. "Was Theodore Parker a Transcendentalist?" *NEQ,* 23 (1950), 351-64.

Smithline, Arnold. *Natural Religion in American Literature.* New Haven: College and University Press, 1966.

Spencer, Benjamin T. *The Quest for Nationality: An American Literary Campaign.* Syracuse: Syracuse Univ. Press, 1957. Biblio.

Sweet, William W. *The Story of Religion in America.* Rev. ed. New York: Harper, 1950.

Swift, Lindsay. *Brook Farm: Its Members, Scholars, and Visitors.* New York: Macmillan, 1900.

*Tanner, Tony. *The Reign of Wonder: Naivety and Reality in American Literature.* Cambridge: Cambridge Univ. Press, 1965. Pb.

*Thompson, Cameron. "John Locke and New England Transcendentalism." *NEQ,* 35 (1962), 435-57.

Thompson, Frank T. "Emerson's Indebtedness to Coleridge." *Studies in Philology,* 23 (1926), 55-76.

Thoreau, Henry David. *The Writings of Henry David Thoreau.* 20 vols. Boston: Houghton, Mifflin, 1906.

Todd, Edgerly W. "Philosophical Ideas at Harvard College, 1817-1837." *NEQ,* 16 (1943), 63-90.

Trueblood, D. E. "The Influence of Emerson's 'Divinity School Address.' " *Harvard Theological Review,* 32 (1939), 41-56.

Tyler, Alice Felt. *Freedom's Ferment: Phases of American Social History From the Colonial Period to the Outbreak of the Civil War.* Minneapolis: Univ. of Minnesota Press, 1944. Pb. Biblio.

Vogel, Stanley M. *German Literary Influences on the American Transcendentalists.* New Haven: Yale Univ. Press, 1955.

Weiss, John. *The Life and Correspondence of Theodore Parker.* 2 vols. New York: Appleton, 1864.

Wellek, René. *Confrontations: Studies in the Intellectual and Literary Relations Between Germany, England, and the United States During the*

Nineteenth Century. Princeton: Princeton Univ. Press, 1965. Contains "Emerson and German Philosophy" and "The Minor Transcendentalists and German Philosophy."

—————. "Emerson and German Philosophy." *NEQ*, 16 (1943), 41-62.

*—————. "The Minor Transcendentalists and German Philosophy." *NEQ*, 15 (1942), 652-80.

Wells, Ronald V. *Three Christian Transcendentalists: James Marsh, Caleb Sprague Henry, Frederick Henry Hedge*. New York: Columbia Univ. Press, 1943.

Werkmeister, W. H. *A History of Philosophical Ideas in America*. New York: Ronald, 1949.

Whicher, George F., and Kennedy, Gail, eds. *The Transcendentalist Revolt*. Rev. ed. Lexington, Mass.: Heath, 1968. Pb. Biblio.

Whicher, Stephen E. *Freedom and Fate: An Inner Life of Ralph Waldo Emerson*. Philadelphia: Univ. of Pennsylvania Press, 1953. Pb.

White, Morton. *Science and Sentiment in America: Philosophical Thought From Jonathan Edwards to John Dewey*. New York: Oxford Univ. Press, 1972.

Williams, George H. *Rethinking the Unitarian Relationship With Protestantism: An Examination of the Thought of Frederick Henry Hedge (1805-1890)*. Boston: Beacon Press, 1949.

Willson, Lawrence. "The Transcendentalist View of the West." *Western Humanities Review*, 14 (1960), 183-91.

Wilson, John B. "Darwin and the Transcendentalists." *JHI*, 26 (1965), 286-90.

—————. "Elizabeth Peabody and Other Transcendentalists on History and Historians." *Historian*, 30 (1967), 72-86.

—————. "Phrenology and the Transcendentalists." *AL*, 28 (1956), 220-25.

*Winters, Yvor. *In Defense of Reason*. Denver: Alan Swallow, 1947. Pb.

Wright, Conrad. *The Beginnings of Unitarianism in America*. Boston: Starr King Press, 1955. Biblio.

Index

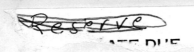